William Ashbrook Kellerman

The Elements of Botany

Embracing organography, histology, vegetable physiology, systematic botany and economic botany, together with a complete glossary of botanical terms

William Ashbrook Kellerman

The Elements of Botany
Embracing organography, histology, vegetable physiology, systematic botany and economic botany, together with a complete glossary of botanical terms

ISBN/EAN: 9783337377229

Printed in Europe, USA, Canada, Australia, Japan

Cover: Foto ©Andreas Hilbeck / pixelio.de

More available books at **www.hansebooks.com**

THE
ELEMENTS OF BOTANY:

EMBRACING

ORGANOGRAPHY, HISTOLOGY, VEGETABLE PHYSIOLOGY, SYSTEMATIC BOTANY AND ECONOMIC BOTANY.

ARRANGED

FOR SCHOOL USE OR FOR INDEPENDENT STUDY.

TOGETHER WITH

A COMPLETE GLOSSARY OF BOTANICAL TERMS.

BY

W. A. KELLERMAN, PH.D.,

PROFESSOR OF BOTANY AND ZOOLOGY IN THE KANSAS STATE AGRICULTURAL COLLEGE. LATE PROFESSOR OF BOTANY IN THE STATE COLLEGE OF KENTUCKY. FORMERLY PROFESSOR OF NATURAL SCIENCE IN THE WISCONSIN STATE NORMAL SCHOOL.

COPIOUSLY ILLUSTRATED.

PHILADELPHIA:
JOHN E. POTTER AND COMPANY,
617 SANSOM STREET.
NEW YORK: 743 & 745 BROADWAY.

PREFACE.

The object in preparing this book has been to present to pupils in our schools and to students generally, in a sufficiently condensed form, a comprehensive view of the Vegetable Kingdom. This includes a general survey of the organs of plants, their structure and functions, of the classification of plants according to their supposed genetic relationship, and, finally, of the uses of plants and the application of botanical knowledge in the various pursuits of life. It is not deemed necessary to apologize for presenting the minute anatomy or histology of plants as seen in the following pages, much less for devoting a separate part of the work to a discussion of the commonest vegetable products found in commerce, as regards their nature, source, and uses. It is believed this new departure will be welcomed by the great mass of intelligent educators of our country, who think this science broad enough and already sufficiently developed to meet the just demand made upon it not only for something disciplinary and pleasurable, but also for something useful. In case of pupils who will afterward pursue collegiate courses of instruction, it is believed this book will offer a suitable introduction to extended botanical study; but it has been prepared especially for pupils who end their school education when, or even before, the ordinary high-school course is completed. It is confidently hoped also that those outside of schools who are desirous of learning something of Botany will find here an attractive introduction to this important science, for the further study of which the works of Gray, Bessey, and others are so admirably adapted.

In Part I. the subject of Structural Botany or Organography is presented in the customary form, yet a slight abridgment of the number of technical terms and the etymologies of the important ones given will, it is believed, be found improvements.

The numerous figures in Part II. will enable the pupils, even without the aid of microscopical appliances, to get a clear idea of the minute structure or histology of plants, upon which, to a large extent, physiology is based.

In Part III. the arrangement of the various groups of plants corresponds quite closely to that in recent publications by eminent botanists. Departures made by Bessey in his Botany seem desirable, and, therefore, have been followed. Only a limited number of representative groups have been mentioned; and should the teacher find this number too great for mastery on the part of his pupils, a further abridgment can readily be made.

In Part IV. only a few, yet in general the most

important, vegetable products have been mentioned and briefly described. The order of sequence of the groups is that used by Weisner in his *Rohstoffe des Pflanzenreiches*, a book which is the source of much of the information, especially of that relating to anatomy, contained in this part.

The Appendix contains suggestions that will, it is hoped, be of advantage, especially to those who study without the assistance of a teacher.

All minute measurements have been given in fractions of an inch, although the great advantage of the use of the metric system is not in the least questioned. But pupils are not, as a rule, familiar with the latter, and can only slowly and gradually be taught to substitute it for what they have learned in early youth and practiced since. The same in substance may be said with reference to the Centigrade and Fahrenheit's thermometers, the familiar scale of the latter being used in this work. Especial attention is called to the tables given in the Appendix of the equivalents of an inch in millimetres, also the equivalents of the degrees of Fahrenheit's scale in degrees on the Centigrade scale.

Nearly three hundred of the illustrations are original. Figs. 223a and 324a were taken, by permission of the publishers, from Wood's *Class-book of Botany*; Figs. 134, 135, and 308 from Gray's *Botany*; Figs. 342, 343, 344, 345, 346, and 347 from Le Conte's *Geology*; Figs. 148,

169, 182, 185, 188, 120, 221, 234, 237, 238, 241, 247, 248, 251, 253, 254, 257, 264, 266, 277a, 282, 300, and 301 from foreign authors, as Sachs, De Bary, and others. Twenty-two illustrations of ornamental plants were furnished by C. W. Seelye, editor of *Vick's Magazine*, from publications of James Vick.

I would say finally that I have been assisted by my wife in the entire preparation of the book, and to her equally with myself is to be attributed any merit that it may contain.

STATE AGRICULTURAL COLLEGE,   W. A. K.
   MANHATTAN, KANSAS, 1883.

CONTENTS.

	PAGE
INTRODUCTION	11

PART I.—ORGANOGRAPHY.

PARTS OF A PLANT	15
THE ROOT	16
THE STEM	21
THE BUD	25
THE LEAF	25
THE FLOWER	39
POLLINATION AND FERTILIZATION	54
THE FRUIT	67

PART II.—HISTOLOGY AND PHYSIOLOGY.

THE CELL	72
THE CELL-CONTENTS	82
TISSUE	87
WATER	100
FOOD-ELEMENTS	104
ASSIMILATION AND METASTASIS	106
RESPIRATION	109
TEMPERATURE	109
LIGHT	111
MOVEMENTS	112

PART III.—SYSTEMATIC BOTANY.

CLASSIFICATION	117
DIVISIONS	121
PROTOPHYTA	122
ZYGOSPOREÆ	126
OÖSPOREÆ	132

CARPOSPOREÆ	136
BRYOPHYTA	148
PTERIDOPHYTA	153
PHÆNOGAMIA	157
GYMNOSPERMÆ	162
ANGIOSPERMÆ	166
MONOCOTYLEDONES	169
DICOTYLEDONES	184
GEOGRAPHICAL DISTRIBUTION	231
FOSSIL PLANTS	234

PART IV.—ECONOMIC BOTANY.

THE GUMS	244
THE RESINS	247
THE CAOUTCHOUC GROUP	261
OPIUM AND CATECHU GROUP	265
VEGETABLE FATS AND WAX	268
CAMPHOR	272
STARCH AND SUGAR	273
FIBRES	278
THE CORTEX OR BARK	291
WOOD	296
ROOTS AND RHIZOMES	303
LEAVES	305
FLOWERS	308
SEEDS AND FRUITS	311
GALLS AND CRYPTOGAMS	320

APPENDIX.

SUGGESTIONS FOR STUDYING	323
SUGGESTIONS FOR COLLECTING	323
THE MICROSCOPE	325
MICROSCOPIC PREPARATIONS	327
THE HERBARIUM	332
GLOSSARY	333
TABLES OF EQUIVALENTS	359, 360

ELEMENTS OF BOTANY.

INTRODUCTION.

BIOLOGY is a term now used to denote the study of all living things or organisms, namely, Plants and Animals. These, as contrasted with minerals or inorganic matter, are, in general, distinguished by the possession of organs, or special parts of their structure, designed to perform certain functions. The very lowest or simplest forms of living matter, however, are often so homogeneous and structureless, or "organless," that they are with difficulty separated from some of the complex, inorganic substances; in other words, there is the most intimate connection between the mineral, or inorganic, and the organic kingdoms. Between the commoner and widely-divergent representatives of these, as, for example, between a crystal of quartz and a tree or a toad, there are numerous patent, distinguishing characteristics, besides the absence or presence of organs; prominent among which is the fact of parentage, or power on the part of organisms to reproduce themselves, and so, by offspring, perpetuate their kind.

That department of *Biology*, which treats of plants, is called BOTANY. It is almost inseparable from ZOOLOGY, which treats of Animals; for the lowest organisms can often be called plants with as much propriety as animals, and animals with as much propriety as plants, on account of the simplicity of their structure and the few characters they present, upon which a systematic classification may be based. It has been proposed to form another Group, called the PROTISTA, to receive these low organisms; the higher representatives of the Vegetable and Animal *Kingdoms* are readily distinguished by many anatomical and physiological characters.

Plants feed on mineral or inorganic substances. Animals derive their food from plants. Many of them, as the herbivorous animals, feed exclusively on vegetation. Carnivorous animals, devouring the vegetable-feeders, depend no less really though indirectly on plants for food.

Plants in general consume carbonic dioxide, and liberate oxygen. This is not true, however, of the parasitic plants, called Fungi. Animals consume in respiration oxygen, and liberate carbonic dioxide. The two kingdoms are thus mutually dependent.

The surface expansion for absorption, etc., is very extensive in case of both plants and animals. In case of plants, however, it is mainly external, as the surface of the roots, rootlets, rhizoids, stems, and leaves; in case of animals it is, in the main, internal, as the alimentary canal, the vascular and respiratory vessels, etc.

Plants possess chlorophyll, that is, green coloring matter, by reason of which they are able to convert the inorganic food into organic matter. Fungi and other parasites and saprophytes are destitute of chlorophyll, and these plants appropriate to their own use the food assimilated by chlorophyll-bearing plants. Animals, with the exception of a very few low forms, do not possess chlorophyll.

Very many vegetable substances or products are ternary compounds, or composed mainly of oxygen, carbon, and hydrogen; while very many of the animal substances or products are quaternary compounds, or composed of oxygen, carbon, hydrogen, and nitrogen.

Most plants, but by no means all of them (especially the lower forms), are stationary, or have no power of locomotion; while animals, also with numerous exceptions, locomote freely from place to place.

Sensation is possessed by plants in a very much less marked degree than by animals.

The study of plants may be solely with reference to their visible parts or organs, and this part of the science is called ORGANOGRAPHY, or *Structural Botany*. When the investigation touches the minute or microscopic structure of plants or their parts and products, it is called *Minute Anatomy*, or HISTOLOGY. The study of the parts of the plant with reference to their functions or office, or their so-called vital actions, comes under the head of VEGETABLE PHYSIOLOGY. The classification of plants and what directly appertains to it constitutes SYSTEMATIC BOTANY. All the plants of any region are called the *Flora* of that region. FOSSIL BOTANY treats of fossil plants, or those which existed in previous geologic times, and whose remains or impressions are found in rock-strata. The application of botanical knowledge in the arts, industries or pursuits of life is designated by the term APPLIED BOTANY. This may be Agricultural, Horticultural, or Medical Botany, etc. ECONOMIC BOTANY is commonly used to indicate a study in general of the vegetable products and their uses.

PART I.

ORGANOGRAPHY.

1. If we examine any common plant, such as a Grass, Rose-bush, Willow, or an Oak, three distinct parts will be found, namely:
   - I. ROOT.
   - II. STEM.
   - III. LEAVES.

2. The **Root**, or descending axis of the plant, generally grows downwards into the ground, sends out numerous branches, and thus firmly fixes the plant in its position. It also absorbs from the soil water or moisture, which contains plant food held in solution. Leaves, or scales representing leaves, are never found on the roots.

3. The **Stem**, or ascending axis, generally grows upwards, and furnishes the support for all the parts which grow above ground. It may be herbaceous,—that is, of soft tissue, like the Pansy,—or it may be woody, like the Lilac, or Willow-tree.

4. The **Leaves** are inserted on the stem or its branches. They are generally of a deep-green color and flattened shape. Their office is to convert the inorganic food, which has been absorbed by the roots and conveyed to them by the stem, into organic matter. From them more or less watery vapor is continually escaping.

5. **Hairs**, or **Trichomes**, may occur on any part of the plant, as on roots, stems, or leaves. They are mostly

16 ORGANOGRAPHY.

hair-like in shape, often very small, but they are sometimes long, and may form a dense covering, and hence afford protection for the plant. They may also take the shape of scales, glands, bristles, prickles, etc.

THE ROOT.

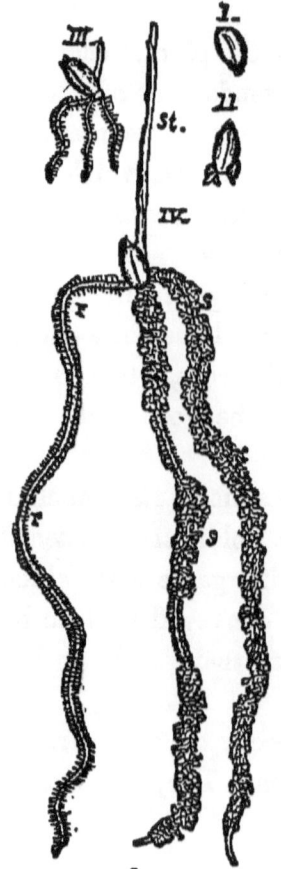

6. The **Root** is present in nearly all of the higher plants, as trees, shrubs, and herbs, but wanting in Mosses, Liverworts, Fungi, and Algæ. It is usually destitute of color, but may be brownish, yellowish, reddish, though never green. In case of some plants (Mosses, Liverworts, etc.), there are *root-hairs*, called *rhizoids* (Gr. *rhiza*, root), which have the same function, but not the same structure, as the true roots.

7. The root is generally found underground, where it sends out numerous branches, without any particular order; and these, in turn, branch again and again into smaller roots, called **Rootlets**. The plant is thus firmly fixed in its place. These rootlets, or their minute branches, are covered with numerous hairs, sometimes called *fibrillæ* (Fig. 1).

In Fig. 2 the terminal portion of a rootlet, with root-hairs much magnified, is shown. In

Fig. 1. Wheat in different stages (I, II, III, IV) of germination: *r*, root with root-hairs; *s*, particles of adhering soil; *st*, stem.

THE ROOT. 17

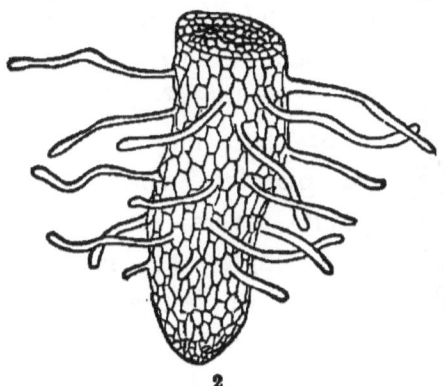

many cases, as in the seedling of Wheat, Flax, etc., these may be seen by the unaided eye, appearing as a woolly covering. The special office of these is to absorb the dissolved food from the soil.

8. When a seed germinates, it generally sends a single root (*radicle*, Fig. 3, *r.d.*) downwards, which is called the **primary root**. This may continue to grow, and remain larger than any of its branches or side-roots which it sends out, and in this case it is called the main, or **tap-root**.

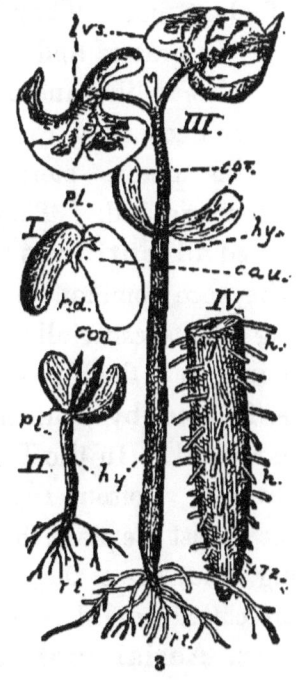

9. The tap-root, when not woody (as in shrubs and trees), may become fleshy, that is, thickened, as, for example, in the Carrot, Turnip, etc. This is in consequence of a deposit of nourishment which has been elaborated or prepared in the green parts of the plant. When it is larger at the top, or where it joins the stem, and tapers gradually downwards, it is said to be *conical* (Fig. 4); if it is turnip-shaped, that is, very large above, tapering abruptly, and becoming very slender below,

Fig. 2. Portion of a root, with root-hairs, highly magnified. Fig. 3. The Bean in different stages of germination: *cot*, cotyledons; *pl*, plumule; *r.d.*, radicle; *cau*, caulicle; *lvs*, leaves.

it is *napiform* (Lat. *napis*, turnip; Fig. 5); when spindle-shaped, or thick in the middle, and tapering to both ends, it is said to be *fusiform* (Lat. *fusis*, spindle; Fig. 6).

10. There may grow from the plantlet, when a seed sprouts, several roots, instead of a single one, as in the Indian Corn, Wheat, Pea, etc. (Fig. 1, etc.) In such case they are called **multiple primary roots**. Sometimes they become enlarged, as in the Sweet-potato, Dahlia, etc., and thus serve as reservoirs of plant food. They are then said to be **tuberous** (Fig. 7). In grasses and many other plants they are numerous and thread-like, and are called **fibrous roots** (Fig. 8).

11. Secondary roots may arise from the different parts of the plant,—stem and branches,—whether above or below ground. They are called **adventitious roots**. They are common in creeping plants especially at the joints, and their production is favored by contact with moist soil. In the Trumpet Creeper, Poison Ivy, etc., they assist the plant in climb-

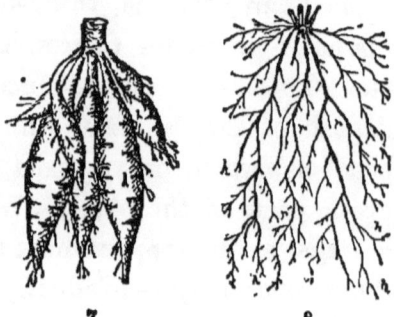

ing, and, since they do not grow into the ground, they are called **aerial roots**.

12. **Aerial roots** are more common in moist tropical

Fig. 4. A conical root.   Fig. 5. A napiform root.   Fig. 6. A fusiform root.
Fig. 7. Tuberous roots.   Fig. 8. Fibrous roots.

countries, especially in deep forests where the light is partially excluded,—it being unfavorable to their development. A notable example is furnished by the *Banyan-tree* of India, and some other Fig-trees, whose outstretched branches send down *adventitious* roots, that grow into the soil, and thus become supporting columns. The Screw-pine is sometimes wholly propped up by roots that originate some distance from the ground. The Sugar-Cane produces aerial roots similar to those of Indian Corn, but they develop from joints higher up. The seeds of the Mangrove of the West Indies sprout before falling from the tree, and send a long root, or radicle, down into the mud, in which these trees grow, thus gaining a foothold before severing their connection with the parent tree.

13. *Aerial roots*, whose function is somewhat different from the above, are found in *epiphytes* (Gr. *epi*, upon; *phyton*, plant), or **air-plants**. They generally grow on other plants, as their name signifies, but their roots serve merely to give the plant attachment, and the food is derived wholly from the air. Many of the beautiful Orchids of the Tropics are of this nature. The Epidendron, or Tree Orchis (growing on a species of Magnolia), and the Tillandsia, or Spanish Moss (hanging in tufts or festoons from trees), of the Southern States, are epiphytes. Many Mosses, Lichens, etc., are epiphytic, though destitute of true roots.

14. Certain plants not only fix themselves to, but also draw their nourishment from, other plants. Such are **parasites**. They send their roots, or what answer functionally to them, into the tissue of their host and absorb the nourishment which the latter had prepared for its own use. True parasites are destitute of the green substance in

leaves, called *chlorophyll* (Gr. *chloros*, green ; *phyllon*, leaf), in whose presence (in sunlight) the plant can convert the inorganic matter into plant food—that is, organic matter.

15. The Fungi (as Moulds, Blights, etc.) are parasitic either on living or decaying substances. The Beech-drops and Indian-pipe are attached to roots and draw their nourishment therefrom. The leafless Cuscuta, or Dodder, is a slender, yellowish parasite of peculiar nature. The seeds sprout in the ground, but the plantlet, as soon as it appears above the surface, seeks for plants around which to twine ; if unsuccessful it soon dies ; but if it finds a proper plant, it sends its rootlets, in the form of suckers, into its host, by means of which it absorbs sufficient nourishment for its growth and development; the stem of the parasite then dies, and thus severs its connection with the soil.

16. The Mistletoe of Europe, and the false Mistletoe of this country, have chlorophyll in their leaves, and are, therefore, capable of *assimilation*, that is, of converting inorganic into organic matter ; or, in other words, of preparing their own food. Yet they do this only in part. They draw a portion of their food from the trees on which they grow, and are to that extent, therefore, parasitic.

The nature of the yellowish or whitish leafless plants, which are fixed to the ground, should not be misunderstood. They do not draw their nourishment from the soil, but from underground roots. Neither should all subterranean parts of plants be regarded as roots, since stems sometimes grow underground. Their true nature, however, is easily determined by the buds and scales (modified leaves) which they produce. Such, for example, are the Irish-potatoes, rootstock of Flag, etc.

THE STEM.

17. The most striking differences in **stems** of various plants is in regard to their size and texture. A stem whose tissue is soft (mostly green) and not woody is said to be **herbaceous**. An herb which completes its growth and dies the same season is called an *annual;* a *biennial* herb, such as the Turnip, Carrot, etc., requires two years to complete its growth and produce seed; an herb is *perennial* when the root continues to live for several years, although the stem every year dies down to the ground, a very small portion only remaining, from the buds of which the shoots arise the following year. If the stem is woody, though not growing to a great height, it is said to be **fruticose** (Lat. *frutex*, shrub), or **shrubby**; when approaching a tree in size it is **arborescent** (Lat. *arbor*, tree), and when forming a proper tree-trunk it is **arboreous**.

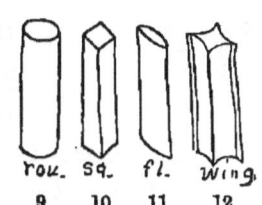

18. The stem of every plant is vertical in its early stages of development; this direction is often maintained, when the stem is said to be **erect**. If it is prostrate or trailing it is said to be **procumbent**. A **decumbent** stem is one that reclines on the ground after having arisen at the base somewhat above it. A stem, climbing by tendrils or rootlets, is said to be **scandent**; when twining around other objects it is **voluble**. Stems which grow underground are called **subterranean** stems.

19. The majority of stems and branches are more or less round (Fig. 9), but many of our common plants, for example, the whole family *Labiatæ* ("lip-shaped flowers"), have

Fig. 9. A round stem. Fig. 10. A square stem. Fig. 11. A flattened stem. Fig. 12. A winged stem.

22 ORGANOGRAPHY.

square stems (Fig 10). Some plants, as the Wire-Grass (*Poa compressa*, L.), have flattened stems (Fig. 11); others may be winged (Fig. 12). Those of Grasses and Sedges are conspicuously jointed and sometimes hollow, and have received the special name of **culm** (Fig. 13). The trunk of the Palms, and the like, is called **caudex**.

20. Certain forms of branches are used by gardeners for the purpose of propagating by buds. Such are Suckers, Stolons, Offsets, and Runners. **Suckers** arise from underground stems. **Stolons** are trailing or reclining branches which take root where they touch the soil. **Offsets** are short Stolons, like those of the House-leek. **Runners** are slender, leafless creeping branches, which, when the full length is attained, take root at the tip, form a bud, and develop an independent plant.

21. Some **tendrils** are slender branches destitute of leaves and intended for assistance in climbing. Examples are furnished by the Grape-Vine, Virginia Creeper, Squash, etc. (Fig. 14). They generally grow out straight until some slender object is reached, around which the tips

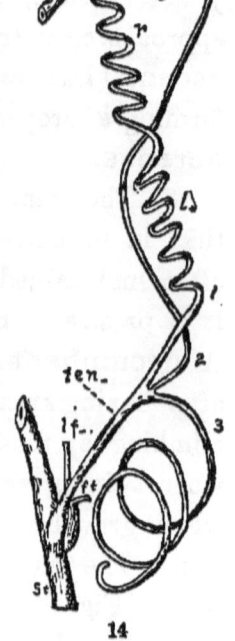

Fig. 13. Culm or stem of Grass. Fig. 14. Tendril (*t*) of the Wild Balsam-apple (*Echinocystis*), attached at the tip and coiled to the right (*r*) and to the left (*l*).

hook. Then the whole tendril shortens by coiling up spirally, thus bringing the plant nearer the support. The Virginia Creeper develops the tendril-tips into adhering disks when it climbs walls or smooth trees (Fig. 15). Other tendrils, as of the Pea, etc., are modified leaves instead of branches. **Spines,**

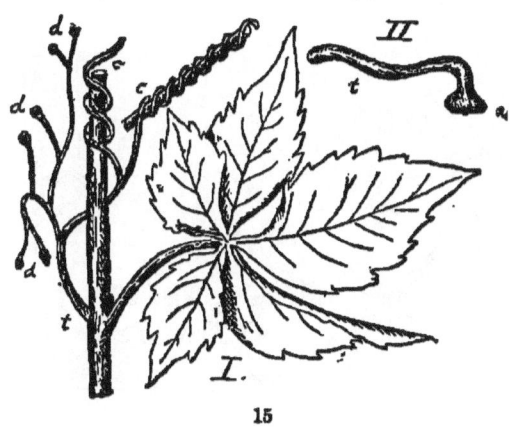

or thorns, are sometimes stunted and hardened branches, as in neglected Pear-trees, Plum-trees, etc. (Fig. 16).

22. *Subterranean* stems and branches may seem on cursory examination to be little, if at all, different from roots. But they are jointed, and roots are not; they have modified leaves in the form of scales—always absent in roots; buds may generally be found on them, but roots never produce buds. Four common types of subterranean stems are the Rhizome, Tuber, Corm, and Bulb. The rhizome (Gr. *rhiza*,

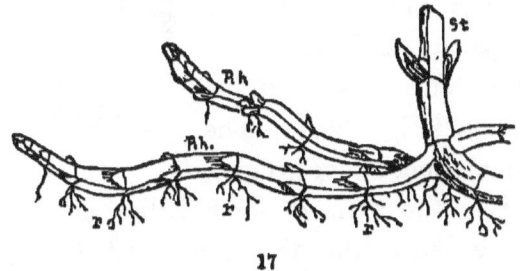

Fig. 15. Tendril, which ends in coils (*t*) and disks (*d*) of the *Ampelopsis*, or Virginia Creeper. Fig. 16. Spine or stunted branch of the Crab-apple. Fig. 17. Rhizome (*rh*) of Mint: *r*, roots; *st*, stem.

root) is very common, as in the Mint, Couch-grass, etc.; it is merely a root-stock, or stem growing under the surface

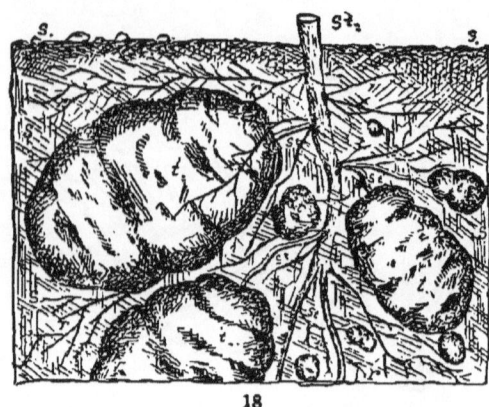

of the ground, producing roots, also leaf-scales and buds (Fig. 17). A **tuber** is a thickened portion of a root-stock. The Potato is the commonest example, the "eyes" being buds (Fig. 18). The **corm** is a very short, thickened root-stock, with roots below and buds above.

23. The **bulb** is an extremely short root-stock, producing, like the corm, roots from the under side. It is covered with leaves, or the base of leaves, in the form of thickened scales. If the latter are broad, and cover all that is within, the bulb is said to be *coated* (Fig. 19), or *tunicated* (Lat. *tunica*, covering). But if the scales are narrow and separate, as in the Lily, the bulb is said to be *scaly* (Fig. 20). The small buds above ground,

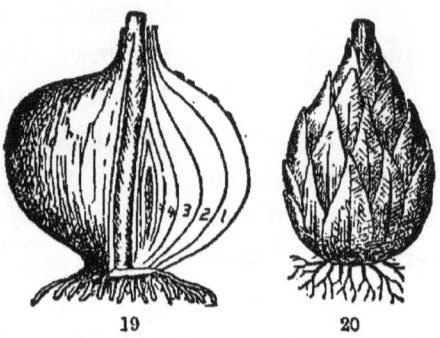

as in the axils of some Lilies, etc., are called **bulblets**. The bulb, like the corm and tuber, is a reservoir of

Fig. 18. Potato tuber (*t*); *r*, roots; *st*, stems. Fig. 19. A coated bulb. Fig. 20. A scaly bulb.

nourishment. The former contains the nourishment in the leaves (base of leaves), and the two latter have it in the thickened stem itself.

24. **The Bud.**—At definite places on the stem occur **buds,** which are simply undeveloped branches or shoots. The scales of the buds are small leaves, and that on which they are situated is the stem (as yet undeveloped). The bud at the end of the stem is called the **terminal** bud (Fig. 21, *ter*); the others are the **lateral** buds. Of these, the majority occur in the axils of the leaves (or if the leaves have fallen, they may be seen just above the leaf-scar), and for this reason they are called **axillary** buds (Fig. 21, *ax*). Sometimes one or two are produced on either side of or above the axillary bud, and in such case they are called **accessory** buds (Fig. 21, *ac*). Occasionally their place of origin is indefinite or irregular; they are then called **adventitious** buds (Fig. 21, *ad*). Many of the lateral buds fail to develop into branches the following year, often remaining dormant for several years; such are **latent** buds.

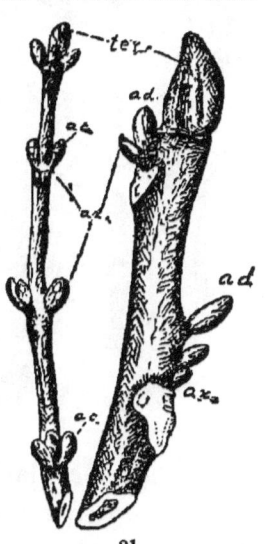

THE LEAF.

25. The **Leaf** is that organ of the plant which is intended primarily for the presentation of a large amount of surface expansion. Accordingly, we find it, as a rule, very broad and long compared with its thickness. Ordinary leaves, or foliage (Lat. *folium*, leaf), exhibit this

Fig. 21. Buds: *ter*, terminal; *ax*, axillary; *ac*, accessory; *ad*, adventitious.

typical form; besides these there are many modified forms, some of which have departed so far from the type that their true nature can be understood only when we see all the intermediate forms or gradations connecting the two extremes. Such are Cotyledons, Scales, Spines, Tendrils, Pitchers, and Fly-traps.

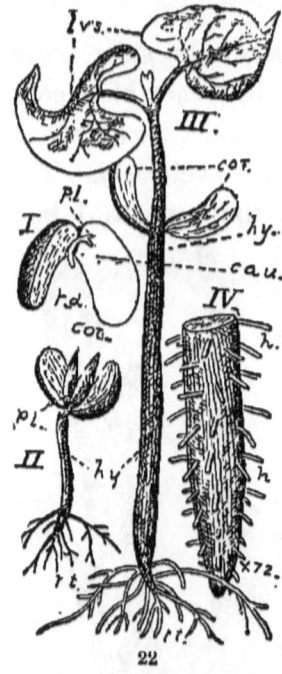

26. The two halves into which a Pea, Bean, etc., readily divide are called the **cotyledons** (Gr. *kotula*, cup), or **seed-leaves** (Fig 22, *cot*). If they be observed, in case of the Pumpkin and certain other plants, some time after germination they will be found to have changed their shape somewhat and become green, like ordinary leaves. As a rule, however, the cotyledons are simply to nourish the plantlet during germination. In the *bulb-scales* is stored up food for the early growth of the plant the following season. This nourishment is consumed, in such bulbous plants as the Hyacinth, etc., by the production of flowers in advance of the leaves.

27. The leaves of underground stems are generally reduced to mere scales. These *bud-scales*, which protect the tender parts within, are modified leaves. A gradual transition between them and the

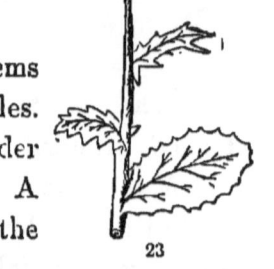

Fig. 22. Different stages in the germination of the Bean: *cot*, cotyledons; *r*, radicle; *pl*, plumule. Fig. 23. Spines, which are modified leaves, of the Barberry.

first foliage leaves may often be traced, as in the Lilac, Hickory, etc. When **spines** occupy the place of leaves, they are modified forms of the latter. In the Barberry all gradations may be seen on a single shoot (Fig. 23). The leaf, or a portion of it, may become changed into a **tendril** for climbing, as in the Pea, Vetch, etc. (Fig. 24).

28. Very interesting modifications of leaves are furnished by the Pitcher-plant (*Sarracenia*), Sundew (*Drosera*), and the Venus's Fly-trap (*Dionœa*). The leaves of Sarracenia are hollow cups or tubes (Fig. 25), covered within with hairs directed downwards. They are generally half-full of a liquid, into which insects may fall, and become macerated, and their juices are then absorbed by the plant. The Drosera is also carnivorous, feeding on small insects which alight on and are held fast by viscid tentacles or hairs on the upper side of the leaf. The leaves of *Dionœa* (Fig. 25a) have at the top two or three lobes furnished with a marginal

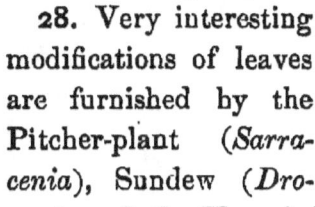

Fig. 24. Tendril of the Pea-leaf.   Fig. 25. Leaf, having the form of a pitcher, of Sarracenia, or the Side-saddle Flower.   Fig. 25a. Leaves of Venus's Fly-trap.

row of stout bristles, and three or four slender ones on the upper surface. When the bristles on the upper surface are touched by a small insect, the lobes suddenly close in on it and the prisoner is then digested and consumed.

29. The leaves are said to be **alternate** (Fig. 26) when there is but a single leaf at each node or joint of the stem. Examples of this arrangement are very numerous, as the Apple, Oak, Elm, Willow, Dock, etc. If two leaves occur at each node, they are said to be **opposite** (Fig. 27), as the Maple, Ash, Peppermint, Catnip, etc. Sometimes there are three or more leaves at each

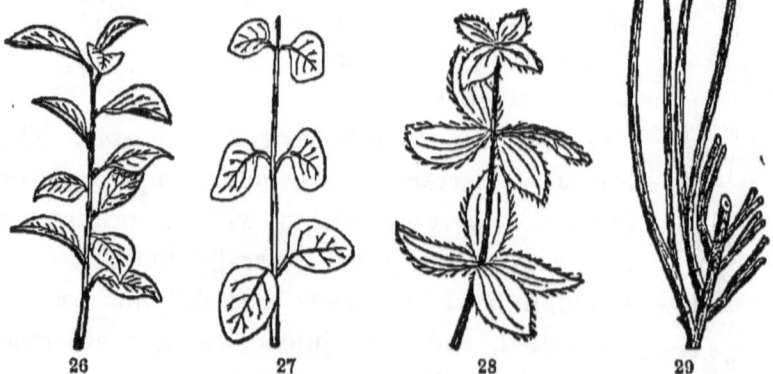

joint, as in Cleavers (*Galium*), Trumpet-weed (*Eupatorium purpureum*, *L.*), etc. In this case the leaves are said to be **verticillate** (Fig. 28). In the Pines and Larch the needle-shaped leaves are in clusters, that is, they are **fasciculate** (Fig. 29). If leaves grow from the base of the stem, but appearing to come out of the ground, they are **radical** (Lat. *radix*, root). Those leaves inserted on the stem are **cauline** (Lat. *caulis*, stem).

30. If on a straight, leafy shoot of an Elm, Cherry, Apple, Oak, Willow, etc., a thread be passed from the

Fig. 26. Alternate leaves. Fig. 27. Opposite leaves. Fig. 28. Verticillate leaves. Fig. 29. Fasciculate leaves.

lowest leaf to the one next above, and continued around the stem in the same direction to the successive leaves above, the thread will be found to take a spiral course; thus the leaves are seen to be spiral in their arrangement on the stem. In the Elm the third leaf stands directly over the first, and to reach it the thread has passed once around the stem, or, as it is usually said, the cycle is complete when the third leaf is reached, and it is expressed by the fraction $\frac{1}{2}$. The numerator denotes the number of turns; the denominator, the number of leaves encountered. Experimenting in a similar manner with the Alder, the fraction $\frac{1}{3}$ is obtained, and with the Cherry, $\frac{2}{5}$. In the latter case the stem would be encircled twice before a leaf is found (the sixth), which is inserted directly over the first, and five leaves are contained in the cycle. In a similar manner the fractions $\frac{3}{8}$ with the Flax, $\frac{5}{13}$ with the Flea-bane, $\frac{8}{21}$ with the House-leek, $\frac{13}{34}$ with cones of some Pines, and $\frac{21}{55}$ with some Firs, would be obtained.

31. If now vertical planes be passed through the points of insertion of the several leaves and the axis of the shoot, the angle formed by any two planes, in case of the Elm, whose cycle is $\frac{1}{2}$, will be one-half of 360°, or 180°—that is to say, the **angular divergence** of the leaves is 180°. In like manner, the angle formed by the planes through the points of insertion of the leaves and the axis of the shoot of the Alder, whose cycle is $\frac{1}{3}$, will be found to be one-third of 360°, or 120°—or the angular divergence of the leaves in this case is 120°. And with the $\frac{2}{5}$ cycle, the angular divergence of the leaves is two-fifths of 360°; with the $\frac{3}{8}$ cycle it is three-eights of 360°, and so on for every cycle.

32. If the fractions $\frac{1}{2}$, $\frac{1}{3}$, $\frac{2}{5}$, $\frac{3}{8}$, $\frac{5}{13}$, $\frac{8}{21}$, $\frac{13}{34}$, etc., be examined, certain definite relations will be seen to exist. For

instance, the numerator and denominator of any fraction may be obtained by adding respectively the numerators and denominators of the two preceding fractions. The numerator of any fraction is the same as the denominator of the second preceding fraction. Spirals may be constructed which will show the arrangements indicated by the several fractions, and exhibit at the same time the angular divergence of the leaves (Figs. 30–33). Such

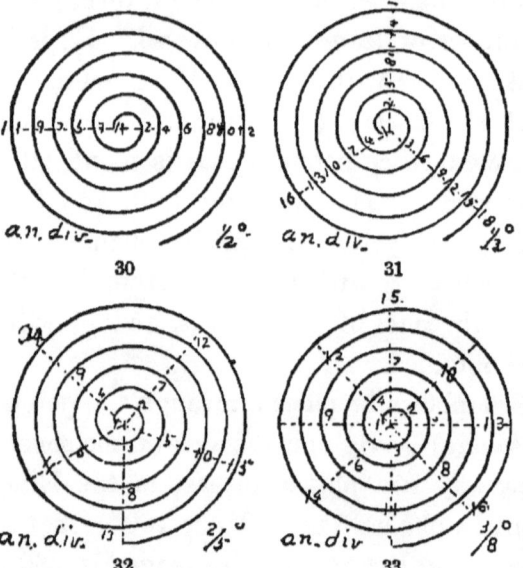

a view may actually be obtained by looking from above at the shoot in the direction of its axis.

33. If a number of leaf-buds be dissected it will be found that a difference prevails in regard to the **vernation** (Lat. *ver*, Spring), or the disposition of the scales or leaves in the bud. The arrangement of these leaves in reference to each other is, in general, like their arrangement on the stem, but more will be said of this hereafter, when treating of flower-buds. Each separate leaf is generally bent or folded or rolled up. When the upper part is bent down upon the lower (e.g. Tulip-tree) it is said to be **inflexed**, or **recline**. When the two halves are folded together, face to face, it is **conduplicate**

Figs. 30-33. Spirals showing angular divergence of leaves, ½, ⅓, ⅖, ⅜.

THE LEAF. 31

(Fig. 34). If the leaf is folded like a fan (e.g. Maple) it is said to be **plicate**, or plaited. It is **circinate** (e.g. Ferns) when rolled from the tip downwards (Fig. 35); **convolute** (e.g. Plum) when

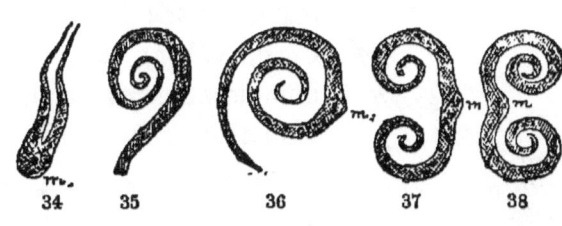

rolled from one edge into a coil (Fig. 36); when rolled from both edges inwards (e.g. Violet) it is **involute** (Fig. 37); when rolled outwards (e.g. Azalea) it is **revolute** (Fig. 38).

34. A leaf may have three parts, namely: the **blade**, or **lamina**, which is the expanded portion (Fig. 39, *bl*); the **petiole** (Fig. 39, *pet*), which is the stem of the leaf; and **stipules**, which are the appendages at the base of the petiole (Fig. 39, *stip*). The stipules are very often wanting, in which case the leaf is said to be **exstipulate**. If the blade is inserted directly on the stem (which is the case when the petiole is absent), the leaf is said to be **sessile**. The blade consists of a net-work of veins or skeleton of woody tissue, and the soft, green tissue between the veins called **parenchyma** (Gr. *para*, by; *enchein*, to fill in). When one vein surpasses the others in size it is called the **midrib** (Fig. 39, *m.r.*); its branches are the **veins** (Fig. 39, *vn*), and the branches from the veins are the **veinlets** (Fig. 39, *vnl*).

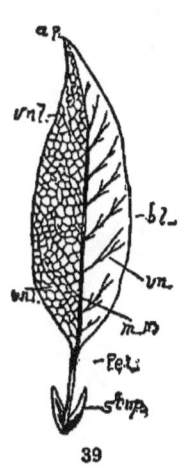

35. If the venation of a large number

Figs. 34–38. Vernation: 34. Conduplicate; 35. Circinate; 36. Convolute; 37. Involute; 38. Revolute. Fig. 39. A leaf: *bl*, blade; *pet*, petiole; *stip*, stipules; *m.r.*, midrib; *vn*, veins; *vnl*, veinlets; *ap*, apex.

of different kinds of leaves be examined, it will be found that two types prevail. The one is represented by such

leaves as the Lily, Flag, Grass, Corn, Wheat, etc., in which a number of conspicuous veins extend from the base to the apex of each leaf, approximately parallel to each other, and this fact has suggested the name **parallel-veined** (Fig. 40). The other type is seen in the Oak, Elm, Maple, Catnip, Mallow, Dock, etc. The veins here form a network, and are said to be **netted-veined**, or *reticulated*. Of the latter there are two sorts: the veins may

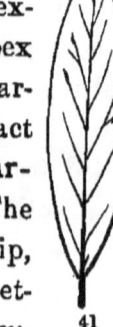

branch from a midrib (Fig. 41), when they are **pinnately-veined** (Lat. *pinna*, feather); or they may branch from 3, 5, 7, etc., ribs (Fig. 42), in which case they are **palmately-veined** (Lat. *palma*, palm).

36. The principal shapes assumed by leaves are: **linear**, narrow, long, and of the same breadth throughout (Fig. 43); **lanceolate** (Lat. *lancea*, lance),

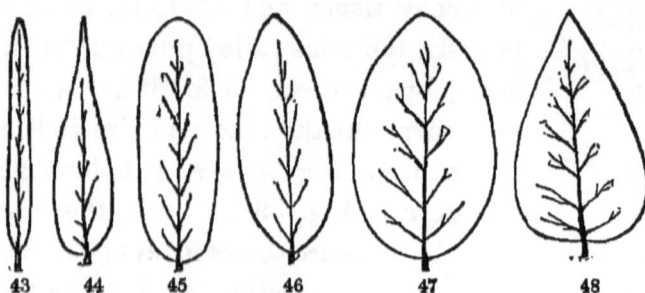

Fig. 40. Parallel-veined leaf. Fig. 41. Pinnately-veined leaf. Fig. 42. Palmately-veined leaf. Figs. 43-48. Shapes of leaves: 43. Linear; 44. Lanceolate; 45. Oblong; 46. Elliptical; 47. Oval; 48. Ovate.

THE LEAF.

long and narrow, tapering upwards and downwards (Fig. 44); **oblong**, twice, or thrice, as long as broad (Fig. 45);

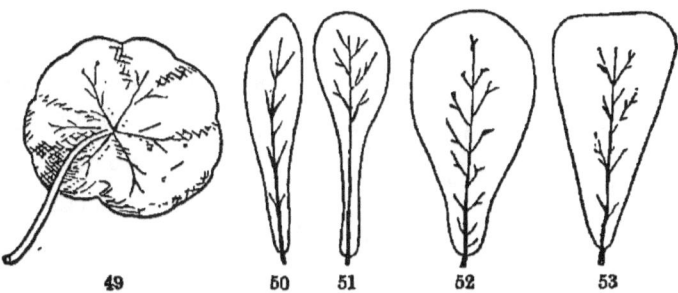

elliptical, oblong, with a flowing outline (Fig. 46); **oval**, broadly elliptical (Fig. 47); **ovate**, shaped like an egg, the broader end downwards (Fig. 48); **orbicular**, circular in outline, or nearly so (Fig. 49); **oblanceolate**, like lanceolate, except with the more-tapering end downwards (Fig. 50); **spatulate**, shaped like a spatula, that is, round above and narrow below (Fig. 51); **obovate**, ovate, with the narrow end downwards (Fig. 52); **cuneate** (Lat. *cunea*, wedge), shaped like a wedge (Fig. 53).

37. As to the *base*, leaves may be: **cordate** (Lat. *cor*, heart), heart-shaped (Fig. 54); **reniform** (Lat. *renes*, kidneys), kidney-shaped (Fig. 55); **auriculate** (Lat. *auricula*, little ear), with ears or blunt projections (Fig. 56); **sagittate** (Lat. *sagitta*, arrow), with pointed projections downwards (Fig. 57); **hastate** (Lat. *hasta*, spear), with pointed projections outwards

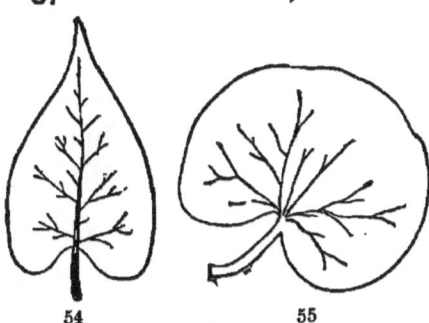

Figs. 49–53. Shapes of leaves: 49. Orbicular; 50. Oblanceolate; 51. Spatulate; 52. Obovate; 53. Cuneate. Figs. 54, 55. Base of leaves: 54. Cordate; 55. Reniform.

(Fig. 58); **peltate** (Lat. *pelta*, shield), when the petiole is attached to the under-surface near the middle (Fig. 49).

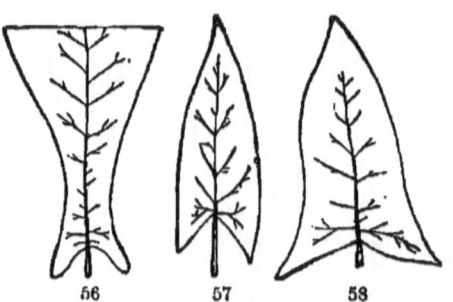

38. The *apex* of leaves may be: **acuminate**, ending in a prolonged point (Fig. 59); **acute**, ending in an acute angle (Fig. 60); **obtuse**, with a blunt point (Fig. 61); **truncate**, with the end as if cut square off (Fig. 62); **emarginate**, notched at the end (Fig. 63); **obcordate**, with a deep notch, or inversely heart-shaped (Fig. 64); **cuspidate** (Lat. *cuspis*, point), tipped with a sharp, stiff point (Fig. 65); **aristate** (Lat. *arista*, awn), with a long bristle or awn (Fig. 66).

39. The *margin* of leaves may be: **entire**, that is, the edge is an even line without any notches or teeth (Fig. 58); **serrate** (Lat. *serra*, saw), with teeth like a saw projecting towards the apex (Fig. 67); **dentate** (Lat. *dens*, tooth), with teeth pointing outwards instead of forwards

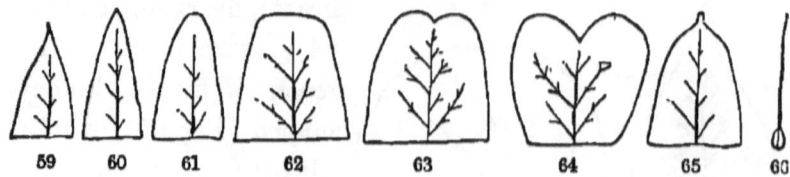

(Fig. 68); **crenate** (Lat. *crena*, scallop), scalloped (Fig. 69); **undulate** (Lat. *undula*, wave), wavy (Fig. 70); **incised**, when the edge is cut or jagged (Fig. 71).

40. When leaves are deeply and regularly cut, the

Figs. 56–58. Base of leaves: 56. Auriculate; 57. Sagittate; 58. Hastate. Figs. 59–66. Apex of leaves: 59. Acuminate; 60. Acute; 61. Obtuse; 62. Truncate; 63. Emarginate; 64. Obcordate; 65. Cuspidate; 66. Aristate.

divisions are called **lobes**. If the incisions extend more than half-way from the margin to the midrib, the leaf is

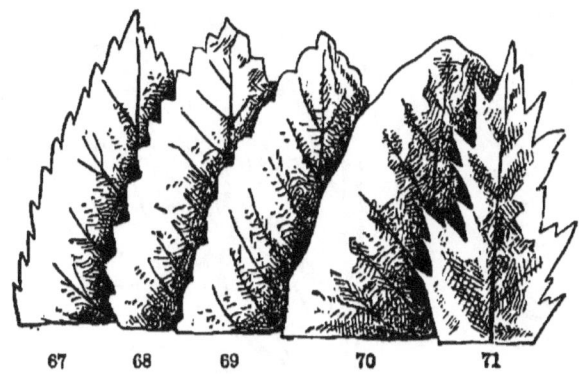

said to be **cleft** (Fig. 72); the number of segments are indicated by the terms **bifid** (two-cleft), **trifid** (three-cleft), **multifid** (many-cleft), etc. If the divisions extend almost to the midrib, the leaf is said to be **parted**; if they extend quite to the midrib, the leaf is **divided**; and thus a **simple** leaf, or one with lamina in a single piece, is converted into a **compound** leaf, that is, one with the blade divided into several parts (Fig. 73). Each of the latter is called a **leaflet** (Fig. 73, *lft*), and the stem or midrib, which supports the leaflets, is called the **rachis** (Fig. 73, *rach*).

41. Corresponding with the pinnate and palmate type of venation, there are pinnately and palmately compound

Figs. 67–71. Margin of leaves: 67. Serrate; 68. Dentate; 69. Crenate; 70. Undulate; 71. Incised. Fig. 72. A Cleft leaf. Fig. 73. A divided, *i.e.* compound, leaf of the rose: *lft*, leaflets; *rach*, rachis; *stip*, stipules.

36 ORGANOGRAPHY.

leaves. The **pinnate** leaves have the leaflets or *pinnæ* arranged on each side of the rachis. If the leaflets are in

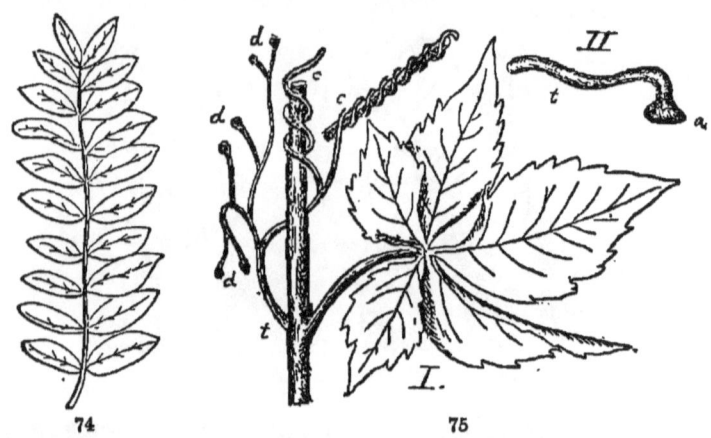

pairs throughout, the leaf is said to be **abruptly-pinnate** (Fig. 74); if a single leaflet terminates the rachis, the leaf is said to be **odd-pinnate** (Fig. 73). **Palmate** (sometimes called **digitate**) leaves have the leaflets borne on the extreme tip of the leaf-stalk (Fig. 75).

42. The leaflets themselves may be divided, which is expressed by the terms **bi-pinnate** (twice pinnate, Fig. 76), or thrice pinnate. When the leaf is several times compound, it is called **de-compound**. Of numerous other forms not yet mentioned, the following are conspicuous. **Perfoliate** (Lat. *per*, through; *folium*, leaf), in which the stem appears to pass through the leaf near its base

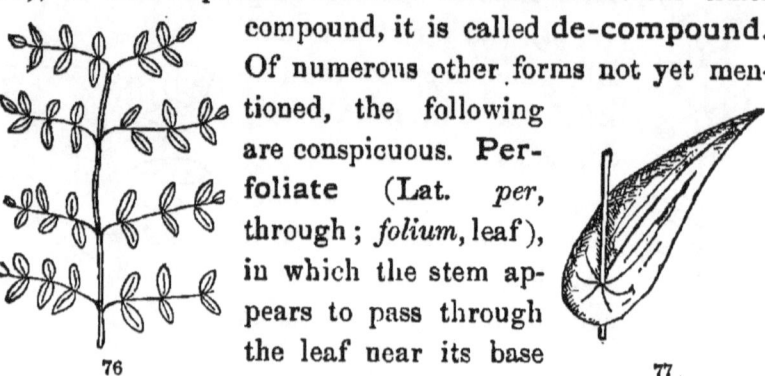

Fig. 74. An Abruptly-pinnate leaf. Fig. 75. A Palmate (or Digitate) leaf. Fig. 76. A Bi-pinnate leaf. Fig. 77. A Perfoliate leaf.

(Fig. 77), as in the Uvularia. In the Honeysuckles the opposite leaves are sometimes united at their bases, rendering them con- nate-perfoliate (Fig. 78). The leaves of the Iris are **equitant**, that is, straddling over each other. Several kinds of leaves have no distinction of blade and petiole; as the sword-shaped, **ensiform** (Lat. *ensis*, sword), leaves of the Daffodils; the needle-shaped, **acicular** (Lat. *acus*, needle), leaves of the Pines (Fig. 29); and the scale-shaped, **squamose** (Lat. *squama*, scale), leaves of the Junipers. If petioles become laminoid, or expanded like a blade, and take the place of the latter, they are called **phyllodia**.

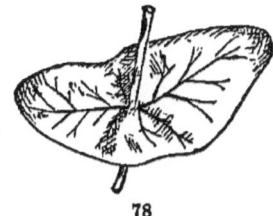

43. The **stipules** are sometimes free, leaf-like appendages, as in the Pea (Fig. 79), and perform the ordinary function of leaves; in Galium they are interpetiolar, and as large as the leaves and exactly resemble them, so that the leaves are usually said to be *whorled;* but in reality they are *opposite*, the two intermediate leaves on each side being free stipules. Ordinarily, however, the stipules are very much reduced in size, as in the Bean; sometimes they take the shape of bristles or prickles, as in the Locust (Fig. 80). In the Smilax they take on the shape of tendrils (Fig. 81). When united to the base of the

Fig. 78. A Connate-perfoliate leaf. Fig. 79. Leaf of the Pea, with large, *free* stipules (*stip*).

petioles, as in the Rose and Clover, they are said to be

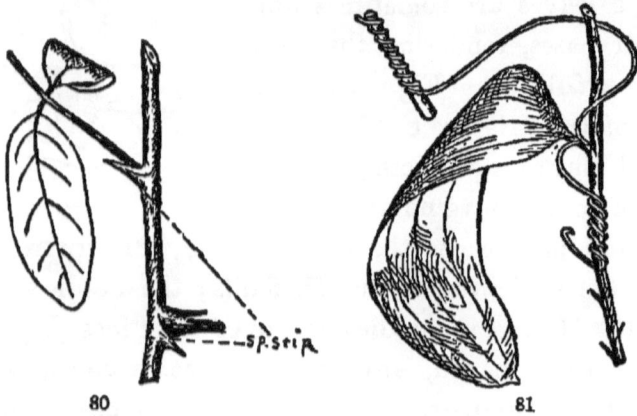

adnate (Fig. 73, *stip*). The stipules of the Tulip-tree serve as bud-scales, falling off soon after the leaves unfold.

44. In the Dock and the Buckwheat family the stipules unite and form a sheath around the stem (Fig. 82), which is called *Ochrea*. If the outer margins only unite, as in the Buttonwood, a double stipule opposite the leaf is formed. If the inner margin only unite, as in the Pondweed (Potamogeton), the double stipule is situated in the axil of the leaf. The sheaths of the grasses represent the petiole, for they bear the blade at their summit; but the small appendages, commonly found at the top of the sheath, called a ligule (Fig. 83), is of the nature of a stipule.

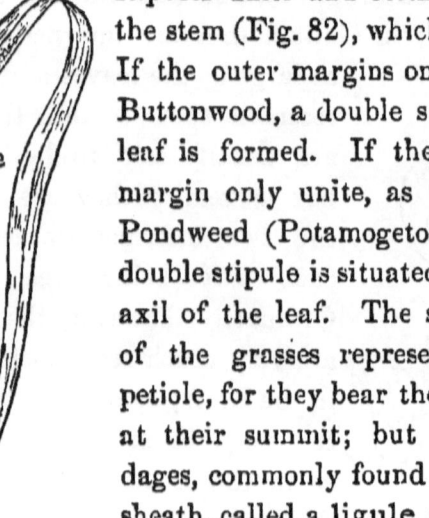

Fig. 80. Spinous stipules (*st. stip*) of the Locust. Fig. 81. Tendril stipules of Smilax. Fig. 82. An Ochrea, or Sheathing stipule, of Polygonum. Fig. 83. Grass leaf, with the ligule (*lig*) representing a stipule.

THE FLOWER.

45. The Flower.—If a leafy shoot be reduced in length, the leaves will be brought close together; if the internodes (portions of the stem between the joints) are wanting entirely, the leaves will be in whorls, or form a rosette. If now these leaves undergo cer-

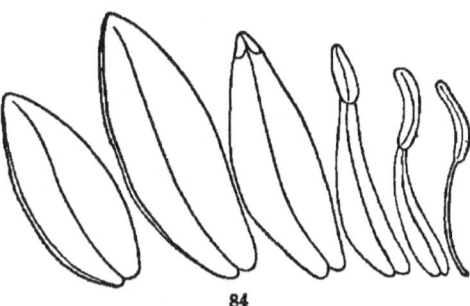

tain changes in form and function, a **Flower** will be formed. This change or modification of one part or organ into another, is called *metamorphosis* (Gr. *meta*, beyond; *morpha*, form); the flower is a metamorphosed branch, and the different organs are modified leaves (Fig. 84). Proofs of this are found in the partial or complete reversion of floral organs back into ordinary leaves; indeed, numerous intermediate forms may readily be found which form a gradual transition from a foliage leaf to the most highly differentiated organ of the flower.

46. The axis and leaves, belonging to or near the flower-

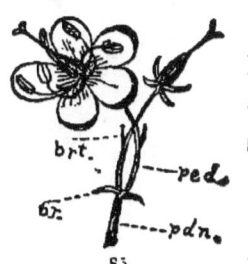

cluster, undergo modifications to form **peduncles** and **pedicels**, and **bracts** and **bractlets**. The stem, or stalk, which supports a flower-cluster, or a single flower, is called the **peduncle** (Fig. 85, *pdn*). If the peduncle is wanting, that is, if the flower is inserted directly on the stem, it (the flower) is said to be **sessile**. When the peduncle arises from the ground, it is called a **scape**.

Fig. 84. Transformation of petals into stamens. Fig. 85. Flowers supported by pedicels (*ped*), which are branches of the peduncle (*pdn*): *br*, bracts; *brt*, bractlets.

The minute branches of the peduncle, or slender stalks which support the individual flowers, are called **pedicels** (Fig. 85, *ped*).

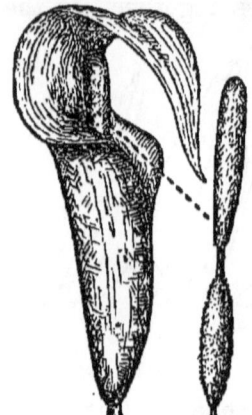

47. The **bracts** are generally diminutive leaves which subtend the flower-cluster, or from whose axil the flower stem proceeds (Fig. 85, *br*). The secondary or small bracts on the pedicels are called the **bractlets** (Fig. 85, *brt*). They have generally lost the ordinary function of leaves, and in some cases become highly colored like the flower, as in the Painted-cup (*Castelleia*), etc. If a single, enlarged bract enclose the flower-cluster, it is called a **spathe** (Fig. 86). If the bracts are numerous and form a conspicuous cup under the flowers, or an imbricated covering around a head of flowers, they form an **involucre** (Fig. 87, *in*). The axis of an elongated flower-cluster is called the **rachis**. When the axis is short, or abortive, so that the flowers are crowded into a head, it is called the **receptacle** (Fig. 87, *rec*).

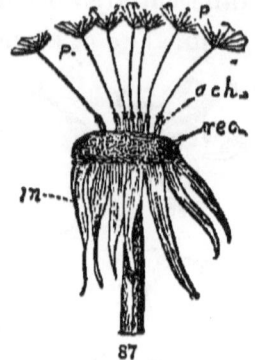

48. **Inflorescence** (Lat. *flos*, flower) is the mode of flowering, or the situation and arrangement of the blossoms on the plant. If the flowers develop from lateral buds, the inflorescence is called **indeterminate**, for the shoot, terminated by a bud, may continue to grow in length. If the flowers develop from terminal buds, the

Fig. 86. Spathe of the Indian Turnip. Fig. 87. Reflexed involucre (*in*) and receptacle (*rec*) of the Dandelion.

inflorescence is **determinate**, because the length of the axis is thereby determined; it cannot grow longer. The indeterminate inflorescence is also **centripetal**, that is, the outermost flowers (when the cluster is level-topped), or the lowest on the stem, open first, and those higher follow in regular succession, until finally the one in the centre or at the top expands. Examples are furnished by the Lily of the Valley, Currant, Plantain, Shepherd's-Purse, etc. The determinate inflorescence is **centrifugal**, inasmuch as the flowering begins in the centre or top and proceeds outwards

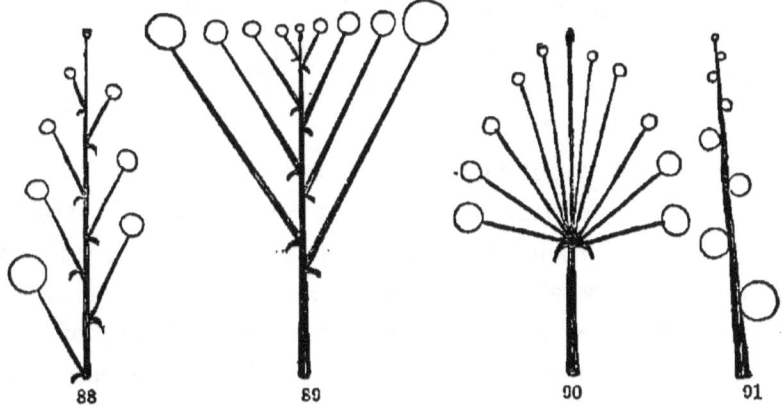

or downwards. This is exhibited in the Chickweed, Dianthus, Hydrangea, etc.

49. The following are varieties of *indeterminate inflorescence:* Raceme, Corymb, Umbel, Spike, Spadix, Catkin, Head, and Panicle. The **raceme** has the pedicellate flowers scattered on an elongated axis (Fig. 88). The **corymb** is the same as a raceme, with the lower pedicels elongated so as to make the flower-cluster level-topped (Fig. 89). In an **umbel** the axis is reduced, and all the pedicels proceed from a common point (Fig. 90). The

Figs. 88-91. Diagrams, illustrating forms of inflorescence: 88. Raceme; 89. Corymb; 90. Umbel; 91. Spike.

spike is similar to a crowded raceme, with the flowers *sessile* (Fig. 91). Two special forms of the spike have peculiar names, namely, the **spadix** (Fig. 86), which is fleshy (and commonly surrounded by a spathe); and the **catkin**, or **ament**, which is scaly (Fig. 92). The **head** differs from a spike in that the axis is reduced, crowding the flowers into a head-like cluster (Fig. 93). A **panicle** is an open and more or less compounded raceme or corymb (Fig. 94).

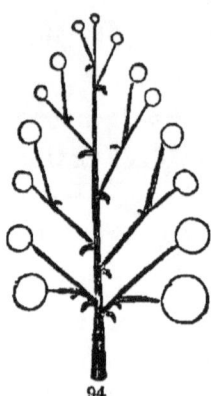

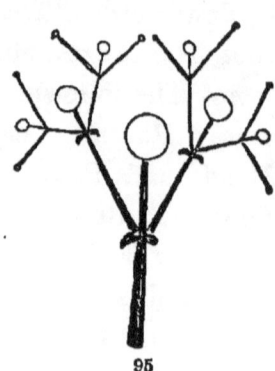

50. The **cyme** is a determinate or definite flower-cluster, with a flat or convex top. It resembles the corymb somewhat, except that in the latter the flowering is centripetal, while in the cyme it is centrifugal (Fig. 95). A crowded cyme is called a **fascicle**. Many of the clusters are often compound, as compound umbels, compound cymes, etc. The two classes of inflorescence may be represented in one and the same plant; thus the Mint Family has cymes or fascicles, which are *centrifugal* in their flowering, but these are

Fig. 92. Catkin of the American Hazel. Fig. 93. Head of Clover-flowers. Fig. 94. Diagram of a Panicle. Fig. 95. Diagram of a Cyme.

generally composed of spikes or racemes, which are centripetal in their flowering.

51. The flower is that organ of the plant which is designed for the production of seed, and thereby the continued existence of its kind. In a complete flower, such as the Buttercup, Rose, Phlox, etc., there is externally the **calyx** (Fig. 96, *ca*), or cup-like portion, which consists of several parts, either distinct or united, which more or less resemble ordinary foliage leaves (Fig. 96). Each leaf, or portion of the calyx, is called a **sepal**; within this whorl of leaves forming the calyx is a second whorl, either of distinct or more or less united parts, called the **corolla** (Fig. 96, *cor*). This is commonly the most showy part of the flower. Its component parts are called **petals**, and they usually depart farther from the ordinary form and texture of foliage leaves than do the sepals.

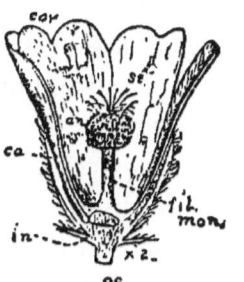

52. Within the corolla are slender bodies called **stamens** (Figs. 96, 101, etc). They sometimes revert to petals or sepals (Fig. 84), showing that they are also modified leaves. These bodies are sometimes excessively numerous; and when few, are rarely less in number than the parts of the corolla or calyx. Within these, and occupying the central part of the flower, are the **pistils** (Figs. 96, 101, etc.); in the lower enlarged part of which (called the **ovary**) the seeds are produced. The pistils, like the stamens, may be numerous, but are very often reduced to one or two. It is very common for the pistils to revert to ordinary green foliage leaves. There can be no production of seed without both stamens and pistils, and for this reason

Fig. 96. A Flower : *ca*, calyx; *cor*, corolla; *in*, involucre.

they are together called the **essential organs** of the flower. The calyx and corolla may or may not be present without directly influencing the production of seed. When present, they surround the essential organs and protect them, hence they are called **protecting organs.** They are also called the **perianth** (Gr. *peri*, around; *anthos*, flower).

53. A flower with the four parts present is called a **complete flower**; but if one or more of the parts are absent, the flower is said to be **incomplete.** If the essential organs are present it is called a **perfect flower.** Those with stamens only (called **staminate** flowers), and those with pistils only (called **pistillate** flowers), are **imperfect.** If the parts are alike among themselves,—that is, all the sepals alike in shape and size, all the petals alike in shape and size, and all the stamens alike in shape and size,—the flower is said to be **regular** (Fig. 97). If this likeness in shape and size does not obtain in any one set of organs, the flower is said to be **irregular** (Fig. 98). If the petals, sepals, and stamens are of the same number, or the latter twice or thrice that number, the flower is said to be **symmetrical**; but if the number is not the same in each whorl, the flower is **unsymmetrical.**

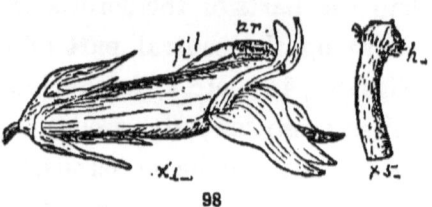

54. If the relative insertion of the floral parts be examined, two types will be found to prevail. In the one case each petal is inserted directly in front of or within a sepal, and each

Fig. 97. Kalmia blossom, a regular flower. Fig. 98. Flower of Lobelia, irregular.

stamen directly in front of or within a petal; and the parts are said to be **opposite** (Fig. 99). But in the other case the petals are in front of or within the spaces between, that is, alternate with the sepals, and the stamens alternate with the petals; then the parts of the flower are said to be

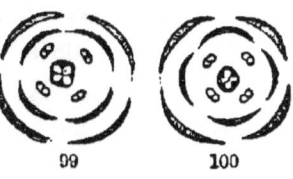

alternate (Fig. 100). When the parts of the flower, especially of the calyx and corolla, are each three in number, the flower is said to be three-parted; and it is generally found that three-parted flowers are borne on plants which

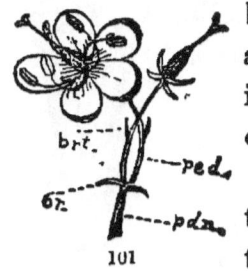

have parellel-veined leaves. If the parts are in 4's or 5's, the flowers are respectively four or five-parted; such flowers generally accompany netted-veined leaves.

55. When the sepals are free, or distinct from one another, the calyx is said to be **polysepalous** (Gr. *polus*, many); and when the petals are free, the corolla is **polypetalous** (Fig. 101). The sepals may be united edge to edge, so that only their upper ends are free, by which the number forming the cup or calyx may be determined. The calyx in such case is said to be **monosepalous** (Gr. *monos*, one), or **gamosepalous** (Gr. *gamos*, union). When the petals are united, the corolla is **monopetalous**, or **gamopetalous** (Fig. 102). This union of similar parts or cohesion, as it is called, gives rise to a

Fig. 99. Diagram of a flower with parts opposite. Fig. 100. Diagram of a flower with parts alternate. Fig. 101. A polysepalous and polypetalous flower. Fig. 102. A Rotate corolla.

variety of forms of the calyx and corolla; prominent among which are: Rotate, Salverform, Campanulate, Funnelform, Tubular, Labiate, and Ligulate.

56. A **rotate** (Lat. *rota*, wheel), or wheel-shaped calyx or corolla, is one in which the tube is very short or wanting, and the lobes spread at once (Fig. 102). In the **salverform** corolla, the spreading limb or border is raised on a narrow tube, and forms a right angle with the latter (Fig. 103). The **campanulate** (Lat. *campanula*, bell) denotes a bell-shaped calyx or corolla (Fig. 104). In the **funnelform**, the tube is narrow below, but gradually spreading above like a funnel. The **tubular** form spreads scarcely any above (Fig. 106). The two upper petals may unite closely and form a kind of upper lip, and the three lower ones unite to form a lower lip (Fig. 105.) In such case the corolla is **labiate** (Lat. *labium*, lip). The calyx may also be labiate, or two-lipped.

57. If a flower-head of a Sunflower be examined, it will be found to consist of numerous florets, with tubular corollas interspersed with the bristles or chaff (Fig. 106), and a row of marginal flowers called *ray flowers;* these ray flowers have strap-shaped corollas (Fig. 106, *lig*), which are called **ligulate** (Lat. *ligula*, tongue). A curious shape is presented by the Pea or Bean (Fig. 107). The corolla

Fig. 103. A Salverform corolla. Fig. 104. A Campanulate corolla. Fig. 105. A Labiate corolla of Toad-flax.

THE FLOWER.

is polypetalous; very irregular and resembles more or less remotely a butterfly, and for this reason it has received the name *Papilionaceous* (Lat. *papilio*, butterfly); the upper and larger petal is called the *banner*, or *vexillum* (Fig. 107, *v*); the two side petals are called the *wings*, or *alæ* (Fig. 107, *a*); and the two anterior

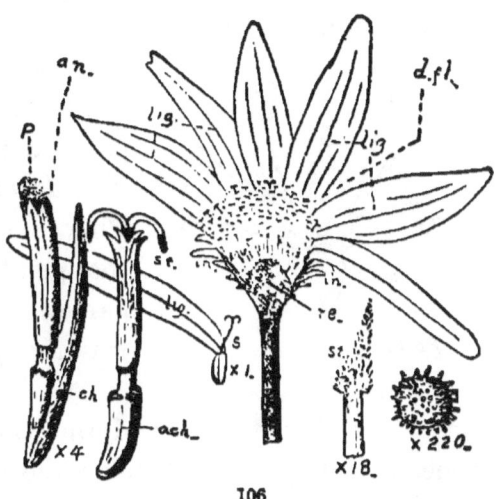

ones, generally cohering slightly (and enclosing the stamens and pistil), are called the *keel* (Fig. 107, *k*). The flowers of the Cress, Mustard, Cabbage, etc., have four petals, arranged two and two opposite, somewhat like a cross, and they are said to be **cruciform** (Lat. *crux*, cross; Fig. 108).

58. A conspicuous irregularity in the flower is caused by the production of appendages of various kinds. One petal in the Violet is prolonged so as to form a **spur**; this organ is tubular, and generally contains Nectar, or sweet substance secreted by the flower. One species of Dicentra is two-spurred. All the petals of

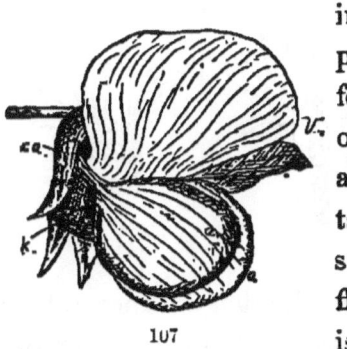

Fig. 106. A head of flowers of Heliopsis: *in*, involucre; *d.fl*, disk-flowers; *lig*, ray-flowers; *ch*, chaff; *ach*, achenia. Fig. 107. A Papilionaceous flower of Pea: *v*, vexillum; *a*, wings; *k*, keel. Fig. 108. A Cruciform corolla.

the Columbine have spurs. Sometimes there is only a gentle swelling or blunt, outward projection (as in Adlumia), which is denoted by the word **saccate**. Sometimes sepals or petals are eared or *crested;* or they have, like the Pink, a projection (corona) at the point where the *claw* or narrow part of the petal joins with the spreading lobe or limb.

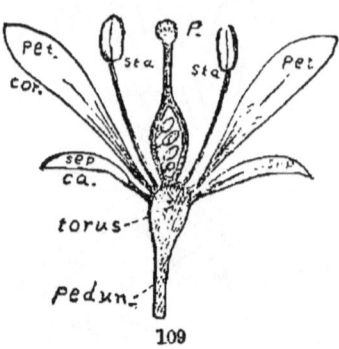

59. When there is no adhesion or growing together of the calyx and corolla, the former is plainly inserted below the points of insertion of the corolla, stamens, and pistils. In such case (Fig. 109), the calyx is said to be **free** or **inferior**; or the calyx and corolla are said to be **hypogynous** (Gr. *hypo*, under; *guna*, pistil). The cohesion may be to the extent shown in Fig. 110, where the petals and stamens are inserted on the calyx-tube. The petals are then said to be **perigynous** (Gr. *peri*, around), though the calyx is *free.* The calyx-tube may be consolidated with the lower part of the pistil or ovary, when it is said to be **adherent** or **superior**; in this case the parts appear to be inserted upon the pistil (ovary), and are therefore said to be **epigynous**

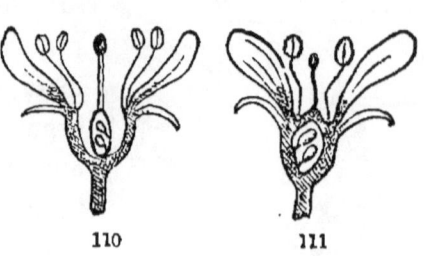

(Gr. *epi*, upon; Fig. 111). If the adhesion does not extend so far up (half-way), the calyx is said to be **half-superior.**

Figs. 109–111. Diagrammatic sections of flowers: 109. Hypogynous; 110. Perigynous; 111. Epigynous.

THE FLOWER.

60. The arrangement of the sepals and petals in the flower-bud, or æstivation (Lat. *æstas*, summer), may best be seen in transverse sections of the bud when it is about ready to expand. If the pieces do not overlap each other, but simply meet edge to edge, the æstivation is **valvate** (Fig. 112). Examples are furnished by the calyx of the Basswood and the Mallow, and the corolla of Grape and Virginia Creeper. In the valvate calyx, or corolla, if the edges turn inwards, it is said to be **induplicate**; if outwards, it is said to be **reduplicate**. In the corolla of the Potato is an example of the former; and in the sepals of the Althea of the latter. In case the parts overlap each other (as in the corolla of Mallows), so that one edge of each is covered, and the other not, the æstivation is **convolute** (Fig. 113). When the overlapping is such that some pieces are wholly inside and others wholly outside, like the shingles on a roof (as in the corolla of the Basswood), the æstivation is **imbricate** (Lat. *imbrex*, tile; Fig. 114).

61. The stamens consist of two parts (Fig. 121), namely, the **filament** (Lat. *filum*, thread), or slender stem; and the **anther**, or enlarged upper end. That portion of the filament between the anther lobes is called the *connective*. The filament is not an essential part, and when wanting, the anther is sessile. When the filaments are united into a tube surrounding the pistil, as in the Mallow (Fig. 115), they are said to be

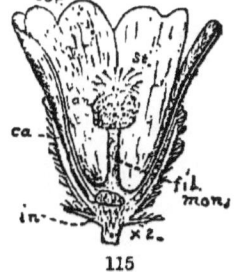

Figs. 112–114. Diagrams illustrating æstivation: 112. Valvate; 113. Convolute; 114. Imbricate. Fig. 115. Monadelphous stamens (*fil. mon.*) in Mallow.

monadelphous (Gr. *monos*, one; *adelphos*, brotherhood). If they are united into two sets, as in Dicentra, they are

diadelphous; if in three sets, **triadelphous**; and so on. When the anthers are united into a tube, as in the Composite family (Sunflower, Dandelion, etc.), they are said to be **syngenesious** (Gr. *syn*, with; *genesis*, birth). If a transverse section of the anther be made (Fig. 116), two or four cavities, called cells, will be seen, and these are filled with a yellow dust, which, on examination with the microscope, proves to be small, round bodies, called **pollen** (Fig. 117). Each pollen grain has two coats: the outer, thicker and often ornamented; the inner, more delicate and elastic.

62. The opening of the anther at maturity, for the discharge of the pollen, is called **dehiscence.** This commonly takes place by a line along the whole length of each cell (Fig. 118). In the Sassafras, Barberry, etc., the opening is by a lid or valve (Fig. 119). In the Azalea, Pyrola, etc., the pollen escapes by a pore at the top of the anther (Fig. 120). As regards the attachment of the anther to the filament, it may be **innate**, or inserted by its base on the top of the filament (as in Fig. 121); or **adnate**, when attached by one face its whole length (Fig. 122). It is **versatile** when inserted near its middle point to the top of the filament, so that it may swing

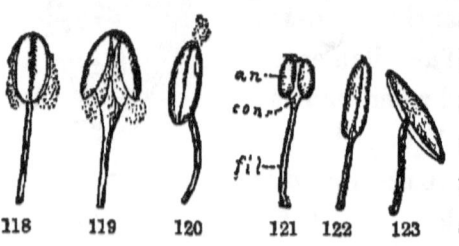

Fig. 116. Transverse section of an anther. Fig. 117. A pollen grain. Figs. 118–120. Dehiscence of anthers: by splitting longitudinally; by lids or valves; by pores. Figs. 121–123. Attachment of anthers: 121. Innate; 122. Adnate; 123. Versatile.

THE FLOWER. 51

loosely (Fig. 123). If the anther is attached to the side of the filament towards the pistil, it is said to be introrse; if from it, extrorse.

63. If a single stamen is present, the flower is said to be **monandrous** (Gr. *monos*, one; *ander*, stamen); if two stamens are present, it is **diandrous**; if three, **triandrous**; if four, **tetrandrous**; and so on. If the stamens are numerous or indefinite, the flower is **polyandrous**. In the Labiate family often two of the stamens are long and the other two short; they are then called **didynamous** (Gr. *di*, two; *dunamis*, power, strong). In the Crucifer family four stamens are long and two short (Fig. 124), and are called **tetradynamous** (Gr. *tetra*, four). As regards the insertion of the stamens, they are **hypogynous** when attached below the pistils (Fig. 109); **perigynous** when attached to the calyx-tube surrounding the pistil (Fig. 110); and **epigynous** when situated with the sepals on the ovary (Fig. 111). They are **epipetalous** when attached to the corolla (Fig. 125).

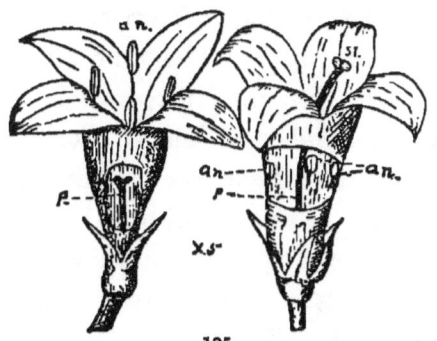

64. The pistil (Fig. 126) consists of three parts: namely, the **ovary** (Fig. 126, *ova*), or lower enlarged part which contains the ovules or seeds; the **style** (Fig. 126, *sty*), or slender part above

Fig. 124. Tetradynamous stamens. Fig. 125. Flowers, with stamens on the corolla (epipetalous). Fig. 126. A pistil: *ova*, ovary; *ovu*, ovules; *sty*, style; *stig*, stigma; *pla*, placenta.

the ovary; and the **stigma** (Fig. 126, *stig*), the more or less enlarged upper end of the style. The style may be wanting, which renders the stigma sessile. According as the pistil, or **carpel**, as it is sometimes called, is formed of a single leaf or of several leaves, it is simple or compound. In a **simple pistil**, formed by a single leaf folded edge to edge, the seeds are borne on the part of the inner wall, which corresponds to the line of union of the edges, and is called the **placenta** (Fig. 126, *pla*). If two placentæ are present, they must have resulted from the union of two leaves, edge to edge; if three placentæ, from the union of three leaves, etc. Therefore the presence of two or more placentæ is proof of a compound pistil. The number of styles generally corresponds to the number of leaves entering into the formation of the carpel.

127   128

65. **Compound pistils** may have a single cell, or they may have many cells. When the latter have simply united with each other, edge to edge (Fig. 127), there will be but *one* cell, and the placentæ, or seed-bearing lines, will be situated on the ovary wall, as in the simple pistil; that is, they will be **parietal** (Lat. *paries*, wall). If each separate carpellary leaf unites edge to edge, and then all the carpels join (Fig. 128), the ovary will have as many cells as there were carpellary leaves, the seed-bearing lines will be crowded to the centre and form **central placentæ**. The dissepiments or walls which separate the cells from one another may become obliterated, leaving the seed-bearing column in the centre of a continuous or one-celled cavity,

Figs. 127, 128. Diagrammatic sections of compound ovaries: 127. One-celled ovary, parietal placentæ; 128. Many-celled ovary, placentæ central.

and thus a free central placenta is formed (Fig. 129). Examples of this are found in the Purslane, Chickweed, Pinks, etc.

66. The number of pistils in a flower is expressed by the Greek words: **monogynous**, meaning one pistil; **digynous**, meaning two pistils; **trigynous**, meaning three pistils; **tetragynous**, meaning four pistils; **pentagynous**, meaning five pistils; **polygynous**, meaning many pistils. The ovary and calyx-tube may be united, when the former is said to be **adherent**, or **inferior** (Fig. 111). If the adhesion extends half-way up, the ovary is said to be **half-inferior**. If there is no adhesion of the ovary with other parts, it is said to be **free**, or **superior** (Fig. 109). The ovules, or small bodies which are to become seeds, are enclosed by the pistil; the latter is, therefore, said to be **angiospermous** (Gr. *angios*, vessel; *sperma*, seed).

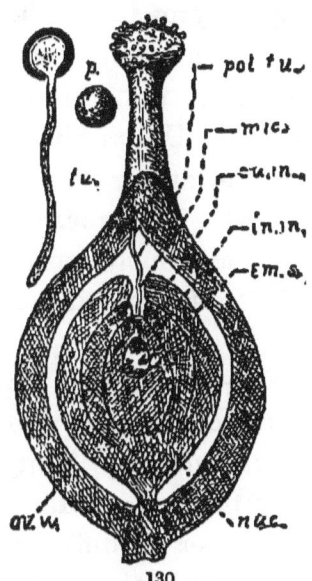

67. In the Pine family the ovules lie exposed in the cone, on the upper surface of the base of the scales. The scale is, therefore, the pistil, and it is said to be **gymnospermous** (Gr. *gymnos*, naked; *sperma*, seed). If ovules, either of gymnospermous or angiospermous pistils, be examined, they will be found to consist of a central

Fig. 129. Diagrammatic section of compound ovaries: One-celled, placenta free, central. Fig. 130. Diagrammatic section of an ovule: *pol tu*, pollen-tube; *mic*, micropyle; *ou. in*, outer integument; *in. in*, inner integument; *em. s*, embryo-sac; *nuc*, nucleus.

part, called the **nucleus**, surrounded by one or two **integuments** (Fig. 130, *in*). These integuments do not close entirely above, but leave a small orifice, called the **micropyle** (Fig. 130, *mic*). This is for the entrance of the pollen-tube (Fig. 130, *pol tu*), which grows from the pollen grain that has been transported from the anther to the stigma.

68. In the upper part of the nucleus of the ovule is the embryo-sac (Fig. 130, *em. s*), in which the embryo of the seed is to be developed. This development, however, does not take place till the ovules become **fertilized**, that is, until the tube emitted by the pollen grain grows from the stigma down through the style, enters the micropyle, and reaches the embryo-sac, where the contents of the grain or tube passes by osmosis into the embryo-sac. Unless, therefore, the pollen finds transport from the anther to the stigma, there will be no production of seed. This transference of the pollen is called **pollination**, and many contrivances and agencies exist to effect it, the most important of which will now be mentioned.

69. **Pollination and Fertilization.**—When both the essential organs, *stamens* and *pistils*, are contained in one and the same flower, as the Rose, Lily, Buttercup, Mint, and Grass, it is called an **hermaphrodite** flower. Many plants possess, either in the same cluster or on different branchlets, both *fertile* (pistillate, that is, with pistils, but no stamens) and *sterile* (staminate, that is, with stamens, but no pistils) flowers, and they are said to be **monœcious** (Gr. *monos*, one; *oikos*, house), such as the Oaks, Hickories, Alder, Corn, Nettle, etc. Others have the fertile and sterile flowers on different trees, as the Willows, Poplars, Ash, Hemp, etc., and they are called **diœcious** (Gr.

di, two; *oikos*, house). In monœcious and diœcious plants it is evident that the transport of the pollen from the staminate to the pistillate flowers must in some way be effected in order to accomplish fertilization. Even in hermaphrodite flowers it is found to be a rare case that the pollen, wholly unaided, falls on the stigma of the same flower.

70. When the pollen of a flower is applied to, and acts on, the stigma of the same flower, the process is called **close-fertilization**, or **self-fertilization**. But if the pollen of one flower is applied to, and acts upon, the stigma of a different flower, it is called **cross-fertilization**. It would naturally be expected that in hermaphrodite flowers self-fertilization would almost invariably obtain. So it was taught until very recently. Now it is known that cross-fertilization is the rule, and self-fertilization the exception. In fact, there is in the majority of cases something in the structure of the flower to prevent self-fertilization. Many plants, as the Oxalis, Violet, etc., have two sets of hermaphrodite flowers—a showy form, in which cross-fertilization occurs, and an inconspicuous form, where close-fertilization necessarily takes place.

71. When the transport of the pollen is effected by the wind, the flowers are said to be **anemophilous** (Gr. *anemos*, wind; *philos*, loving). Such are the Pines, Oaks, Hickory, Walnut, Alder, Grasses, Sedges, Hemp, Hops, etc. They are characterized by the production of an enormous quantity of pollen. This insures the contact with the stigma of at least a small portion of the pollen. It is light, dry, incoherent, and readily transported great distances, sometimes forming "showers of sulphur." The flowers are mostly greenish, or of dull colors, and inconspicuous. The

stigmas are generally large, often furnished with hairs or dissected into plumes (Fig. 131) for the retention of the grains that may come in contact with them. The anthers are often suspended on capillary filaments, so as to be more directly exposed to the action of the wind.

72. When pollination is effected by *insects*, the flowers are said to be **entomophilous** (Gr. *entomon*, insect; *philos*, loving). In these the amount of pollen produced is not so great, there being but little waste as compared with the loss when transported by the wind. It is not so dry and incoherent as in the anemophilous flowers; the grains

are generally moist or slightly viscid, often provided with projections or entangling threads. In the Orchids and Milkweeds the pollen is in masses, supplied with viscid pedicels (Fig. 148). All these contrivances tend to insure the adherence of the pollen grains or masses to the head, legs, or body of the insects which visit the flowers, and thus effect the transportation of the pollen to the stigmas of other flowers. Such flowers are further characterized by the possession of a large, showy perianth, or of odor, or by the secretion of nectar; or they may furnish all these attractions combined.

73. Of the special adaptations in hermaphrodite flowers, to insure cross-fertilization, **dichogamy** (Gr. *dichos*, asunder; *gamos*, union) is an important one; it means that the stamens and pistil of the same flower do not come to maturity at the same time, hence self-fertilization is impossible. The flower is **proterandrous** (Gr. *protos*, first; *andres*, stamens) when the anther ripens and discharges the pollen

Fig. 131. Plumose stigma of a grass-flower (*Poa pratensis*).

before the stigma reaches maturity. If the stigma is in a receptive condition before the pollen escapes, the flower is **proterogynous** (Gr. *guna*, pistil). Among the anemophilous flowers the common Plantain furnishes an example of Proterogyny. The long, slender, hairy stigmas may be seen protruding from the unopened perianth while the anthers are yet enclosed. Only pollen from other flowers, therefore, can effect the fertilization. Later the stigmas wither, and the corolla expands; the four anthers now appear supported on long, delicate filaments, and their pollen is carried to stigmas of other Plantain-flowers which may have a synchronous maturity.

74. A Proterogynous example among entomophilous flowers is furnished by the *Scrophularia*. The flowers are visited by bees for the nectar, which is secreted by glands at the bottom of the corolla.

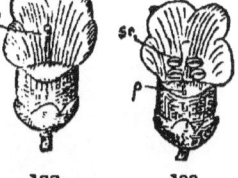

The lower lobe of the irregular corolla serves as a landing-place for the bees. The mature pistil projects, as seen in Fig. 132, when the flower first opens; and fertilization now takes place, the pollen coming from another flower of the same sort. The position of the unripe stamens at this time is not seen in the figure, for the filaments are curved and the unripe anthers are deep down in the corolla. A day or two later the anthers, now mature, appear at the mouth of the corolla, as is shown in Fig. 133. By this time the stigma, previously fertilized, is no longer in a receptive condition, and lies half-withered on the lower petal. Bees, visiting the flower, would come in contact with the anthers, and the pollen grains that adhered

Figs. 132, 133. Proterogynous flowers of *Scrophularia nodosa*: 132. First stage: Stigma mature; 133. Second stage: Anthers mature: *p*, pistil; *an*, anthers.

to them would be carried to the next *Scrophularia* visited by them, and the pistil, if ripe, would receive and be fertilized by them.

75. As an example of proterandrous flower, may be mentioned "*Clerodendron Thompsoniæ*, a Verbenaceous, tropical African climber, now common in conservatories. The adaptations in this flower (which we indicated long ago) are exquisite. The crimson corolla, and bright, white calyx in combination, are very conspicuous. The long filiform filaments and style, upwardly enrolled in the bud,

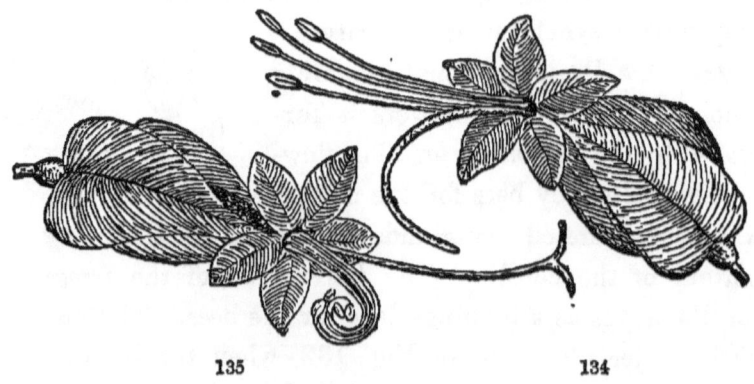

straighten and project when the corolla opens; the stamens remain straight, but the style proceeds to curve downwards and backwards, as in Fig. 134. The anthers are now discharging pollen; the stigmas are immature and closed. Fig. 135 represents the flower on the second day, the anthers effete and the filaments recurved and rolled up spirally, while the style has taken the position of the filaments, and the two stigmas, now separated and receptive, are in the very position of the anthers the previous day. The entrance, by which the proboscis of a butterfly may

Fig. 134, 135. Proterandrous flowers of *Clerodendron Thompsoniæ*; 134. First stage: Anthers mature; 135. Second stage: Stigma mature.

reach the nectar at the bottom, is at the upper side of the orifice. The flower cannot self-fertilize. A good-sized insect, flying from blossom to blossom and plant to plant, must transport pollen from the one to the stigma of the other."—(Gray.)

76. The composite flowers, such as the Rudbeckia, Heliopsis (Fig. 136), Sunflower, etc., are additional examples of proterandry. The anthers are syngenesious, and discharge the pollen early, which is pushed out of the tube by the elongating pistil (Fig. 136, *II*, *p*). The latter is not as yet in a receptive condition, and moreover the pollen cannot be applied to the stigmatic surfaces, for they are on the inner sides of the forks or branches of the tip of the style. These do not spread until the pistil has acquired its full length, and then curving outwards, the adjacent pollen is still prevented from access to the stigma (Fig. 136, *III*, *st*). The conspicuous ray-flowers (Fig. 136, *lig*) doubtless serve for the attraction of the many visiting insects, and they, by their more or less hairy bodies, convey the adhering pollen (Fig. 136, *IV*) from some flowers to the exposed stigmas of others; and thus cross-fertilization is effected. Other proterandrous

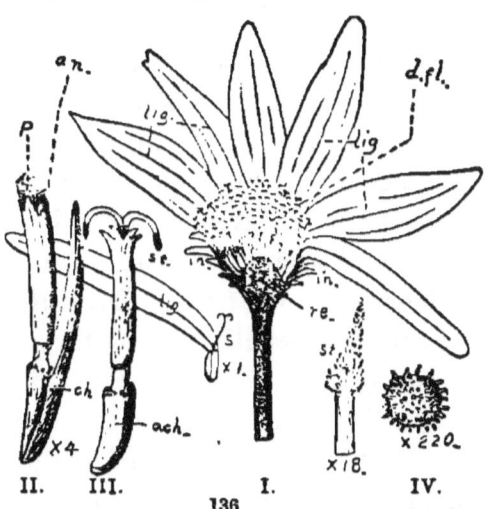

Fig. 136. *Heliopsis lævis*: *I*, Section of head of flowers; *II*, Floret immature; *III*, Floret, with mature stigma; *IV*, Pollen grain; *in*, involucre; *d.fl*, disk-floret; *lig*, ray-flowers; *ach*, achenia; *ch*, pale or chaff; *p*, pollen; *st*, stigma.

flowers are the Gentians, Epilobium, Campanula, Parnassia, Lobelia, etc. The anthers in Lobelia are like those in the

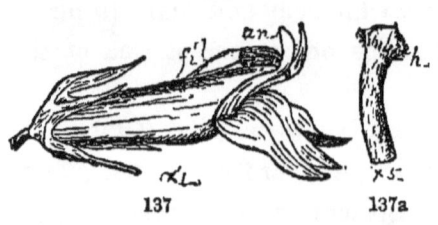

Sunflower family, that is, syngenesious, or united by their anthers forming a tube around the upper portion of the style. The pollen is discharged while the style is yet so short (Fig. 137) as to be concealed deep down in the tube. As the stigma approaches maturity, the style elongates and pushes the pollen out before it; the mouth of the tube is so situated that insects entering the throat of the corolla, for the purpose of getting nectar, would necessarily brush the pollen onto their body from the end of the protected stigma (Fig. 137a). The stigmatic surface finally becomes exposed (Fig. 138). It is evident from the description and figures that self-fertilization is impossible; and cross-fertilization by the insects, which transport the pollen from flowers in the first stage of maturity to those in the second stage, must take place.

77. **Dimorphism** (Gr. *di*, two; *morpha*, form) denotes two kinds of hermaphrodite flowers of the same species. It is often an adaptation for intercrossing. An example is furnished by the Houstonia. One set of flowers has long stamens and a short pistil (Fig. 139), and the other set has short stamens and a long pistil (Fig. 140).

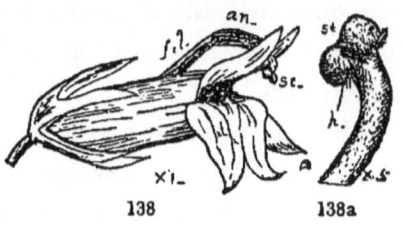

Figs. 137, 138. Proterandrous flowers of *Lobelia syphilitica*: 137. First stage: Anthers mature; 138. Second stage: Stigma mature; *an*, anthers; *fil*, filament; *st*, stigma; *h*, hairs. Figs. 137a, 138a: Stigma slightly magnified.

A bee visiting the different flowers would brush some part of the body against the anthers of the long stamens, and another part against the anthers of the short stamens; and these same parts (which, of course, would have pollen adhering to them) coming in contact with long and short pistils respectively, the pollen of one flower would in each case be applied to a stigma of another flower; or, in other words, cross-fertilization would necessarily result. It is found, besides, that the pollen grains of the two sets of stamens are of different size, and each less active upon its own stigma than upon the stigma of another flower. In some genera three sets of flowers with stamens and pistils of differing lengths exist (*trimorphism*), evidently designed for intercrossing.

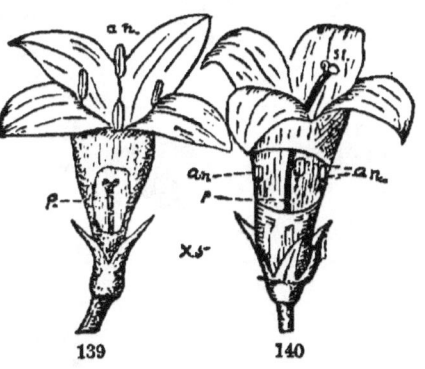

78. There are other adaptations for cross-fertilization besides dichogamy and dimorphism. An interesting case is furnished by *papilionaceous flowers;* for example, the Pea (Figs. 141–143). The ten stamens and single pistil are enclosed within the keel (Fig. 141). There are hairs on the style below the stigma, and these loosely retain the pollen which is discharged early by the anthers, the latter remaining in the keel. When a bee alights on the wings (Fig. 142, *a*) and keel (Fig. 142, *k*) they are together

Figs. 139, 140. Dimorphic flowers of Houstonia: 139. Pistil short; 140. Pistil long.

pressed downwards, and the pistil protrudes in consequence (Fig. 143, *A*). The stigma strikes the abdomen of the bee, and the style also brushes against it. When the bee visits the next flower, the stigma of that strikes the abdomen as before, but it has been dusted with pollen from the previous flower, and of course a portion of it is retained by the stigma, thereby effecting cross-fertilization. In like manner pollen from that flower is carried to the next, and so on.

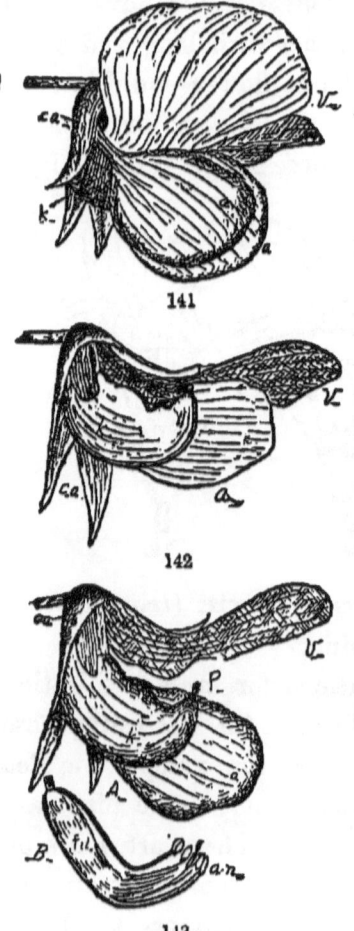

79. A slight variation from the foregoing is seen in the Bean blossom, where the keel is coiled into a snout (Fig. 144). Within this are the stamens, also the pistil, with an oblique stigma and hairy style (Fig. 145), the latter loosely retaining the early discharged pollen. When a bee, in alighting to search for nectar, presses the wing-petals downwards, the stigma and hairy style, loaded with pollen, protrude, striking the front part or side of the insect. Therefore visiting a succession of flowers the bee transports pollen

Figs. 141-143. Papilionaceous flower of the Pea: 141. The flower entire; 142. The alæ, or wings, removed, exposing the keel; 143. *A*, the keel depressed, causing the stigma to protrude; *B*, the diadelphous filaments; *v*, vexillum; *a*, alæ; *k*, keel; *fil*, filaments.

from one to another. In the Kalmia blossom the anthers of the ten stamens are lodged in cavities in the corolla, and the filaments are curved backwards as the flower expands (Fig. 146). Bumble-bees, hovering over the flowers, searching for nectar, liberate the stamens by occasional contact, which, in springing back straight, discharge the pollen from pores at the top of the anthers (Fig. 147).

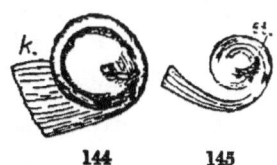

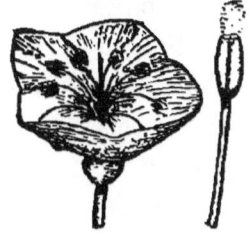

Some of the pollen grains which strike the under side of the bumble-bee and adhere to it, will, when the next flower is approached, be deposited on its stigma, thus bringing about cross-fertilization.

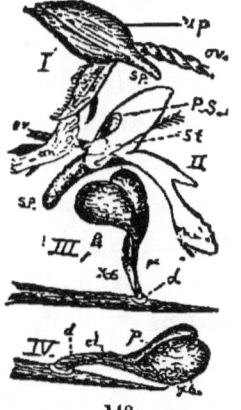

80. The most varied and wonderful contrivances for cross-fertilization are found in the family of Orchids (Fig. 148). The stamens are generally reduced to one, and this is united in a column with the pistil, indicated by the term **gynandrous** (Gr. *guna*, pistil; *andres*, stamens). The pollen in each anther-cell is united into a mass, and furnished with a little stem or caudicle, which has a very viscid disk (Fig. 148, *III, IV, d*). These two disks are so placed that when an insect visits the flower, and thrusts its proboscis into the spur for the nectar (as shown by the arrow, Fig.

Fig. 144. The coiled tip of the keel of a Bean-flower. Fig. 145. The terminal portion of the style of the same flower. Fig. 146. Flower of *Kalmia latifolia*. Fig. 147. One of its stamens discharging pollen, slightly magnified. Fig. 148. Orchid flower: *I*, flower entire; *II*, some parts removed; *III* and *IV*, pollinia attached to a lead pencil; *d*, disk; *p*, pollinia; *st*, stigma; *P.S.*, anther or pollen-sac; *cl*, caudicle; *III* and *IV*, slightly magnified.

148, *II*), they will touch and adhere to its head, and be dragged from their places when the insect departs (Fig. 148, *III*). The pedicels dry quickly, and curve downwards (Fig. 148, *IV*); when, therefore, the insect approaches another flower of the same kind, the pollen masses, or *polli-nia*, as they are called, strike against its viscid stigma, and a portion of the pollen is retained. The pollinia of this flower are in the same manner transferred to the next visited, and so on. When the access of insects is prevented, no seeds are produced, showing that self-fertilization is impossible.

81. Many tropical plants cultivated in the conservatories invariably fail to produce seed. The cause of this is to be found in the fact that the tropical insects which alone can effect their pollination are not present. It is not at all seldom that only a certain species, or, at most, only a few species, of insects can fertilize a particular kind of flower, as in the case of bumble-bees and Red Clover. Many of the adaptations for cross-fertilization, it should be remembered, do not absolutely prevent self-fertilization, so that if insects fail to visit the flowers a few seeds may, nevertheless, be produced. When the flowers are evidently arranged to favor self-fertilization, and prevent cross-fertilization, they are said to be **cleistogamous** (Gr. *kleistos*, closed). But no known species is altogether cleistogamous.

82. Examples of cleistogamy are furnished by one set of flowers of Viola, Oxalis, some Grasses, etc. "Their petals are rudimentary, or quite aborted; their stamens are often reduced in number with anthers of very small size, containing very few pollen grains, which have remarkably thin transparent coats, and generally emit their tubes while still inclosed within the anther-cells; and, lastly, the pistil is

much reduced in size, with the stigma in some cases hardly at all developed. These flowers do not secrete nectar, or emit any odor; from their small size, as well as from the corolla being rudimentary, they are singularly inconspicuous; consequently insects do not visit them, nor could they find an entrance if they did. Such flowers are, therefore, self-fertilized, yet they produce an abundance of seed. In several cases the young capsules bury themselves beneath the ground, and the seeds are there matured."—(Darwin.)

83. After fertilization an embryo is developed in the embryo-sac; the ovary enlarges, and the ovules or seeds grow to the normal size. The **embryo** is the initial plantlet (Fig. 149, *I*), and consists of an axis, called the **caulicle** (Lat. *caulis*, stem); one end of which, in germination, grows downwards, and is called the **radicle**; the other end grows upwards, and is terminated by a bud, which is called the **plumule**; and of seed-leaves, called **cotyledons**

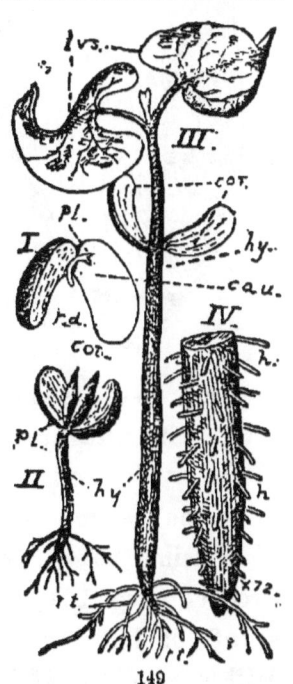

(Gr. *kotula*, cup). In case of the Grasses, Sedges, Lilies, Flags, etc., there is a single cotyledon to each embryo, and the group of plants to which they belong is said to be **monocotyledonous** (Fig. 150). In case of the Pea, Bean, Buttercup, Rose, Ash, Maple, Oak, Chestnut, etc., there are two cotyledons to each embryo, and the

Fig. 149. A dicotyledonous seed (Bean) in different stages of germination: *rd*, radicle; *pl*, plumule; *cot*, cotyledons; *hy*, hypocotyledonary portion of stem.

5

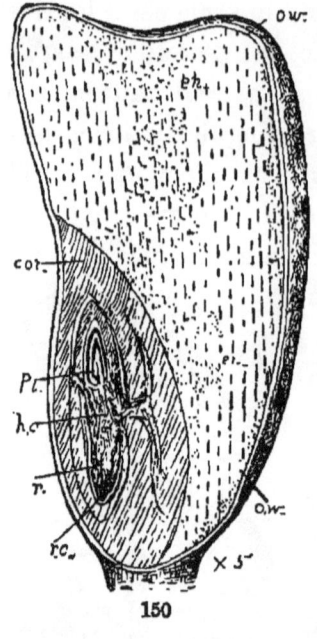

group to which they belong is said to be **dicotyledonous** (Fig. 149.) Most of the cone-bearing plants (*Coniferæ*) have **polycotyledonous** embryos. The nourishment for the plantlet during germination is stored up wholly (Pea, Bean, Maple), or in part (Corn, Wheat), in the cotyledons. The portion, if any, stored within the embryo-sac, but not in the cotyledons (Fig. 150, *en*), is called **endosperm** (Gr. *endon*, within); that, if any, outside the embryo-sac is called the **perisperm** (Gr. *peri*, around).

84. The integuments of the seed correspond with those of the ovule, and are called the **testa**. It often has, to assist the dissemination of the seed, *outgrowths*, in the shape of a wing, as in the Pine, Trumpet Creeper (Fig. 151) etc., or it may have a tuft of hairs, called **coma**, as the Milkweed (Fig. 152) and Epilobium; or a hairy covering, as the Cotton-seeds. The testa in many seeds is crustaceous, in others it becomes berry-like, and the edible pulp causes the seeds to be eaten and disseminated by birds. The seed is

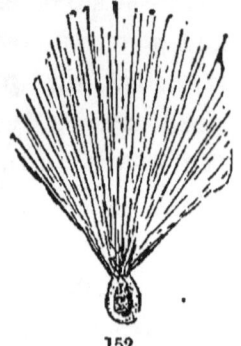

Fig. 150. Section of a monocotyledonous seed (grain of Indian Corn): *cot*, cotyledon; *r*, radicle; *pl*, plumule; *en*, endosperm. Fig. 151. Winged seed of Trumpet Creeper (*Tecoma radicans*). Fig. 152. Comose seed of Milkweed (*Asclepias Cornuti*).

THE FRUIT.

sometimes more or less covered by an outgrowth called the **aril**, as in the Nutmeg (where it is called Mace), the Burning-bush, the Climbing Bitter-Sweet, etc.

85. The **torus** is the name given to the end of the axis which supports the floral organs (Fig. 109). It is generally somewhat enlarged and rounded. It may be much elongated, as in the Magnolia (Fig. 153); or very much broadened, as in the Flowering Raspberry (Rubus). In the Strawberry it is broadened and elongated (Fig. 154). Exactly the reverse of this, namely, deeply concave, is exemplified by the Rose (Fig. 155). In the figures (Figs. 163, 164) the receptacle is hollowed out and almost completely closed at the top. In some plants of the Pink family an internode is developed between the calyx and corolla, called the **stipe**. The elongation may continue between the carpels, as in the *Geranium* and in the *Umbelliferæ*. In *Nelumbium* it is inversely conical with isolated immersed carpels. A **disk** is a development of the receptacle under or around the pistil.

86. **The Fruit.**—The Fruit may consist simply of the ripened ovary, with the enclosed seeds, as the Buttercup, Bean, Wheat, etc., or it may consist of the ovary and seeds together with the adnate parts. The Apple, for instance, consists of the ovary with the adherent calyx-tube (Fig. 156); the

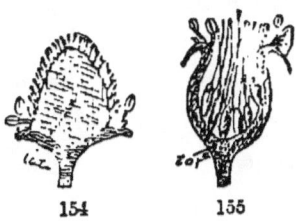

Fig. 153. Elongated torus of Tulip-tree (*Liriodendron Tulipifera*). Fig. 154. Enlarged torus of Strawberry. Fig. 155. Depressed torus of Rose.

Strawberry consists very largely of the enlarged and juicy torus. If the fruit is composed of a single pistil, either simple or compound, it is called a **simple fruit**. Those are called **aggregate fruits** which consist of a mass of carpels all belonging to one flower; and **multiple fruits** are formed by the union of pistils of several flowers.

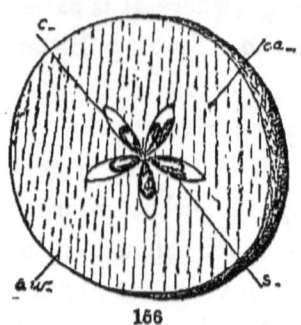

87. Simple fruits are either **dry**, as the Bean-pod; or **fleshy**, as the Plum. Some of the dry fruits spontaneously open at maturity, and are called **dehiscent** (Lat. *dehiscere*, to gape), as the Columbine, Larkspur, Shepherd's-Purse, etc. Others do not open, and are called **indehiscent**, as the winged fruit of the Maple, seeds of the Thistle, etc. Dehiscent fruits are the Follicle, Legume, Capsule, Silique, and Silicle. Indehiscent fruits are the Samara, Achenium, Utricle, Caryopsis, and Nut.

88. The **follicle** (Fig. 157) is formed of a simple pistil, and dehiscent by the *ventral suture*, that is, the line corresponding to the united edges of the carpellary leaf (Peony). A **legume** (Fig. 158) is like the above, except that it opens not only at the ventral, but also at the *dorsal suture*, or line corresponding to the midrib of the carpellary leaf (Pea-pod). A **capsule** is the dehiscent fruit of any compound pistil (Purslane). A modification of this is called

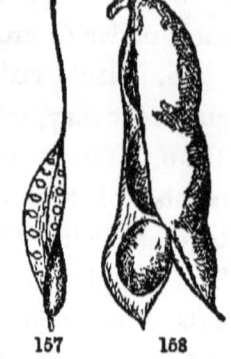

Fig. 156. Section of an Apple: *s*, seeds; *ca*, calyx; *c*, carpel; *aw*, wall of ovary. Fig. 157. Follicle of Columbine. Fig. 158. Legume of the Pea.

THE FRUIT.

the silique (Fig. 159), or two-valved fruit of the family *Cruciferæ*, where the pod has two parietal placentæ; and often a false partition from which the valves separate (Mustard). A silicle (Fig. 160) is a short silique (Shepherd's-Purse).

89. The **samara** (Fig. 161) is a winged, one-seeded, indehiscent fruit (Ash, Elm, Maple). The **achenium**, or **akene** (Fig. 136, *ach*), is a seed-like fruit, dry, naked, and indehiscent (*Anemone, Compositæ*). The **utricle** is like the akene, but with a thin and bladdery loose covering (Goosefoot). The **caryopsis** (Fig. 1, *I*) is the grain; it completely fills the thin-walled cell, and is consolidated with it (Wheat, Indian Corn). A **nut** is like an akene, but larger, and often enclosed or surrounded by a kind of involucre (Fig. 162), called a *cupule* (Acorn, Hazelnut, Hickory).

90. The **drupe** is a fruit, the outer part of which becomes fleshy, called the *sarcocarp* (Gr. *sarx*, flesh; *karpos*, fruit); and the inner, stony, called the *putamen* (Cherry, Peach). The **pome** (Fig. 156) is a fruit with several carpels of parchment-like or stony texture, covered by flesh (Apple, Pear, Quince). The **pepo** is the fleshy gourd-fruit, surrounded with a firm rind (Squash, Cucumber, Melon). The **berry** is a fruit which is fleshy throughout (Tomato, Grape, Currant).

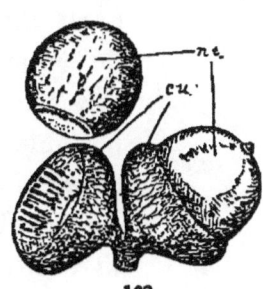

Fig. 159. A Silique. Fig. 160. A Silicle. Fig. 161. A Samara of Maple. Fig. 162. Acorn, with cupule, of Shingle Oak (*Quercus imbricaria*).

ORGANOGRAPHY.

91. Examples of **aggregate fruits**, or those in which many carpels belonging to one flower are crowded in a mass, are furnished by the Raspberry, Blackberry, Magnolia, etc. Examples of **multiple fruits**, or those resulting from the union of several flowers, are furnished by the Pine-Apple, Mulberry, Fig (Figs. 163, 164), Pine, etc. The **cone** (Fig. 165) is a special kind of multiple fruit.

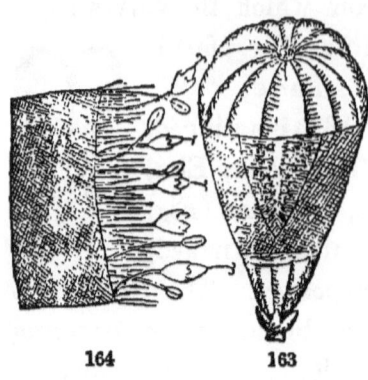

164   163

The name is improperly given to the Hop, where the large bracts represent the scales. The cone of the Pine consists of crowded scales, on the upper surface of which the naked seeds are borne. The various forms assumed by fruits, have, in many cases, evident reference to the dispersion of seeds.

92. The **wing** of the fruit of the Elm, Maple, Ash, Hop-tree, Birch, Pine, etc., enables the seed to be scattered great distances by the wind. The wing-like, floriferous bract of the Basswood renders the fruit more buoyant and transportable by the wind. The **pappus** (Fig. 87), or persistent calyx of the Thistle, Dandelion, and other *Compositæ*, often finely dissected and downy, causes the seeds to be transported for miles. The Beggar-ticks (*Bidens*, Fig. 166), Tickseed (*Coreopsis*), and Burdock, have **barbs** or **hooks**, which,

165   166

Figs. 163, 164. A Fig: 163. Natural size; 164. A portion slightly magnified. Fig. 165. Cone of Hemlock. Fig. 166. Achenium, with barbed pappus, of *Bidens frondosa*.

adhering to the coats of animals or plumage of birds, often effect a wide dissemination of seeds (Fig. 166). The seeds of **fleshy** fruits, eaten by birds, are generally uninjured by the process of digestion, and are carried sometimes to great distances from the place of growth. Of the multitude of nuts transported by the rodents to their habitations, some would escape injury, and might give rise to trees at considerable distance from the place of their production.

93. In Witch-Hazel the seeds are scattered by the bursting elastically of the pod; so also the Touch-me-not. The seeds, together with the pulp, are ejected with force from the Squirting Cucumber (*Ecbalium*). These, though but moderately efficient contrivances, are evidently designed for the dispersal of seeds. Many seed-coats are so firm as to resist for a long time the action of water, and may, therefore, germinate after being transported great distances by river and ocean currents. Seeds may lie dormant for a long time, and then finally germinate when favorable conditions obtain. The spores of Fungi, or Moulds, Puffballs, etc., are produced in countless thousands, and are readily transportable by even gentle winds. It is estimated that an Elm-tree produces upwards of half a million, and a single Tobacco plant forty thousand seeds, numbers which are small in comparison with those of the spores of many cryptogamous plants. This great fecundity is an important factor in effecting the dissemination of seeds,

PART II.

HISTOLOGY AND PHYSIOLOGY.

THE CELL.

94. If a thin, transverse section of a stem or leaf be examined under the microscope, it will be found to consist

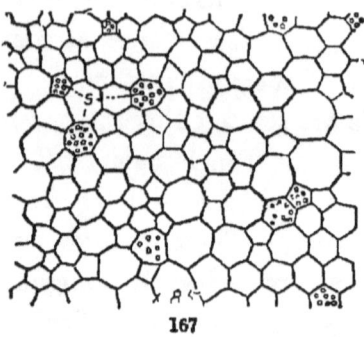

of a multitude of globular or more or less elongated and flattened bodies, called **cells** (Fig. 167). These vary in shape in different plants, or even in different parts of the same plant. They may be globular, as in many unicellular plants, pollen grains, etc. (Fig. 168); they are pyriform, or pear-shaped, in case of some swarm spores (Fig. 169); they are many-sided, or elongated, in tissue of ordinary plants; they may take

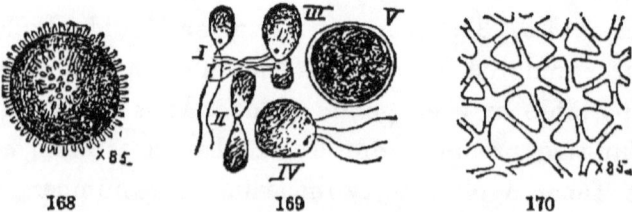

on a very irregular shape, as *stellate* (Lat. *stella*, star), in the tissue of the Rush (Fig. 170); or *ramose* (Lat. *ramus*,

Fig. 167. Section of stem of *Clematis*. Fig. 168. Pollen grain of Morning-Glory. Fig. 169. Swarm spores. Fig. 170. Stellate cells from the stem of Rush (*Juncus*).

branch), as in common mould (Fig. 171). The variation is as striking in regard to size; the cells of *Bacterium termo*, the common fungus of putrefaction, are about .00009 inch long and .00005 inch broad; the Yeast-plant cells are about .0003 inch in diameter; the average size of cells of ordinary plants is .005 to .0005 inch; many cells, as of bast, plant-hairs, etc., are not microscopic as those mentioned above, but attain a length of several inches.

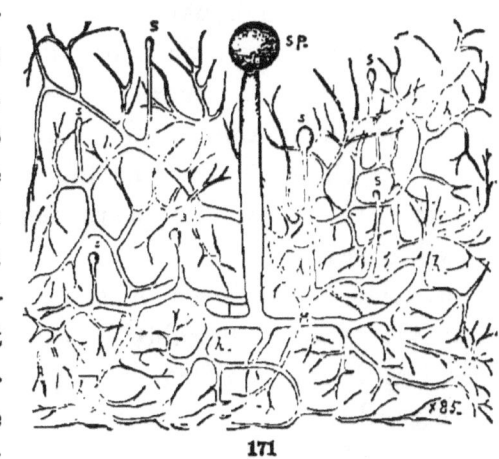

95. A **cell** consists of four parts, namely: (1) the **cell-wall** (Fig. 172, *w*), or cell-membrane, a covering enclosing the cell-contents, which are (2) the **protoplasm** (Gr. *protos*, first or primitive; *plasma*, form), a transparent, semi-fluid substance (Fig. 172, *pr*), containing (3) the **nucleus**, a spherical or oval body, denser than the protoplasm (Fig. 172, *n*), and (4) the **cell-sap**, a watery fluid occupying cavities, called *vacuoles* (Fig. 172, *v*). Of these four parts the protoplasm is the only one essential to the growing cell; the other parts may be wanting; swarm spores have no cell-wall;

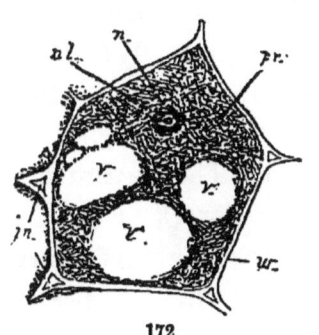

Fig. 171. Common Mould (partially diagrammatic). Fig. 172. A cell showing the four parts: *w*, cell-wall; *pr*, protoplasm; *n*, nucleus; *nl*, nucleolus; *v*, vacuoles.

the nucleus has not been detected in the cells of all the lower plants, though never absent in the higher; in very young tissue the cell-sap is not differentiated. From the protoplasm the other parts are secreted or formed; and while the protoplasm remains, the cell continues to live. With age, the cell-wall often thickens, as in woody tissue, and the protoplasm disappears, immediately after which growth ceases.

96. The cell-wall, which is very thin in young cells, often increases considerably in thickness. This thickness is seldom, if ever, uniform throughout the whole wall, and there results, therefore, a variety in its sculpturing. The direction of the thickening may be centrifugal, or outwards; or it may be centripetal, or inwards. The first is illustrated by the projections, ridges, etc., on isolated or exposed cells, as in many spores, pollen grains, etc. (Fig. 168). The centripetal thickening is seen in ordinary woody tissue, whose elongated cells are compacted together. The portion thickened may be in the form of rings (Fig. 173, *an*), when the thickening is said to be **annular** (Lat. *annulus*, ring). The thickened band may be **spiral** (Fig. 173, *sp*), and either closely or loosely wound. When the tissue is rudely torn asunder, these spiral bands often uncoil, the thin portion of the wall giving way. The spiral thickening is the most common. The **reticulate** wall has thickenings so as to present a net-work (Fig. 173, *ret*). In the **scalariform** (Lat. *scalaria*, flight of stairs, or ladder) the thickening is at the longitudinal angles of the cells, and extends across, so as to give approximately the appearance of rounds of a ladder (Fig. 173, *sca*).

97. When the thickening of the cell-wall is intercepted at numerous isolated spots, it becomes **pitted** (Fig. 173,

THE CELL.

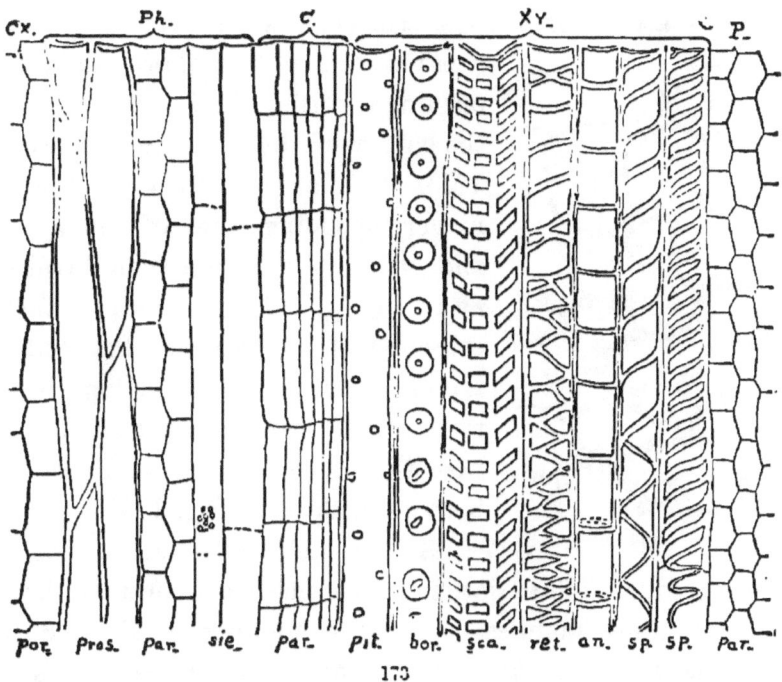

pit). These pits or channels may be simple or branched (Fig. 180), and in cross-section appear oval, round, etc.; or they may be elongated fissures. The woody tissue of the Pine family is characterized by **bordered pits** (Figs. 174–178), where each pit is surrounded, when viewed from without, with a ring (Figs. 173, *bor*, and 174); this result is brought about thus: a circular portion of the wall remains thin (Fig. 175), and around this a wall arises and grows inwards (Fig. 176),

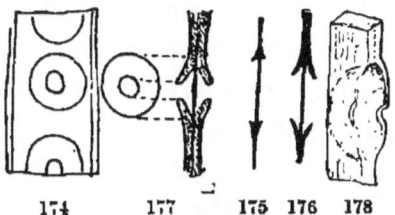

Fig. 173. Diagrammatic section through ducts and cells, showing various modes of thickening: *P*, pith; *xy*, wood; *C*, cambium; *Ph*, bast; *Cx*, cortex; *par*, parenchyma; *pros*, prosenchyma; *sie*, sieve tubes; *pit*, pitted; *bor*, bordered pits; *sca*, scalariform; *ret*, reticulated; *an*, annular; *sp*, spiral. Figs. 174–178. Bordered pits, and their development.

76   HISTOLOGY AND PHYSIOLOGY.

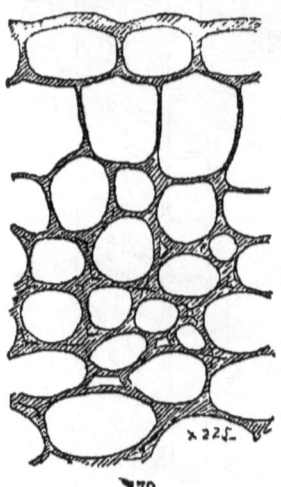

forming a low dome (Figs. 176, 177); the overarching wall does not meet in the middle; and this opening furnishes the inner ring, and the bottom of the pit the outer (Fig. 177). Similar growth takes place in corresponding sides of the wall, and the thin partition soon breaks away (Fig. 178), allowing free communication between the cells. Another method of thickening gives rise to tissue, called **collenchyma**; here the corners of the cell alone become thickened (Fig. 179).

98. In cell-walls considerably thickened, a differentiation into numerous concentric layers is plainly manifest under the microscope (Fig. 180). This is called **stratification**, and it is due to the fact that alternate layers contain different amounts of water of organization. The dark layers contain less, and the light layers contain more, water. From a study of the stratification in starch grains, Nägeli was led to the conclusion that the molecules of the cell-wall are aggregated into small particles in the form of crystals (each of which he called a *micella*), each surrounded by a layer of water. With larger amounts of water these particles, or *micellæ*, are pushed further apart, and the layer appears light under the microscope. With a decrease of the amount of water the

Fig. 179. Collenchyma. Fig. 180. Hardened cells of the Pear, in which stratification is shown.

particles approach each other, making a dense layer, and appearing dark under the microscope. Sometimes a system of layers at right angles to the layers of stratification is evident, due likewise to varying amounts of water contained. This is called **striation**. Owing to chemical changes a cell-wall may actually become separated into two or more layers or shells, as in pollen grains, spores, etc.; but this has no necessary connection with stratification or striation.

99. The cell-wall is composed of **cellulose** (which consists of carbon, hydrogen, and oxygen, and whose formula is $C_{12} H_{20} O_{10}$), water of organization, and ash constituents. The ash or mineral constituents constitute often less than one per cent. of the whole weight of the plant. Three to five per cent. may be considered the average, though it may run as high as twenty or thirty per cent. Potassium, calcium, magnesium, iron, phosphorous, sulphur, sodium (traces of manganese), silicon, and chlorine exist in the ash. In addition to these, bromine and iodine are found in the tissue of marine plants. The chemical changes, or metamorphoses, which the cell-wall often undergoes are (1) conversion into **mucilage**; (2) conversion into **cork**; and (3) conversion into **wood**, or **lignification** (Lat. *lignum*, wood). The seeds of Flax and Quince furnish an example of the first. **Corky layers** are developed abundantly in some plants, as in the Cork-Oak. Cork is impervious to water. When a plant is wounded slightly on the surface, layers of cork are developed immediately under the wound, and thus protection is afforded to the parts beneath. **Lignification** of the cell-walls takes place in all but herbaceous plants, and consists in the impregnation of the cellulose, with a substance called lignin; the tissue resulting being ordinary wood or woody tissue, of indispensable use in the industries of life.

100. Growth of the cell-wall does not take place by the addition or apposition of new layers concentrically around the one first formed, as was for a long time believed. It takes place, as is now quite generally held, by a process called **intussusception**. This may be understood by a reference to Fig. 181, which is a diagrammatic representation of the theoretical structure of the cell-wall. The small squares represent the particles (*micellæ*), or crystal-molecules (aggregates of molecules of cellulose); and surrounding each there are layers of water. The nutrient solution from the protoplasm passes between the particles, and from it new particles, or micellæ, arise between those already existing. It is evident that growth can thus take place only when the cell-wall is in a turgid state, that is, distended by water. An increased amount of water pushing the already existing particles further asunder, affords space for the formation and existence of new ones.

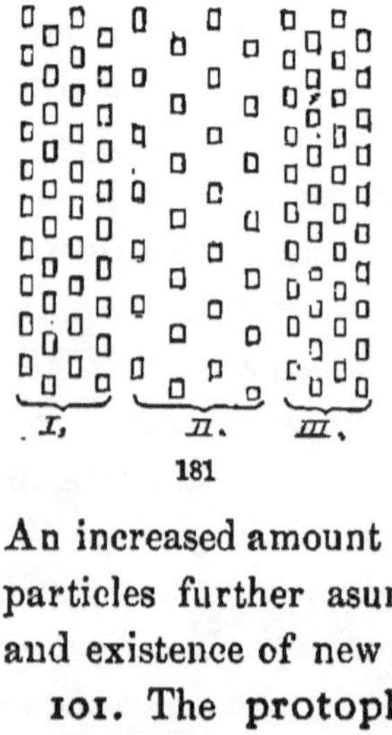

101. The **protoplasm** is a very complex substance, whose exact chemical composition has not been as yet satisfactorily determined. It consists of albuminoids (containing oxygen, hydrogen, carbon, and nitrogen), with a variable amount of water and a small amount of ash or mineral constituents. It is transparent, often slightly yellowish, and more or less granular under the microscope. Living protoplasm often exhibits movements both when

Fig. 181. Diagrammatic representation of the minute structure of a cell-wall; *I* and *III*, with less water; *II*, with more water surrounding the *micellæ*.

THE CELL. 79

free and when confined by a cell-wall. Swarm-spores (Fig. 169), which consist of a mass of protoplasm destitute of a covering, swim through water by means of their cilia, or hair-like protoplasmic elongations. The slime moulds consist, in their vegetative or growing stage, of naked protoplasm, and this is able to creep slowly about over rotten wood in damp forests, where they usually grow. Diatoms (Fig. 182), which are one-celled plants, move freely about in the water, though in exactly what manner they accomplish the movement is as yet not satisfactorily determined. The protoplasm confined in cell-walls exhibit two kinds of movement, called **circulation** and **rotation**.

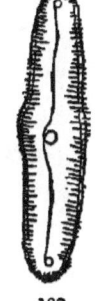

182

102. The **circulation** of the protoplasm (Fig. 183) takes place in cells having a large sap-cavity, the protoplasm existing as a parietal layer, connected by strings and bands with a more or less central mass; it consists of a movement (shown by the granules) in streams, mainly to and from the nucleus. The currents may be in opposite directions, though side by side, and often contiguous; they may gradually cease and then begin again in an opposite direction without apparent cause. The movement called **rotation** (Fig. 184) differs from this, in that the whole mass of the protoplasm rotates or moves as a broad stream around the cell-wall, passing up one side and down the other, carrying the granules

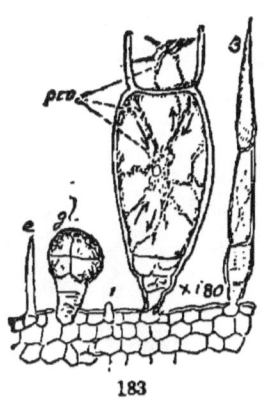

183

Fig. 182. A Diatom, *Navicula viridis.* Fig. 183. Circulation of Protoplasm in a cell; the arrows indicate the direction of the currents.

80 HISTOLOGY AND PHYSIOLOGY.

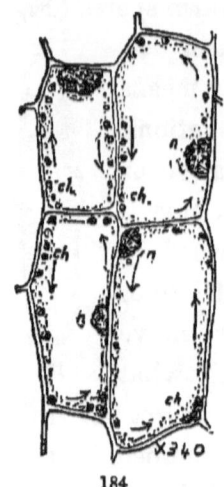

184

and nucleus along with it. The nucleus, the roundish or elongated body usually present and imbedded in the protoplasm, seems to be of the same chemical composition as the latter, and is, therefore, considered a somewhat differentiated portion of it. Its function is not well understood, though it seems to take a prominent part in the initial processes of cell-multiplication. Sometimes it contains a smaller body within it, called the *nucleolus*. In all ordinary tissue one nucleus is present in each cell; but in a few Algæ each cell may contain several nuclei.

103. There are four typical methods of cell-formation. In the method called **rejuvenescence**, the whole protoplasmic mass within the cell contracts, expels a portion of its water, escapes through the broken cell-wall, and begins an existence as a young cell (Fig. 185). Some of the fresh-water Algæ, as *Œdogonium*, illustrate this process. In another common and beautiful fresh-water Alga (*Spirogyra*) new cells arise by **conjugation** (Fig. 186). Two cells lying near each other begin to protrude their walls (Fig. 186, 1) until they touch, then unite (Fig. 186, 2), and the partition between them becomes absorbed, allowing free communication (Fig. 186, 3 and 4). In the meantime

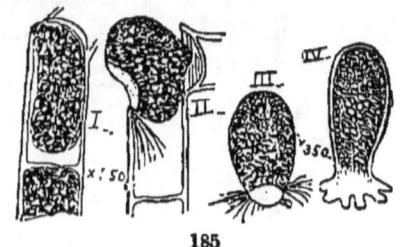

185

Fig. 184. Rotation of Protoplasm, the arrows indicating the direction: *n*, nucleus: *ch*, chlorophyll grains. Fig. 185. Cell-formation, by rejuvenescence, in *Œdogonium*.

THE CELL.

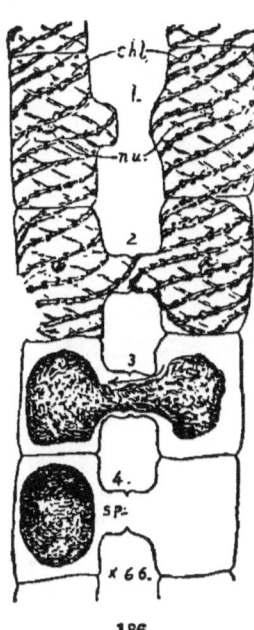

186

the protoplasm in each cell contracts, that in one cell gradually passes over to the other, and the two masses unite into one, forming a new cell or spore (Fig. 186, *sp*). A cell-wall is secreted, and the spore, after some length of time, begins to grow, and another plant like the adult form is the result.

104. **Free cell-formation** is exhibited in the production of spores in some Fungi, Lichens, in the embryo-sac of the flowering plants, etc. New centres of formation arise in the mass, and around each of these a portion of the protoplasm collects and forms a new cell (Fig. 187); only a part of the protoplasm is consumed, a portion remaining over. One or many cells may thus arise in any cell. A fourth method of cell-formation is by **division**. Here the protoplasm separates into two masses, a partition wall is secreted which separates the two portions, and thus two new cells are formed. Recent investigations of Strasburger show that the process, when a nucleus is present, is very complicated. It is illustrated in Fig. 188, which represents the successive stages (*I, II, III, IV, V, VI*) in the formation of spores (in *Psilotum triquetrum*). The nucleus appears filamentous in structure, and the threads arrange themselves approximately parallel to

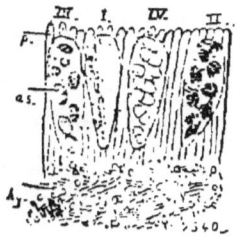

187

Fig. 186. Cell-formation by conjugation in *Spirogyra:* *1, 2, 3. 4*, the successive stages. Fig. 187. Free cell-formation in the asci of a Lichen (*Cladonia*).

HISTOLOGY AND PHYSIOLOGY.

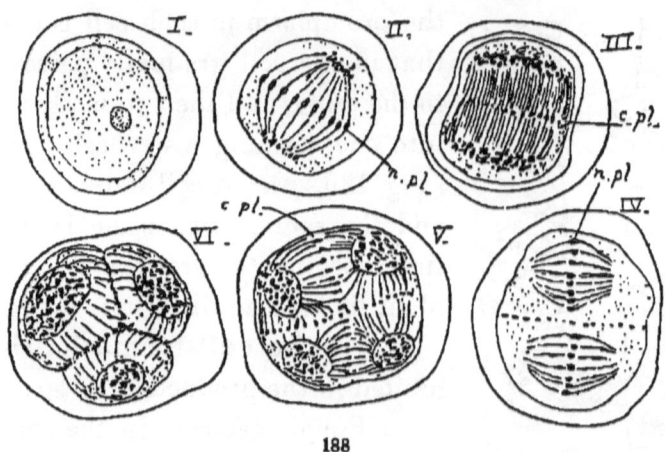

each other. In the middle they enlarge, and finally coalesce to form a *nucleus-plate* (Fig. 188, *n. pl.*); the latter divides, and the two halves recede to the poles to form the two nuclei. Then where the nucleus-plate originally arose, a *cell-plate* (Fig. 188, *c. pl.*) now is formed, and this indicates the partition wall between the two new cells.

105. **The cell-contents.**—Of the cell products, the **chlorophyll** (Gr. *chloros*, green; *phyllon*, leaf) is the first in importance. It is the green coloring matter in the cells. In ordinary tissue it is in the form of *grains* (Fig. 184, *ch*); in *Spirogyra* it is in the form of *spiral bands* (Fig. 189); and in *Zygnema*, another fresh-water Alga, it is in star-like

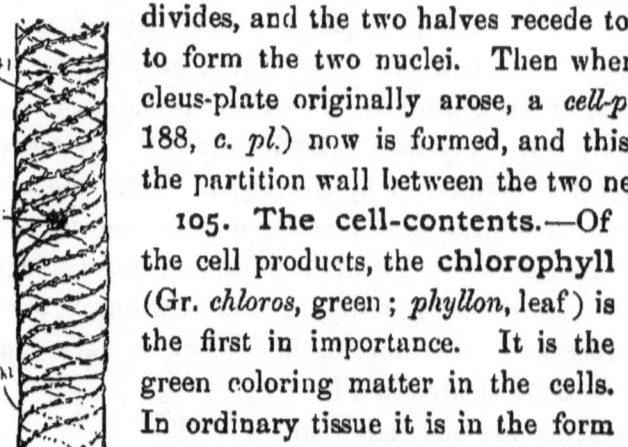
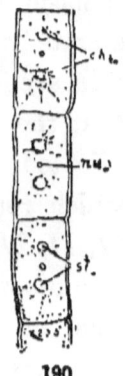

Fig. 188. Cell-formation by division, in case of Spores of *Psilotum triquetrum*; *I, II, III, IV, V, VI*, successive stages; *n. pl*, nucleus-plate; *c. pl*, cell-plate. Fig. 189. *Spirogyra*, with chlorophyll in spiral bands. Fig. 190. *Zygnema*, with chlorophyll in stellate masses.

masses (Fig. 190); in *Ulothix*, also a fresh-water Alga, it is in the form of a ring or zone. It is very seldom, though sometimes, found dissolved in the cell. The chlorophyll is soluble in alcohol, ether, chloroform, etc., and when removed by these solvents a protoplasmic body remains behind. The chlorophyll thus extracted has recently been obtained in the form of crystals. Only cells exposed to the light have chlorophyll developed in them. If chlorophyll-bearing cells be placed in the dark, they gradually lose their green color. If the plant food be deprived of iron, the chlorophyll will not be developed. The importance of this compound is great, for only in cells containing chlorophyll (and exposed to sunlight) does **assimilation**—which is the change of the crude sap, or inorganic food, into organic matter—take place. Those plants are destitute of chlorophyll which do not assimilate food, but absorb it, already "digested" (assimilated), from others; for example, parasitic plants (Fungi, etc.).

106. The following are regarded as modifications of chlorophyll: **xanthophyll**, which is the yellow coloring matter of the autumn leaves; **anthozanthin** is the coloring matter of the yellow petals of flowers; **phycozanthin** is a brown coloring matter associated with chlorophyll in many Algæ, as in Diatoms and *Fucus;* **phycocyan** is the blue coloring matter in the cells of Nostocs; **phycoerythrin** is the red coloring matter of the Red Algæ. The last two are soluble in water. The red orange and yellow coloring matters of flowers are found in the form of rounded protoplasmic bodies. Other coloring matters are dissolved in the cell-sap, as many which are found in flowers. Of this kind also is the red of many autumn leaves, as the *Cornus* and *Ampelopsis*. The pigments of

flowers differ from chlorophyll in that the former appear to be independent of light for their production. Flowers expanding in the dark have their natural colors.

107. The **starch** grains arise in the chlorophyll as a product of assimilation. They may be of various shapes, as lenticular in Wheat grains, oval in the Potato, many-sided in Indian Corn, elongated, with enlarged ends, in the milky juice of *Euphorbia splendens*. The average size and shape of the grains are characteristic for the different plants; and, therefore, when starch is examined microscopically, it can be determined from what plant it was obtained.

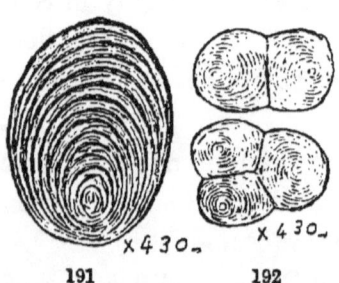

Some grains have one nucleus, and are, therefore, simple (Fig. 191); others have two or more nuclei, and are compound (Fig. 192). Surrounding the nucleus are concentric layers, light and dark alternating, as in the cell-wall, and due to the same cause, namely, greater and lesser amounts of water contained. The molecular structure is the same as that of the cell-wall, and growth takes place by intussusception, or intercalation of particles between those already existing. Chemically, starch resembles sugar and cellulose, and is composed of carbon, hydrogen, and oxygen. It turns a deep blue color when a solution of iodine is applied to it.

108. After starch has been formed in the chlorophyll-bearing cells, it becomes dissolved, and is either consumed at once in the formation of vegetable fabric, or is transported to some other part of the plant, where it reappears

Figs. 191, 192. Starch grains from a Potato: 191. Simple; 192. Compound grains.

in the form of starch grains. Here it is stored for subsequent use by the plant, and from this reservoir the plant draws nourishment as needed. The tubers of the Potato, Hyacinth bulbs, and seeds of various plants, are examples of an accumulation of this reserve material. Besides starch, *aleurone grains* (or *proteine grains*) are formed in ripe seeds and tubers. These are minute grains of albuminous matter (Fig. 193), often containing roundish or clustered granules, called *globoids* (Fig. 193, *gl*). Other inclusions are sometimes present, called *Crystalloids* (Fig. 193, *cr*); these are bounded by plane surfaces, and they, therefore, resemble crystals, except in their behavior with re-agents. They absorb water, and change their angles. Their exact nature, like that of aleurone, is not well understood, though they appear to be modifications of protoplasm.

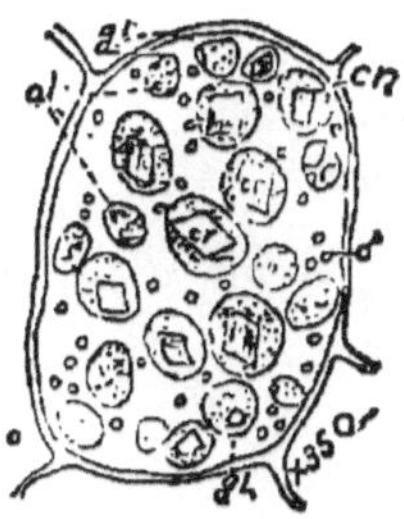

109. The **cell-sap** (Fig. 172, *v*) is the watery fluid contained in the vacuoles of the protoplasm. It holds in solution the food materials absorbed by the plant, as well as the surplus of the products of assimilation. One important constituent is sugar. There are two varieties: the sucrose, or cane sugar, existing in abundance in Sugar-Cane, Sugar-Maple, Sugar Beet, Indian Corn, and other plants; and the glucose, or fruit sugar, found in Grapes, Cherries, Gooseberries, and Figs. The two kinds may exist together, as in Apricots, Peaches, Strawberries. A substance related to starch and sugar, and dissolved in the cell-sap, is **inuline**. It may be precipitated, when it takes the form of sphere-crystals (Fig.

Fig. 193. Aleurone grains in the cells of the endosperm of the Castor Oil Bean; *gl*, globoids; *cr*, crystalloids.

194), which consist of crystalline elements disposed in a radiate manner. Inuline is abundant in the tubers of Elecampane, common Sunflower, roots of Dandelion, and other *Compositæ*.

110. In many plant-cells, particularly in seeds, **fixed oils**, as Olive, Castor, Linseed, and Palm Oil, are secreted and exist in the form of drops, mingled with the other cell-contents. The **essential oils** and **resins** are generally the products of special cells. Of the former, Oil of Turpentine, Oil of Lemons, Oil of Thyme, represent one class; Camphor, Essence of Cinnamon, etc., a second; and the

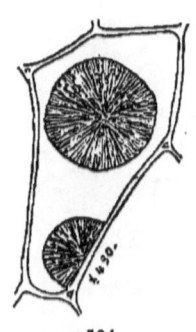
194

essential oils in Mustard, Onions, Asafœtida, etc., represent a third class. Resins are generally associated with, and dissolved in, the essential oils. They may be separated by heat, when they take the form of transparent, or translucent, little bodies. **Oxalic acid** is generally combined with calcium, in the form of crystals. Other vegetable acids are: **malic acid**, abundant in many sour fruits, Apples, Cherries, Strawberries, etc.; **tartaric acid** occurs in the Grape, unripe berries of Mountain Ash, etc.; **citric acid** is abundant in the Lime and Lemon, also associated with malic acid in Gooseberries, Cherries, etc.; **tannic acid**, in the bark and leaves of Oak, Elm, Willow, etc.; **quinic acid**, nearly related to the last, occurs in Peruvian Bark (*Cinchona*).

111. Calcic oxalate may occur in cell-walls, or within the cell, either in granules, or in the form of **crystals**. Of the latter, the needle-shaped forms are called **raphides** (Fig. 195); they occur in the cavities of parenchymous

Fig. 104. Inuline crystals from the roots of the Thistle.

cells, and lie parallel in bundles. Still other forms are prisms, octohedra, etc. They may be either simple (Figs.

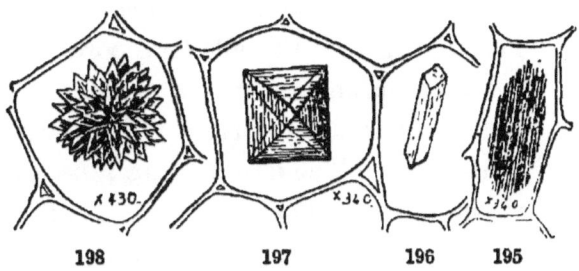

196, 197), or compound (Fig. 198). Crystals of calcic carbonate are not so common. A peculiar form, called **cystoliths** (Gr. *cystis*, bladder; *lithos*, stone), occurs in the leaves of the *Urticaceæ* (Nettle, Fig, Mulberry, Hop, etc.), a club-shaped outgrowth of cellulose projects into the cell, and in this multitudes of small crystals are grouped (Fig. 199). It is said that crystals of calcic phosphate, calcic sulphate, and silica, are occasionally to be met with. It is probable that crystals are residual products of chemical action in the plants, and are, therefore, to be regarded as of the nature of excretions.

TISSUE.

112. Some of the lower plants consist of but a single cell, and are, therefore, called unicellular plants. Such are the *Protococcus, Desmids, Bacteria,* etc. Many of the unicellular plants are more or less bound together by a jelly-like substance, and thus form cell-colonies, as in *Gleocapsa*

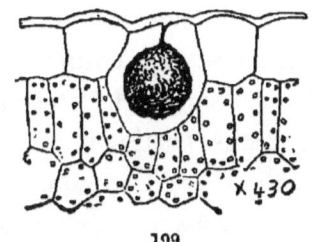

Figs. 195–198. Crystals in cells: 195. Raphides; 196, 197. Simple crystals; 198. Compound crystal. Fig. 199. A cystolith in a Nettle leaf.

(Fig. 200), *Nostoc* (Fig. 201). A common example of a cell-colony, or spurious tissue, is furnished by the fresh-water Alga, Water-net (*Hydrodictyon*). The separate motile cells (zoöspores) into which the protoplasm breaks up arrange themselves and unite so as to form a net while yet in the mother-cell. The term **tissue** is used to denote a permanent union of cells. They may be united end to end, so as to form a row, or filament, as in the filamentous Algæ (*Spyrogyra*, *Zygnema*, Figs. 189, 190), jointed hyphæ (or vegetative threads of Fungi), and many hairs of the higher plants. When cell-fission takes place in two directions, a cell-surface, or single layer of cells, is the result. Examples are furnished by some Algæ (*Ulva*), and the leaves of some of the Mosses. In ordinary tissue, cell-fission takes place in three directions, resulting in a mass of greater or less solidity.

113. It sometimes happens that the partition wall between two adjacent cells becomes absorbed, and the two cells fuse, as it were, into one. Thus by *cell-fusion* of many cells, long tubes, or **ducts** may arise. Aside from cavities so formed, and those of the individual cells, there are others, called **intercellular spaces**. Rapidly growing parenchymous tissue exhibits numerous small intercellular spaces at the corners of the cells, which have resulted by the splitting of the walls and the partial receding of the cells from each other (Fig. 203, *in*). In like manner continuous vessels are sometimes found, as in the tissue of the Pine family, where they

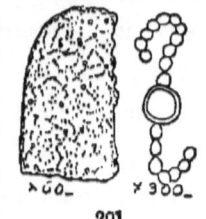

Fig. 200. Gleocapsa forming a cell-colony. Fig. 201. Nostoc, a cell-colony.

serve as resin canals (Fig. 202, transverse section); in the Compositæ, where they are oil-passages; and in the Umbelliferæ, where they are filled with a mixture of gum-mucilage, and oily or resinous substances. The adjacent cells may assume the function of glands, and secrete the substances found in the canals.

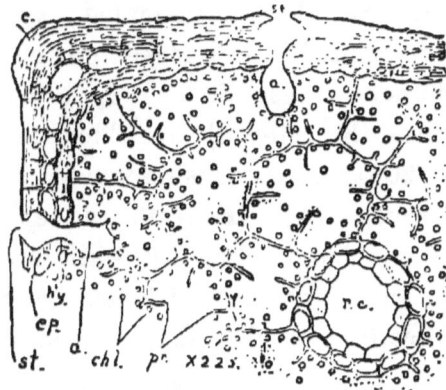

The large air canals in many water plants are intercellular spaces, whose origin is referable to the splitting apart of cells. But the large cavities in the stems of many plants (as Grasses and Umbelliferæ) arise by a breaking of some of the cells.

114. Although the several kinds of tissue merge into one another, they may generally be referred to two typical forms, namely, **parenchyma** and **prosenchyma**. In **parenchyma** the cells are polyhedrical and generally isodiametric; or, if elongated, the ends are truncate, or, at least, never pointed and wedged into one another (Fig. 203). The tissue of some Fungi, formed of hyphæ, or threads placed closely together, resembles parenchymous tissue, and is called

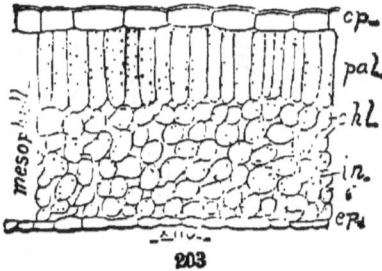

Fig. 202. Transverse section of a Pine leaf, showing a Resin canal (*r.c.*); *st*, stomata; *hy*, hypoderm; *chl*, chlorophyll; *a*, air-cavity. Fig. 203. Section of a Potato leaf, showing Parenchyma; *ep*, epidermis; *in*, intercellular spaces; *chl*, chlorophyll.

pseudo-parenchyma (Fig. 204). In **prosenchyma** the

cells are always elongated, and have pointed ends wedged into one another (Figs. 205, 209, *pros*). When the cell-walls are thickened and excessively hard (Fig. 206), the tissue is designated as **sclerenchyma** (Gr. *scleros*, hard). Beneath the epidermis of some plants tissue is found, whose cell-walls are thin, except at the corners, where they are thickened; and the word **collenchyma** has been used to designate such (Fig. 207).

115. Vessels containing a milky juice (latex) are called **laticiferous vessels** (Fig. 208). Most of them arise by cell-fusion, and may form a net-work, penetrating the other tissue. The walls are generally thicker than that of the surrounding tissue. The latex is an emulsion of several substances. Some of these, as Caoutchouc (India Rubber), Gutta-Percha, and Opium, are of great economic importance. In *Euphorbia* elongated grains of starch are found in the latex. **Glands** are secreting-cells,

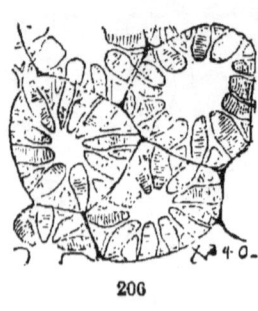

or clusters of cells, with characteristic contents, either odoriferous, acrid, colored, oily, or resinous, which "find no further use in changes connected with nutrition or growth." The secretion may collect in the interior of the gland, as in case of Oil of Camphor; or it may be discharged exter-

Fig. 204. Pseudo-parenchyma. Fig. 205. Prosenchyma of Indian Mallow (*Abutilon Avicennæ*). Fig. 206. Sclerenchyma from a Pear.

nally, as the viscid excretion of some stems, and the nectar of nectaries.

116. **Sieve-tubes** (Fig. 209, *sie*) are ducts, not lignified, colorless, having at long intervals horizontal, or oblique septa, which are perforated. Sometimes the lateral walls are at different places perforated, and these are called **sieve-discs**. Through the perforations the protoplasmic contents of the cells freely unite. In **latticed cells** the markings, but not the perforations of the sieve-discs, are present. They may, therefore, be regarded as undeveloped sieve-tissue. The **tracheary tissue** (Fig. 209) comprises vessels, or ducts, with walls thickened in a spiral (Fig. 209, *sp*),—often modified so as to be ringed (Fig. 209, *an*),—reticulated (Fig. 209, *ret*), scalariform (Fig. 209, *sca*), or pitted manner. The diameter is usually much greater than that of the surrounding cells. They contain protoplasm when young, which disappears later, and then they are filled with air. Single closed cells, which otherwise possess the characters of vessels, are called **tracheides**.

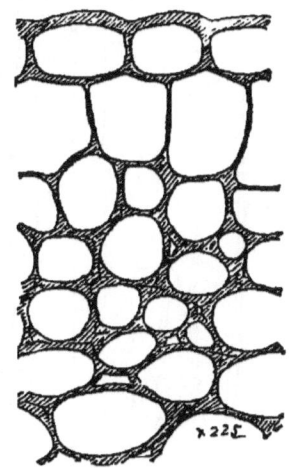

207

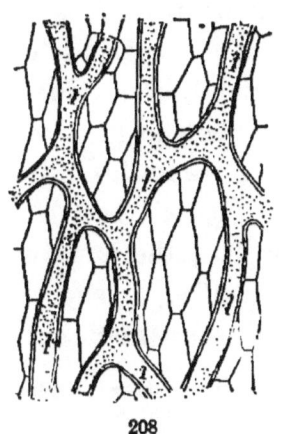

208

117. In the lowest plants (and in the earliest stage in the development of higher plants) the cells are all alike, and the tissue is, therefore, uniform throughout. But as we

Fig. 207. Collenchyma. Fig. 208. Laticiferous vessels.

92 HISTOLOGY AND PHYSIOLOGY.

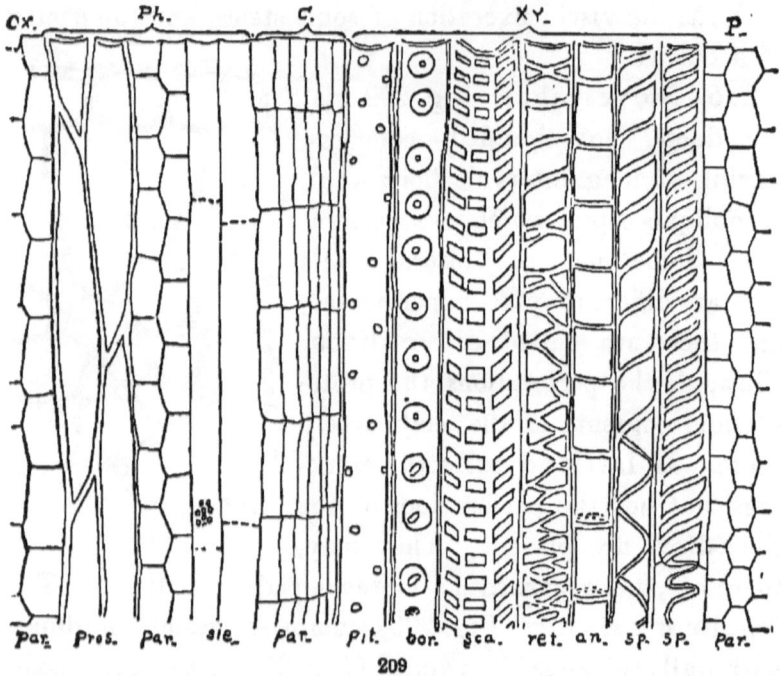

Fig. 209. Diagrammatic longitudinal section through tracheary tissue; *P*, pith; *xy*, wood; *C*, cambium; *Ph*, bast; *Cx*, cortex; *par*, parenchyma; *pros*, prosenchyma; *sie*, sieve-tubes; *pit*, pitted; *bor*, bordered pits; *sca*, scalariform; *ret*, reticulated, *an*, annular; *sp*, spiral.

ascend from the lowest to the highest, we find a gradual modification of the tissue for special purposes. The outer cells form a boundary tissue, and, together with their appendages, constitute the **epidermal system.** This includes the *epidermis, trichomes,* and *stomates.* Certain other cells, or rows of cells, become modified into tubes or ducts, and form the string-like masses, or form fibers in the stems of the higher plants. These are the **fibro-vascular bundles.** They contain a woody portion (*xylem*), bast portion (*phloëm*), and *cambium;* from the last, the first two are formed. All the other tissue, unmodified, or slightly modified, is designated by the term **fundamental tissue.**

118. The **epidermis** is the external, compact layer of cells, rarely containing chlorophyll, destitute of intercellular spaces, and with their outer walls more or less thickened (Figs. 203, 210). When the walls are much thickened, the outer portion becomes cuticularized (impregnated with cutin) and impervious to water. Often the outermost portion becomes separated as a continuous pellicle, and is called the **cuticle**. A waxy, or resinous matter, often forms on the cuticle, and constitutes the *bloom* found on some leaves and fruits. When the walls become much thickened, the protoplasm disappears from the cells. But in aquatic plants, and the roots of ordinary plants, there is but slight modification from the other cells. The epidermis at first consists of but one layer of cells; but later may split into two or more layers. The inner layers may resemble the outer ones, as in the Oleander; or they may be thin-walled cells, with watery contents (called aqueous tissue), as in the Begonia.

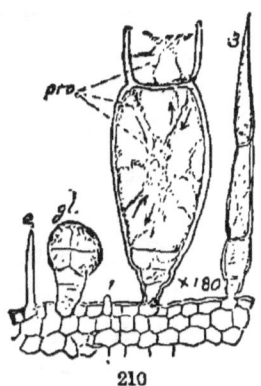

119. The outgrowths of the epidermis are called **trichomes** (Gr. *thriches*, hairs), and may have the form of hairs, scales, bristles, prickles, etc. (Fig. 210). They are at first enlargements, or protrusions, of an epidermal cell. They elongate and may remain one-celled, or become many-celled, and take on an endless variety in shape, as may be seen by examining these structures on many different plants. Those elongated, unicellular hairs on the young roots of plants, called **root-hairs**, have very thin walls, and absorb the plant food which is dissolved in the water of the soil.

Fig. 210. Epidermis and hairs from the ovary of the Squash flower.

94 HISTOLOGY AND PHYSIOLOGY.

In Mosses, hairs, called **rhizoids** (Gr. *rhiza*, root), perform

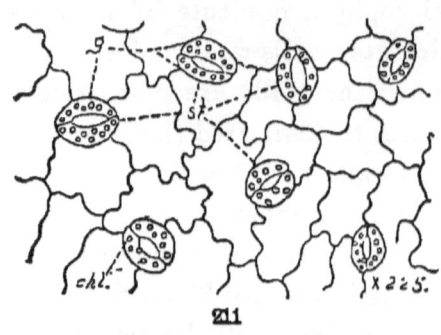

the function of roots exclusively, the latter being absent in these plants. In many hairs on aerial parts of plants, the terminal cell, or cluster of cells, becomes transformed into a secreting organ, in which gummy, resinous, or other substances are produced. These are termed **glandular hairs** (Fig. 210, *gl*). Related to these are the hairs of some Thistles, with elongated lashes. The leaves of the Sundew (*Drosera*) have stalked, sensitive glands, for the capture of insects upon which these plants partially feed.

120. The **stomates** (Gr. *stoma*, mouth) are minute orifices (Figs. 211, 212) in the epidermis, surrounded by two chlorophyll-bearing cells, called guard-cells (Fig. 211, *g*). Immediately under each stomate is an air cavity (Fig. 212, *a*). Stomates are never present in roots, seldom in submerged or underground stems; but **exceedingly numerous on aerial stems and leaves.**

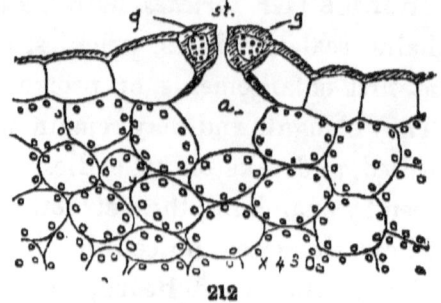

They are also met with at times on sepals, petals, and carpels of flowers. As a rule, they are more numerous on the lower than on the upper side of the leaf. On the upper

Fig. 211. Epidermis of Potato leaf, showing stomates (*st*) and guard-cells (*g*).
Fig. 212. Section through the epidermis and stomate (*st*) of Potato leaf: *a*, air cavity.

side of the leaf of *Anemone nemorosa*, for example, there are none; on the lower side there are 42,215 to the square inch; on the leaves of Indian Corn there are on every square inch on the upper side 60,630, and on the lower side 101,910 stomates; on the Sycamore leaf there are none on the upper side, but on the lower side 179,310 to the square inch. In the leaf of the common Sunflower there are in each square inch: above, 112,875; below, 209,625. Through the stomates, or breathing pores, an interchange of gases takes place.

121. The *fibro-vascular bundles* are composed of tracheary tissue, sieve-tubes, and parenchyma. They may be easily separated from the other tissue in the petioles of the Plantain, in the stems of Indian Corn, etc. When examined in section, they are seen to consist of two parts, namely, **wood**, called **xylem**; and **bast**, called **phloem** (Fig. 213). When cambium (delicate cells, rich in protoplasm, capable of division) is present between them, the bundle is said to be *open* (Fig. 214, a diagram); if it is absent, it is said to be a *closed* bundle (Fig. 215, a diagram). Open bundles continue to increase in size, new layers of wood and new layers of bast being formed from the cambium. The bundles, which are isolated when the plantlet is very young, increase

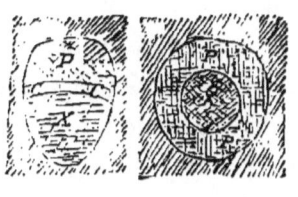

Fig. 213. Transverse section of a fibro-vascular bundle: *Ph*, phloēm; *Xy*, xylem; *C*, cambium. Figs. 214, 215. Diagrams illustrating open (*214*) and closed (*215*) bundles.

96   HISTOLOGY AND PHYSIOLOGY.

in size, fuse laterally into a continuous mass, the cambium in each joining with that of the adjacent bundle, thus forming a *cambium zone*, or layer, which annually produces a ring of wood, as in forest trees. (See *Angiospermæ*, Part III). Closed bundles do not increase in size, and plants having such (as the Asparagus, etc.) do not form an annual ring of growth.

122. The **fundamental tissue** includes all except the epidermal tissue and the fibro-vascular bundles. It consists mainly of parenchyma of various forms, in contact

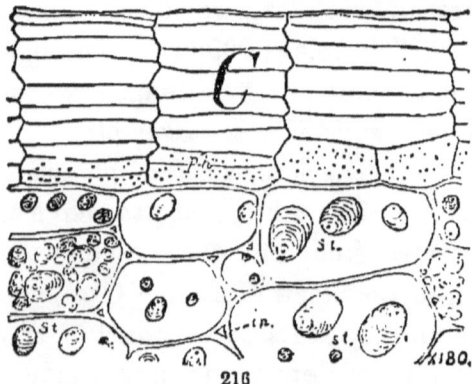

with or near the epidermis. Collenchyma is sometimes present. This is replaced by sclerenchyma in parts requiring greater firmness than that given by the former. The term **hypoderm** (Gr. *hypo*, under; *derma*, skin) has been used to designate those differentiated portions lying immediately beneath the epidermis (Fig. 202, *hy*). Laticiferous vessels may also occur in the fundamental tissue. To this tissue belong the **medullary rays** in woody plants. Within the zone of the hypoderm, or immediately below the epidermis, layers of **cork** may be developed (Fig. 216, *C*). The cells are generally four-sided in section, filled with air, have thin walls, impermeable to water. The generating tissue (Fig. 216, *ph*) is called **cork-cambium**, or *phellogen* (Gr. *phellos*, cork; *genein*, to be produced). When a plant is slightly cut or injured,

Fig. 216. A layer of cork-cells (*C*) forming the covering of the Potato.

the parenchyma-cells immediately under the wound become a mass of phellogen, and a protecting mass of cork, called wound-cork, is developed. The epidermis may be replaced entirely by a continuous corky layer, called the **periderm** (Gr. *peri*, around). Restricted corky growths below stomates may push out the epidermis, as in Elder; and thus roundish, or elongated masses of cork, called **lenticels**, are formed.

123. At the growing ends of stems and leaves (and roots) is found a tissue composed of cells, with delicate walls, filled with protoplasm, capable of division. This is called primary **meristem** (Gr. *meros*, part; *temnein*, to cut off,, and from it the various tissues are developed. As growth proceeds, portions of the primary meristem become transformed into permanent tissue, which is incapable of division. The terminal portion of an organ consisting of primary meristem, and having permanent apical growth, is called the **punctum vegetationis**, or **growing point**. As it often projects in a conical elongation it is sometimes called the **vegetative cone**. The *punctum vegetationis* may consist of a single cell, called the **apical cell** (Figs. 217, 218, *ap*), or it may be composed of a multitude of cells (Fig. 219). Many of the Algæ grow from an apical cell. This elongates and divides, the upper portion continuing as the apical cell, which, in turn, elongates, and divides as before; and so on. The other portion, appearing like a piece or disc cut off from the apical cell, is called a segment. The segments may remain undivided (Fig. 217). They may

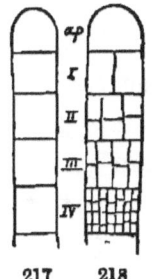

Figs. 217, 218. Diagrams showing growth from an apical cell; segments (*I, II, III, IV*) divided (*218*) and undivided (*217*).

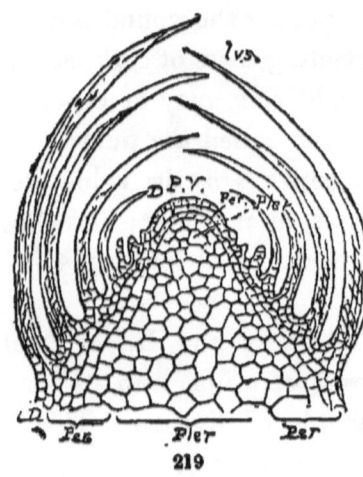

divide into two cells, which, in turn, divide, and so on indefinitely (Fig. 218).

124. In the higher plants, the *punctum vegetationis* has no apical cell. Here the primary meristem consists of cells which are very small and numerous. The outermost layer of cells is continuous, with the epidermis of the older portion further back. In fact, it produces it. Hence it is called the **primordial epidermis** (Fig. 219, *D*), or **dermatogen** (Gr. *derma*, skin; *genein*, to be produced). Beneath the dermatogen are generally found several continuous layers out of which the cortex originates. These are called the *primordial cortex* (Fig. 219, *Per*), or **periblem** (Gr. *periblema*, cloak). The nucleus of tissue, enclosed by the periblem, and out of which the fibro-vascular bundles and pith are produced (Fig. 219, *Pler*), is called the **plerome** (Gr. *pleroma*, a filling up). A short distance back from the apex of the *punctum vegetationis* the leaves (and buds) take their origin as **exogenous structures**, that is, from the external cell-layer, or dermatogen.

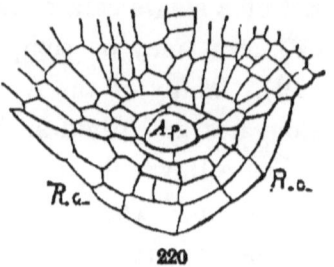

125. The root, like the stem, is furnished with a *punctum vege-*

Fig. 219. The growing point, or *punctum vegetationis*, in longitudinal section: *D*, dermatogen; *Per*, periblem; *Pler*, plerome. Fig. 220. Diagram of longitudinal section through the root-tip, showing the apical cells (*Ap*) and the root-cap (*R.c*).

tationis, either with or without an apical cell. The Fern root furnishes an example of the first (Fig. 220), and the root of any of the higher plants an example of the second (Fig. 221). While the tender *punctum vegetationis* of the stem is protected by the overarching of the young leaves, that of the root is furnished with a peculiar shielding structure, called the **root-cap** (Fig. 221, *R.c*). This consists of a mass of cells developed from the dermatogen. The latter divides into two layers, the innermost continuing as the dermatogen, to be subsequently divided in the same manner. The outermost multiplies its cells copiously, and constitutes the root-cap.

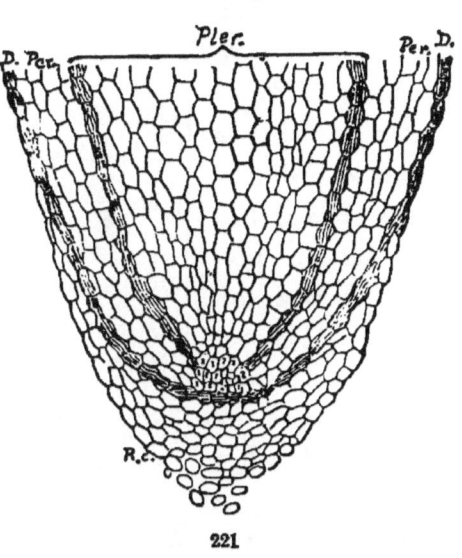

221

The outer cells of this are, of course, continually abraded as the rootlets push their way through the soil, but as constantly replenished from behind. The root is further distinguished from the stem in having its branches (side roots) developed as **endogenous structures**, that is, from cells a distance below the epidermis; having no stomates, no joints, no chlorophyll, and no leaves.

Fig. 221. Diagram of longitudinal section through the root-tip, showing the initial cells (*i.i.*), and the root-cap (*R.c*).

WATER.

126. All living vegetable tissue is abundantly supplied with **water**. In aquatic plants it may constitute as much as ninety-five per cent. of the whole weight. In the terrestrial plants it generally averages about seventy-five per cent. In consequence of this quantity of water the cells are rendered turgid, without which growth would be impossible. If green plants be dried in the air at ordinary temperatures, they lose only a portion of their water. Thus Red Clover contains seventy-nine per cent. of water, and when air-dry (hay) it contains seventeen per cent. Fresh Pine-wood contains forty per cent. of water, and the same dry contains twenty per cent. The first quantity in each case may be called the **free water of vegetation**. The second represents the **water of organization**. The rootlets and root-hairs which penetrate the soil, growing between the more or less minute soil-particles, where water is contained (Fig. 222), are the organs of absorption.

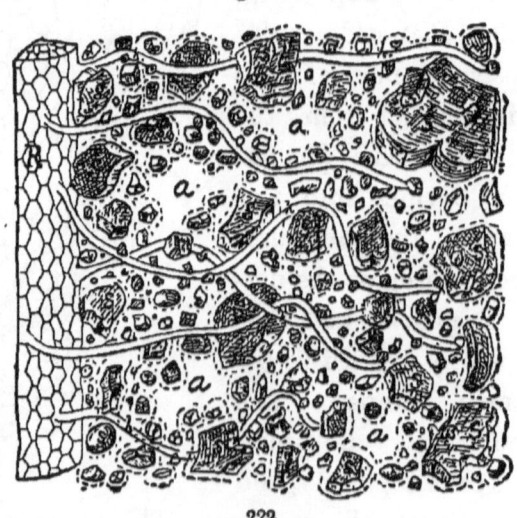

127. The tendency of the water in plants to assume a state of equilibrium is disturbed by three causes; namely,

Fig. 222. Diagram representing a root, with root-hairs penetrating the soil: *s*, soil-particles; *h*, root-hairs; *a*, air.

(1) chemical processes within the cells; (2) the imbibition of water by the protoplasm and cell-walls; and (3) the evaporation of a portion of the water. All these are in almost constant operation; and, therefore, there is a perpetual movement of water in the growing plant. The **chemical processes** include the actual consumption of water by breaking the molecule up into oxygen and hydrogen, the formation of substances which are more soluble than those from which they were formed, and the formation of others less soluble than the substances from which they were formed. The protoplasm has **imbibing power** in a marked degree. It imbibes more water than it can retain, the surplus being separated in drops, the so-called vacuoles. The protoplasm of rapidly growing tissue is more watery than that in a dormant state, as in seeds. The cells are kept turgid, and succulent parts made rigid.

128. The **evaporation** (called also exhalation and transpiration) of water from the surface of plants is a more potent agency disturbing the equilibrium than the two previously mentioned. No evaporation, however, can take place when the air is saturated with moisture. The further below the point of saturation the amount of moisture falls, the greater is the amount of evaporation. The epidermis offers considerable hindrance to the process; and the thicker and less impermeable they are, the less the amount of water which escapes. In such case the escape is mainly through the stomates, which may be considered special organs of exhalation (and breathing). They are placed over intercellular spaces (Fig. 212), and these are connected with intercellular passages, which, of course, are filled with moist air and gases. Stomates open more widely the greater the amount of light, and the greater

the amount of moisture on the epidermis. Another partial hindrance to more rapid evaporation lies in the fact that the water contains many substances in solution, which, as is known, evaporates more slowly than pure water.

129. The **rate** of evaporation is very slow. It was long ago found that the amount of water evaporated from a vine in twelve hours of daylight was equal to a film only .005 inch thick, with an extent equalling the evaporating surface; the amount from a Cabbage in the same time equalled a film .012 inch thick; from an Apple-tree .01 inch. The evaporation from most leaves is estimated to be about one-third that from equal areas of water. A close-topped Oak-tree, twenty feet high, having about 700,000 leaves, evaporated (according to calculation) 246,630 pounds of water during the growing season of five and a half months. This amounted to a layer of water 1.31 inches deep over the whole evaporating surface. Considered with reference to the area of ground covered by the tree-top, it was found that the evaporation from the tree was eight times as great as the annual amount of water which fell beneath it. The evaporation would be much less in dense forests, yet even there it is sufficient to deprive the ground of its moisture in a short time in a dry, hot season.

130. To supply the loss by evaporation there must be a **movement of water** through the roots, stems, and branches to the leaves. This is demonstrated by cutting off a leafy shoot when evaporation is going on rapidly; the leaves wither quickly from loss of water, but if the cut end be placed in water, the latter passes up through the stem and supplies the loss from the leaves, which then retain their normal condition. If in this experiment a colored watery solution be used, it will be evident that some kinds

of tissue conduct more rapidly than others. In ordinary plants the elongated wood-cells convey the water mainly. The rapidity of the ascent is dependent on the rate of evaporation; but in general it may be considered to vary between the limits of five and fifty inches per hour. The so-called **root pressure** may be shown by cutting off a vigorously growing plant at the ground, and attaching a glass tube in which the water will rise to a considerable height (36 inches in *Vitis*, 84 inches in *Betula*). This is supposed to be due to a purely physical (endosmotic) force.

131. The water absorbed from the soil by the rootlets holds, in solution, inorganic food-materials for the plant. Even pure water is a solvent for many kinds of rocks and minerals, which, in a more or less finely divided state, constitute **soil**. In consequence of this fine state of division, the surface exposed to the action of water, and consequently the amount of material dissolved is enormously increased. Water charged with carbonic dioxide (called carbonated water), as the soil water invariably is, has its solvent power greatly increased. When such water is heated, or so exposed as to loose its carbonic dioxide, it is forced to precipitate the minerals contained, as illustrated by the lime-coating in boilers and in tea-kettles. The solvent power is still greater when the water contains alkalis—ammonia, potash, and soda: in fact, up to a certain point, "its solvent power increases with the amount and number of matters dissolved." Besides, the root-hairs themselves (Fig. 223) attack and dissolve the

Fig. 223. A root-hair highly magnified, showing its attachment to the soil-particles (*s*).

soil-particles. If a polished granite, or marble slab, be placed under the soil, exposed to the action of the rootlets, and then examined at the end of the growing season, it will be found to be sensibly roughened and dissolved wherever the rootlets came in contact with it.

FOOD-ELEMENTS.

132. The food-elements, which plants consume, may be determined in two ways: (1) by chemical analysis of vegetable tissue; or (2) by causing plants to grow in pure water, to which are added the compounds containing the elements that will nourish them. They have been found to be **carbon, hydrogen, oxygen, nitrogen, sulphur, iron,** and **potassium.** If all these are present, the plant will grow; if any one or more are absent, the plant will die of starvation. Besides these seven elements, plants appropriate **phosphorous, calcium, sodium, magnesium, chlorine,** and **silica.** These six are of secondary importance, for without them the plant may grow. In marine plants, **iodine** and **bromine** are always present. In special cases are found also at times small quantities of **aluminum, copper, zinc, lithium, manganese, nickel, cobalt, strontium,** and **barium.** Calcic fluoride is contained in the bones of animals; and, as their food is furnished wholly by plants, the presence of fluorine in the latter is inferred.

133. Oxygen may enter the plant in a free or uncombined state. All the other elements are absorbed in the condition of compounds, namely, water, carbonic dioxide, and the nitrates, sulphates, carbonates, phosphates, silicates, and chlorides of ammonia, potash, lime, iron, soda, and magnesia. **Carbon** constitutes usually about one-half of the entire dried substance of the plant. Yet this large quantity is derived mainly from the decomposition of carbonic dioxide (CO_2), taken into the leaves through the stomates from the surrounding air, of which it constitutes on an average only four hundredths of one per cent. **Hydrogen** is present in much smaller quantity than carbon. It is probably derived mainly from the decomposition of water (H_2O). **Oxygen** forms the largest proportion, after carbon, of the weight of the dried vegetable substance. It is introduced into the plant in excessive quantities, in the form of water, carbonic dioxide, and oxygen-salts, and also absorbed directly from the atmospheric oxygen. The small quantity of **nitrogen** is obtained from the compounds of ammonia (NH_3) and nitric acid. **Sulphur** is furnished by the salts of sulphuric acid.

134. The elements, carbon, hydrogen, oxygen, nitrogen, and sulphur, compose the greater (combustible) part of the substance of plants. They are constituents of cellulose, and the albuminoids which form protoplasm. "They mainly form the organized and organizable part of the plant, and of every individual cell. Their importance, therefore, lies in the fact that they furnish the chief materials for the construction of the plant." **Iron** is indispensable for the production of the chlorophyll, though extraordinarily small quantities suffice. If large quantities of solutions of iron become distributed in the tissues of plants, the cells quickly die. The importance of this food-element is great, since without chlorophyll no assimilation takes place. It has also been demonstrated that the presence of *potassium* is necessary to the assimilating activity of chlorophyll. If it is absent, the plants do not increase in weight, but behave as if absorbing only pure water.

ASSIMILATION AND METASTASIS.

135. The change into organic matter of the mineral or inorganic substances taken into the plant as food is called **assimilation**. The process takes place only in sunlight, and then only in cells containing chlorophyll. It is, however, as yet but imperfectly understood. It appears that water and carbonic dioxide become decomposed in the chlorophyll-mass, and their elements recombined to form carbo-hydrates. In most plants **starch** is the first visible product of assimilation in the chlorophyll grains. Sometimes no starch is formed, but instead, oily or sugary matters, which are chemically similar. The oxygen in starch is less than in water and carbonic dioxide, therefore assimilation is a deoxidizing process, large quantities of free oxygen being given off by the plant. Plants, destitute of chlorophyll (as Indian-pipe, Beech-drops, Fungi, etc.), are compelled to live on the assimilated products of other plants, as in case of *Parasites* (Gr. *para*, beside; *sitein*, to feed), or on the juices or products of decaying organic matter, as in case of *Saprophytes* (Gr. *sapros*, rotten; *phyton*, plant).

136. Of the plants which obtain their food partly or wholly from some other source than assimilation, there is, besides the parasites and saprophytes, a group called **insectivorous plants**. A common example is the Sundew (*Drosera*), which grows in bogs and wet places. The radical leaves are furnished with stalked glands, whose glistening secretion imprisons flies which alight thereon. The flies soon die, and are then digested by the acidulous secretion, which is at such time more copiously poured forth. The nutritive portion is absorbed into the plant,

ASSIMILATION AND METASTASIS.

and thus furnishes a portion of its (nitrogenous) food. Venus's Fly-trap, the lobes of whose leaves close and capture insects when the latter touch the slender hairs on the upper side (Fig. 223a), is likewise capable of digesting animal food. The numerous sessile glands

provide the digestive secretion, and also absorb into the plant the digested portions of the insects. Glands, whose viscid secretion is capable of digesting nitrogenous material, are also found on the leaves of the Butterwort (*Pinguicula*), which grows on wet rocks and damp soils. The curious little bladders (Fig. 224) of the Bladderwort

(*Utricularia*) capture small water-animals. In the pitchers (Fig. 225) of the *Sarracenia* and *Nepenthes*, insects fall and drown; these animals, by their decay, probably furnish food to be absorbed by the plants.

137. The immediate products of assimilation undergo further (though but slightly understood) chemical changes to form the various substances found in vegetable tissue. All these changes, subsequent to assimilation, are collectively termed **metastasis** (Gr. *meta*, over; *istamai*, to place). Metastasis is a process of oxidation;

Fig. 223a. Leaves of Venus's Fly-trap (*Dionæa*). Fig. 224. Bladder from the stem of the Bladderwort (*Utricularia*), slightly magnified. Fig. 225. A leaf, having the form of a pitcher or cup, of *Sarracenia*.

it, therefore, consumes oxygen instead of liberating it, as in assimilation. Instead of increasing the weight of the plant, as is the case in assimilation, it decreases it; it takes place in all cells, and in darkness as well as in sunlight. At the expense of the elaborated materials,—called **formative material**,—growth of tissue, that is, the multiplication of cells, takes place. This may occur at once, or a portion of the formative materials may be stored up for subsequent use. Thus, in case of the Potato-plant, starch, which is formed in the chlorophyll grains in sunlight, becomes dissolved when darkness sets in, and is transported through the parenchyma and thin-walled cells of the phloëm to the reservoir of reserve material. The tuber, bulb, rhizome, stem, seeds, and spores hold in store varying amounts of reserve material.

138. This **reserve material** furnishes the elaborated food for the beginning of the subsequent period of growth; thus, from that stored up in stems and roots, the buds develop in the spring; from that in the bulb, a cluster of flowers may form; from that in the tuber, the "eyes" (buds) develop into branches; from that in the seed, the embryo unfolds into a self-supporting plantlet. The reservoirs are emptied gradually as the growth of the new organs progresses. When they are entirely empty, growth ceases, unless the conditions of assimilation (presence of chlorophyll and sunlight) render the formation of new organic material possible. The direction of the **transport** of assimilated materials is from the assimilating organs directly to the growing parts, or to the reservoir of reserve materials, thence to the growing parts. The movement is mainly one of **diffusion**. "The pressure caused by the tension and turgescence of the tissues has, in addition, a

tendency to propel the fluids in the direction of least resistance, which is also that in which they are consumed."

RESPIRATION.

139. The **respiration** of plants consists in the absorption of atmospheric oxygen and the liberation of carbonic dioxide. This cannot be readily detected while assimilation is going on, for then much larger quantities of oxygen escape. Nevertheless, respiration is constantly performed, causing oxidation of the assimilated substances and other chemical changes resulting from this. "The loss of assimilated substance caused by respiration would appear purposeless if we had only to do with the accumulation of assimilated products; but these are themselves produced only for the purpose of growth, and of all the changes with life; the whole life of the plant consists in complicated movements of the molecules and atoms; and the forces necessary for these movements are set free by respiration." In the absence of oxygen, the chemical changes connected with growth, the movements of the protoplasm, and the power of motion of motile and irritable organs cease. The heat generated by oxidation seldom causes a sensible increase in the temperature of the tissue. But in a mass of germinating seeds, or unfolding flowers, or a spadix during anthesis, the elevation of temperature may be observed. The phenomenon of **phosphorescence** also depends—in a manner not clearly demonstrated—on the respiration of oxygen.

140. The **degree of temperature** at which assimilation and metastasis may take place varies in different plants. Some plants live wholly in very low temperatures, as the Red-snow plant. In Polar waters myriads of

Diatoms and some of the higher Sea-weeds (*Fucaceæ, Florideæ*) flourish. Of our ordinary land plants, subjected to different temperatures, the greatest growth of the plumules took place as follows:

Pea . . . . 78.8° F.
Wheat . . . . 92.7° F.
Indian Corn . . . . 92.7° F.
Scarlet Bean . . . . 92.7° F.

In other experiments it was found that the most rapid growth of roots was at the following temperatures:

Scarlet Bean . . . . 78.8° F.
Pea . . . . 79.9° F.
Flax . . . . 81.3° F.
Wheat . . . . 83.3° F.
Indian Corn . . . . 92.7° F.

The following table shows the lowest (minimum), the most favorable (optimum), and the highest (maximum) degree of temperature at which seeds of several plants will germinate:

Seeds.	Minimum.	Optimum.	Maximum.
Indian Corn	48.8° F.	92.7° F.	115.2° F.
Scarlet Bean	48.8° F.	92.7° F.	115.2° F.
Pumpkin	56.7° F.	92.7° F.	115.2° F.
Wheat	41° F.	83.7° F.	108.5° F.
Barley	41° F.	83.7° F.	99.5° F.
Flax	35° F.	81° F.	. . . .
Pea	43° F.	80° F.	. . . .
Hemp	. . . .	88.7° F.	. . . .
Watermelon	. . . .	99.5° F.	. . . .

Metastasis may take place at lower temperatures than assimilation. In the growth of many plants in spring, at the expense of the reserve material, metastasis takes place at quite low temperatures, as many plants begin to grow and develop flowers simultaneously with the disappearance of the snow.

141. Plants may be killed by too high a temperature, as well as by too low a temperature. Those which contain least water can best endure high temperatures; many dry spores and seeds are uninjured at 149° to 177° F., but in water they are generally killed when the temperature exceeds 122° or 131° F. Aquatic plants can seldom endure a prolonged temperature above 104° F.; most terrestrial plants are killed at 122° F. At such temperatures the albuminoids of the protoplasm coagulate, lose their power of imbibing water, and the cells, therefore, lose their turgidity. Similar results follow too great a reduction of temperature. Those tissues containing most water are more quickly killed; seeds when dry endure almost any low degree of temperature, but, when they have become watery and germinated, a reduction to, or a little below, 32° F. generally kills them. Succulent tissues when frozen may sometimes survive by being subjected to a very slow thawing. In this case the water of the melting ice-crystals could be reabsorbed by the protoplasm or other substances which originally yielded it, and no injury done; but in rapid thawing the reabsorption of all the water could not take place.

142. The presence of **light** is a necessary condition upon which vegetable growth, either directly or indirectly, depends. Assimilation takes place in the chlorophyll-mass, and this is developed only under the influence of light. The assimilated products may undergo the metastatic changes in darkness as well as light; and those organisms (parasites and saprophytes), whose food is furnished by chlorophyll-

bearing plants, may pass their entire existence in darkness. The degree and kind of light influences the amount of assimilation. There is here, as in case of temperature, a minimum, optimum, and maximum intensity. If the amount of assimilation in white light be taken as 100, that for each of the isolated rays of the solar spectrum is found on the average to be as follows: Red, 9.5; Orange, 23.5; Yellow, 27.3; Green, 14; Blue, 8.2; Indigo, 5; Violet, 2.5.

The more refrangible rays are less efficacious; from the yellow and orange rays there is a decrease in both directions; and in the heat and actinic rays, found respectively beyond the red and violet, no assimilation whatever takes place.

MOVEMENTS.

143. If all other conditions are made constant, the rapidity of growth of most aerial stems is greater in darkness than in light. This is due to the retarding influence of the rays of high refrangibility (blue, indigo, violet, and ultra-violet). When, therefore, the illumination is greater on one side of the stem than on the other, a curvature arises in consequence of the retarding influence of light. Thus, when plants are grown in windows, they curve strongly towards the light. This phenomenon has received the name of **heliotropism** (Gr. *helios*, sun; *trepein*, to turn). It is due to the fact that the growth of the cells on the illuminated side is retarded, while on the opposite side the cells elongate, causing a curvature. Some organs, however, bend away from the light, indicated by the term **negative heliotropism** (the former being **positive heliotropism**), the explanation of which is not as yet clear. Thus the tendrils of the Grape-Vine and Virginia

Creeper are negatively heliotropic; and they, therefore, turn to walls or trees, to which they attach themselves for support of the plant.

144. The stems of most of the higher plants grow upwards, or from the earth, and the roots grow downwards, or towards the earth; the stems of most Mosses grow upwards, and their rhizoids downwards; the spore-bearing (conidia) filaments or hyphæ of some Fungi grow upwards, and the root-like hyphæ downwards. To designate these phenomena of growth, the term **geotropism** (Gr. *ge*, earth; *trepein*, to turn) has been used. The organ is **positively geotropic** if it grows downwards; and **negatively geotropic** if it grows upwards. That geotropism is due to the influence of gravitation may be demonstrated by placing germinating seeds on rapidly rotating wheels. If the rotation is vertical, the centrifugal force is substituted for gravitation, and the roots grow away from the centre or hub of the wheel, and the stems grow towards it; if the rotation is horizontal, the centrifugal force and gravitation act at right angles, and the roots will grow in a line coinciding with a diagonal, or resultant of the two forces, outwards and downwards, and the stems will grow upwards and inwards. If geotropic organs are placed horizontally, they will curve upwards or downwards, even when considerable resistance is offered. The cells are more elongated upon the convex than upon the concave side; but how gravitation causes this has not as yet been explained.

145. A few plants exhibit **spontaneous movements** of some of their foliar organs. In *Desmodium gyrans*, a plant of India, with trifoliate leaves, the small lateral leaflets bend continually upon their slender stalks in such

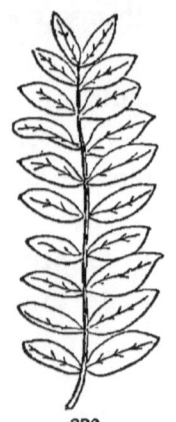

a way that their apices describe nearly a circle in from two to five minutes. Less conspicuous spontaneous movements take place in Clover, Mimosa, Oxalis; but they are generally concealed by more marked movements due to other causes. Thin walled cells compose the tissue of the active part of the moving organ. "The cells are turgid, and the tissues are in a state of tension, when movements occur it appears that the protoplasm in certain layers of cells permits the escape into the intercellular spaces of a portion of the water of the vacuoles; it is, however, quickly absorbed again, and the cells rendered thereby turgid, while the escape of water takes place in contiguous layers, to be quickly absorbed again, and so on regularly around the axis of the contracting organ."

146. Certain other movements depend upon external stimuli. The leaves of many plants assume a position (Fig. 227) at night (sleep) different from the ordinary or diurnal position (Fig. 226), in consequence of sensitiveness to light. Thus the leaves of Clover, Vicia, Lathyrus, and Honey-Locust fold upwards at night; those of the Locust and Oxalis downwards. The common petiole of Mimosa turns downwards at night; that of Phaseolus becomes erect. The leaflets of Mimosa turn laterally forwards and upwards in the dark; those of Tephrosia backwards. The petals of the Tulip, Oxalis, Portulaca, etc., open and close alternately in the

Fig. 226. Diurnal position of the leaflets of the Honey-Locust. Fig. 227. Nocturnal position of the same.

morning and evening, or upon a change of weather. The leaves of various species of Oxalis, Mimosa, etc., are sensitive to contact and concussion. A violent or repeated concussion, in some cases even gentle contact, causes the parts to assume the position of sleep. The stamens of the Barberry, in contact with the corolla when at rest, curve inwards when lightly touched near the base, bringing the anther in contact with the stigma. The stamens of the *Centaurea* and other *Compositæ* are sensitive to irritation. When at rest, their free filaments, bearing syngenesious anthers, curve concavely outwards; on contact or concussion, they contract and straighten, lengthening again after some minutes, and resuming their curved form. "This phenomenon occurs only while the style is growing through the anther-tube, and the pollen is being emptied into the tube. The motion of the filaments effected by insects causes the anther-tube to be drawn downwards, and a portion of the pollen thus to escape above it, which is then carried away by insects to other flowers and capitula when the stigmas are already unfolded."

147. It often happens that growth takes place more rapidly first on one side of an organ, and then on the other side; and then by the alternating rate of elongation on the two sides, a **movement of nutation** in one plane will take place. Many leaves furnish a good example; in the bud the greater growth is on the under or outer side of the leaf, the latter bending upwards; but on the opening of the bud the greater growth takes place on the upper side. Floral leaves often exhibit such nutations, as do also many stamens and styles. If the parts of unequal growth, instead of alternating from side to side, pass regularly around the organ, a **revolving nutation** will be the

consequence. This is illustrated in twining plants and tendrils. The former generally rotate to the left; though the Hop, Honeysuckle, and others, rotate to the right.

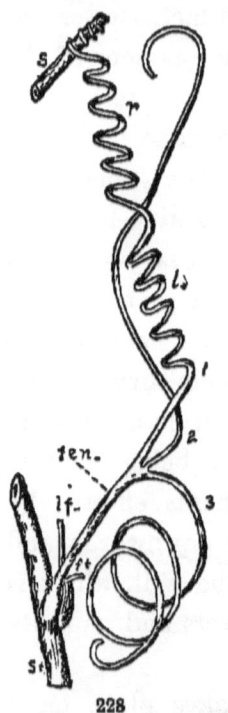

Fig. 228.

When they touch an upright object they continue their rotation, and thus twine around a support. Tendrils (Fig. 228) grow straight until they have attained about three-fourths of their size. They are then sensitive to contact, and are continually revolving; when they come in contact with any object, a curvature takes place, and a number of revolutions are performed around the support (Fig. 228, *s*); whether the coils are few or many, they become attached with considerable force; that portion between the point of contact and base also coils in a cork-screw manner (in two directions, Fig. 228, *l* and *r*, since both ends are attached), and this brings the plant nearer the support. Tendrils which do not find an object to encircle, become abortive and fall off (in the Grape-Vine and Virginia Creeper), or roll up slowly from the apex to the base, and form a spiral (in *Cardiospermum*), or a helix (in *Cucurbita*), then dry up and become woody.

Fig. 228. Tendril of Wild Balsam-apple; *1, 2, 3,* the three branches; *ten*, tendril; *s,* support; *r,* coil to the right; *l,* coil to the left; *lf,* petiole of leaf; *ft,* stem of a fruit; *st,* branch.

PART III.

SYSTEMATIC BOTANY.

CLASSIFICATION.

148. All individuals which very closely resemble each other in every particular (as regards the stem, leaves, flowers, fruit, etc.), or are so nearly alike that they may without hesitancy be referred to an immediate common parentage, constitute what botanists call a **species**. Thus all the Red Clover plants are—unless subjected to some abnormal or peculiar influences—so nearly alike that a minute description, or an exact figure of any one, would be an accurate account or representation of any other individual; the same may be said of the individual White Oaks, Locusts, Dogwoods, May-Apples, Dandelions, or any other plants; each of these, therefore, is a separate species. That individuals of different species occasionly pass, by a series of immediate forms, into one another cannot be denied. The large majority of species now existing, however, are well marked; and though closely related to some others, their characters appear constant, and they do not perceptibly tend to vary into each other.

149. The seeds of any species of plants will, when sown, produce individuals exactly, or approximately, like the adult. The same is true for all succeeding generations, so far as is known by actual experiment or observation. It sometimes happens, however, that certain individuals differ slightly, but evidently, from the typical form; the latter may be smooth, and the individuals in question hairy; the difference may be in the size of the plants, or in the color of the flowers, shape of the leaves, or any other minor character. If the descendants of these individuals differ in the same respect from the typical form; or, in other words, if their characters are constant, they constitute a **variety** of that species. Thus, one of the wild Buttercups (*Ranunculus abortivus*) has smooth, rather large stems; but a form of it (*Ranunculus abortivus, var. micranthus*) has smaller, hairy stems. The cultivated Snow-ball is a variety of the wild High Cranberry (*Viburnum Opulus*); the latter has only the outer flowers of the cluster enlarged and conspicuous (neutral); in the former, they are all thus characterized. The amount of variation, within varietal limits, cannot of course be conventionally determined; some botanists may, in particular cases, call *species* what others designate as merely good *varieties*.

150. An individual of any species may occasionally show a conspicuous variation from the typical form; as, a Violet without a spur, a Strawberry plant with simple leaves, a regular flower, when the flowers of the plant are labiate; and so on. Such characters are not transmitted to descendants; the latter present the typical form. Individuals behaving in this manner are called **sports**. Exaggerations of such tendencies often produce monstrosities. These are sometimes instructive, especially in cases of *reversion*. Thus in a monstrous flower, the several organs may revert to the form of leaves, of which evidently, therefore, they must be considered modifications; or a flower-bud may develop into a branch, showing that the flower is homologous with the latter. The influence of cultivation (sub-

jecting the plant often to conditions abnormal to it) in producing monstrosities, sports, races, and varieties (in the sense understood by gardeners) is very marked. Thus, there are hosts of forms of the Dahlia in cultivation, all derived since 1802 from *Dahlia variabilis;* the Pansies, from *Viola tricolor,* are also numerous; "some Melons are no larger than small Plums, others weigh as much as 66 pounds; one variety has scarlet fruit, another is only one inch in diameter, but three feet long; one variety can scarcely be distinguished externally or internally from Cucumbers; one Algerian variety suddenly splits up into sections when ripe."

151. The several species of Willows have a marked resemblance to each other: the same may be said of the various Oaks, Osiers, Clovers, Violets, etc. A group of such nearly-related species is designated by the word **genus**. Thus, there is a genus of Oaks (*Quercus*), a genus of Roses (*Rosa*), a genus of Toad-stools (*Agaricus*), a genus of Rusts (*Puccinia*), and so on. The genera including the Bean (*Phaseolus*), Pea (*Pisum*), Vetch (*Vicia*), Lathyrus (*Lathyrus*), and several others, have a general resemblance in foliage, flowers, fruit, etc.; and they are, therefore, grouped together, and constitute a **family**, called, in this case, *Leguminosæ*. Others, as the Iron-weeds (*Vernonia*), Thistles (*Cirsium*), Dandelion (*Taraxacum*), *Hieracium, Lactuca,* etc.—characterized by having the flowers in an involucrate head with syngyuesious anthers—form the family *Compositæ*. In like manner, that is, by more or less closely related genera, other families, as *Ranunculaceæ, Cruciferæ, Labiatæ, Gramineæ,* etc., are formed. Larger groups, or **orders**, are formed of families, and still more comprehensive are the so-called **classes**.

The names, Division, Class, Tribe, Cohort, Order, and Family are not always used with exactly the same signification by different botanists.

152. The system of nomenclature, perfected by Linnæus, and used since his time, is **binomial**; that is, every plant is designated by a double name, the name of the genus followed by the name of the species, both being Latin, or Latinized words. Thus the botanical name of Black Walnut is *Juglans nigra, L.*; of Sugar-Maple, *Acer saccharinum, Wang.*; of Ground Ivy, *Nepeta Glechoma, Benth.*, etc. The specific name is generally an adjective, and, therefore, is not to be capitalized, unless it is a proper adjective, as in *Sanguinaria Canadensis;* sometimes it is an old substantive, or the name of a person, in which cases the capital is retained, as in *Magnolia Umbrella,* Lam.; *Phacelia Purshii,* Buck. The generic name is a substantive, always capitalized, and may be the old classical name, as *Platanus, Acer, Nepeta;* a name formed from Latin, Greek, or other words, as *Trifolium* (Lat. *tri*, three; *folium*, leaf), *Zea* (Gr. *zao*, to live), *Datura* (Arabic *Tatorah*); or the name of a person, as *Claytonia* (after John Clayton, an early botanist of Virginia); *Linnæa* (after Linnæus, the immortal Swedish botanist, born 1707, died 1778). The abbreviation of the author's name is also added when botanical names are written. Thus, *L., Wang., Benth.,* in the names above are for *Linnæus, Wangenheim, Bentham,* who described and named the several species.

153. Many attempts have been made to classify plants, but until recently the arrangement was very artificial, in as much as undue stress was laid on one, or a few characters, to the exclusion of all others. By this method plants, very much unlike in general, were often brought near together, or into the same group; and plants closely related were sometimes widely separated—in other words, the classification was far from being *natural;* it was *artificial.* By taking into account all the characters of the adult form, and its development, or embryonic changes it passes through to reach that form, an approximation to a **natural system** of classification can be made, even in the present state of botanical science. Many of the lower plants are as yet very imperfectly understood, and, therefore, not really classifiable. They have been temporarily placed in a separate division, called *Protophyta* (Gr. *protos*, first, simple; *phyton*, plant).

DIVISIONS.

154. The Vegetable Kingdom may be grouped into the following Divisions:

1. **Protophyta**, such as Slime-Moulds, Bacteria, Yeast-plant, etc.
2. **Zygosporeæ** (Gr. *zugon*, yoke), Water-net, Diatoms, Spirogyra, Moulds, etc.
3. **Oosporeæ** (Gr. *oön*, egg), Peronospora, Fucus, Sargassum, etc.
4. **Carposporeæ** (Gr. *karpos*, fruit), Erysiphe, Lichens, Wheat Rust, Toad-stools, etc.
5. **Bryophyta** (Gr. *bryon*, moss), Mosses and Liverworts.
6. **Pteridophyta** (Gr. *pteron*, wing), the Ferns.
7. **Phanerogamia** (Gr. *phainos*, visible; *gamos*, union), ordinary flowering plants, herbs, shrubs, etc.

The first four groups are called *Thallophyta* (Gr. *thallos*, frond), or plants without distinction of stem and leaves; and the last three groups are called *Cormophyta* (Gr.

kormos, trunk), or plants with differentiation of stem and leaves. It will be noticed that the old groups of Algæ and Fungi are abandoned in this classification, though the two are physiologically quite distinct. The terms will be frequently used; Algæ, denoting thallophytes with chlorophyll (and, therefore, assimilating inorganic matter); and Fungi, thallophytes destitute of chlorophyll, and hence parasitic or saprophytic. The first six groups are sometimes called **cryptogams** (*cryptogamia*, Gr. *kruptos*, hidden; *gamos*, marriage, or union), or **flowerless plants**, and they produce *spores* (destitute of an embryo); the last group is called **phenogams**, or **flowering plants**, and they produce seeds (having an embryo).

PROTOPHYTA.

155. The lowest and simplest plants are included in the group **Protophyta**. They are often exceedingly small, and can be seen only with the high powers of the microscope. The nucleus has not been detected in the cells of all of them, and some are destitue of a cellwall. The cells are either isolated or but loosely united into families. The usual mode of multiplying is by fission; that is, a cell, after attaining a certain size (Fig. 229), begins to constrict in the middle (Fig. 230), and this continues (Fig. 231) till it is separated into two portions (Fig. 232), each of which is a new cell. A modification of the method of reproduction by fission is exhibited in the so-called **budding**. On the adult cell (*mother-cell*) is produced a small cell (*daughter-cell*) which eventually becomes separated (Fig. 235). Still another mode of reproduction

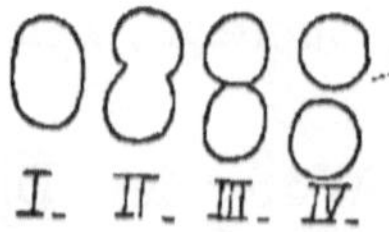

Figs. 229-232. Successive stages in the process of multiplication by Fission.

PROTOPHYTA.

is presented by some of the members of this group, viz. by the formation of **spores** (Fig. 233).

156. As representatives of this division (Protophyta), the **Myxomycetes**, or **Slime-Moulds**, are the most remarkable. During their growing, or vegetative stage, they consist of a homogeneous mass of colored (but never green) protoplasm, which has received the name of *plasmodium*. There is no cell-wall; there is a streaming or circulation in the mass of protoplasm, and the latter can, by constant change of form, move slowly around on the damp decaying wood, or vegetable mould, where these plants are often to be met with. In their vegetative state they are so much like the lower animals (*Monera*) that they were, for a long time, considered as belonging to the animal kingdom. If they are brought to rest by absence of proper moisture and temperature, they become changed into rounded masses, and secrete a cellulose wall. This is called the *sclerotium* stage. Upon return of suitable conditions, the plasmodium form is again assumed. The reproductive stage is also one of rest; the mass becomes compact, heaped up into definite shapes (Fig. 233, *I*) surrounded by cellulose; the protoplasm within becomes separated into multitudes of spores (Fig. 233, *V*), which, in many species, are commingled with an irregular net-work of (often ornamented) filaments, called the *capillitium* (Fig. 233, *III, IV*). Under proper conditions the

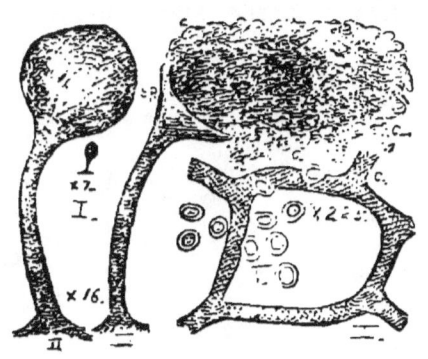

Fig. 233. *Arcyria pomiformis*, a Slime-Mould; *c*, capillitium; *sp*, sporangium; *I*, plant, natural size; *II* and *III*, magnified sixteen diameters; *IV*, capillitium; *V*, spores, more highly magnified.

spores burst open, the protoplasm of each escapes as a swarm-spore with one cilium, and undergoes fission. Coalescence of a number of these takes place in a few days to form the plasmodium.

157. The **Bacteria** (*Schizomycetes*) are Protophyta, destitute of chlorophyll. They are exceedingly small and simple organisms (Fig. 234), present in fermenting and putrefying matter, and sometimes in the blood of diseased animals. They occur isolated, or in cell-families, and multiply exclusively by transverse fission; most of them have a motile and a motionless stage. The unicellular Bacteria sometimes form a jelly-like mass or colony, probably in consequence of the swelling up of their cell-walls, and this is called the zoöglea stage (Fig. 234, *Bct*). The common agent of putrefaction is *Bacterium termo*, which consists of very small cylindrical cells. *B. æruginosum* is found in blue-green pus. The genus *Micrococcus*, consists of spherical cells (Fig. 234, *Micr*). *M. prodigiosus* causes the blood-like patches on bread, paste, etc. *M. diptheric us* causes, or at least accompanies, diptheria. There are two genera, with filiform cells; *Bacillus*, with the filament straight (Fig. 234, *Bcl*); and *Vibrio*, with the filament curved or undulated (Fig. 234, *Vib*). *B. subtilis* is the butyric ferment, and *B. anthracis* causes the anthrax or splenic fever. The genus *Spirillum* (Fig. 234, *spl*) has spirally twisted cells. *S. volutans* is a comparatively large species with a flagellum or cilium at each end.

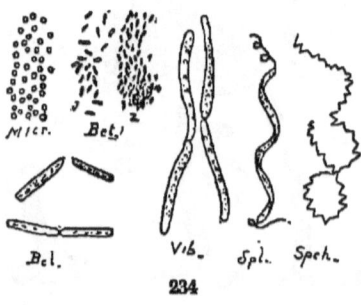

Fig. 234. Bacteria; *Micr, Micrococcus prodigiosus; Bct, Bacterium termo; Bcl, Bacillus ulna; Vib, Vibrio rugula; Spl, Spirillum volutans; Spch, Spirochæte plicatilis.*

PROTOPHYTA. 125

158. Another family of plants belonging to the Protophyta is the **Saccharomyces**, including the Yeast-plant (*Saccharomyces cerevisiæ*) and other species, which produce fermentation in sugar solutions. The transparent cells are more or less round, oval, or elongated, and multiply by budding (Fig. 235). When the supply of nourishment  is less abundant (as when yeast is grown on slices of potato or carrot), the cells are larger, and divide internally into four new cells with cell-walls. These may be called spores; they escape and grow into cells of the ordinary kind, capable of multiplication by budding. *Saccharomyces cerevisiæ* produces the alcholic fermentation; that is, the sugar in the solution is converted into alcohol with the escape of carbonic dioxide. *S. ellipsoides, S. conglomeratæ*, and others, live on grapes, and find their way into the juice in the manufacture of wine, and cause the fermentation of the latter. *S. mycoderma* is found on the surface of spoiled beer or wine; it does not produce fermentation like the others, but putrefaction instead.

159. Another family of the Protophyta containing (unlike the preceding) chlorophyll is the **Nostocs** (*Nostocaceæ*). The plants consist of rounded cells loosely united into filaments, and imbedded in a jelly-like mass (Fig. 236). At intervals are large, clear cells, called heterocysts, whose

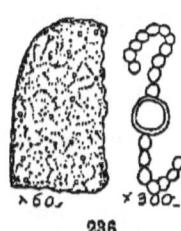

function is not clearly known. The plants grow in fresh water, or in damp places. They multiply usually by fission of the cells. Filaments sometimes break in pieces capable of motion; and from these, when at rest, new colonies are formed. The

Fig. 235. Yeast-plant (*Saccharomyces cerevisiæ*). Fig. 236. A colony of Nostoc; the figure on the left moderately magnified; the one on the right (a single filament) highly magnified.

Oscillatoria have the cells of the filament more closely united. They form dark-green masses in water, or on wet earth, and exhibit an oscillating movement of the filaments. The *Nostocs, Oscillatoria*, with several other genera, as *Rivularia, Scytonema*, etc., have, in addition to chlorophyll, a soluble coloring matter, called *phycocyanine*, and a less soluble one, called *phycoxanthine*. They are blue-green, verdigris-green, brownish-green, or even purple-red, and live in fresh or stagnant water, on damp ground, rocks, or decaying wood.

ZYGOSPOREÆ.

160. The second division, or **Zygosporeæ**, is composed mostly of many-celled, filamentous organisms, but some of them are unicellular, and others a flat thalloid mass; nearly all of them contain chlorophyll, and are aquatic. They are the common Algæ of our ponds and streams. The modes of reproduction are by (1) **fission**, (2) **non-sexual spores** (*swarm-spores*), and (3) **zygospores**. The swarm-spores (Fig. 237) are motile, naked masses of protoplasm, furnished with cilia. They escape from the cell in which they are produced, and after swimming about for a time, fuse two and two, and a spore with a thick wall is the result. Very simple, yet undoubted, sexual organs exist in the members of this group. The difference between the male and female organs, however, is not appreciable. The result of the union of the two sexual cells is the formation of a zygospore, with thick, firm walls; the process is illustrated in the Moulds (Fig. 238).

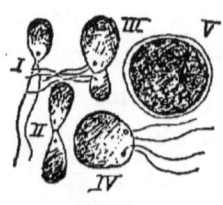

Fig. 237. Swarm-spores.

ZYGOSPOREÆ.

Two small branches from the vegetative threads, or *mycelium*, unite end to end (Fig. 238, *I*); continue to grow larger (Fig. 238, *II*); the terminal portion of each becomes separated by a partition wall (Fig. 238, *III*); the common wall between these cell-ends becomes absorbed (Fig. 238, *IV*); their contents fuse; a firm, thick cell-wall is secreted; and thus is formed the zygospore (Fig. 238, *V*), or *resting-spore*, as it is sometimes called, for it often remains quiescent and retains its vitality for a great length of time.

161. The Hydrodictyon, or Water-net, a fresh-water Alga, is a representative of the division, Zygosporeæ. It sometimes occurs in abundance in ponds and slow streams. It is composed of a multitude of cells, arranged so as to form a tubular 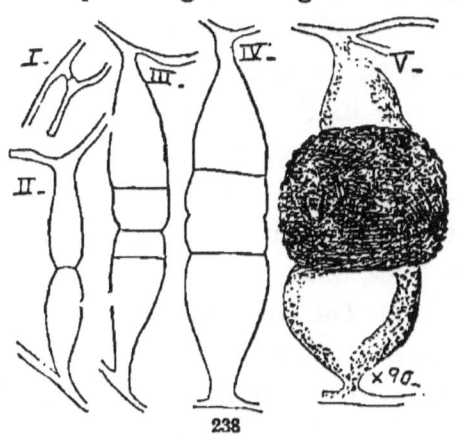 net, whose meshes in the full-grown plant—when it may be eight or ten inches long—are plainly visible to the naked eye. It reproduces by the protoplasm of certain cells breaking up into several thousand small masses, or daughter-cells, which presently unite so as to form a miniature net; the wall of the mother-cell becomes absorbed, and the little plant is set free. It is said also to reproduce by means of swarm-spores. The Desmids (*Desmidiaceæ*) are motile unicellular fresh-water Algæ (Figs. 239, 240), belonging also to this division. The cells are

Fig. 238. Successive stages (*I, II, III, IV, V*) in the formation of a zygospore in case of *Mucor stolonifera*.

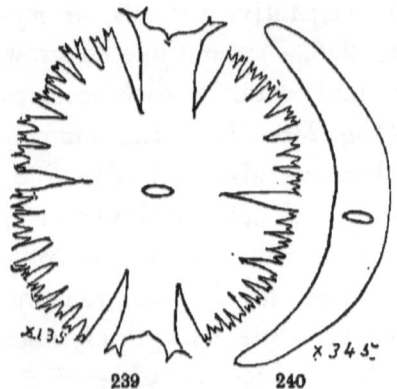

generally more or less constricted in the middle, and divided into two symmetrical half-cells. A sexual reproduction takes place by the elongation and fission of the neck, uniting the two halves of the cells. The two small half-cells grow until they are as large as the original ones, when they separate. Sexual reproduction results in the formation of a zygospore; thus, elongations, or conjugating tubes, of two adjacent cells grow out till they meet, their protoplasm fuses upon the absorption of the partition between them, and this becomes covered with a thick wall, or exospore.

162. The **Diatoms** (*Diatomaceæ*), as are also the Desmids, are microscopic, unicellular Algæ (Fig. 241), with a multitude of ornamental forms. They differ, however, in having silicious cells, and their chlorophyll concealed by a brownish or yellowish coloring matter, called *phycoxanthine*. The cell (called a *frustule*) consists of two portions, called valves, one of which is slightly larger and fits over the other like the lid of a pill-box. Reproduction takes place very similar to that in the Desmids, the protoplasm divides in a plane parallel to the valves, each portion secretes a shell or valve, which, in every case, is slightly smaller and fits into the old or outer valve. It is evident, therefore, that as multiplication by fission con-

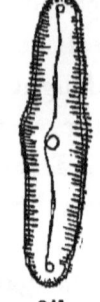

Fig. 239. *Micrasterias furcata*, a Desmid. Fig. 240. *Cosmarium parvula*, a Desmid. Fig. 241. *Navicula viridis*, a Diatom.

tinues, the resulting plants become smaller and smaller. When a certain limit is reached, reproduction by another process, namely, by *auxospores* (Gr. *auxano*, to increase), takes place, by which the original size is again attained; two plants approach each other, their valves separate, the protoplasm of the two fuses into one mass, and this grows to a large size, secretes a shell or valves of the normal form. Like the Desmids, the Diatoms locomote freely; but the mechanism of the process is not understood. They are excessively abundant, and inhabit both salt and fresh water, often forming a yellowish layer at the bottom. As fossils they are also abundant, their silicified shells forming vast beds. Their beautiful and very fine markings make them desirable as test objects for the microscope.

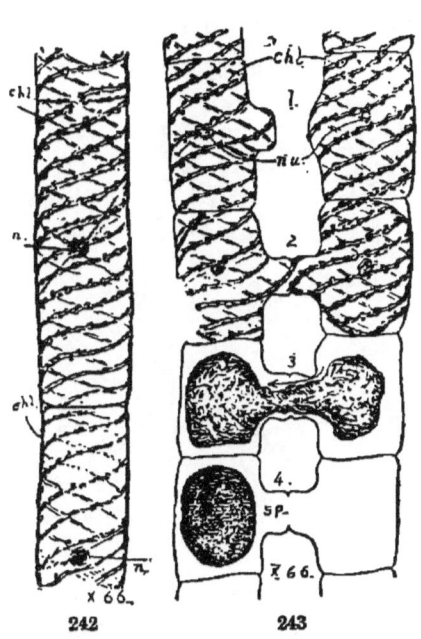

163. Another very common, abundant and beautiful fresh-water Alga, belonging to the division Zygosporeæ, is the **Spirogyra** (Fig. 242, 243). It is a many-celled, filamentous Alga, with the chlorophyll in spiral bands, and a conspicuous nucleus in each cell, which is imbedded in the small central protoplasmic mass, and suspended by extensions to the parietal protoplasm (Fig. 242). The

Fig. 242. A vegetative filament of Spirogyra. Fig. 243. Spirogyra in the process of conjugation.

filaments elongate by the fission of the cells; the protoplasm divides, a cellulose wall is at the same time secreted, and the two daughter-cells then elongate to the normal length. Sometimes the filaments break up spontaneously, and each part gives rise to a new filament. The sexual reproduction takes place by a process called *conjugation* (Fig. 243). From each of the cells of two filaments lying parallel to each other, slight protrusions arise (Fig. 243, 1), and these grow towards each other until they come in contact and unite (Fig. 243, 2). The partition between them becomes absorbed (Fig. 243, 2); in the meantime, the protoplasm in each of the two cells contracts, rounds itself, and one mass passes gradually through the channel (Fig. 243, 3) over into the other cell, where the two unite and form the zygospore (Fig. 243, *sp*). The old cell-walls decay, and the zygospore falls to the bottom of the water and remains till the process of germination commences. The latter begins by the bursting of the outer hard wall of the spore, the mass within extends in columnar form, secretes cross-partitions, and elongates to the normal form.

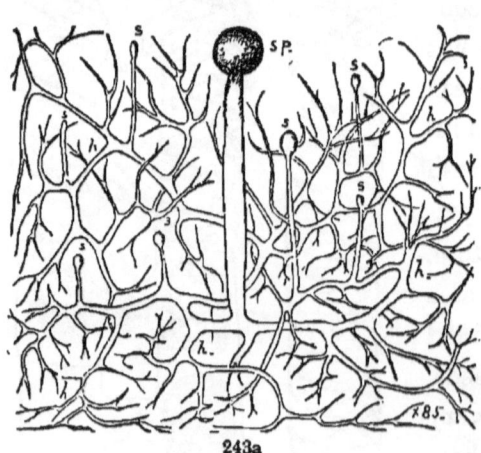

164. The common Fungi, called **Moulds** (*Mucorini*),

Fig. 243a. Common Mould, partially diagrammatic; *h*, hyphæ; *sp*, sporangium; *s*, young sporangia.

are also Zygosporeæ. They are saprophytic (or rarely parasitic), and, of course, destitute of chlorophyll. Their branching vegetative filaments, or hyphæ, are numerous, and form a somewhat felted mass, or mycelium (Fig. 243a). Their vegetative, or non-sexual, reproduction takes place thus: erect hyphæ are sent up from the mycelium, at the top of which a sporangium is formed by the terminal portion becoming enlarged and cut off by a partition wall (Fig. 244). This partition arches upwards, the terminal cell becomes larger (Fig. 245), and the former extends far up into the latter, and forms what is called a *columella* (Fig. 246, c). The protoplasm of the terminal cell, or sporangium, breaks up into a multitude of minute masses, each of which becomes surrounded with a cell-wall, and thus the spores are formed. 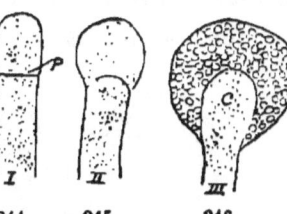 The latter germinate when on a proper nourishing substance, by sending out one or two hyphæ, which soon branch and form a mycelium. The sexual reproduction of the Moulds has been illustrated in paragraph 160, above. The zygospore, after a period of rest and desiccation, will, in a moist atmosphere, send out hyphæ, which do not form a mycelium, but produce sporangia, in which spores develop capable of germinating and forming a mycelium.

Figs. 244-246. Diagrammatic representation of successive stages in the formation of a sporangium in case of the Mould *Mucor*.

OOSPOREÆ.

165. The third division is the **Oosporeæ**, or plants characterized by the production of a large female cell, called the *oögonium* (Fig. 247, *o*), in which is contained one or more round masses of protoplasm, the *oöspheres*. These are fertilized by the contents of special, smaller male cells, called *antheridia* (Fig. 247, *a*). In some cases the protoplasm of the latter is transferred to the oösphere by direct contact; in other cases, it is first broken up into motile bodies, called *spermatozoids*, which approach and fuse with the oösphere. The oösphere becomes the

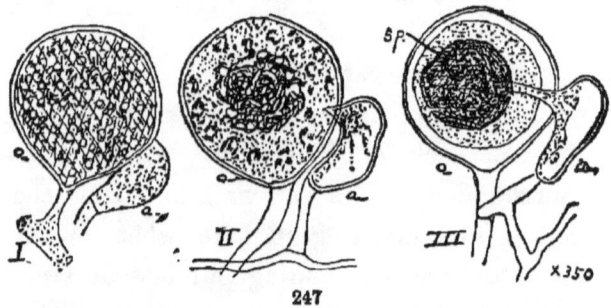

247

oöspore, with a hard (and generally colored) covering, or exospore, and is capable of germinating after a certain period of rest. One mode of non-sexual reproduction in this group is presented by the genus *Œdogonium*, where large zoöspores are produced (Fig. 248). Another mode is the formation of *conidia*, as in the White Rust (*Cystopus*), where they are formed under the epidermis, and in the genus *Peronospora* (to which the potato disease, *Peronospora infestans*, belongs), where they are produced on the ends of branching hyphæ that grow through the stomates (Fig. 250).

Fig. 247. Reproduction by the formation of an oöspore in *Peronospora Alsinearum*; *o*, the oögonium; *a*, antheridium; *sp*, the oöspore.

166. As a representative of the Oösporeæ, the filamentous fresh-water Alga, *Œdogonium*, may be mentioned. It grows in ponds and streams, and forms green masses attached to sticks or other objects. When examined under the microscope, 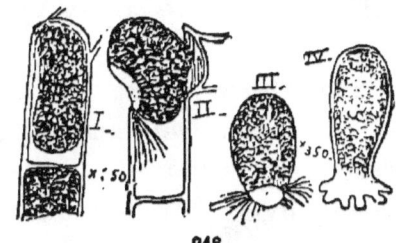 a number of transverse parallel lines near one end of the cell will be seen, and in section they appear as so many cups slipped over each other (Fig. 249). This results from its peculiar mode of *intercalary* growth, as follows: an inward growth from the wall takes place in such a way as to form a cylindrical ring (Fig. 249, *I*). After a time, the cell-wall splits circularly through the exterior portion of the ring, and the two portions of the cell-wall recede from each other, connected by the unfolded cylinder (Fig. 249, *II*). The cell elongates again by the formation of a new ring below the previous one, and so on. The non-sexual reproduction takes place by the formation of ciliated, motile zoöspores (Fig. 248); when the spore (zoöspore) comes to rest, and forms a cell-wall, it sends out 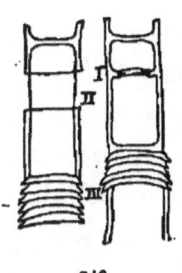 root-like projections for attachment, then elongates, forms cross-partitions, and takes on the form of the adult filament. The sexual reproduction takes place by the formation of an oösphere in an enlarged cell of the filament, the oögonium; this then opens, and allows the entrance of the spermatozoids, which have a crown of cilia, like

Fig. 248. Non-sexual reproduction of Œdogonium. Fig. 249. Diagrammatic representation of intercalary growth of the Œdogonium.

the zoöspores. The spermatozoids are produced in small cells which have arisen by simple fission of one of the larger cells.

167. Other representatives of the Oösporeæ are the unicellular *Saprolegnia*, and allied genera, which grow on dead fishes, cray-fishes, etc., and may be found parasitic on young, living fish in aquaria. They are often extremely abundant, and then cause immense losses in fish breeding. They multiply non-sexually by the production of ciliated zoöspores, which are formed from the protoplasm in the end of a branch. The zoöspores swim about for a few minutes, come to rest, their cilia disappear, and after a few hours they germinate by sending out a filament which produces a new plant. The sexual reproduction is by means of oögonia and antheridia. When the two arise on the same plant, fertilization takes place by direct contact of the antheridia with the oögonia, and the passage of the contents of the former into the latter through the tubular process of the antheridium. When the plants are diœcious, motile spermatozoids are produced for the purpose of fertilization. The oöspores have a thick, double integument (exospore and endospore), and germinate by sending out a tube after a period of rest.

168. The **Peronosporeæ** (division Oösporeæ) deserve special attention on account of the great damage they do by their parasitism on living plants, and many of these are common in cultivation, as the Potato, Clover, Spinach, Grape-Vine, etc. The branching mycelium is unicellular, and grows into the tissue of the higher plants, sending minute branches, called *haustoria*, into the cells themselves for nourishment. They multiply with great rapidity by non-sexual spores, called conidia. In the genus *Cystopus*, which may be seen on Shepherd's-Purse, and other *Cruci-*

feræ, as white, blister-like patches, the conidia are produced just beneath the epidermis, which becomes ruptured, and allows their escape. In *Peronospora*, as the Grape-Mildew (*P. viticola*), the Potato Fungus (*P. infestans*), the white, frost-like down on Peppergrass (*P. parasitica*), etc., the conidia are produced on aerial branches of the hyphæ growing from the stomates (Fig. 250). The conidia quickly germinate, and in some species give rise directly to a filament; in other species, swarm-spores, each with two cilia, are formed, which, after coming to rest, send out germinating filaments; these pass into the host-plant, either growing through the stomates, or boring directly through the epidermis, where numerous hyphæ are again produced. The sexual reproduction takes place by means of oögonia and antheridia (Fig. 247).

169. The **Fucoideæ** are also representatives of the Oösporeæ. They are marine Algæ, whose green, or chlorophyll, is concealed by a reddish-brown coloring matter. They are often of

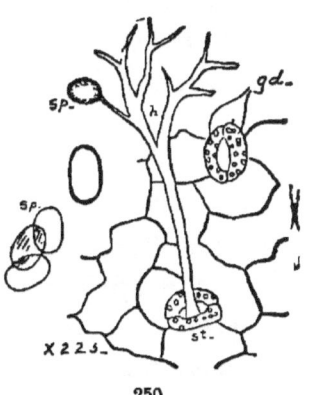

great size and present considerable differentiation of tissue, not found in the Thallophytes previously mentioned. They may be flat, or strap-shaped, and several yards in length, as in *Laminaria*; they may be tree-like in form and size, twenty to thirty feet in height, as in *Lessonia*; or, like a gigantic pinnate leaf, sometimes more than three hundred feet long, as *Macrocystis*. The outer tissues are generally dense, and formed of small and crowded cells; the inner cells are mostly elongated and loosely joined, so as to

Fig. 250. Conidia of Peronospora; *h*, hyphæ; *sp*, conidia; *st*, stomates; *gd*, guard-cells.

leave intercellular spaces. There is also considerable differentiation into reproductive organs, somewhat analogous to the floral branches in the higher plants. The reproductive organs, that is, oögonia and antheridia, are borne on modified branches, which differ more or less from the ordinary ones; they are generally contained in hollows (called *conceptacles*) of the epidermis. Some species are monœcious; others, diœcious. No non-sexnal reproduction takes place. While most Thallophytes are short-lived, the plants of this group often live many years. The species of *Fucus* and *Sargassum* are washed ashore in great quantities and used as a fertilizer for soil, and also for obtaining alkalies and iodine. *Sargassum bacciferum* is the Gulfweed, which covers a large area in the Atlantic, called the *Sargasso Sea*.

CARPOSPOREÆ.

170. The fourth division of the vegetable kingdom, viz. the **Carposporeæ**, is characterized by the production of a **sporocarp**, which consists in general of two parts: (1) a fertile part, which directly or indirectly produces the spores; and (2) a sterile part, which is composed of cells or tissue developed from the cells adjacent to the fertile part and envelopes the latter. Some of the representatives are chlorophyll-bearing, as the Red Marine Algæ; others are destitute of chlorophyll and parasitic, as the Wheat Rust, Corn-Smut, etc.; or saprophytic, as the Toad-stools and Puff-balls. In the higher members of the group there is a considerable differentiation into *caulome* (or stem) and *phyllome* (or leaf). The non-sexual reproduction may take place by the production of (1) zoöspores, (2) non-motile tetraspores (so called because they are mostly formed by the division of the mother-cell into four parts or spores), or (3) conidia. The female organ in the sexual reproduction is called the carpogonium, and the male organ antheridium. Where two filaments cross each other, or come in contact, they enlarge (as in *Sphærotheca*); one assumes an oval form, becomes separated from the filament by a partition, and represents the carpogonium (Fig. 251, *car*); the other grows up in contact with the carpogonium, cuts off a small terminal cell, the antheridium (Fig. 251, *an*). After fertilization the cells at the base of the reproductive organs grow upwards, unite, and completely invest the carpogonium with a many-celled struct-

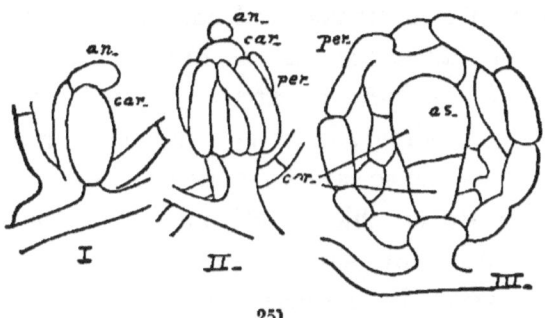

ure, called the *perithecium* (Fig. 251, *per*). The carpogonium (Fig. 251, *car*) then undergoes cell-division, and from it one *ascus* (Fig. 251, *as*), or several (asci), are formed, which contain the spores, sometimes called ascospores.

171. The **Florideæ**, or Red Algæ of salt water, are chlorophyll-bearing representatives of the division Carposporeæ. The chlorophyll is concealed by a red pigment (called *phycoërythrine*), which is soluble in cold, fresh water. When it is extracted the plants are green. These Algæ are very numerous and beautiful; inhabit deep waters generally; and are, therefore, difficult to obtain for study. The

Fig. 251. Successive stages (*I, II, III*) in the development of the sporocarp in *Sphærotheca pannosa; car,* carpogonium; *an,* antheridium; *per,* peridium.

non-sexual reproduction is by means of tetraspores. The carpogonium is peculiar in having a long filamentous appendage (trichogyne) to which the spermatozoids attach themselves when set free from the antheridium. Fertilization takes place in consequence of this contact, and the result is the production of the sporocarp. This, in some species, is very simple, and consists of the spores and the short branches which bear them; in others the mass is surrounded by a covering, or pericarp, developed from peripheral cells of the carpogonium. Some orders of the Florideæ contain "species which display the most exquisite combination of ramification and coloring." The "Dulse" (*Rhodymenia palmata*) is used as human food. The Irish Moss (*Chondrus crispus*) is extensively used also for food.

172. An exceedingly large and important group of the Carposporeæ is the so-called **Ascomycetes**. The plants are all destitute of chlorophyll, but differ among themselves to great extent as to size and appearance. They are all alike, however, in producing their spores in sacs, called asci; the spores are, therefore, called ascospores. The following are the most important orders:

1. **Erysiphaceæ.** The plants of this order are mainly parasitic, and consist of a mass of branching, jointed filaments, which form a white web-like film on the surface of the leaves and stems on which they grow and from which they draw their nourishment. They are very abundant, and often do great injury to the Apple, Cherry, Grape, Pea, etc. The conidial spores are produced in great abundance during the summer. Later, the sexual reproduction takes place in the manner described in paragraph 170 (Fig. 251). The sporocarp, or perithecium, has at its base radiating filaments, or appendages (*ambulacra*); they

are, in some cases, straight and prismatic, or they may be dichotomous, or hooked (Fig. 252) at the free ends.

2. **Pyronomycetes.** This order differs from the preceding in having the asci embedded in deep cavities (called

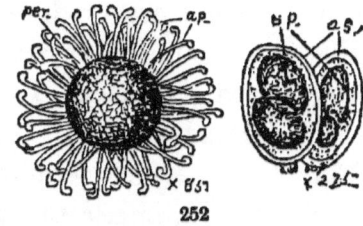

perithecia) with narrow openings, instead of being completely enclosed in perithecia. The pyronomycetous Fungi are very numerous, and exceedingly injurious not only to plants, but to insects also. A common representative is the

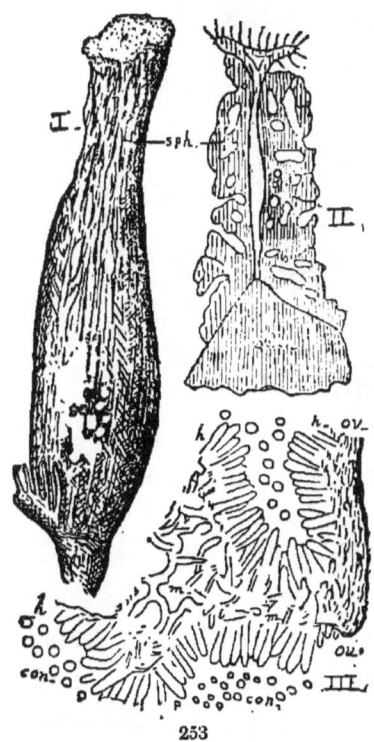

Fungus (*Claviceps purpurea;* Fig. 253), which produces the Ergot on Rye and other Grasses. In its earliest stage, it consists of a mass of mycelium (Fig. 253, *m*), in and upon the young ovary. Conidia (Fig. 253, *con*) are produced in great abundance, which quickly germinate. Following the conidial stage, the mycelium, at the base of the ovary (Fig. 253, *ov*), assumes a hard and compact form, increases in size, bears a horn-shaped and dark-colored body, the so-called Ergot. Such a compact mass of hyphæ is called a *sclerotium*.

Fig. 252. The sporocarp (perithecium), with its appendages and two asci, of *Uncinula macrospora*. Fig. 253. *Claviceps purpurea*, the Fungus which produces the Ergot; *m*, mycelium; *con*, conidia; *ov*, ovary.

This sclerotium usually begins in the spring a new growth; little branches are produced, each with a globular head (Fig. 254, *I*), in the cortical region of which the numerous flask-shaped perithecia (Fig. 254, *II*, *III*) are produced. The elongated asci (Fig. 254, *III*) bear attenuated spores (Fig. 254, *sp*), which germinate and produce the mycelium, which, in turn, infests the young ovaries as before. The

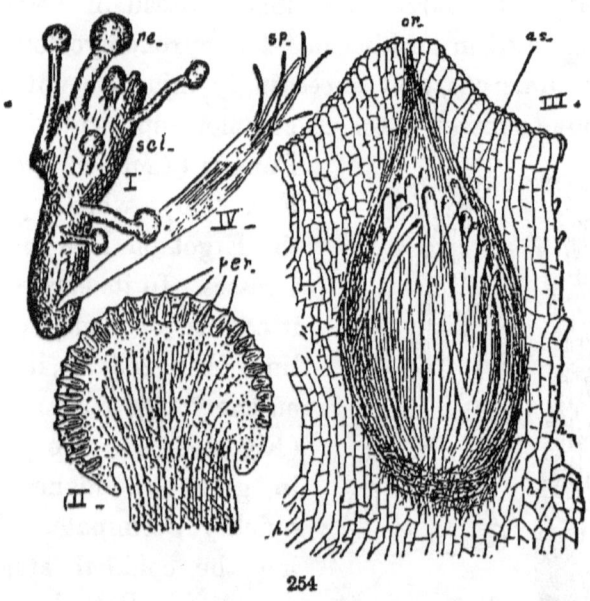

Black-Knot (*Sphaeria morbosa*) is another common and injurious Fungus of this order.

3. Lichenes. The Lichens (Figs. 255, 256) are considered by most botanists to be ascomycetous Fungi, although formerly they were held to be an independent, isolated group. The tissue consists of an aggregation of colorless jointed hyphæ, which, in the cortical portion, are usually

Fig. 254. *Claviceps purpurea* (Ergot); successive stages in the development of the ascospores; *scl*, Ergot (*sclerotium*); *per*, perithecia; *h*, hyphæ; *sp*, spores; *as*, asci.

compacted into a pseudo-parenchyma, and in the medullary portion distinct. Scattered through the interior, or disposed in one or more distinct layers, are numerous green, bluish-green, or brownish-green cells, called *gonidia*. These cells may be isolated, or in groups; or they may be rows, or chains of cells, and are capable of multiplication by fission. They are connected with the hyphæ by one or more branches from the latter, or they may be united directly to an intermediate or terminal cell of the hyphæ. The latter were, for a long time, supposed to produce them. Now it is held that the gonidia are simply imprisoned Algæ, which assimilate the food to be appropriated by the Lichens—a peculiar kind of parasitism which seems to be mutually advantageous to the two plants. The reproduction is similar to the other Ascomycetes (Fig. 256). The asci are either collected in a disk-like surface (gymnocarpous lichens), or enclosed in cavities or perithecia (angiocarpous lichens); and in either case called an *apothecium*. Of the numerous Lichens, a few furnish important commercial products; thus, from *Roccella tinctoria*, the dye orchil and "litmus" are obtained; and food is furnished by the Iceland Moss (*Cetraria islandica*), and others. The Reindeer Moss (*Cladonia rangiferina*) furnishes food to the reindeer.

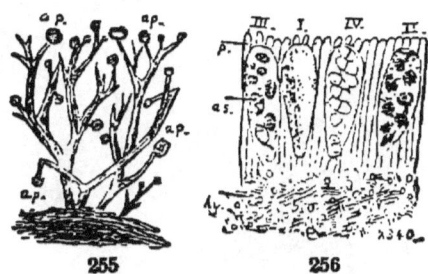

4. **Uredineæ.** The plants are parasitic in habit, and polymorphic; that is, in their life-course they take on at

Fig. 255. Cladonia, a Lichen; *ap*, the fruit, or apothecium. Fig. 256. Asci from the same, highly magnified.

successive periods two or more distinct forms, so unlike each other generally that the different stages were formerly considered as distinct plants. Nothing is yet known as to their sexual organs. The mycelium penetrates between the cells in the tissue of leaves, causing abnormal growth and more or less distortion. There then appear, beneath the epidermis, globular masses (Fig. 257), having within at their base a compact layer of upright hyphæ, each of which produces a chain of conidial spores. The epidermis is ruptured by the growing mass; and the thin layer of cells,

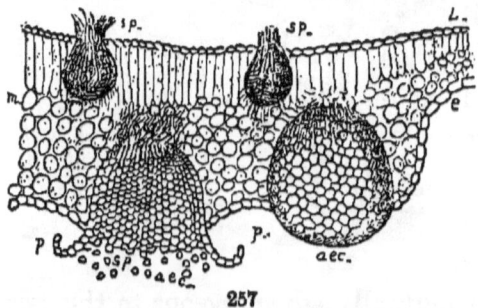

or periderm (Fig. 257, *p*), enclosing the spores, breaks open; the yellow spores, hitherto many-sided from mutual pressure, become round and escape. This stage formerly received the generic name of *Æcidium* (Fig. 257). The spores may, therefore, be called the *œcidiospores*. There are often present also smaller flask-shaped reproductive bodies, called spermogonia (Fig. 257, *sp*), containing hair-like filaments, which break up into exceedingly small bodies, called the *spermatia*. The exact function of these is not accurately known. The æcidiospores, when they fall on the proper host-plants, germinate, penetrate through the stomates, and form a dense mycelium in the parenchyma of the leaf; from this mycelium grow pedicelled spores, called uredo-spores, and form, when they burst through the epidermis, orange-colored spots. This

Fig. 257. Yellow Cluster-cup, or Æcidium (*aec*) of *Puccinia graminis*, and spermogonia (*sp*) on the Barberry leaf; *e*, epidermis; *p*, peridium; *sp*, spermogonia.

stage was formerly called the genus *Uredo* (Fig. 258). The

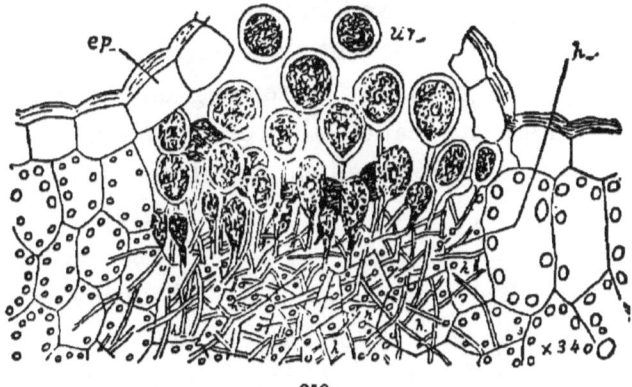

uredo-spores germinate quickly, and from their mycelium other uredo-spores are produced, and this process may continue a great length of time. Finally, from the same mycelium, are produced (Fig. 259) thick-walled, brown or black spores, called *teleutospores* (Gr. *teleuta*, end), which may be one-celled (as in *Uromyces* and *Melampsora*), two-celled (as in *Puccinia*, Fig. 259; and *Podisoma*,

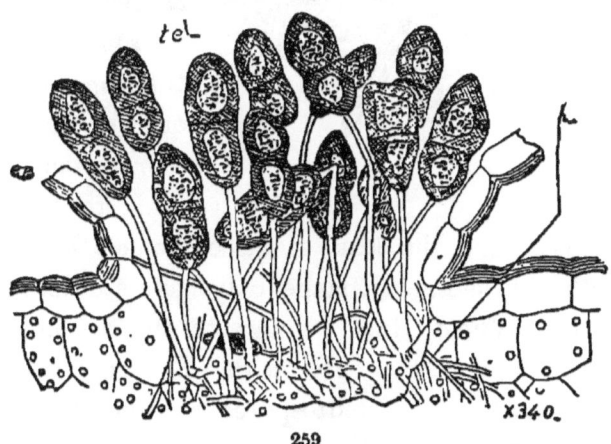

Fig. 258. Rust on Wheat (*Puccinia graminis*); section through the leaf, showing the uredo-spores (*ur*), highly magnified. Fig. 259. Rust on Corn (*Puccinia sorghi*); section through the leaf, showing teleutospores, highly magnified.

Fig. 260), or many-celled (as in *Phragmidium*). They rupture the epidermis and become exposed, but generally remain attached to their host-plant during the winter. In the spring, they germinate by sending out from each cell a jointed filament, called the *promycelium*. In small branches of the promycelium, small terminal cells, or sporidia, are formed. These are carried about by the wind, and germinate on the proper host-plant. They send their filaments into the parenchyma of the leaf, from which a mycelium proceeds that gives rise to an æcidium, and so on, as before described. In some species all the stages may grow on the same plant; more often the æcidial stage is found on one plant, and the other stages on some other one; or, in yet other species, each stage may have a different host-plant. The Wheat Rust belongs to the second group; its æcidial stage occurs only on the Barberry leaves, and the uredo-spores and teleutospores are found on Wheat and other *Gramineæ*.

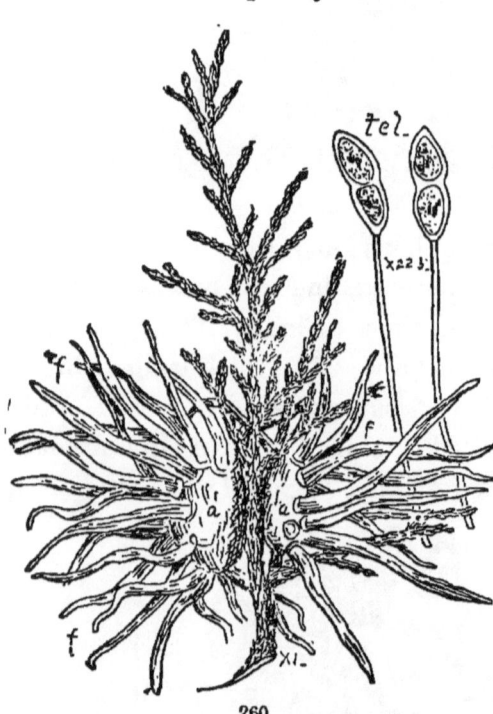

Fig. 260. Cedar-Apple, *Gymnosporangium* (or *Podisoma*) *macropus*, on *Juniperus Virginiana; tel*, teleutospores, highly magnified.

5. **Ustilagineæ.** The plants of this order are also parasitic; the mycelium ramifies through the tissue of the host-plant, and finally produces an abundance of brown, or black, thick-walled spores, which burst through the epidermis. The hyphæ are jointed and branching, grow in the intercellular spaces, and also within the cell-cavities of their host-plants. The mycelium generally begins its growth when the host-plant is quite young, and grows with the latter. The spores are generally produced only in some definite part of the plant, as the young flowers (as in the smut of Wheat, Oats, etc.), ovaries (as in the bunt of Wheat), anthers (as in the smut of Silene), etc. In the smut of Indian Corn they may be formed in any part of the plant. The spores germinate, so far as have been observed, by producing a promycelium on which several sporidia are formed, much as in the Uredineæ. No sexual organs have as yet been detected. Many species of the genera *Ustilago*, *Tilletia*, and *Urocystis* are very destructive to Wheat, Oats, Corn, Grasses, Onions, etc.

173. The large and interesting Fungi, known as Puff-balls and Toad-stools, are additional representatives of the Carposporeæ. But one kind of spores, and these non-sexual, are known, and they are produced on slender out-growths from the ends of enlarged cells, called *basidia* (Fig. 261, *b*); for this reason the group is called the *Basidiomycetes*. The mycelium is mostly saprophytic, very abundant, and from it the spore-bearing growth, or sporocarp, is produced. The two important orders of this class are the *Gasteromycetes* and *Hymenomycetes:*

1. **Gasteromycetes.** The sporocarps in this order are usually more or less globular. The spores are borne within somewhat irregular cavities, from which they escape by the

drying and rupture of the surrounding tissue. The basidia, upon each of which four or more spores are borne, are the rounded or elongated terminal cells of internal hyphæ-branches. The outer wall (peridium) of the sporocarp ruptures irregularly in the common Puff-ball (*Lycoperdon*); but in the Earth-star (*Geaster*), where it consists of two layers, the outer, dense layer splits from the top into segments, which re-curve and expose the inner and more delicate layer. This, in turn, ruptures somewhat irregularly, and allows the escape of the spores. The Giant Puff-ball (*Lycoperdon giganteum*) is a very common and edible species.

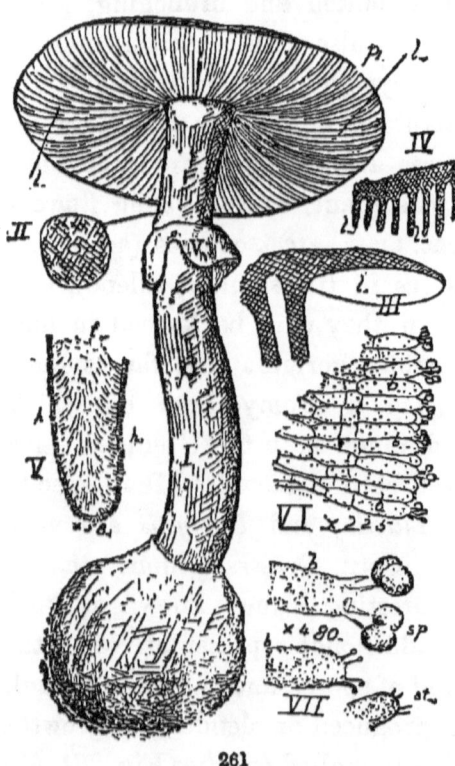

2. **Hymenomycetes.** The sporocarp, in the Fungi of this order, is composed of parallel, vertical hyphæ, which grow upwards, and (as in *Agaricus*) bend out laterally, or send out lateral branches at the top, to form the umbrella-like

Fig. 261. A Mushroom (*Agaricus phalloides*); *I*, the entire plant; *II*, section of stem, or stipe; *III*, gills, in transverse section; *IV*, longitudinal section, showing the gills, or lamellæ; *V*, a single lamella, moderately magnified; *VI*, a portion of the hymenium, highly magnified; *VII*, two basidia, with sterigmata and spores; *p*, pileus, or cap; *l*, lamellæ; *h*, hymenium; *t*, trama; *b*, basidia; *sp*, spores; *st*, sterigmata.

top or pileus (Fig. 261, *p*). On the under side of this are the gills, or lamellæ (Fig. 261, *l*), upon whose surface there is developed a continuous spore-bearing layer, or hymenium (Fig. 261, *h*). The hymenium consist of parallel, compacted, elongated, subclavate cells (Fig. 261, *h*); on some of which, namely, the basidia, four (in some species only two) little pedicels (called *sterigmata*) arise (Fig. 261, *st*), and the ends of these enlarge and become converted into spores; called, therefore, basidiospores (Fig. 261, *sp*). These soon fall off and germinate, and (so far as is known) give rise to a mycelium. The most numerous and common representatives of this order belong to the genus *Agaricus*, which has several hundred species. Other common genera are *Polyporus*, in which the hymenium lines the walls of vertical pores on the under side of the pileus; *Hydnum*, in which the hymenium clothes numerous dependent spines; and *Stereum*, in which the hymenium covers the smooth surface of the sporocorp. Many of the species are edible, and cultivated (as the Mushroom, *Agaricus campestris*) for food. It is said that Dr. M. A. Curtis found in North Carolina thirty-eight edible species of *Agaricus*, eleven of *Boletus*, nine of *Polyporus*, seven of *Hydnum*, and thirteen of *Clavaria*. Many of the common species are poisonous.

174. A small group of slender, submerged, aquatic chlorophyll-bearing plants, called *Characeæ*, should perhaps be mentioned, as additional representatives of the Carposporeæ. They have jointed stems, which bear whorls of leaves at regular intervals. The stems in cross-section are one-celled (as in *Nitella*), or they have a large axial cell, surrounded by many smaller ones, which form a cortical envelope (as in *Chara*). Under the microscope there is

a manifest rotation of the protoplasm in the cells. The sexual organs differ somewhat from those of the Carposporeæ. The "central cell," or carpogonium, is the terminal one of a row of cells; from the basal cells there grow upwards five elongated ones, which surround the carpogonium, and become twisted, so as to form a spiral. The antheridium is globular, enclosed by eight triangular cells, called shields, which are united by zigzag margins. From the centre of each shield, projects inwardly a cylindrical cell, which supports many long, coiled filaments, in each of whose numerous segments a long, slender, spiral, biciliate spermatozoid is produced. The spermatozoids escape, when ripe, by the bursting of the antheridium, and swim about in the water till they find the orifice at the upper end (or " crown"), of the enveloping coat of the carpogonium. Upon their entrance, fertilization is effected, and the enveloping cells become hard and dark-colored. The fruit, or sporocarp, falls to the bottom, where it germinates when favorable conditions obtain; and a proembryo, consisting of a single row of cells, is formed, from which the sexual plant is developed by the growth of a lateral bud.

BRYOPHYTA.

175. The **Bryophyta** (Mosses and Liverworts) constitute the fifth division of the vegetable kingdom. There is a well-marked alternation of sexual and non-sexual generations. The first, or that proceeding from the spore, bears the sexual organs, and is hence called the *sexual generation*. After fertilization, there grows a sporocarp (called sporangium), in which spores arise non-sexually; this, therefore, is the *non-sexual generation*. The sexual organs of the Bryophyta consist of *archegonia* and *anther-*

BRYOPHYTA. 149

idia. The archegonium is flask-shaped, in the bottom of which is a naked mass of protoplasm, the germ-cell, which is the essential part of the female organ. The antheridium is generally club-shaped, or sub-spherical, supported by a pedicel, and filled with many sperm-cells, each of which contains a single, spirally-coiled spermatozoid. The neck of the archegonium is open at the time of fertilization, and into it pass the free spermatozoids, which fuse with the germ-cell. Thereupon a thick wall, or covering, is

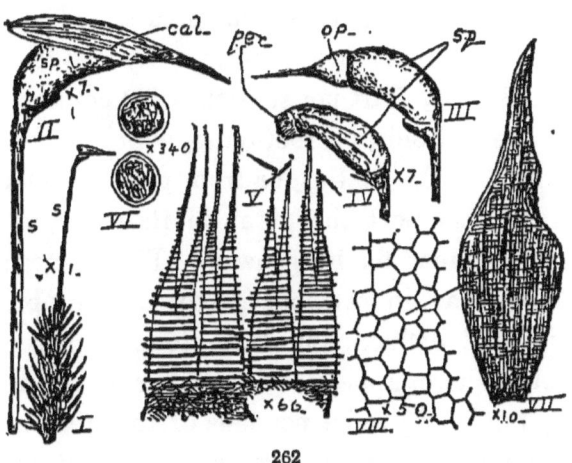

262

formed, and cell-division in the germ-cell takes place. This, the spore-case (sporangium), supported by a pedicel, or *seta*, is nourished by the plant in which it is formed, but yet has no *organic* connection with it; and is, therefore, called the second, or non-sexual generation. Within the sporangium the spores are formed, and contain, besides colorless protoplasm, starch and drops of oil, also chlorophyll grains. When ripe, the spore-case (as, for example, in *Hypnum*) opens by a more or less beaked lid, called the *operculum* (Fig. 262, *op*), which, in many species, is

Fig. 262. A Moss; *Dicranum glaucum;* *op*, operculum; *cal*, calyptra; *per*, peristome; *sp*, sporangium; *s*, seta; *sp*, spores.

surmounted by a hood, called the *calyptra* (Fig. 262, *cal*); surrounding the orifice is a (single or double) row of teeth (Fig. 262, *per*), called the *peristome* (Gr. *peri*, around; *stoma*, mouth); the teeth number four, eight, sixteen, thirty-two, or sixty-four. The spores germinate by the rupture of the firm, outer coat, or exospore, and tube-like protrusion of the delicate, inner coat, or endospore, which, by division, gives rise to the filamentous proembryo, called *protonema*; from this numerous buds arise, which give origin to the upright, leafy, sexual plants.

176. No true roots are produced by the Bryophyta; organs functionally (but not structurally) corresponding to them, are the rhizoids, or root-hairs, which grow from the under surface of the thallus, or from the sides of the stem. They serve to support the plant in its place, and also to absorb nourishment for its growth. The tissues are more differentiated than in previous groups. The epidermis is often quite well defined, and true stomates, absent in the lower groups, here appear. The tissue is mainly parenchymous; but in the axial portions of the stem, and in the veins of the leaf, there is, by the elongated bundles of cells, slight indication of a fibro-vascular system. The two classes into which the Bryophyta are divided are (1) the Liverworts (*Hepaticæ*) and (2) the Mosses (*Musci*).

1. **Hepaticæ.** In this group, the Liverworts (Fig. 263), the plant-body is generally a true thallus, or thalloid structure, with only slight differentiation into stem and leaves. There are usually well-marked dorsal and ventral surfaces; when leaves are present, they consist of a simple layer of cells, with no midrib or other veins. The plants are small, of a bright green or brownish color, and grow in moist places on the ground, on rocks, or on the bark

of trees. Besides the sexual reproduction by means of archegonia and antheridia, they multiply extensively in a non-sexual manner; namely, by the production of peculiar buds, called *gemmæ* (Fig. 263, *gem*). These, in the common Liverwort (*Marchantia*), are little cellular bodies, developed in cups, on the upper surface of the thallus. When the gemmæ are full-grown, they fall to the ground, and grow directly into new plants. The stomates in these plants are not of the ordinary kind found in higher groups; instead of being surrounded, as there, by two guard-cells, there are sixteen (or more) cells, in four (or more) superposed layers, encircling the orifice, which leads into a large air-cavity below the epidermis. In this cavity are branching rows of cells, which contain the chlorophyll-masses (Fig. 264).

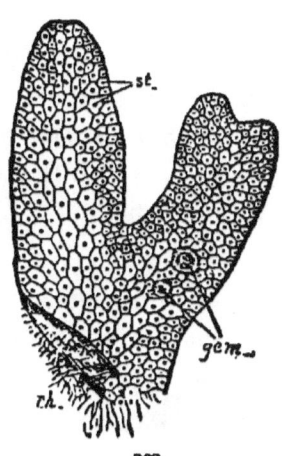

2. **Musci.** This group includes the Sphagnums and the true Mosses. The plants (Fig. 262) have stems, with sessile leaves and articulated root-hairs, or rhizoids; the leaves are composed of a single layer of cells, and may, or may not, have a midrib. The stems may have an outer, thickened layer, or layers (imperfect sclerenchyma); and within, either simply thin-walled parenchyma, or an axial bundle of very narrow, thin-walled cells—imperfect fibro-vascular

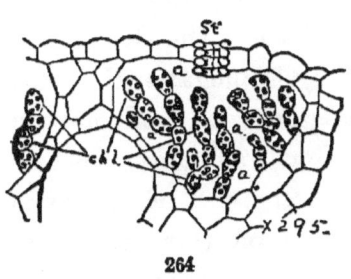

Fig. 263. A portion of a Liverwort, with the gemmæ in cup-like cavities. Fig. 264. Section of a frond of Liverwort, showing the stomate (*st*) and the air-cavity (*a*) below, containing the cells which have the chlorophyll (*chl*).

bundles. Stomates, like those of higher plants, occur only in the capsules, or sporangia. Most of the Mosses are aerial plants, growing on moist earth or rocks, upon the bark of trees, or occasionally in water; they are all chlorophyll-bearing, and usually of a light-green color. They sometimes multiply non-sexually, as in the Liverworts, by the production of gemmæ. These may be produced on the end of the stem; and when they fall off give rise to a kind of protonema, upon which buds arise, and develop into the leafy plants. At times a protonema is formed from the leaves or root-hairs, and new plants then, in the ordinary way, are formed. The Peat Mosses (*Sphagnum*) are large, soft, and pale-colored plants, which grow in bogs and swampy places. The leaves are formed of two kinds of tissue, namely, of small cells, which contain chlorophyll; and of large perforated cells, destitute of chlorophyll, and containing water. By means of the latter, the plants are capable of taking up and retaining moisture, like a sponge. They are, therefore, useful material for "packing" in the transportation of living plants. Twenty or more species of Sphagnum occur in the United States. The true Mosses (Order, *Bryaceæ*) present the highest differentiation of tissue in the Bryophyta, and closely approach the Vascular Cryptogams (the next higher group). The genera are numerous, and have a wide, geographical distribution. In one sub-order, the sporangia, or capsule, is developed at the end of the main axis, and these are called the **Acrocarpæ** (Gr. *akron*, top; *karpos*, fruit); common acrocarpous genera are *Bryum, Minum, Polytrichum*, etc. In the other sub-order, the fruits, or sporangia, are developed laterally, called, therefore, **Pleurocarpæ** (Gr. *pleuron*, side); *Climacium, Hypnum*, etc., are common pleurocarpous genera.

PTERIDOPHYTA.

177. The sixth division, called **Pteridophyta**, include the Ferns (Fig. 265) and their allies. Here, as in the previous division, there is an alternation of sexual and non-sexual generations. But while the conspicuous generation (the Moss) in the Bryophyta is sexual (and the inconspicuous, namely, the sporangium, non-sexual), the reverse is the case in the Pteridophyta, that is, the conspicuous generation (the Fern, etc.) is non-sexual; and the sexual generation, or stage, bearing the sexual reproductive organs (the prothallium) is very much reduced and short-lived. This prothallium is a small, flattened, thallus-like growth from the spore, composed of chlorophyll-bearing parenchymous cells, in one or a few layers; on its under surface are produced rhizoids, by which it is fixed to the ground. On the prothallia are developed the archegonia and antheridia, which are essentially similar to those in the higher plants of the preceding division. The spirally-coiled spermatozoids escape from the antheridium, enter the tube, or neck, of the archegonium, and fertilize the germ-cell therein contained. The result of this is the formation of a young plantlet, which develops into a leafy plant of considerable size, with marked differentiation of tissue, and capable of producing non-sexual spores.

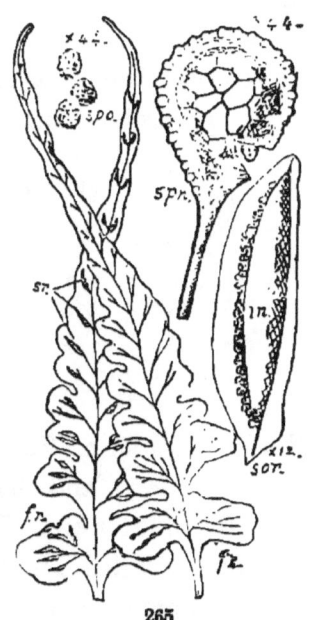

Fig. 265. A Fern (*Camptosorus rhizophyllus*); *fr*, frond; *sor*, sori; *in*, indusium; *spn*, sporangium; *spo*, spores.

178. True roots first make their appearance in the Pteridophyta. They, like the stems, develop from a triangular apical cell (Fig. 266). This gives rise behind to the tissue of the root, and in front to the root-cap (Fig. 266, *R.c*). The three systems of tissue—epidermal, fibro-vascular, and fundamental—are well developed. The epidermis contains stomates of the ordinary kind. Trichomes, or hairs, are often abundantly developed, especially on young leaves, when they take the form of scurfy hairs, or scales. The fibro-vascular bundles are always closed. They generally contain tracheary, parenchymous, and sieve-tissue. The fundamental tissue consists of parenchyma, and sometimes also sclerenchyma; collenchyma and laticiferous tissue are seldom met with. The Pteridophyta are divided into three classes: (1) the Horsetails, or Scouring Rushes (*Equisetineæ*), (2) the Ferns (*Filices*), and (3) the Club-Mosses (*Lycopodineæ*).

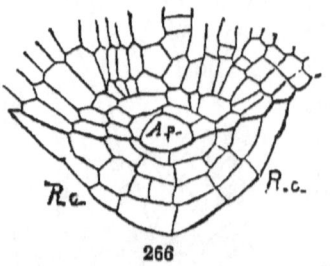

266

1. **Equisetineæ.** The plants (non-sexual generation) of this class (called Horsetails, or Scouring Rushes) have a hollow-jointed, grooved stem, bearing at each node a whorl of narrow, united leaves, which form a sheath. The branches arise in the axils of the leaves, and are, therefore, verticillate. There are underground perennial stems, which each year send up the vegetative and spore-bearing stems. The spores are produced in sporangia, which are modified leaves on the ends of the ordinary green stems, or on early colorless or brownish stems, which die as soon as

Fig. 266. Diagrammatic section through the tip of a Fern root, showing the apical cell (*ap*) and the root-cap (*R.c*).

the spores are ripe. The modified spore-bearing leaves are peltate in form, and collected into cone-shaped clusters; in consequence of pressure each becomes hexagonal in outline; on the under surface of each peltate leaf, or scale, there arise several sac-shaped sporangia, which open at maturity by a slit on the side next to the pedicel, and allow the escape of the spores. "In their development the spores acquire three concentric coats, and as they approach maturity the outer one, which has previously become spirally thickened, splits, from two opposite points, into narrow spiral filaments, which are united with one another and the spore at a common point. These filaments are hygroscopic, and they roll and unroll with the slightest changes in the moisture in the air; when moistened, they tightly wrap around the spore; but when dry, they unroll, and become more or less reflexed. By the changes of position which they undergo, they move the spores very considerably, and are doubtless useful in emptying the sporangia after dehiscence, hence they have been called *elaters*" (Gr. *elater*, driver). The epidermis of the Equisetineæ contains a large amount of silica. The stomates are arranged in longitudinal rows—in the channels between the ridges. The fibro-vascular bundles are arranged in a circle surrounding the central cavity. Each bundle passes isolated down through the internode, and at the node divides into two short branches, which unite right and left, with corresponding branches of other bundles, thus forming the alternating bundles of the next lower internode (Fig. 267). The single bundle from each leaf is applied at the point where the descending

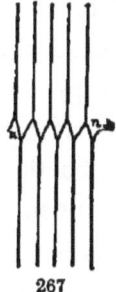

267

Fig. 267. Diagram, showing the course of the fibro-vascular bundles in the stem of *Equisetum*.

branches from the upper bundles unite to form the bundle in the lower internode. The class Equisetineæ has but a single living genus, *Equisetum*, which contains about twenty-five species, most of them being small plants. In the Devonian and Carboniferous Ages there were many genera, forming an order *Calamarieæ*, which became extinct in the Permian Period.

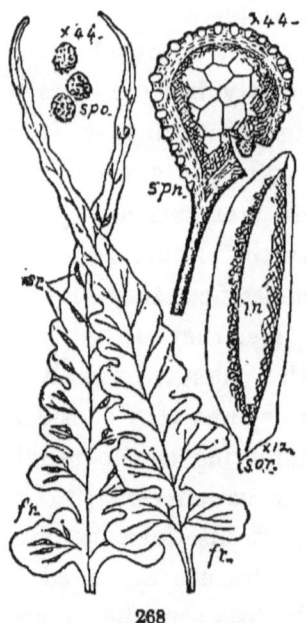

268

2. **Filicinæ.** The plants (non-sexual generation) of this class (Ferns) have a solid stem, with roots and broadly expanded leaves. They are mostly terrestrial, and all richly supplied with chlorophyll. The spores are developed in sporangia on the surface or margins of the ordinary or modified leaves. The leaves, called fronds, are circinate (Fig. 35) in their unfolding, and often divided and several times compound. On their under surface are the clusters of sporangia, or *sori* (Fig. 268, *sr*). The sorus may be naked, or covered by a membrane, called the *indusium* (Fig. 268, *in*), which is of various shapes, and has various modes of attachment in the different genera. The sporangia are generally roundish and pedicelled bodies. Each (in the Order *Filices*) is surrounded by an elastic ring (*annulus*), which contracts, and sets the spores free when ripe. The stems are mostly short, or creeping, but in the Tropics they are often of

Fig. 268. A Fern (*Camptosorus rhizophyollus*); *fr*, frond; *sor*, sori; *in*, indusium; *spn*, sporangium; *spo*, spore.

considerable thickness and height. They contain flat fibro-vascular bundles, usually arranged in a circle. When the stems become thick with increase of growth, a net-work of anastomosing bundles is formed in place of the central bundle. Ferns appeared in the Devonian Age, represented by twelve genera, belonging to extinct families. In the Carboniferous Age they were much more numerous, but decreased to the present time. These plants are very ornamental, but otherwise of comparatively little value economically. The largest and commonest genera are *Asplenium, Aspidium, Botrychium, Cystopteris,* etc.

3. **Lycopodineæ.** The stems of the Club-Mosses are solid, leafy, and mostly erect. The leaves are simple, small, sessile, imbricated, and resemble those of the Mosses. The spores are produced in sporangia, situated in the axils, and are appendages of the leaves. In some of the genera (*Lycopodium*, etc.) the spores are all alike; in others (*Selaginella*, etc.) there are two kinds—large spores (macrospores) and small spores (microspores). The plants of this class, now generally terrestrial, and only a few inches high, were numerous in the Devonian and Carboniferous Ages. Some of them (*Lepidodendron*, etc.; Fig. 345) were of gigantic size, but the order to which they belonged became extinct in the Permian Period. Several species of *Lycopodium* occur in the United States. Many species of *Selaginella*, which are mostly tropical, are cultivated for ornament.

PHÆNOGAMIA.

179. The seventh and last division is called **Phænerogamia**, and includes all the common flowering plants; as herbs, shrubs, and trees. The reproductive organs (Fig.

269) are the stamens (Fig. 269, *sta*), which produce (in the anthers) the pollen grains, the latter homologous with the

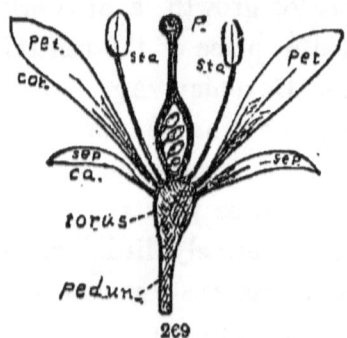

microspores; and the pistils (Fig. 269, *P*), in which (ovary) the ovules are produced, which contain the embryo-sacs corresponding to the macrospores of the previous division. Enclosing and protecting these often grow special organs (slightly modified leaves), called the perianth; or, when two whorls, corolla (Fig. 269, *cor*), and calyx (Fig. 269, *cal*). These, together with the stamens and pistils, and also the axial structure which bears them (Fig. 269, *torus*), constitute the Flower, whose development in general is as follows: At the end of a stem, protected and concealed by the small leaves, called bud-scales, arise minute papillæ, or elevations, forming a peripheral whorl (Fig. 270). These are the first development of the outermost floral organs, namely, sepals (Fig. 270, *s*). Immediately following them appear another whorl of similar papillæ (Fig. 271), situated within the first, and these represent the petals (Fig. 271, *P*). These two sets grow rapidly, arch over, and protect the essential organs which develop within.

180. While the two whorls described above are increasing in size, a third whorl of papillæ

Fig. 269. Longitudinal section of a flower; *ca*, calyx; *cor*, corolla; *sep*, sepals; *pet*, petals; *sta*, stamens; *p*, pistil; *torus*, torus; *pedun*, peduncle. Figs. 270–273. Diagrammatic representations of the successive stages in the early development of a flower; *s*, sepals; *p*, petals; *an*, stamens; *p*, pistil.

(Fig. 272), immediately within the second whorl, makes its appearance. These blunt protuberances (Fig. 272, *an*) develop later into stamens, with anthers, a portion of whose interior tissue undergoes repeated cell-division, and from it are formed isolated double-walled cells—

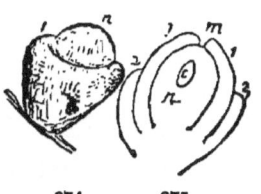

274   275

the pollen grains. In the meantime, there has arisen within the innermost whorl, a circular elevation, or wall (composed of one or several parts, or carpellary leaves), which, arising and arching over at the top, forms a cavity (Fig. 273), destined to contain the ovules later developed from a point, or line (called the placenta, and corresponding to the edge of the carpellary leaf), on the inner side of this cavity, or ovary. This structure, terminating the axis, is the pistil (Fig. 273, *p*). The ovule, at its first appearance, is a blunt protuberance (Fig. 274); after growing to considerable size, an elevation, or ring, near its base appears, and gradually grows as a covering, or integument (Fig. 275), over the nucleus or body of the ovule. In many cases a second integument arises, and in a similar manner encloses the first. At the apex an orifice, the micropyle (Fig. 275, *m*), invariably remains, which,

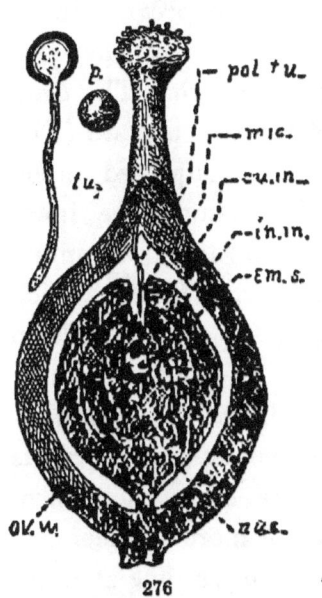

Figs. 274, 275. Successive stages in the early development of the ovule. Fig. 276. Longitudinal section through an ovary and ovule; *p*, pollen; *tu*, pollen-tube; *ov.w*, ovary wall; *pol-tu*, pollen-tube; *mic*, micropyle; *ou. in*, outer integument; *in. in*, inner integument; *em. s*, embryo-sac; *nuc*, nucleus, or body of ovule.

when fertilization is to take place, allows the entrance of the pollen-tube.

181. Simultaneously with the growth of the integuments is developed, near the upper end of the body, or nucleus of the ovule (Fig. 276), the embryo-sac (Fig. 276, *em. s*). This, when first distinguishable from the other tissue, consists of a cell somewhat larger than the adjacent ones. It then enlarges greatly; voluminous vacuoles appear, and the protoplasm condenses at the two extremities. In its apical portion, one or more roundish masses of protoplasm become differentiated, and these are the germ-cells, the impregnation of one of which results in the production of the embryo. The firm, outer coat of the pollen grain (Fig. 276, *p*) becomes ruptured upon absorption of moisture, the inner coat protrudes, and lengthens into a slender tube (Fig. 276, *tu*), which grows (Fig. 276, *pol. tu*) down through the micropyle (Fig. 276, *mic*) till it comes in contact with the embryo-sac (Fig. 276, *em. s*). Fertilization is the result of this contact, whereupon an embryo is formed (Fig. 277, *1*). This consists of a short stem (caulicle, Fig. 277, *cau*), bearing one or more rudimentary leaves, called the cotyledons (Fig. 277, *cot*), at one end, and

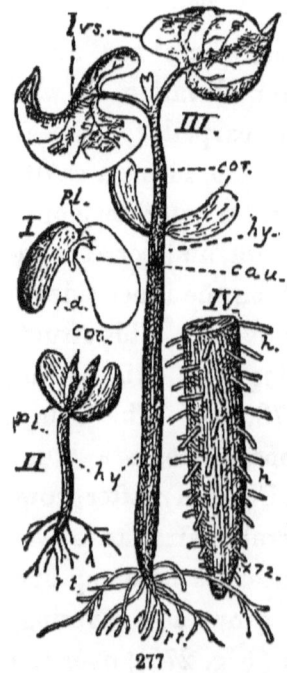

Fig. 277. Successive stages (*I, II, III*) in the development of the Bean plantlet; *cot*, cotyledons; *cau*, caulicle; *pl*, plumule; *rd*, radicle; *hy*, hypocotyledonary stem; *lvs*, the first set of leaves; *IV*, a portion of root, with root-hairs slightly magnified.

a rudimentary root at the other (Fig. 277, *r.d*). The embryo-sac develops within it a mass of cells, called the endosperm, at the expense of which the embryo, or rudimentary plantlet, grows. The ovules become much enlarged while the embryo is forming, and their outer coat generally becomes thickened and more or less hardened. At this stage it is called the *Seed*, and at maturity separates from the parent plant.

182. After a period of rest, the seed, exposed to suitable conditions, germinates; that is, when proper temperature and moisture are supplied, it begins anew its development. It draws on the store of nourishment contained in the endosperm, or cotyledons; the caulicle

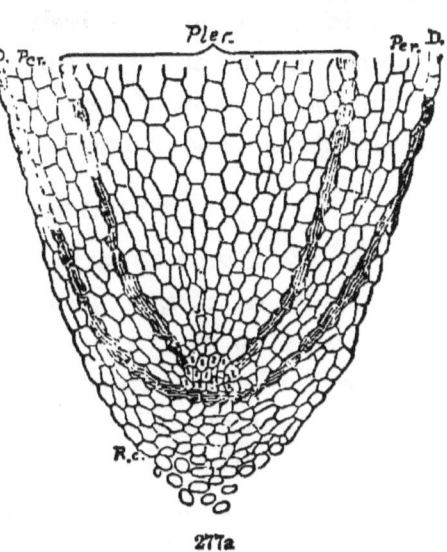

elongates; the radicle, clothed with the root-cap (Fig. 277a, *R.c.*), grows downwards; and the stem, surmounted by the plumule (Fig. 277, *I*, *pl*), grows upwards. By the time the nourishment contained in the seed is exhausted, the plantlet (Fig. 277, *III*) is able to absorb food from the soil, and it develops by successive internodes into the adult form. The three tissue systems are well developed in the Phænerogamia. The epidermis is supplied with numerous stomates; and trichomes of various forms are also copiously

Fig. 277a. Section through the end of a root, highly magnified, and showing the root-cap (*R.c.*); *i, i*, initial cells; *D*, dermatogen; *Per*, periblem; *Pler*, plerome.

developed. The fibro-vascular bundles are either closed, or open, and consist of all kinds of tissue, except collenchyma. The fundamental tissue is mostly parenchyma; but in the hypodermal portions it may contain collenchyma and sclerenchyma. In certain orders laticiferous tissue is also common. But few of the plants are parasitic or saprophytic; they are mostly chlorophyll-bearing. They vary in size from excessively small to excessively large plants, and in duration from a few days or weeks to hundreds of years. They are divided into two classes, *Gymnospermæ* and *Angiospermæ*.

GYMNOSPERMÆ.

183. The **Gymnospermous** plants, which include the Cycads, Pines, Firs, etc., have naked ovules, that is, not enclosed in an ovary; and the endosperm arises in the embryo-sac before fertilization takes place. They are all terrestrial, chlorophyll-bearing, and, with few exceptions, large trees. The flowers are always diclinous, that is, the staminate and pistillate organs are in different flowers. The pollen is transported by the wind (hence, the immense quantity produced) from the anthers to the ovules, whose orifice (micropyle) is at this time filled with a fluid. This drying carries the pollen grains down till they come in contact with the nucleus, or body of the ovule, when they germinate and produce pollen-tubes, which pierce the soft tissue, and reach the elongated bodies, called the corpuscula (which seem to be homologous with the archegonia of previous divisions), which are developed in the embryo-sac; and the result of this contact is fertilization and consequent formation of the embryo-sac. This takes place as follows: The lower, or germ-cell of the corpusculum,

gives rise, by the formation of a transverse partition, to a cell which is the rudiment of the suspensor. This grows and elongates, and at its lower end the embryo is formed; the growing point (*punctum vegetationis*) is opposite to the suspensor; and near it, as lateral members, are produced the cotyledons. At the end next to and under the suspensor, a root, with a few-celled root-cap, is formed. The epidermal system consists of one or more layers of epidermal cells, frequently much thickened. The xylem portions of their fibro-vascular bundles are compacted into a dense woody cylinder, surrounded by the so-called bark or united phloëm portions of the bundles. The generating tissue, or meristem, called cambium, is situated between the phloëm (bast) and xylem (wood). The mass of xylem is formed of tracheïdes, with thickened walls and bordered pits (Fig. 278). 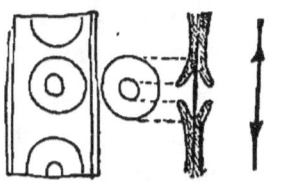 The fundamental tissue consists of parenchyma in the inner portion (pith), which soon loses its vitality; the outer portion (cortex) consists of parenchyma and sclerenchyma, or collenchyma; in it there is considerable development of cork. The narrow radiating plates of tissue (medullary rays) between the fibro-vascular bundles, are parenchymous in the young, and sclerenchymous in the older, stems. The medullary rays have cambium, called interfascicular cambium, corresponding in position and function with that of the fibro-vascular bundles. Most Gymnosperms have intercellular canals, filled with turpentine, containing dissolved resin. The class is divided into three orders, as follows: Cycads (*Cycadeæ*), Conifers (*Coniferæ*), and Joint Firs (*Gnetaceæ*).

Fig. 278. Bordered Pits, and diagrams representing their development.

1. **Cycadeæ.** The **Cycads** have simple (or rarely branched) stems, with large pith. They are large or small trees, with the general appearance of Palms and Tree Ferns. The stem is crowned with wide-spreading pinnate leaves. They are all tropical or sub-tropical species (about fifty or sixty), belonging to nine genera. One genus, *Zamia*, occurs in Florida. A kind of Sago is made from the starch in the roots of some species, and in some cases the seeds also are nutritious. The order originated in the Carboniferous Age, and in the Jurassic had twenty or more large genera.

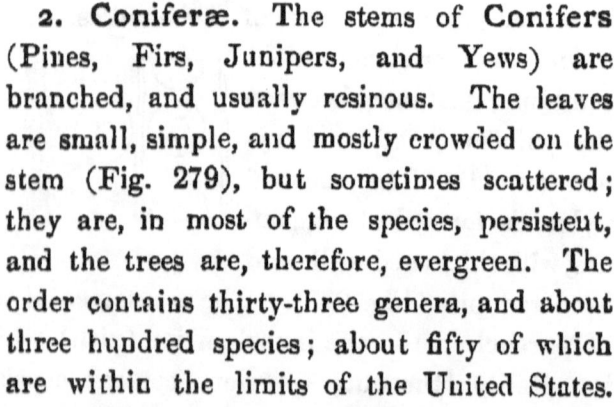

2. **Coniferæ.** The stems of **Conifers** (Pines, Firs, Junipers, and Yews) are branched, and usually resinous. The leaves are small, simple, and mostly crowded on the stem (Fig. 279), but sometimes scattered; they are, in most of the species, persistent, and the trees are, therefore, evergreen. The order contains thirty-three genera, and about three hundred species; about fifty of which are within the limits of the United States. Generally, the Conifers occur in the cooler regions of the globe. Economically, the order is of great value. Most of the Pines (*Pinus*) and Firs (*Abies*) furnish turpentine of varying quality, secreted in resin-passages (Fig. 280, *r.c*). Canada Balsam is obtained from the Balsam-Fir (*Abies balsamea*) of the United States; Venice Turpentine from the European Larch (*Larix Europœa*); Damar Resin from *Dammara alba* of the Malay Islands. The wood of many species, especially that of the White Pine (*Pinus*

Fig. 279. Fascicled leaves of the Pine.

Strobus), is very valuable. Very many of the Cedars, Pines, Firs, Arbor Vitæ, Yews, are very ornamental. The Big-tree of California (*Sequoia gigantea*), growing only on the western slopes of the Sierra Nevada mountains, attains a height of more than three hundred feet, and a diameter of twenty to thirty feet.

3. **Gnetaceæ.** The Joint Firs are undershrubs, or small trees, and, except the peculiar *Welwitschia*, have jointed, rush-like stems, and opposite, setaceous, or oval leaves. Unlike the previous Gymnosperms the flowers have a perianth, or floral envelope. This may be single and bifid, or composed of two or more bract-like bodies (phyllomes). The order in-

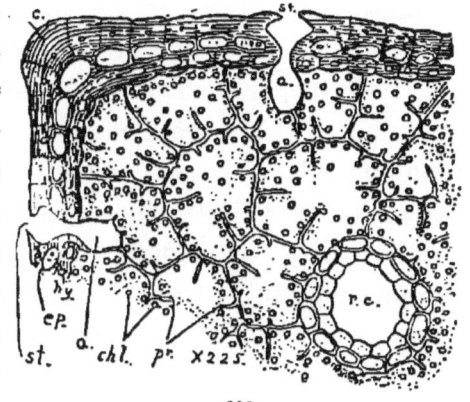

cludes three genera, the most remarkable of which is the *Welwitschia*, which has but one species, growing in South Africa. Its trunk is a foot or two in diameter, and arises one foot above ground. There is a stout tap-root branching below. The top of the stem is flattened with a depression across its diameter. There are only two leaves arising from grooves, near the top of the stem; they seem to be the persistent cotyledons, and grow to be six feet long. Scarlet cones are produced on peduncles arising from the axis of the leaves.

Fig. 280. Transverse section of a Pine leaf, highly magnified, showing the resin canal (*r.c.*); *st*, stomate; *hy*, hypoderm; *chl*, chlorophyll; *a*, air-cavity.

ANGIOSPERMÆ.

184. The second class of the Phænerogamia, namely, the **Angiosperms**, have ovules enclosed in an ovary; they are further distinguished from the Gymnosperms in having, as a rule, much more complex flowers. They are, in the great majority of cases, monoclinous (or hermaphrodite); that is, the male (staminate) and female (pistillate) organs occur in the same flower. The floral axis generally remains very short; at its centre or top is situated the *gynœcium*, as the pistils are collectively called, and immediately below, or without this whorl, is the whorl or whorls of stamens, which are denominated the *andrœcium*. Surrounding these organs closely is generally found the perianth, consisting of one (calyx) or more (calyx and corolla) whorls of modified leaves. The latter are usually conspicuous and attractive (in entomophilous flowers) on account of size, color, odor, or honey secreted in the nectaries, which are usually present at their base. The pollen grains, transported from the anthers by various agencies to the viscid stigma, there germinate, or send down a tube through the loose tissue of the pistil which enters the micropyle of the ovule, and effects the fertilization of the latter.

185. The effect of fertilization is manifest as follows: The germ-cell (called also the embryonic vesicle), situated in the apical region of the embryo-sac, at once develops a cellulose-wall. It then divides transversely one or more times, giving rise to a row of cells, called the suspensor, or proembryo, and the lower end of this, by copious cell-multiplication, forms the embryo. There is, in the meantime, " free cell-formation" of the protoplasm in the basal portion of the embryo-sac, by which the endosperm is formed. The latter, increasing rapidly, fills the embryo-sac, and, besides, encroaches on and displaces, in most cases, the surrounding tissue. It is then more or less completely consumed in the further development of the embryo. After a many-celled body is formed at the lower end of the suspensor, or proembryo, partitions then arise in the cells, parallel to the surface; and thus is formed the primary epidermis, or dermatogen. Simultaneously with this, there is also, as a rule, a differentiation of the inner cells foreshadowing the future tissue systems. A little later, either a depression in one side of the thallus-like structure is formed, which becomes the *punctum vegetationis* of the embryo, and the apical part extending beyond this point, the single cotyledon (Fig. 148); or instead, the apical point of the embryo becomes the *punctum vegetationis*, which is enclosed between the two cotyledons that grow out symmetrically from opposite points below, and adjacent to the same.

186. The growing embryo, embedded in the nutrient endosperm, increases in size at the expense of the latter. In many cases it ceases its growth before all the endosperm is absorbed; as in the Crowfoots (*Ranunculaceæ*), Violets (*Violaceæ*), Palms (*Palmaceæ*), Grasses (*Gramineæ*), etc. Such seeds were formerly designated by the term *albuminous*. Otherwise, the embryo grows till it has absorbed and displaced the whole endosperm, storing its nutrient substances in the much enlarged cotyledons, as in the Mustard family (*Cruciferæ*), the Roses (*Rosaceæ*), the Oaks (*Cupuliferæ*), etc. Seeds containing such an embryo were called *exalbuminous*. It happens in a few cases, for example, in the Water-Lily family (*Nymphaceæ*), that the endosperm is only slightly developed; in such cases the nutriment

for the future growth of the embryo is largely stored up in the tissue of the ovule surrounding the embryo-sac, and this tissue is called *perisperm*. The ovary, as well as the ovule, usually undergoes great changes while the embryo is forming. The outer parenchymous coat of the ovule often becomes more or less sclerenchymous, and forms the testa; or it may become pulpy; in some cases it develops wings, or a tuft of hairs, etc. The ovary may become hard and dry, or pulpy. These two, called now seed and pericarp respectively, spontaneously separate at maturity from the parent plant.

187. The epidermis of the Angiosperms has commonly more stomates than that of the Gymnosperms. The trichomes, or hairs, are more often present, and exhibit a greater variation in form and structure. The fundamental tissue is abundant, and mostly parenchymous in the annual stemmed species; in the perennials there is less of it, and more of the fibro-vascular tissue. In these sclerenchyma is also usually developed. The chlorophyll-bearing parenchyma of the leaf (*mesophyll*) is fundamental tissue; so also are the succulent parts of fruits. The fibro-vascular bundles are either closed or open, and their disposition for the most part is dependent on the position of the leaves. They are usually of the kind called "common bundles," that is, they extend above into the leaf, and below into the stem. In a few cases there are "cauline bundles," or those in the stem which have no connection with the leaf. Based on the number of cotyledons in the embryo, the structure of the stem, etc., the Angiosperms have been divided into two sub-classes, the *Monocotyledones* and the *Dicotyledones*.

MONOCOTYLEDONES.

188. The **Monocotyledones**, so called since the embryo has alternate leaves, of which the first one developed is called a cotyledon, are also called **Endogenæ**, or **Endogenous** plants. A transverse section of the stem (Fig. 281) shows that the fibro-vascular bundles are isolated, numerous, and scattered irregularly throughout the pith or fundamental tissue. Each bundle is closed; that is, there is no zone of meristem tissue (cambium) between the xylem and phloëm when these have reached their maturity, or passed over into permanent tissue. In consequence of this limitation of growth of the bundles, the plants are generally short-lived. In very young plants, where the fibro-vascular bundles are as yet few, their general disposition, or arrangement, may be seen. In the " Palm type," which is illustrated in the accompanying diagram (Fig. 282), the leaves supposed to be opposite, and their bases united with the entire circumference of the stem. The numerous bundles from each leaf pass obliquely into the stem, and then descend through the latter. The middle

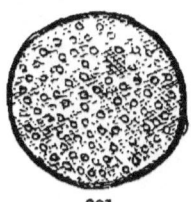

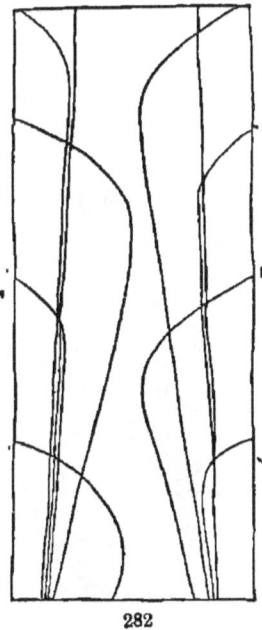

Fig. 281. Transverse section of an endogenous stem. Fig. 282. Diagram showing the course of the fibro-vascular bundles in a stem from four successive leaves, in case of the " Palm-type"

bundle of each leaf (Fig. 282) passes deep towards the centre, and the lateral bundles (Fig. 282) curve downwards in the peripheral portions of the stem. There are many deviations from this type, especially by the bundles having lateral anastomosing branches. The fibro-vascular bundles (or veins) in the leaf are approximately parallel, passing usually from the base to the apex (Fig. 283). The flower in the great majority of cases in the Monocotyledones, or Monocotyls, is three-parted; that is, each whorl consists of three members. As an example of the structure of the seed, the slightly magnified section of a grain of Indian Corn is given (Fig. 284). The germination of the seed is shown in the accompanying figure (Fig. 285). The sub-class is represented by about fifty natural orders, of which the following are interesting or important:

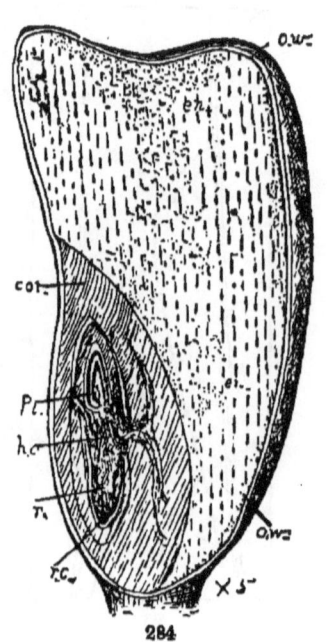

1. Gramineæ. The Grasses are herbaceous, or rarely woody, plants, with round, jointed, and (mostly) hollow stems, which have alternate two-ranked leaves. The leaf below is a split sheath (Fig. 286); above, a narrow, elongated part, called the lamina; and at the junction of these two there is a

Fig. 283. A parallel-veined leaf. Fig. 284. Section of a grain of Indian Corn; *cot*, cotyledon; *pl*, plumule; *r*, radicle; *r.c*, root-cap; *en*, endosperm.

membranous outgrowth, called the ligule. The flowers are in spikes, racemes, or panicles, consisting mostly of numerous spikelets; each of the latter is surrounded at the base by two glumes (Fig. 287), above which are the flowers. The protecting organs, or perianth, consist of an upper palet (Fig. 288) and lower palet (Fig. 288, *lp*); within are the (mostly three) stamens, with slender filaments and versatile anthers. The ovary is simple, contains one ovule, and has two styles, mostly with feathery stigmas (Fig. 289). The fruit is a grain, or caryopsis. This is a very natural and large order, containing about six thousand species, to be found in all climates. All other orders of plants combined probably do not contribute more to the sustenance of man than the Gramineæ. Wheat (*Triticum vulgare*), probably a native of Asia, has been in cultivation from time immemorial. Remains of

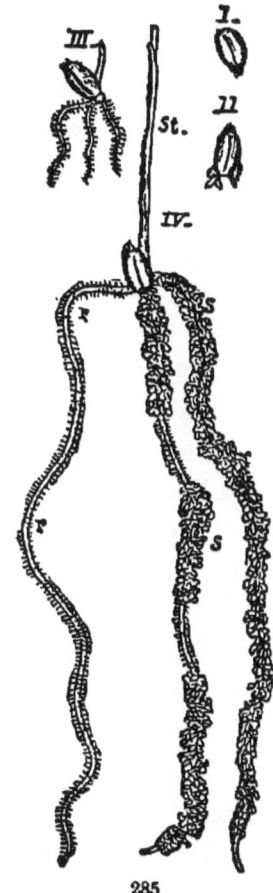

Fig. 285. Successive stages in the germination of Wheat; *r*, roots; *s*, soil-particles; *st*, stem. Fig. 286. Leaf of Grass. Fig. 287. Spikelet of Grass-flowers; *gl*, glumes; *fls*, flowers; *p*, palets.

wheat-grains have been found in the pre-historic Lake Dwellings of Switzerland. Under the influence of cultivation, innumerable "varieties" have arisen, differing much as to the color and quality of the grain, presence or absence of awns, as to the hardiness of the plant, etc. Barley (*Hordeum distichum* and *H. hexastichum*, two-rowed and six-rowed Barley) is now used in making bread; it was cultivated in remote times. The Rye (*Secale cereale*) has also been cultivated for ages, originating probably in Southern Europe and Asia. Rice (*Oryza sativa*), cultivated in many countries, furnishes food to more human beings than any other plant. Indian Corn, or Maize (*Zea Mais*), a native of the warm regions of the New World, was cultivated by the aborigines of North and South America. Under its extensive cultivation many "varieties" have arisen. The Oat (*Avena sativa*), grown more especially in cooler climates, probably originated in North Europe or Asia. Among the important forage Grasses are the Timothy, or Herd's Grass (*Phleum pratense*), Red-top (*Agrostis vulgaris*), Orchard Grass (*Dactylis glomerata*), all natives of Europe; also Kentucky Blue Grass (*Poa pratensis*) of the United States and Europe, and Slough Grass (*Muhlenbergia glomerata* and *M. Mexicana*) of the Mississippi Valley. The Sugar-Cane (*Saccharum officinarum*) is a native of the warm regions of Asia, and is cultivated in all warm regions

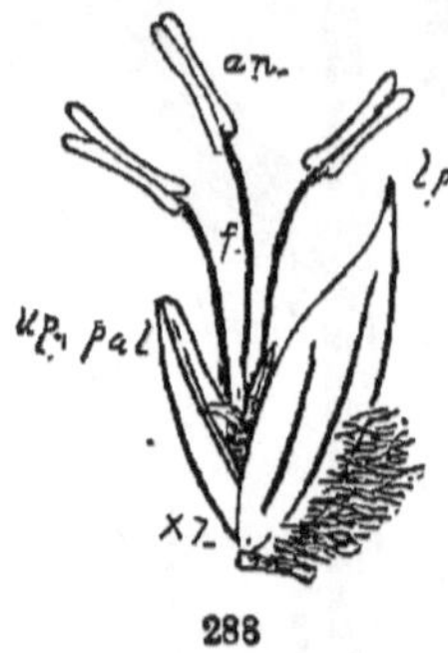

Fig. 288. A gramineous flower (*Poa pratensis*); *up pal*, upper palet; *lp*, lower palet. Fig. 289. Feathery stigma of *Poa pratensis*.

of the world. From its sweet juice most of the sugar and molasses of commerce is made. The Chinese Sugar-Cane (*Sorghum vulgare*) has lately been introduced into the United States, and from it molasses and sugar are made. The Broom-Corn, used in the manufacture of brooms, is a variety of this. The Bamboo (*Bambusa arundinacea*), sometimes attaining the height of even one hundred feet, has innumerable uses in India, where it is employed in manufacturing ornamental trinkets, house building, fences, water-pipes, and various other things.

2. **Cyperaceæ.** The **Sedges** differ from the Grasses in having solid, three-angled stems, three-ranked leaves with entire sheaths. The spiked flowers have no perianth, or only hypogynous setæ, or a cup-shaped or sac-shaped perigynium. Stamens mostly three, pistil simple, and fruit a utricle. The order comprises about two thousand widely distributed species. They never form continuous mats like most of the Grasses, but grow in tufts, preferably in wet places. As forage plants they are very inferior, or mostly quite unfit. A Sedge (*Cyperus textilis*) is used in India for making ropes and mats; and other species are used in Egypt for the same purpose. The Bulrush (*Scirpus lacustris*) of Europe and Asia is used extensively in making mats, ropes, chair-bottoms, and hassocks. The Papyrus (*Papyrus antiquorum*) of Egypt and adjacent countries, a tall plant, diameter one inch, was used in ancient times for making paper. This was done by slicing the cellular pith, and then hammering and smoothing it. A Carex, or true Sedge (*Carex arenaria*), has deep and extensive roots, grows in tufts, and binds the soil of the dikes and the moving sands of the sea-shore.

3. **Juncaceæ.** The Rushes grow in temperate and cold regions. They are herbaceous and grass-like, often leafless, with inconspicuous green or dry flowers. The perianth is glume-like, six-parted, stamens six (or three), and pistil three-carpelled. The order includes about two hundred and fifty species of which the Rushes (*Juncus*) are used extensively in making mats, chair-bottoms, baskets, hassocks, etc. A curious aquatic plant of South Africa, with serrated leaves two or three feet long, has a stem, composed of a firm fibre, capable of conversion into paper; it has been also used for brushes. The Asphodel (*Narthecium ossifragum*) is cultivated for ornament.

4. **Liliaceæ.** The Lily family contains mostly herbaceous plants, with showy flowers and entire leaves. The flowers are perfect, regular, and six-parted (rarely four-parted), stamens perigynous, ovary superior, and fruit a capsule or berry. There are about two thousand species found in all climates; some of them furnish food, others medicine, and many of them are very fine ornamental plants. The Onion (*Allium Cepa*), from the Mediterranean region, is cultivated all over the world. Asparagus (*Asparagus officinalis*), native of Europe and Asia, was cultivated by the Romans before the Christian Era. In this long period of cultivation it has exhibited but little variation. The curious Grass Gum-trees (*Xanthorrhœa*) of Australia, six to ten feet high, with grass-like leaves, yield a fragrant resin, and contain an abundance of picric acid. The latter is used in dyeing silk and wool yellow. The gum resin is made into candles, used in some churches as incense. Aloes is the inspissated juice of several species of *Aloe*. This genus contains about one hundred and fifty species, mostly from South Africa and adjacent islands.

Many species are cultivated. Several species of Smilax (*Smilax officinalis*, etc.) of South America furnish sarsaparilla root. The Squill (*Scilla maritima*) comes from the sandy regions of the Mediterranean; its sliced bulbs form the dry squill. The Lily of the Valley (*Convallaria majalis*) is a native of Europe and Asia. The Crown Imperial (*Fritillaria imperialis*) of Europe and Asia, and the Day-Lilies (*Hemerocallis flava*, and *H. fulva*) of Europe, are coarse, ornamental plants. The Hyacinth (*Hyacinthus orientalis*), a native of Asia Minor, was introduced into England before the end of the sixteenth century; and under cultivation, has developed many varieties. Of the true Lilies (*Lilium*), the following are most common in cultivation: The Orange Lily (*L. bulbiferum*), Tiger Lily (*L. tigrinun*), the Turban Lily (*L. Pomponium*), the Golden Lily (*L. auratum*), the White Lily (*L. candidum*). A delicate climber in conservatories, called Smilax (*Myrsiphyllum asparagoides*), is from the Cape of Good Hope. The Star-of-Bethlehem (*Ornithogalum umbellatum*) from Europe, the Tube Rose (*Polianthes tuberosa*) from the East Indies, are also common in cultivation. The Tulip (*Tulipa Gesneriana*), whose specific name was given in honor of the botanist Conrad Gesner, who was the first to describe and figure it (in 1559), was brought into Europe

Fig. 290. A cultivated species of Yucca.

more than three hundred years ago. The Dutch improved it very much; and single bulbs of choice varieties sold at enormous prices. The original yellow flowers have been greatly enlarged. Several species of Yucca (Fig. 290), a genus from Mexico and adjacent regions, are found in cultivation, as Adam's Needle, Spanish Bayonet, Bear-Grass, etc.

5. **Lemnaceæ.** The **Duckweeds** are the smallest of the Phænogams; they consist of floating parenchymous disks, with several or one (*Lemna*), or no (*Wolffia*) roots beneath. Their flower-clusters are sunken into pits in the top, or edge, of the disks, and have one or two stamens and one pistil, each representing a flower. There are about twenty species, widely distributed in the Northern Hemisphere.

6. **Aroideæ.** The **Arum** family includes mainly tropical herbs, which are often large and palm-like, with large leaves, having reticulated venation, and the flower-cluster usually surrounded by a spathe. The flowers are borne on a spadix (Fig. 291); the perianth consists of from four to six scales, or is wanting; stamens hypogynous; stigma sessile; fruit baccate (or dry). There are about one thousand species of Aroids, some of which attain a height of from six to twelve feet; one recently discovered in Sumatra (*Amorphophallus Titanum*) has a spathe six feet in depth, and two and a half feet in diameter. The Indian Turnip (*Arisæma triphyllum*, and *A.*

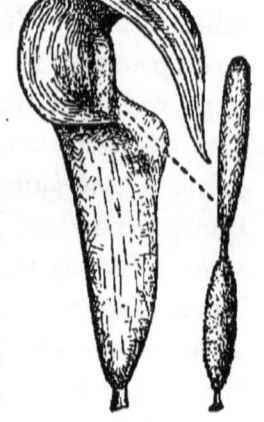

Fig. 291. Spathe and spadix of Indian Turnip.

Dracontium) and Sweet Flag (*Acorus Calamus*) are medicinal. The Calla, or Ethiopian Lily (*Richardia Africana*), native of Africa, has been in cultivation about one hundred and fifty years. Recently, species of *Alocasia* and *Caladium* have been introduced as hot-house plants. The Skunk Cabbage (*Symplocarpus fœtidus*) belongs to this family.

7. **Palmaceæ.** The **Palm** family includes trees, shrubs, or woody climbers, with the monœcious or diœcious flowers in a spadix (or a panicle or spike), generally enclosed in a hard, or leathery spathe. The perianth is six-parted; stamens six; pistil of three carpellary leaves; fruit a berry, or stone-fruit. The plants occur in the Tropics, or adjacent warm regions. No plants are more majestic than the arboreous species, which rise often to the height of one hundred feet, bearing at their summit spreading crowns of large leaves and drooping clusters of fruit. There are nearly a thousand species; and, except the Grasses, no family of plants surpasses them in the importance of their products. An arboreous Brazilian species (*Atalea funifera*) furnishes in its fibrous leaves material for making ropes, mats, and coarse brooms; the hard nuts (Coquilla-nuts), about three inches long, are used for making door-handles, bell-pulls, etc. The Cocoa-nut Palm (*Cocos nucifera*) is a native of the coasts of Tropical Africa, India, and Malay, and cultivated in all tropical countries. It produces the cocoa-nuts of commerce; each tree may yield one hundred to one hundred and fifty nuts annually, and continue to bear forty years. The white albumen and the milk furnish the natives of some parts of India and other countries with nearly their entire food and drink. The uses of the various parts of this tree are manifold, as in constructing huts,

fences, baskets, ropes, making drums and ornaments. The tender terminal bud is highly prized for food. From the juice of the flower-stems, rich in sugar, by fermentation, wine is made; and by distillation, a spirit is produced, called arrack. The fibre from the sheaths (leaves) is made into "coir" rope, floor-matting, brushes, and brooms; and is used also for stuffing cushions. The Palm (*Elæis guineënsis*) of West Africa produces nuts, from which is manufactured palm oil, used in the manufacture of candles, soap, etc. The Wax Palm (*Copernica cerifera*) of Brazil furnishes a wood which takes a fine polish, and is used for veneering, and a waxy secretion (on the leaves) used for making candles. For ages the Date Palm (*Phœnix dactylifera*) has been cultivated in Arabia and North Africa, and furnishes a large portion of the food of the people of these countries. The Dates are also imported into the United States, after having been picked before quite ripe and dried in the sun. The Ginger-bread Palm (*Hyphæne thebaica*) is a branching species of the upper Nile region, which produces fruits the size of an apple, with the flavor of ginger-bread. The tree furnishes a resin called Egyptian Bdellium. A giant Palm, growing on the Seychelle Islands of the Indian Ocean, is the Double Cocoa-nut (*Lodoicea Sechellarum*). The nuts are oblong, appear as if double, and weigh thirty to forty pounds; a single branch will sometimes weigh four hundred pounds. It takes ten years to ripen the fruit; but the albumen is too hard and horny to serve as food. The leaves are made into hats, baskets, etc. The Rattan, or Cane Palms (*Calamus Rotang*), of India and the Malayan Islands, have slender, reed-like stems, which often grow two hundred to three hundred feet high. They are used in making chair-bottoms, umbrellas, etc. Dragon's Blood, used for coloring varnishes and staining horn, is a secretion coating the surface of the small fruits of *Calamus Draco*, which grows in the same region with *C. Rotang*. The Sago Palms (*Sagus lævis*, and *S. Rumphii*) are natives of Siam, Indian Archipelago, etc. The soft, white pith taken from the trunks is thrown into tanks of water, in which it is washed and strained till a pure pulpy paste is obtained. It is preserved under water by the natives, who use it for food. For exportation it is dried, and granulated through sieves. The Betel-nut, or Pinang, of the far East, is a fruit of the size of a hen's egg, produced by the Betel Palm (*Areca Catechu*). It is cut into pieces, and rolled up in a leaf of Betel-pepper, with lime, gambier, etc., and chewed, as tobacco in this country. The Wax Palm (*Ceroxylon andicola*) grows on the mountain sides, nearly to the snow limits. A resinous wax is scraped off from the trunk, and used by the natives in making candles. The stems of several species of Climbing Palms (*Chamædorea*) of New Granada are used in making suspension bridges. A Sago Palm, of the Malayan Archipelago (*Saguerus saccharifer*), has enormous pinnate leaves (sometimes forty feet long); from the juice, which flows from the wounded spadix, sugar is obtained. In the Southeastern United States grow the Cabbage Palmetto (*Sabal Palmetto*), the Sun Palmetto (*S. serrulata*), and the Blue Palmetto (*Chamærops Hystrix*); and in California and Arizona, *Washingtonia filifera*.

8. Dioscoreaceæ. The **Yam** family has twining stems, ribbed and netted-veined leaves, and small diœcious, regular flowers, with a calyx-like, six-parted perianth, and a three-celled ovary, with three distinct styles. There are about one hundred and fifty species, growing mostly in the

Tropics. The Yam is the edible tuberous root of several species of *Dioscorea* (*D. sativa, D. aculeata*, etc). In the West Indies they take the place of the Irish Potato in the cooler climates. The Chinese Yam (*Dioscorea Batatas*) is extensively cultivated in China and Japan. The Tortoise-plant (*Testudinaria elephantipes*), a green-house plant from South Africa, is curious on account of its large woody corm-stem, three or four feet in diameter, and the same in height; it is covered with a hard tessellated coat, composed of numerous angular protuberances, and at the top grows a twining herbaceous vine.

9. **Amaryllidaceæ. Amaryllis family.** These are chiefly bulbous and scape-bearing herbs, with linear, flat root-leaves, flowers six-androus, ovary inferior. The species (about four hundred in number) are found in temperate and tropical climates. The Century-plant of Mexico (*Agave Americana*), grown in conservatories, in California and its native countries, blooms at the age of from ten to fifteen years; but in cool climates not till thirty to seventy years. The strong fibres of the leaves are used for cordage. From the juice, which flows abundantly when the central bud is cut out just before the lengthening of the flower-stem, the Mexicans obtain, by fermentation, their national drink, called "Pulque;" or, by distillation, that which is called "Mescal." *Hæmanthus toxicaria* has a poisonous bulb, which the Hottentots in South Africa use for poisoning their arrows. There are many ornamental genera, as Amaryllis (from South Africa and South America; Fig. 292) and Narcissus (from Europe). The latter includes the Daffodil, Jonquil, Polyanthus, etc. The Snowdrop (*Galanthus nivalis*) and Snowflake (*Leucojum vernum*) of Europe belong to this family.

10. **Iridaceæ.** The Iris family differs from the preceding in having but three stamens, and equitant three-ranked leaves. There are about five hundred species, mainly found in the south temperate climates. Many species of Iris, Gladiolus, and Crocus, are cultivated for the beauty of their flowers. The dye Saffron is obtained from the stigmas of *Crocus sativus;* upwards of four thousand flowers are required to produce one ounce of Saffron.

11. **Orchidaceæ. Orchis** family. The Orchids (Fig. 293) are terrestrial and epiphytic plants, with irregular, generally showy, flowers; a six-parted perianth; one segment of the inner whorl usually much modified, and called the *labellum;* one or two gynandrous stamens; pollen in cohering masses (pollinia); stigma generally broad and glutinous; seeds minute; containing a rudimentary embryo; and no endosperm. A large order (three thousand species), yet possessing but a few economic uses. It is, however, highly esteemed in cultivation for the hundreds of curious flowers, both as regards color and shape. The latter have reference to their pollination; none of them are able unaided

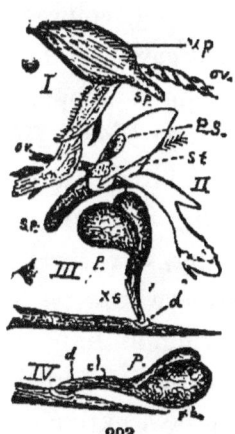

Fig. 292. Amaryllis. Fig. 293. An Orchid (*Orchis fusca*); *up*, upper lip; *un*, labellum; *ov*, ovary; *sp*, spur; *P.s*, pollen-sac; *st*, stigma; *p*, pollinia; *cl*, caulicle; *d*, disk; *I* and *II*, natural size; *III* and *IV*, magnified.

to effect self-fertilization, but depend on insects for the transport of the pollen from the anthers to the stigmas. Vanilla is the pod-like fruit, five to ten inches long, of *Vanilla planifolia*, an epiphytic plant, with thick, laurel-like leaves; native of the West Indies and Tropical America. When introduced into the East Indies it failed to perfect fruit until artificial fertilization was resorted to. From the tubers of *Orchis mascula*, and other species of Europe and Asia, a starchy, mucilaginous, and highly nutritious substance, "Salep," is obtained. The cultivated genera are too numerous to mention. Single rare plants sometimes command enormous prices—their weight in gold. The largest private collections are now to be found in France, Belgium, and England. In the United States there are showy native representatives of *Cypripedium, Calopogon, Pogonia, Orchis, Habenaria, Epidendrum, Corallorhiza*, etc.

12. **Bromeliaceæ.** The **Pine-Apple** family consists of herbs, chiefly epiphytic, with persistent, often scurvy, leaves; calyx three-parted; corolla three-parted, colored; stamens six, perigynous; style single; seeds numerous. The species number about two hundred, and belong to Tropical or sub-Tropical America. One genus, the Long Moss (*Tillandsia*), is represented in the Southern United States. The black, tough, elastic stem of this Long, Spanish, or Black Moss (*T. usneoides*), hanging in long, dark, gray tufts and festoons from trees in the Southern States, is used, after removal of the bark by hammering, as hair in upholstering. The Pine-Apple (*Ananassa sativa*), now cultivated throughout the world, is supposed to be a native of Brazil. The fleshy fruits are aggregated into solid, edible, cone-like masses.

13. **Scitamineæ.** The Banana family. These plants have irregular flowers; a six-parted perianth; six stamens (generally), few of which are fertile; fruit with no endosperm, but with much perisperm. They are found principally in the Tropics. The Banana (*Musa sapientum*) and the Plantain (*M. paradisiaca*) are large herbs, ten to fifteen feet high. Their fruit constitutes almost the entire food for millions of people in the Tropics. Large quantities are also exported. The Manilla Hemp is obtained from *M. textilis* of the East Indies. The dye Turmeric is the yellow-colored rhizome of *Curcuma longa* of the East Indies and Pacific Islands. The Ginger-plant (*Zingiber officinale*), probably a native of India, is cultivated in most tropical countries. Its aromatic rhizome, dried and powdered, constitutes the ginger of commerce. From the fleshy rhizomes of *Maranta arundinacea*, a native of Tropical America, the starch called Arrow-root is obtained. Common cultivated plants of this family are the many species of *Canna* (Fig. 294) and *Strelitzia Regina*, the latter from South Africa.

Fig. 294. Canna; rhizome and flower natural size; plant reduced.

14. Hydrocharidaceæ. The **Frog's-bit** family consists of small aquatic plants, with inconspicuous diœcious or polygamous flowers; stamens three to twelve, ovary inferior, fruit ripening under water. The American Water-weed (*Anacharis Canadensis*) is a slender herb, with opposite whorled leaves, growing under water; upon its advent into Europe a few years ago, it multiplied so rapidly as to be troublesome to navigation. The Grass-wrack (*Zostera marina*), found in tidal rivers, is used for packing, cushions, etc. The Tape, or Eel-grass (*Vallisneria spiralis*), growing at the bottom of the water, has long tape-like leaves and diœcious flowers. The staminate flowers become detached early, floating on the water, where they expand and shed their pollen. The latter finds its way to the pistillate flowers, whose elongated peduncles allow them also to reach the surface of the water. After fertilization, the peduncles again coil and draw the ovary beneath the water, where its development is completed.

DICOTYLEDONES.

189. The **Dicotyledones** are so called because the first leaves (seed-leaves or cotyledons) of the embryo, or plantlet, are two and opposite (Fig. 277, *cot*); this sub-class is also called **Exogenæ,** or **Exogenous** plants, because the growth or increase of the wood each year (in case of the perennial woody species) is in the form of a concentric ring, or cylinder, external to that previously formed. A transverse section of a very young plant will show the presence of a few open fibro-vascular bundles, arranged in the form of a circle (Fig. 295). Other bundles soon arise between these first formed (Fig. 296), and finally become so numerous as to lie against each other, and form a cylinder, the tissue within which constitutiug the pith, and that without, the cortex. The thin parenchyma here and there persisting between the bundles, and radiating from the centre, forms the Medullary Rays. The cambium of each bundle

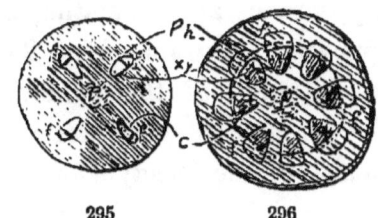

295   296

joins that of the adjacent bundles on either side, and thus arises a cambium ring, or zone, sometimes called "zone of life." From this cambium, xylem, or wood, is formed on the inner side; and phloëm, or bast, on the outside. The new layer of wood produced during the year (annual ring) has generally larger pores, or ducts, in that portion, found early in the season, and much smaller ones formed later. To this fact largely is due the phenomenon of well marked annual rings, whose number, as counted in cross section (Fig. 297), indicates the age of the tree.

190. There is great diversity in the general disposition or arrangement of the fibro-vascular bundles, as may be observed in the study of different young Dicotyledonous plants before they have become so numerous, or fused laterally so as to form a solid cylinder. There are very few "cauline bundles," that is, such as have no connection with the leaves; they are mostly "common bundles," or

297

extend both up into the leaf and down into the stem. There may be several entering the leaf, and these descending in the stem may for a time remain isolated, but further down unite laterally with those from other leaves. If the bundle-cylinder

Figs. 295, 296. Fibro-vascular bundles in young stems, diagrammatically represented. Fig. 297. Transverse section of an exogenous stem, showing pith, annual rings, medullary rays, and bark.

be split down one side and spread out into a plane, an appearance approximating more or less that in the accompanying diagram (Fig. 298) will be presented. The distribution of the bundles or midrib and veins in the leaves is such as to form a distinct net-work; and the leaves of the Dicotyledones, or Dicotyls, are, therefore, said to be reticulate, or netted-veined.

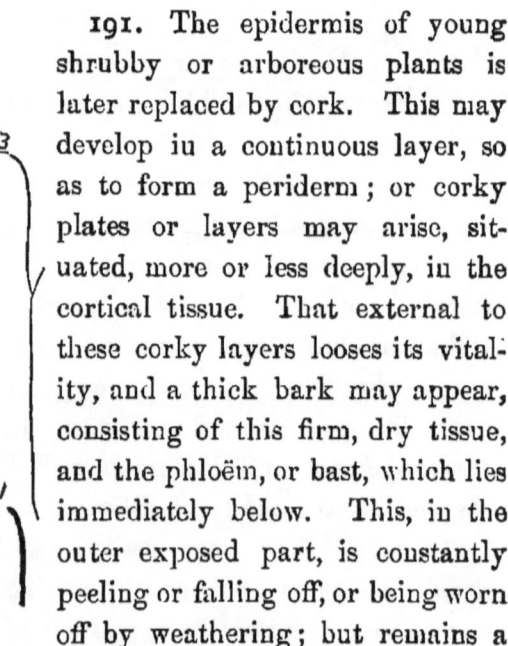

191. The epidermis of young shrubby or arboreous plants is later replaced by cork. This may develop in a continuous layer, so as to form a periderm; or corky plates or layers may arise, situated, more or less deeply, in the cortical tissue. That external to these corky layers looses its vitality, and a thick bark may appear, consisting of this firm, dry tissue, and the phloëm, or bast, which lies immediately below. This, in the outer exposed part, is constantly peeling or falling off, or being worn off by weathering; but remains a constant thickness, due to the fact that it is ever replenished within by the cambium. The flowers are generally four or five-parted; that is, each floral whorl contains four or five members. The embryo and germination of a Dicotyl is shown in Fig. 277. The sub-class is very large, embracing all of our forest trees except the *Coniferæ* (Pines, Firs, etc.), and divisible into three groups, namely, *Apetalæ, Gamopetalæ,* and *Polypetalæ* or *Choripetalæ.*

Fig. 298. Diagram, showing the course of the fibro-vascular bundles in an exogenous stem (of *Stachys*); the figures indicate the position of the leaves.

192. The **Apetalæ** embrace those Dicotyledonous, or Exogenous, plants whose flowers are destitute of a corolla, or of both corolla and calyx. Of this group the most interesting and important families are as follows:

1. **Santalaceæ.** The plants of this small family (about two hundred species) are mostly parasitic herbs, shrubs, or trees, in temperate and tropical regions. The ovule is destitute of integuments; our common representative is the Bastard Toad-Flax (*Comandra umbellata*). The Sandalwood-tree of South Asia, a tree about twenty-five feet high, furnishes a dark-red wood, used in cabinet-making, and for incense-burning in Buddhist temples. Species from the Pacific Islands also furnish Sandalwood.

2. **Loranthaceæ.** The **Mistletoe** family comprise parasitic evergreens, which live on other Dicotyledons. Their flowers are quite insignificant, more reduced than those of the previous family. The four hundred and fifty species are mostly tropical. The Mistletoe of Europe (*Viscum album*) grows on the Apple, and a few other trees. It has viscid berries, used in making bird-lime. The plant is generally used in England for Christmas decoration, and was formerly held sacred by the Druids. The American Mistletoe (*Phoradendron flavescens*), growing on the Elm, Walnut, Wild Cherry, etc., occurs in the Southern States.

3. **Cupuliferæ.** The **Oak** family, with about three hundred species of trees and shrubs, with simple leaves, mostly in the Northern Hemisphere, furnishes an important part of the wood used for fuel and in the manufacture of implements and utensils, houses, ships, etc. The sterile flowers are in slender catkins (Fig. 299). The fruit is a nut or acorn, surrounded by a scaly, indurated cup or

cupule (Fig. 300). Most of the species contain in the bark, etc., much tannin. The Filbert is the fruit of *Corylus Avellana*, a native of Europe and Asia, but cultivated also in this country. There are many varieties, as White Filberts, Red Filberts, Barcelona-nuts, etc. Its branches are used in making hoops, crates for merchandise, etc. The common, wild Hazel of United States is *Corylus Americana;* it is smaller, both the shrub and nut, than the preceding. The Iron-wood (*Ostrya Virginica*) has a hard, fine-grained wood, suitable for fuel and various uses in the arts. The trunks are often used for levers, whence the popular name Lever-wood. The Spanish Chestnut (*Castanea vesca*) was introduced into Europe from Asia probably two thousand years ago, and furnishes a valuable, coarse-grained wood and edible fruit. The Chestnut of the Eastern United States is a variety (*var. Americana*) of the Spanish Chestnut. The wood is light, and easily worked, it is used in making doors, various kinds of furniture, etc. The Beech of the United States (*Fagus ferruginea*), has wood of a reddish color, and great hardness when dry; it is extensively used in making carpenter's tools. The Oaks (genus *Quercus*) includes about two hundred and fifty species, scattered over the Northern Hemisphere. The British Oak of Europe (*Q. Robur*) furnishes timber considered to be superior to all other kinds of Oak; it is used extensively for all kinds of construct-

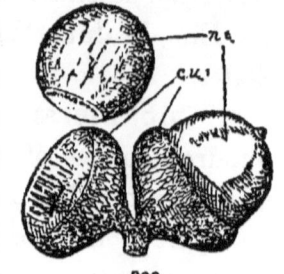

ive purposes. The bark also is used in tanning. The

Fig. 209. Catkin of the American Hazel.   Fig. 300. Acorn and cup; *cu*, cupule.

Nut-Galls of commerce, are morbid growths on the leaves of *Q. Lusitanica, var. infectoria*, caused by the punctures made by an insect (genus *Cynips*). The tree grows in the Mediterranean region, and the galls are valuable for the tannin they contain. The White Oak (*Q. alba*) of the United States is of great importance for its timber. The Live Oak of the Southeastern United States, having small evergreen leaves, has heavy, strong, and durable wood, used in ship-building. The Cork Oak (*Q. suber*) grows in Southern Europe and Northern Africa; the corky layers of the bark increase much in thickness, and are carefully removed every eight or ten years, and furnish the cork of commerce. The Black Oaks, as Black-Jack (*Q. nigra*), Red Oak (*Q. rubra*), Scarlet Oak (*Q. coccinea*), etc., produce a less durable and coarser grained wood than the preceding (White Oaks). From the bark of the Scarlet and Quercitron (*Q. coccinea, var. tinctoria*) Oak, a yellow dye, Quercitron, is obtained. The California Tan-bark Oak (*Q. densiflora*) is a beautiful tree one hundred feet high, and bears fruit in curious chestnut-like, spiny cups.

4. **Juglandaceæ.** The Walnut family comprises trees and shrubs, with pinnate leaves, and a hard one-seeded nut. This small family (about thirty species) has representatives in North America and Asia. The light brown wood of the Walnut of the Old World (*Juglans regia*) is highly prized in the manufacture of furniture, piano-cases, gun-stocks, etc. The thin-shelled nuts are imported to this country under the name of English Walnuts. The Black Walnut (*J. nigra*), a giant tree of the United States, furnishes a dark-brown timber, as valuable as the preceding; and like it, extensively used in

cabinet-making, the manufacture of furniture, etc. The wood of the smaller White Walnut, or Butternut (*J. cinerea*), is lighter colored than that of the preceding. The wood of the Shell-bark Hickories (*Carya alba* and *C. sulcata*) is white, hard, tough, and used extensively in the manufacture of agricultural implements, where great strength is required. The fruits (Hickory-nuts) are found in our markets, and exported to England. The Pecan-nut

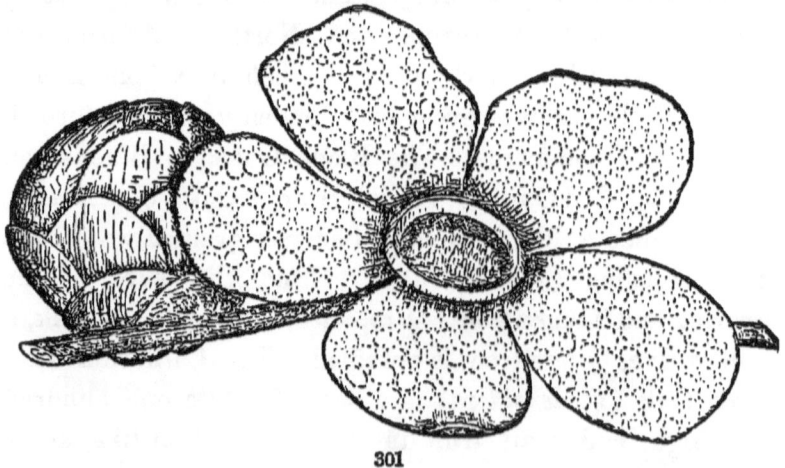

301

is furnished by a small tree (*C. olivæformis*) of the Southern States.

5. Rafflesiaceæ. This family comprises twenty or more species, found in the Tropics, growing parasitically on the stems and roots of Dicotyledons. The most remarkable representative was discovered in 1818 in Sumatra, by Dr. Arnold, and is called *Rafflesia Arnoldi* (Fig. 301). It is parasitic on a woody climber, and produces the largest flower known, which is three feet in diameter; it has five mottled-red petals.

6. **Piperaceæ.** The **Pepper** family is almost confined to the Tropics. The plants are herbs, shrubs, or small trees, with spiked flowers, and generally provided with a pungent and aromatic principle. There are over a thousand species, six hundred and twenty of which are included in the genus *Piper*, and three hundred and eighty-two in the genus *Piperomia*. A climbing plant (*Piper nigrum*) of East India, now cultivated also in the West Indies, with heart-shaped leaves and spikes of berries, furnishes the pepper of commerce. The fruit, gathered green and dried, constitutes the black pepper; gathered ripe and dried, it is the white pepper. The dried, unripe berries of *P. cubeba*, of the East Indies, constitute cubebs.

7. **Euphorbiaceæ. Spurge** family. A large and important group of three thousand species, varying in size from small herbs to gigantic trees, and having a wide geographical distribution, though most numerous in the Tropics. They generally have a milky or watery (mostly acrid and poisonous) juice, and a free three-celled ovary. Arrow-root is furnished by *Manihot palmata* and *M. altissima*; these slender plants (of Tropical America) have thick roots, containing much starch, called, when separated, arrow-root; this, when heated on hot plates and granulated, is called tapioca; the dried pulp without separation of the starch is cassava. These three products are important articles of food in the country in which they are produced, and are exported into this country. The Castor-Oil Plant (*Ricinus communis*), a native of India, is extensively cultivated for it's seeds, from which castor-oil is obtained by pressure (Fig. 302). In Germany its leaves are fed to silk-worms. It also occurs in cultivation as an ornamental plant. From the seeds of *Croton Tiglium*, a plant of India,

croton-oil is expressed. From *Jatropha Curcas*, a native of Tropical America, pinhœn-oil is obtained. From several species of plants of this family (especially *Hevea Guinensis*), Caoutchouc, or India Rubber, is obtained, which, in its crude state, consists of the dried, milky juice exuding from incisions made into the tree. The Tallow-tree of China (*Excœcaria sebifera*), now cultivated in America, has its seeds coated with a white greasy substance, from which candles are manufactured. The Box-tree of Europe and Asia (*Buxus sempervirens*), attaining a height of ten to thirty feet, and a diameter of eight to ten inches, furnishes the important, hard, and fine-grained timber called box-wood, used in wood-engraving, the manufacture of mathematical instruments, etc. The Dwarf Box, used for bordering garden walks, is a variety of this species. The African Teak (*Oldfieldia Africana*) is a wood so hard and heavy that it is now no longer in general use in ship-building, for which it was introduced into England in 1819. It is adapted for steam vessels, as it stands a great degree of heat. The genus *Euphorbia*, containing seven hundred species, furnishes very many ornamental plants; conspicuous among these are *Euphorbia splendens* from Madagascar, *E. punicea* from the West Indies, *E. pulcherrima* (called also Poinsettia) from Mexico, and *E. marginata* from the western United States (Fig. 303).

Fig. 302. *Ricinus communis*, the Castor-Oil Plant.

DICOTYLEDONES.

8. Salicaceæ. The **Willow** family comprises diœcious trees and shrubs whose amentaceous flowers are destitute of a perianth. There are two genera and one hundred and eighty species, found principally in the North Temperate and Arctic Zones. Many species of Willow (*Salix*) are cultivated for basket-making. The charcoal obtained from them by charring the wood is extensively used in the manufacture of gunpowder. The Weeping Willow (*S. Babylonica*) is a native of Persia, but common in cultivation. The Poplars (*Populus*) have a light, white wood, used much in manufacturing. The Lombardy Poplar (*P. dilatata*) is the commonest one cultivated for ornament.

9. Platanaceæ. The **Plane-tree** family consists of five monœcious plants of the genus *Platanus*, whose flowers are in globose catkins. The Plane-tree, or Sycamore (*P. occidentalis*), whose wood, though valuable, is not much used, is found in the Eastern United States; one species occurs in California, two in Mexico, and the fifth (*P. orientalis*) is found in the Old World.

10. Betulaceæ. Birch family. Of these monœcious, amentaceous trees, numbering over forty species, the most useful perhaps is the White Birch (*Betula alba*) of Northern Europe, Asia, and North America. Its wood is used for fuel, also in

Fig. 303. *Euphorbia marginata.*

manufactories, and in making charcoal. Its bark is made into shoes, boxes, etc. It is used in tanning leather, and from it an oil is distilled which gives the peculiar scent to Russian leather. The Indians use the bark of the Paper Birch (*B. papyracea*) for making the "birch-bark canoes." The wood of the Alder (*Alnus*) is very durable only under the ground or water, used also for charcoal. Sometimes it is manufactured into wooden bowls and other utensils, and the bark is used in dyeing and tanning.

11. **Urticaceæ.** A large family (more than two thousand species), including the Elms, Mulberries, Nettles, Hemp, Hop, etc. They are mostly diclinous plants, with superior one-celled ovary. The American, or White Elm (*Ulmus Americana*), is one of the most magnificent of all trees, and is everywhere found as an ornament in large grounds. The timber is durable only when kept continuously dry, or else entirely under water or in the ground. The timber from the Slippery Elm (*Ulmus fulva*) is more valuable, its mucilaginous inner bark is used in medicine and surgery. The Hemp (*Cannabis sativa*) is a native of India, where the inhabitants make from the dried leaves, stems, and flowers an intoxicating drink called *Hashish*. The plant is cultivated in all temperate and warm countries for its fibre, which is used for cordage. The Hop (*Humulus Lupulus*) is indigenous to North America, temperate Europe, and Asia. It is cultivated for *Lupulin*, a bitter substance developed in fertile flower-clusters, and used in the manufacture of beer, ale, etc. The Bread-Fruit-tree (*Artocarpus incisa*) of the Pacific Islands, twenty to thirty feet high, has a fleshy receptacle, and agglomerated carpels in the form of a mass as large as a man's head. This is gathered before ripe, baked, and

DICOTYLEDONES. 195

eaten by the people of the Tropics. The Fig-tree (*Ficus Carica*) has been cultivated for ages, and is now to be met with in all tropical and sub-tropical countries. The tree is sixteen to twenty feet high, and the ripened and dried receptacles, which are pear-shaped and closed (Figs. 304, 305), constitute the figs of commerce; other species of the genus (as *F. elastica*, etc.) yield Caoutchouc. From one species the resinous exudation called gum-lac is collected. The Banyan-tree (*F. Indica*) is remarkable for its adventitious roots, which proceed from, and ultimately support, the branches. The Cow-tree (*Galactodendron utile*) flourishes in Venezuela; its milky juice is used by the natives for milk, which it resembles much. Several species of the Mulberry (*Morus*) are cultivated for the edible fruit, and for the leaves as food for the silk-worm 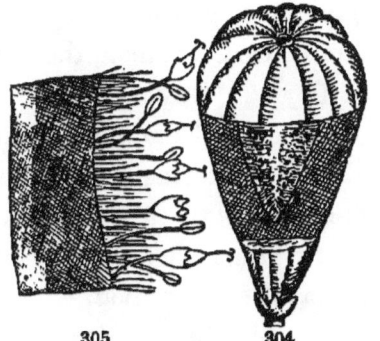 The Osage Orange (*Maclura aurantiaca*) of Arkansas, Texas, etc., is an important hedge plant. From its wood a coloring matter is obtained for dyeing. From *M. tinctoria* of the West Indies, the dye Fustic is obtained. The Chinese make paper, and the Pacific Islanders make cloth, from the fibres of the Paper Mulberry (*Broussonetia papyrifera*). The China Grass, or *Ramie* (*Bœhmeria nivea*), a perennial herb, introduced into the Southern States and California, furnishes a fibre approaching flax in fineness and durability. Our common Stinging Nettles belong to the genera *Urtica* and *Laportea*. To the latter belongs the

---

Figs. 304, 305. The Fig, natural size (*304*), and a portion with the flowers (*305*) slightly magnified.

true Nettle (*L. gigas*) of Australia. This obtains a height of fifty to one hundred and thirty feet, and the sting produces dangerous results.

12. **Lauraceæ.** The **Laurel** family includes aromatic trees and shrubs, and a few parasitic herbs, in all about one thousand species. The pendulous seed has no endosperm. The Bay, or Laurel, of Europe is an evergreen tree forty to fifty feet high. The leaves were formerly used to crown heroes. They are now used in flavoring custards, puddings, figs packed in boxes, etc. Other important products furnished by representatives of this family are Cinnamon, the bark of *Cinnamomum Zeylanicum* of Ceylon; Cassia bark and Cassia buds, from *C. Cassia* of Ceylon; Camphor, from *C. camphora* of China and Japan; Sassafras bark, from the *Sassafras officinale* of the United States. The Greenheart-tree of Guiana (*Nectandra Rodiei*) furnishes a dark, heavy, and durable timber, used in naval construction.

13. **Myristicaceæ. Nutmeg** family. These plants are aromatic trees, with monadelphous stamens; there are seventy-five species, all tropical, and belonging to the genus *Myristica*. The most important representative is the Nutmeg-tree of the Malay Archipelago (*M. fragrans*), twenty to thirty feet high, and whose fruit, or seed, deprived of its integuments, is the nutmeg of commerce. The reddish branching aril (a fleshy growth outside of the integuments) when dry constitutes the *mace* of commerce.

14. **Chenopodiaceæ.** The **Goosefoot** family consists of about five hundred herbs, shrubs, or, sometimes, trees, whose flowers have an herbaceous perianth and one seed. The most important representatives are the common Beet (*Beta vulgaris*), Sugar-Beet, and Mangel Wurzel,

both varieties of the former; also common garden Spinach (*Spinacia oleracea*), and several species of *Chenipodium*, as Quinoa, (*C. Quinoa*) an important article of food in Peru and Chili, and Wormseed (*C. ambrosioides*), from Tropical America, used in medicine.

15. **Polygonaceæ.** The **Buckwheat** family consists of herbs and shrubs, rarely trees, with knotted-jointed stems, and sheathing stipules, or ochreæ (Fig. 306). They are mostly found in temperate regions, and number about six hundred species. Representatives of this family furnish the Pie-plant (*Rheum Rhaponticum*), from Western Asia; the Rhubarb (*R. officinale*), from Southeastern Asia; and the Buckwheat (*Fagopyrum esculentum*), from Central or Northern Asia. Much tannin is contained in the leaves of *Polygonum amphibium, var. terrestre*, a native of the United States; and they have been occasionally used as a substitute for bark in the process of tanning.

193. The **Gamopetalæ** are Dicotyledons, or Exogenous plants, whose flowers generally have both sepals and petals present, and the latter connately united. Of this group the following are the most interesting or important families:

1. **Labiatæ.** The **Mint** family has about twenty-five hundred species, widely distributed, except in cool regions. The plants are aromatic herbs, or shrubs, with square stems, opposite leaves, a deeply four-parted ovary, and often labiate flowers. The family is of no great economic importance. Lavender (*Lavendula vera*), a shrub of South Europe, yields, on distillation, Oil of Lavender. In the same manner Oil of Peppermint is obtained from *Mentha*

Fig. 306. Ochrea of Polygonum.

piperita. Many species are used as domestic medicines, etc., as Pennyroyal (*Hedeoma pulegioides*), Hoarhound (*Marrubium vulgare*), Thyme (*Thymus vulgare*), Sage (*Salvia officinalis*), Catnip (*Nepeta Cataria*), etc. Several species, grown as ornamental plants, belong to the genera *Salvia*, *Cedronella* (Fig. 307), *Coleus*, etc.

2. Verbenaceæ.

Vervain family; herbs, shrubs, and trees, mostly square stems. The ovary is not four-lobed, and the plants are seldom aromatic. Among its ornamental representatives are various species of *Verbena*, from South America; the Lemon Verbena (*Lippia citroidora*), from Chili; several species of *Lantana*, from Tropical America; and of Clerodendron, from Asia and South America (Fig. 308). The

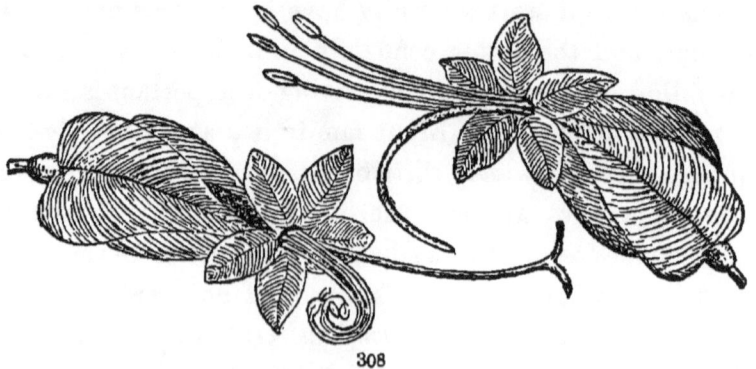

gigantic Teak-tree of India (*Tectona grandis*), furnishes a yellowish, durable wood, much used in ship-building.

Fig. 307. Cedronella, an ornamental plant. Fig. 308. *Clerodendron Thompsoniæ.*

3. **Bignoniaceæ. Bignonia** family; mostly woody plants, with stamens didynamous or diandrous, ovary commonly two-celled, many-seeded. The family numbers about five hundred species, found mostly in the Tropics. The Trumpet-flower (*Tecoma radicans*), as well as the common Catalpa (*C. bignonioides*), occurs both wild and cultivated in the United States.  The western Catalpa (*C. speciosa*) is much hardier than the preceding, and furnishes a rapid growing and durable wood.

4. **Lentibulariaceæ.** The **Bladderwort** family, comprising aquatic or marsh plants, of temperate and cold regions. 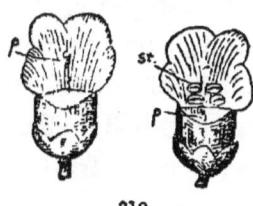 The flowers are labiate, and spurred; stamens two; ovary one-celled. The aquatic species (as *Utricularia*) have insect catching bladders (Fig. 309), others are also insectivorous.

5. **Scrophulariaceæ. Figwort** family; herbs or shrubs, rarely trees; corolla irregular (Figs. 310, 311); ovary two-celled. The two thousand species are widely distributed. The family is of little economic importance. The drug Digitalis is obtained from the Foxglove (*Digitalis purpurea*) of Europe. Many cultivated species have showy flowers, as Snapdragon (*Antirrhinum*), Monkey-flower (*Mimulus*), *Veronica*, etc. *Paulownia imperialis* is a cultivated tree in the Southern States, introduced from Japan. Many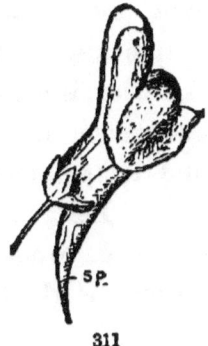

Fig. 309. Bladder on the stem of Utricularia. Fig. 310. Flowers of *Scrophularia nodosa*. Fig. 311. Flower of Toad-Flax (*Linaria vulgaris*).

of our common weeds belong to this family, as Mullein (*Verbascum*), Toad-Flax (*Linaria*), Lousewort (*Pedicularis*), etc.

6. **Solanaceæ.** The **Nightshade** family comprises from twelve hundred to fifteen hundred species, found chiefly in the Tropics. The plants have often a suspicious look, and contain a poisonous principle. The flowers are five-merous and regular (Fig. 312), and the fruit is a two-celled pod or berry. The Potato (*Solanum tuberosum*) is a native of America, from Mexico to Chili; but in its wild state the tubers are very small. By culture and selection, for two or three hundred years, they have been enormously increased (Fig. 313), and are now cultivated in nearly all countries. The cells of the tubers are filled with large, oval starch grains (Fig. 348). The Egg-plant (*S. Melongena*), cultivated for its edible fruit, is a native of South America. For its wholesome fruit, the Tomato (*Lycopersicum esculentum*), a native also of South America, is generally cultivated in warm and temperate countries. Belladonna is obtained from the Deadly Nightshade (*Atropa Belladonna*), a plant of the

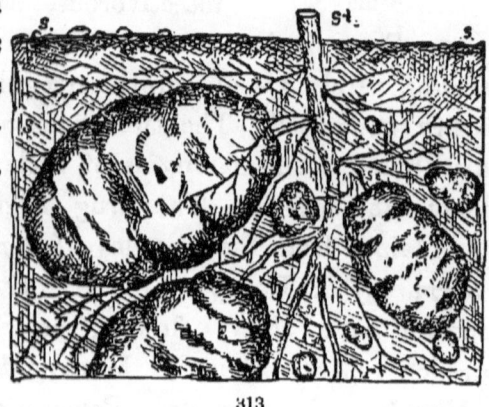

Fig. 312. Rotate corolla of the Potato-plant. Fig. 313. Potato Tubers; *st*, stem; *s*, soil; *r*, roots.

Old World. Supplying similarly very narcotic medicines, and growing in the same countries, are also the Henbane (*Hyoscyamus niger*) and the Thorn-Apple (*Datura stramonium*). The South American Tobacco (*Nicotiana Tabacum*), cultivated by the American aborigines, is extensively grown in the United States and elsewhere, and used in immense quantities by many nations of the globe. *Datura* from South America and Mexico, *Lycium* from Europe, *Nierembergia* (Fig. 314), etc., are cultivated for ornament.

7. **Convolvulaceæ.** The **Convolvulus** family has about eight hundred species, in tropical and warm countries generally. They are mostly twining or trailing herbs, often with a milky juice. The corolla is showy and convolute in the bud. The most important representative is the Sweet Potato of India (*Ipomœa Batatas*). The Morning-Glory (Fig. 315), from Tropical America, is universally cultivated; and the twining parasitic Dodder (*Cuscuta*, Fig. 316), with its numerous species, often does much injury to

Fig. 314. Nierembergia, a cultivated species. Fig. 315. The Morning-Glory.

crops. Scammony is the dried juice of *Convolvulus scammonia* of Asia. Oil of Rhodium is obtained from *C. Scoparius* and *C. floridus* of the Canary Islands; from the scent of the wood of these two, it is called "Rosewood," and from it oil is extracted and used in adulterating attar of Roses.

8. **Borraginaceæ.** The **Borage** family (twelve hundred species) are, for the most part, hispid herbs, shrubs, or trees, with a four-parted ovary. They are found all over the world; but few are of importance, as that whose roots yield the red dye Alkanet (*Anchusa tinctoria* of Europe), and ornamental plants, as Forget-me-not (*Myosotis palustris*) from Europe, and Heliotrope (Fig. 317; *Heliotropum Peruvianum*) from Peru. Comfrey (*Symphytum officinale*) is supposed to be medicinal. Many weeds belong to this family, as Stickweed (*Echinospermum*), Hound's-Tongue, and Beggar's Lice (*Cynoglossum*), Puccoon (*Lithospermum*), etc.

9. **Loganiaceæ.** This small family (three hundred and fifty species) of the Tropics deserves mention, as including the *Strychnos nux-vomica* of India, which produces an

Fig. 316. The Dodder or *Cuscuta*.   Fig. 317. Heliotrope.

orange-like fruit, containing large flattish seeds, the latter being the poisonous drug Nux-vomica. From these two alkaloids, Strychnia and Brucia are obtained, the sulphate of the former being kept in the shops. The poison variously known as Curare, Ourari, or Woorara, is obtained from *S. toxifera* of South America. A Japanese Climber (*S. Tieute*) furnishes Upas Tieuté, or Tjettek, which the natives use to poison their arrows.

10. **Asclepiadaceæ.** The **Milkweed** family comprises woody or herbaceous plants, with a milky juice, which is generally acrid and poisonous; ovaries two, but with a single common stigma; peculiar flowers and pollinia, adapted for pollination by insects. This large family (about thirteen hundred species) is mostly tropical, but of slight economic importance. Of the ornamental plants, the Wax-plant of India (*Hoya carnosa*, Fig. 318) is the most common. Our common Milkweeds (*Asclepias*) belong to this family.

Fig. 318. Wax-plant (*Hoya carnosa*).

11. **Apocynaceæ.** The **Dogbane** family is much like the preceding, but the pollen is granular and the corolla convolute. There are about nine hundred, mostly tropical, species. The tough fibrous bark of our native species of Apocynum was used by the Indians for making cordage, nets, etc. Caoutchouc is obtained from species of *Siphonia* of South America, of *Vahea* and *Urceola*, natives of Madagascar, Borneo, etc. The Ordeal-tree of

Madagascar (*Tanghinia venenifera*) furnishes the very poisonous seeds called Ordeal poison, or Tanghin. The most common ornamental plant of this family is the Oleander (*Nereum oleander*), from the Levant, which has been cultivated in England and this country for two or three hundred years. The whole plant is somewhat poisonous.

12. **Oleaceæ.** The **Olive** family contains two hundred and eighty widely distributed species, with four-parted flowers, two stamens, and two-celled ovaries. The Olive (*Olea Europœa*) is an important representative, now cultivated in all warm countries. It came probably from Asia originally. It is a small evergreen tree, bearing bluish oily drupes, from which olive-oil or sweet-oil is expressed. The hard wood is sometimes used in turnery, etc. Valuable timber, for use in turnery, manufacture of implements, etc., is supplied by various species of Ash (*Fraxinus*). Of the ornamental representatives, the following are common: Jessamine (*Jasminum*), Lilac (*Syringa*), Fringe-tree (*Chionanthus*), Privet (*Ligustrum*), *Forsythia*, etc.

13. **Ebenaceæ.** The **Ebony** family. Mostly tropical plants, trees, or shrubs; about two hundred and fifty species. Our only representative is the Persimmon (*Diospyros Virginiana*), a small tree with edible fruit. The hard, black wood, known as ebony, is furnished by several species of *Diospyros*. That of *D. reticulata*, from the island of Mauritius, is considered the best.

14. **Primulaceæ.** The two hundred and fifty species of the **Primrose** family are mostly found in the North Temperate Zone. They are herbs with simple, and mostly radical, leaves, and a many-seeded ovary, with a free central placenta. This family furnishes very many

ornamental plants, as the English Primrose (*Primula vulgaris*), English Cowslip (*P. veris*), Chinese Primrose (*P. sinensis*), *Cyclamen* (Fig. 319), *Dodecatheon, Lysimachia,* etc.

15. **Ericaceæ.** The **Heath** family comprises about seventeen hundred species, mostly shrubs, or small trees, many evergreen, with anthers usually opening by a terminal pore, and pollen grains compound. The Madroñia of the Pacific Coast of the United States is an evergreen tree, eighty to a hundred feet high, whose hard wood is useful in cabinet-making. *Arctostaphylos pungens* and *A. glauca* are evergreen shrubs of California, whose heavy dark-colored, fine-grained wood is used in turnery. The leaves of the Bearberry (*A. Uva-ursi*) of the colder regions of North America, Europe, and Asia are bitter, astringent, and medicinal. The stems of the Heath of Europe (*Calluna vulgaris*), a straggling evergreen undershrub, are made use of for brooms, and the flowers are rich in honey. The Wintergreen, or Checkerberry (*Gaultheria procumbens*), has aromatic fruit and foliage; the latter yields oil in distillation. The genus *Erica* includes four hundred species, all in Europe, Asia, and Africa; many of them are found

Fig. 319. Cyclamen.

in conservatories. Other very showy plants belong to the genera *Kalmia*, *Rhododendron*, and *Azalea*. The Black Huckleberries are the fruit of *Gaylussacia resinosa*; Early Blueberry, of *Vaccinium Pennsylvanicum*; Late Blueberry, of *V. vacillans*; Swamp-Blueberry, of *V. corymbosum*; Small Cranberry, of *V. Oxycoccus*; Large Cranberry, of *V. macrocarpon*, which is extensively cultivated. The Pipsissewa, or Prince's Pine (*Chimaphila maculata*), used by the Indians as a medicine, the parasitic or saprophytic Indian-pipe (*Monotropa uniflora*), and Pine-sap (*M. Hypopitys*), the Trailing Arbutus (*Epigæa repens*), are among our other common representatives of this family.

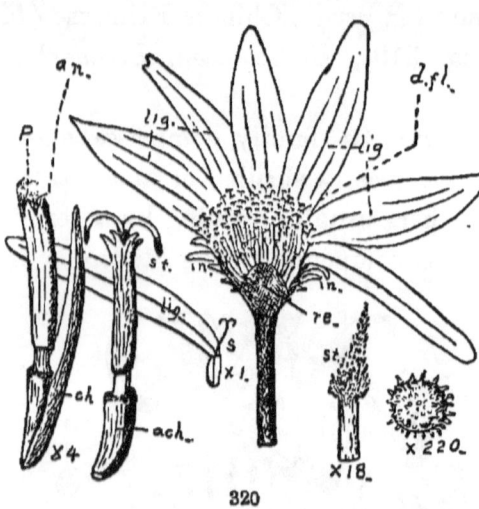

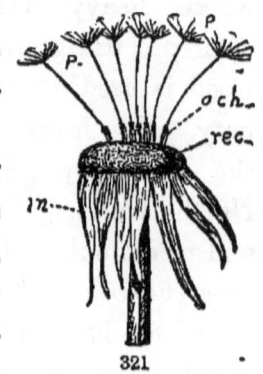

16. **Compositæ.** The Sunflower family comprises ten thousand species of herbs and shrubs (rarely trees), easily recognized (Fig. 320, 321) by involucrate heads of flowers and syngenesious stamens. They are widely distributed, many possess great beauty, but few are other-

Fig. 320. A composite flower (*Heliopsis lævis*); *re*, receptacle; *in*, involucre; *lig.* ray-flowers; *d.fl*, disk-flowers; *an*, anthers; *p*, pollen; *ach*, achenium; *ch*, chaff. *st*, stigma; the florets magnified 4, the stigma 18, and the pollen grain 220 diameters. Fig. 321. Reflexed involucre (*in*) of the Dandelion, showing the receptacle (*rec*), and a few achenia (*ach*) with pappus (*P*).

wise of any utility. Among the latter are Chicory (or roots of *Cichorium Intybus* of Europe), Garden Lettuce (*Lactuca sativa,* native of Asia), Salsify, or Oyster-plant (*Tragopogon porrifolius* of Europe), Safflower (or red flowers of *Carthamnus tinctoria,* used as a dye), Arnica (flowers and root of *Arnica montana* of Europe and Siberia), Flea-powder or Persian insect-powder (the pulverized leaves and flowers of *Pyrethrum*), Chamomile (*Anthemis nobilis*), Tansy (*Tanacetum vulgare*), and Elecampane (*Inula Helenium*). The Tasmanian *Bedfordia salicina,* attaining a height of fifteen feet, possesses hard and beautifully grained wood, prized in cabinet work. The Musk-tree (*Olearia argophylla*), also of Tasmania, twenty feet high, one foot in diameter, is used in turnery and the manufacture of agricultural implements because of the hardness of its wood. Other species of Olearia in New Zealand are equally valuable. Among the many ornamental plants the commonest are species of *Centaurea, Dahlia, Zinnia, Coreopsis, Helianthus, Aster, Solidago, Eupatorium, Chrysanthemum,* etc. Among vile weeds may be noticed the Thistles (*Cirsium*), Ragweeds (*Ambrosia*), Spanish Needles (*Bidens*), etc. The Sage Brush (*Artemisia*) of the Rocky Mountains consists of tall shrubs.

17. **Rubiaceæ.** The **Madder** family includes over four thousand species of herbs, shrubs, and trees. They have opposite, or whorled, stipulate entire leaves, regular corolla, and epipetalous stamens (Fig. 322); the most important members grow in the Tropics. There are thirty or more species of *Cinchona* belonging to South America. Several of them furnish Peruvian Bark, or Jesuits' Bark, which contains two important alkaloids, namely, Cinchonia and Quinia; the sulphate of the

208 SYSTEMATIC BOTANY.

latter is Quinine. The emetic Ipecacuanha, or "Ipecac,"

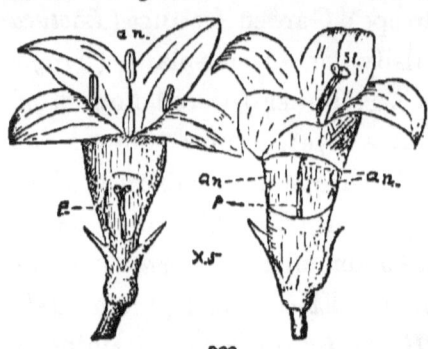

is from the root of *Cephœlis Ipecacuanha*, a small shrub of Brazil. The Coffee-tree (*Coffea Arabica*) is a native of Abyssinia, has glossy evergreen leaves, white axillary flowers, and red berries, each with two seeds, the coffee of commerce. It has varied much under the extensive cultivation to which it has been subjected. The Madder-plant (*Rubia tinctoria*) is a perennial herb of Europe, now cultivated in many parts of the world for the red dye, or Madder, which its roots yield. The family furnishes a few ornamental plants, as Asperula (Fig. 323), etc. Our common wild representatives are Cleavers, or Bedstraw (*Galium*), Partridgeberry (*Mitchella*), Bluets (*Houstonia*, Fig. 322), Button-bush (*Cephalanthus*), etc.

18. **Caprifoliaceæ.** The Honeysuckle family. Mostly woody plants; flowers generally zygomorphic; stamens epipetalous. There are two hundred species, found

Fig. 322. *Houstonia purpurea;* *an*, anthers; *st*, stigma; *p*, pistil. Fig. 323. Asperula.

mainly in the Northern Hemisphere. They are of little use except for ornament. The commonest in cultivation are the Honeysuckle (*Lonicera*), Snowberries (*Symphoricarpus*), Bush-Honeysuckles (*Diervilla*), the Snowball (*Viburnum*), Weigelia from Japan, etc. The berries of the Elder (*Sambucus*) are sometimes used for making pies, jellies, wine, etc. The beautiful *Linnæa borealis*, which was a favorite of, and dedicated to, the immortal Linnæus, belongs to this family.

194. The **Polypetalæ**, or **Choripetalæ**, are Dicotyledonous, or Exogenous plants, whose flowers generally have both sepals and petals, the latter not connately united, but separate. Of this group the following families are interesting or important:

1. **Cornaceæ.** The **Dogwood** family comprises but seventy-five species, mainly in the North Temperate Zone. They have simple leaves, and an adherent calyx, whose limb is minute. The wood of the Flowering Dogwood (*Cornus florida*) is hard and fine-grained, and sometimes used as a substitute for box-wood. Many species of *Cornus* are ornamental plants. The wood of the Sour-Gum (*Nyssa multiflora*) is much used for hubs for wagon-wheels, being difficult to split.

2. **Araliaceæ.** The **Ginseng** family; three hundred and forty species; mostly tropical; shrubs or trees, rarely herbs. Leaves alternate, compound; fruit a berry, or drupe. The European Ivy (*Hedera Helix*) and *Aralia spinosa* are common in cultivation as ornamental plants. The root of Ginseng (*Aralia quinquefolia*) of the United States is medicinal. The pith of *Aralia papyrifera* of China is cut into thin sheets, pressed flat, and forms the Chinese rice-paper.

3. **Umbelliferæ.** The **Parsley** family. Flowers in umbels, styles two. Fruit consists of two seed-like dry carpels (*mericarps*). Leaves usually much dissected. Herbs, rarely shrubs or trees. Species thirteen hundred, widely distributed; most abundant in Northern Europe and Asia. Many contain an acrid poisonous principle, especially in the green parts; fruits often aromatic and innoxious. Among the aromatic and medicinal fruits are Caraway (*Carum carvi*), Coriander (*Coriandrum sativum*), Cumin (*Cuminum sativum*), Anise-seed (*Pimpinella Anisum*). Edible roots are furnished by the Carrot (*Daucus carota*), Parsnip (*Pastinaca sativa*); edible stems and leaves, used as salads or for flavoring, are Celery (*Apium graveolens*), Parsley (*A. petroselinum*), Fennel (*Fœniculum vulgare*), etc. The important resinous gums obtained from the milky juice are Asafœtida (from *Ferula Asafœtida* of Thibet), Gum-Ammoniacum (from *Dorema ammoniaca* of Western Asia), and Gum-Galbanum (from *Ferula galbaniflora* of Asia). Some of our native species, as Poison Hemlock (*Conium maculatum*), Water Hemlock (*Cicuta maculata*), and Fool's Parsley (*Æthusa Cynapium*), are very poisonous. Some shrubby or arborescent representatives grow in the Madeiras and Australia.

4. **Cactaceæ.** The **Cactus** family consists of about one thousand, mostly Tropical American, species of succulent herbs, shrubs or trees, often spiny, and generally leafless, with solitary sessile flowers. The family is remarkable for the curious aspect of the plants, and for the fine flowers furnished by such as the Night Blooming Cereus (*Cereus grandiflorus*), and other species of the genera *Cereus, Opuntia, Echinocactus*, etc. The Cochineal insect inhabits *Opuntia coccinellifera* and other species found in Mexico.

5. **Begoniaceæ.** A small tropical family of three hundred and fifty, mostly American, species, deserving of mention because it includes the genus *Begonia*, many species of which furnish us with very fine ornamental green-house plants.

6. **Cucurbitaceæ.** The **Gourd** family; climbing or trailing herbs or undershrubs, with diœcious or monœcious flowers, and stamens mostly with united tortuous anthers. The majority of the four hundred and seventy species are tropical. The important representatives of this order are the Winter Squash (*Cucurbita maxima*), Crook-necked Squash (*C. verrucosa*), Pumpkin (*C. Pepo*), Muskmelon (*Cucumis Melo*), Cucumber (*C. sativus*), and Watermelon (*Citrullus vulgaris*). The nativity of the first three is unknown; the last three are from India. The common Gourd (*Lagenaria vulgaris*) is a native of Asia and Africa. The Towel-Gourd of Egypt (*Luffa Ægyptica*) has fruit larger than a Cucumber; the internal fibrous portion of which is used as a bathing spouge. The Wild Balsam-apple (*Echinocystis lobata*) and Star-Cucumber (*Sicyos angulatus*) are natives of the United States, and often grown over arbors, screens, etc.

7. **Onagraceæ.** The **Evening Primrose** family; three hundred herbaceous species, of temperate regions; flowers often four-parted; petals convolute in the bud. Our native wild species, as Willow-herb (*Epilobium angustifolium*), Common Evening Primrose (*Œnothera biennis*), etc., are not so showy as the splendid exotics (Fig. 324) from Mexico and South America. *Fuchsia coccinea* was brought from Chili in 1788; *F. decussata*, from the same place, followed in 1823. Other Chilian species were soon after introduced, and also the fine

Mexican species, *F. fulgens, F. cordata, F. corymbiflora*, etc. Edible fruits are produced by *Trapa natans* of Europe, *T. bispinosa* of India, and *T. bicornis* of China.

8. Myrtaceæ. Myrtle family. Mostly trees and shrubs, with opposite glandular-dotted leaves; calyx adherent, stamens indefinite. An important family of eighteen hundred species of the Tropics and Southern Hemisphere. Valuable fruits called Guavas are furnished by *Psidium pomiferum* and *P. pyriferum* of the West Indies, and *P. Cattleyanum* of Brazil. The Malay-Apple and Rose-Apple are the fruits of *Eugenia malaccensis* and *E. Jambos* respectively, much used in the East. The fruit of *E. pimenta* of the West Indies, gathered and dried before ripening, is the Pimento, or Allspice, in common use. *E. aromatica* is the Clove-tree of the Moluccas, whose flower-buds are collected and dried, and constitute the cloves of commerce. The Brazil-nuts are the rough oily seeds contained in the woody-shelled fruit of *Bertholletia excelsa*, a Tropical American tree one hundred to one hundred and fifty feet high. The hard-mottled wood of *Myrtus communis*, the Myrtle-tree of Western Asia, is much used in turnery. Various species of the vast genus *Eucalyptus*, of Australia and Tasmania, are large and important timber trees; the wood is tough and durable, and much used in structures exposed to sea-water. The Blue-Gum (*E. globulus*) is now being planted in California. From

Fig. 324. Clarkia, a cultivated species.

E. resinifera and other species Gum-Kino is obtained. In conservatories are seen species of *Myrtus, Eugenia*, etc.

9. **Droseraceæ.** The Sundew family consists of about one hundred and ten widely distributed species, mostly bog-herbs, with radical gland-bearing leaves, and regular pentamerous flowers. They are interesting because of their power of catching and digesting insects. Not only the Venus's Fly-trap (*Dionæa muscipula*, Fig. 324a) and the Sundews (*Drosera*), but also the other genera are insectivorous.

324a.

10. **Saxifragaceæ.** The **Saxifrage** family. Flowers usually with five petals, and definite stamens inserted on the calyx. There are five hundred and forty species of herbs, shrubs, and trees, mostly of temperate and cold climates. The Gooseberry (*Ribes Grossularia*) and Currant (*R. rubrum*) are common in cultivation. The ornamental representatives are numerous, among which may be mentioned the Strawberry Geranium of China (*Saxifraga sarmentosa*), the Mock Orange of the Old World (*Philadelphus*), the Flowering Currants of the United States (*Ribes*), *Deutzia* from China and Japan, *Hydrangia* from Japan and the United States, etc.

11. **Rosaceæ.** The **Rose** family. Flowers with five petals and many stamens, perigynous. An important family of one thousand herbs, shrubs, and trees, widely distributed. The genus *Pyrus* furnishes the Apple (*P. Malus*), the Pear (*P. communis*), American Crab-Apple

Fig. 324a. Leaves of Venus's Fly-trap (*Dionæa*).

(*P. coronaria*), the Siberian Crab-Apple (*P. prunifolia* and *P. baccata*), and the Quince (*P. Cydonia* or *Cydonia vulgaris*). The first two have been cultivated for ages; the last is from the Levant. The Hawthorns (*Cratægus*) and Serviceberries (*Amelanchier*) have small, edible fruits. Some are ornamental, and some of use for hedges. From species of *Fragaria*, the cultivated varieties of the Strawberry have been obtained, and several species of *Rubus*

furnish Raspberries and Blackberries. *Rubus occidentalis*, the wild Black Raspberry; *R. strigosus*, the Red Raspberry; and *R. villosus*, the Blackberry, are natives of the Eastern United States. To the genus *Prunus* belong the Almond, a native of Asia (*P. communis*); the Peach (*P. Persica*), the Apricot (*P. Armeniaca*, originally from Armenia), the European Plum (*P. domestica*), the common Wild Plum (*P. Americana*), the Cherry. (*P. Cerasus* and *P. avium*), and the Wild Cherry (*P. serotina*). The wood

Fig. 325. A Double Rose.

of the last two is much used in the manufacture of furniture. The double-flowered Dwarf Almond is *P. nana.*

326

The many Roses (genus *Rosa*) are among the most highly prized of all ornamental plants (Figs. 325, 326.)

12. **Leguminosæ.** The **Pulse** or **Bean** family. Herbs, shrubs, and trees, with usually compound leaves, often papilionaceous flowers (Fig. 327), and fruit a legume (Fig. 328). A large and important family of sixty-five hundred species, widely distributed. Some of the food-plants are the Pea (*Pisum sativum*), English Bean (*Vicia Faba*),

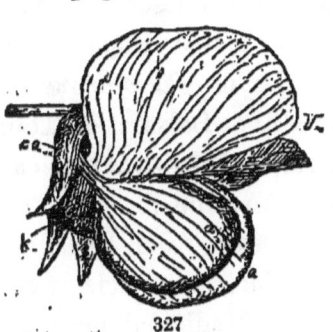

Fig. 326. A Moss-Rose. Fig. 327. A Papilionaceous flower (of the Pea). Fig. 328. A legume (Bean).

Pole Bean (*Phaseolus vulgaris*), Field Bean (*P. nana*), Lima Bean (*P. lunatus*), all from Asia. The Peanut (*Arachis hypogæa*) is a native of South America; its peduncles, after fertilization of the yellow flowers, have the curious habit (as if for protection) of bending down and thrusting the young pods into the ground, where they ripen. Among the many forage plants may be mentioned the Red Clover (*Trifolium pratense*), White Clover (*T. repens*), Lupine (*Lupinus albus*), Lucerne (*Medicago sativa*), Sanfoin (*Onobrychis sativa*), Vetch (*Vicia sativa*), all from countries adjacent to the Mediterranean region. The timber trees include the Locust-tree of the United States (*Robinia Pseudacacia*); the Rosewood of Brazil (*Dalbergia nigra*) and of India (*D. latifolia*); the Mora-tree of Guiana (*Dimorphandra Mora*); the Honey Locust of the United States (*Gleditschia triacanthos*); Kentucky Coffee-tree (*Gymnocladus Canadensis*); *Acacia melanoxylon* of Australia (considered equal to the best walnut); *Lysiloma Sabicu* of Cuba, etc. Dyes yielded by members of this family are Indigo, from *Indigofera tinctoria* of India; Red Sandalwood, or chips, from *Pterocarpus santalinus;* Brazil-wood, from *Cæsalpina echinata* of Brazil; and Logwood, from *Hæmatoxylon Campechianum* of Central America. The gums deserving mention are Gum-Tragacanth from *Astragalus tragacantha*, etc., of Asia; Gum-Kino from species of *Pterocarpus* of India and Africa; Balsam of Peru and Balsam of Tolu from species of *Myroxylon* of Central and South America; Gum-Copal from species of *Trachylobium* and *Hymenœa* of Africa and Madagascar; Copaiva Balsam from Brazilian species of *Copaifera;* and Gum-Arabic, or Acacia, from Asiatic and Africa species of *Acacia*. Medicinal products are the roots of *Glycyrrhiza glabra* (Liquorice) and the foliage of African and East Indian species of Cassia (*Senna*). The fibres of *Crotalaria* are strong, durable, and used for making cordage and coarse cloth. The Tamarind (*Tamarindus Indica*) grows in North Africa and East India. Very many representatives of the family are cultivated for ornament, as species of *Lupinus, Laburnum, Petalostemon, Robinia, Wistaria, Phaseolus, Lathyrus, Acacia, Mimosa,* etc. The Sensitive-plant is *Mimosa pudica*, from South America (Fig. 329).

13. **Anacardiaceæ.** The **Cashew** family. Trees and shrubs, with milky resinous juice, often poisonous. Flowers small, regular, pentandrous. Species chiefly tropical, numbering about four hundred and fifty. The fruit called Mango is produced by a species from India, *Mangifera Indica*, now cultivated in most warm countries. The Cashew-nut is the fruit of *Anacardium occidentale*, a tree of the West Indies; and the Pistachio-nut of *Pistacia vera*, a tree of Asia. The resinous substance Mastic is obtained from *Pistacia Lentiscus* from the Mediterranean region. Our common representatives of this family belong to the genus *Rhus*. The Sumac (*R. typhina* and *R. glabra*) contains much tannin in the leaves, which are, therefore, used in tanning. The Poison Ivy (*R. Toxicodendron*), the

Fig. 329. The Sensitive-plant.

Poison Sumac (*R. venenata*), both of the Eastern United States, and the Poison Oak (*R. diversiloba*) of California, are to most people quite poisonous.

14. **Sapindaceæ. Soapberry** family. Trees and shrubs, rarely herbs. Leaves mostly compound or lobed. The five to ten stamens inserted on a fleshy disk, sepals and petals four or five; six hundred or seven hundred widely distributed species. An important genus of this family is the *Acer*, or Maples; many of them are planted for ornament, as *Acer campestre* (European Maple), *A. Pseudo-Platanus* (Sycamore Maple), and *A. platanoides* (Norway Maple), all of Europe; and the Sugar-Maple (*A. saccharinum*), the Red Maple (*A. rubrum*), and Silver Maple (*A. dasycarpum*). The Box-Elder (*Negundo aceroides*) is also cultivated for ornament. The Sugar-Maple (*A. saccharinum*) yields an abundance of sweet, watery juice, or sap, from which Maple Sugar is made. The wood is hard, as is also that of the Large-leaved Maple (*A. macrophyllum*) and the Vine Maple (*A. circinatum*) of California and Oregon. The wood of the other species is soft and of much less value. That called Bird's-eye Maple is the distorted growth of *A. saccharinum*. Other important trees of this order are the Soapberry of Tropical America (*Sapindus Sapindaria*), the rind of whose hard globose seeds is saponaceous, and used by the natives as a substitute for soap; Horse-chestnut (*Æsculus Hippocastanum*), a valuable ornamental tree, in cultivation about three hundred years, obtained originally, perhaps, from the Himalayan range, etc. Other ornamental species are the Balloon-Vine (*Cardiospermum Halicacabum*), the Bladder-nut (*Staphylea trifolia*), the Buckeyes (*Æsculus*), etc.

15. **Ampelidæ.** The **Vine** family consists of about two hundred and fifty species of, mostly climbing, shrubs (Fig. 330); the majority found in the Tropics. Tendrils and flower-clusters opposite the leaves, the latter alternate. Stamens opposite the valvate petals. The most important genus is *Vitis*. The Vine of the Old World (*V. vinifera*) has been cultivated from time immemorial, and from its fruit (Grapes) wine is made by fermentation, and brandy by distillation. It has been carried from its native country (Southern Asia) to nearly all parts of the world, and under cultivation has developed numberless "varieties." In some countries (Southern Europe and the Pacific Coast States) raisins (or sun-dried Grapes) are made. Our important native species are the Northern Fox-Grape (*V. Labrusca*), from which most of our common varieties, as the Catawba, Concord, and Isabella, have arisen; the Summer Grape (*V. æstivalis*), from which have been obtained the Virginia Seedling, Herbemont, etc.; the River-bank Grape (*V. riparia*), which has produced the Taylor Bullit, Delaware, and Clinton; the Southern Fox-Grape (*V. vulpina*), from which was derived the Scuppernong and other varieties. The Virginia Creeper (*Ampelopsis quinquefolia*) is a native climber, unsurpassed for

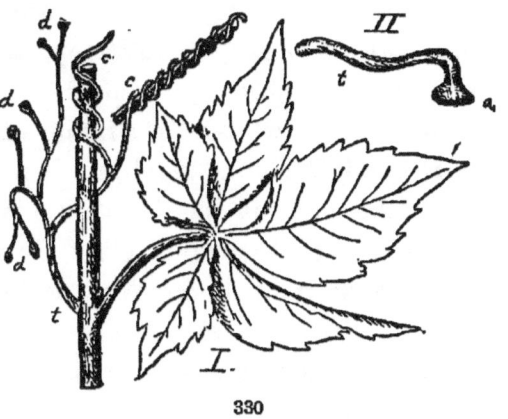

Fig. 330. The Virginia Creeper (*Ampelopsis quinquefolia*); *t*, tendril; *d*, disk; *c*, coil.

ornamental purposes, and often seen in cultivation. Species of *Vitis*, from Java and Sumatra, are to be seen in conservatories.

16. **Burseraceæ.** The **Myrrh** family. Trees and shrubs, with resinous or oily secretion. Species one hundred and forty-five, mostly tropical. Several important dyes are furnished by members of this group. Myrrh is yielded by two small Arabian trees, *Balsamodendron Myrrha* and *B. Katif.* Bdellium is produced by an African species, *Bd. Africanum.* Olibanum is from *Boswellia thurifera*, a tree of Central India. Gum Elemi is obtained from several trees of the West Indies and South America (*Amyris Elaphrium*, etc). A species of Guiana (*Icica altisonia*) attains a height of one hundred feet and a diameter of four or five feet, and produces a wood that is light, and much used in making household furniture.

17. **Rutaceæ.** The **Rue** family is a group of about six hundred and fifty shrubs and trees (rarely herbs), found in tropical and temperate regions. Leaves with pellucid glands, containing a pungent or bitter-aromatic acrid oil. The common Rue (*Ruta graveolens*) was cultivated by the ancients on account of its reputed medicinal qualities, and is still found in gardens cultivated as a domestic medicine. It is a native of Southern Europe and Western Asia. A number of valuable fruits are furnished by the genus *Citrus*, as the Sweet Orange (*C. aurantium*, native of India), the Lemon (*C. limonum*, went from Northern India to Europe during the Crusades), the Citron (*C. medica*), the Lime (*C. Limetta*), the Shaddock (*C. decumana*), the Seville, or Bitter Orange (*C. Bigardia*), etc. The wood of the Orange is hard, and used for inlaying. The medicinal Angustura Bark is from *Galipea cusparia*,

a large tree in Guiaua and Brazil. The bark of our native Prickly Ash (*Zanthoxylum Americanum*) is used medicinally. A few species are cultivated for ornament, as *Dictamnus* (Fig. 331), etc.

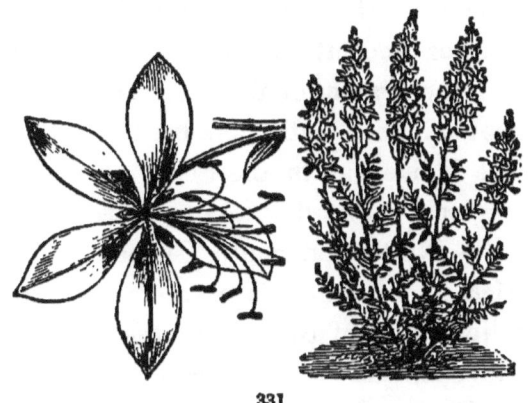

18. **Geraniaceæ.** The **Geranium** family consists mostly of herbs, seven hundred and fifty species, found in the temperate and hot tropical regions, many of which are ornamental. The Garden Balsam, or Touch-me-not (*Impatiens Balsamina* of India), has been cultivated for nearly three hundred years. Many exotic species (from South Africa, etc.) of *Oxalis* are found in cultivation. The South American genus *Tropæolum* furnishes the Nasturtion (*T. magus*); also edible tuberous roots (from *T. tuberosum*), used instead of Potatoes in Peru. Most of our fine cultivated "Geraniums" belong to the South African genus *Pelargonium*. The Alfilaria of California (*Erodium cicutarium*) is said to be a nutritious forage plant.

19. **Linaceæ.** The **Flax** family. Species one hundred and thirty-five, widely distributed. Herbs, shrubs, and a few trees, with single sessile leaves, and regular,

Fig. 331. Dictamnus, an ornamental species.

symmetrical, hypogynous flowers. "The most important plant of the order, and one of the most important in the vegetable kingdom, is the Flax (*Linum usitatissimum*), cultivated from time immemorial for its fibres, called linen, (the bast fibres of the cortical part of the stem). The mummy-cloth of ancient Egypt was composed of Flax fibres; and in the remains of the Lake Dwellers in Switzerland fragments of linen-cloth have been found. The plant appears to be indigenous in the South of Europe, as well as in the regions eastward in Asia; it is now cultivated throughout the North and South Temperate Zones. The seeds are rich in oil, which is extracted by pressure, producing the linseed-oil of commerce; the compressed refuse is called oil-cake, and is much used as food for cattle. *Erythoxylon Coca*, a South American shrub, is cultivated in Bolivia and New Granada for its stimulating leaves, which are chewed like tobacco."

20. **Tiliaceæ.** The three hundred and thirty species of the **Linden** family are, in the main, tropical trees and shrubs. They have mucilaginous properties, fibrous bark, valvate sepals, imbricated petals, and usually polyadelphous stamens. Here belongs the Jute-plant (*Corchorus capsularis*), whose fibre is extensively used in making gunny-bags, coarse carpets, etc. At present, finer fabrics are being made from it. The wood of the Lime, or Linden-tree (*T. Europæa* of Europe, and *T. Americana* of the United States), is light and white, much used in carving, in the manufacture of musical instruments, etc. Both species are cultivated in parks.

21. **Sterculiaceæ.** A tropical family of two hundred and fifty species, important as including the Chocolate-tree of Tropical America (*Theobroma Cacao*). This small tree

bears ribbed fruits, each containing forty or fifty oily seeds. The latter are ground, after being roasted, then made into a paste, flavored with vanilla, etc., and this constitutes the chocolate and cocoa of commerce.

22. **Malvaceæ. Mallow** family. Herbs, shrubs, and trees, with simple leaves, regular flowers, convolute petals, and monadelphous stamens (Fig. 332). The majority of the seven hundred species are found in the Tropics. The Cotton-plant (*Gossypium herbaceum*, and other species) produces a fibre (hairs covering the seeds) that is of immense importance in the manufacture of cloth, etc. The Cotton-plant was cultivated many centuries before the Christian Era. It is now extensively grown in the United States, West Indies, Brazil, Egypt, and India. The Silk-trees of the East and West Indies (*Bombax*) produce a similar fibre, fine and silky, not suitable for weaving, but for stuffing cushions, etc. Many species (of *Sida, Hibiscus*, etc.) furnish valuable bast. Valuable fruits are furnished by species of *Durio* in the Malay Archipelago, and of *Matisia* in New Granada; they are eaten by the inhabitants of those countries. The Okra, or Gumbo, of Tropical America (*Hibiscus esculentus*), is cultivated in the Southern States for its mucilaginous, edible pods. The Cork-wood of Jamaica (*Ochroma Lagopus*) is so soft and compressible that it is used as a substitute for cork. "The Baobab, or Monkey-bread, called also Sour-gourd (*Adansonia digitata*), is a native of Tropical Africa, extending from east to west. It is a remarkable

Fig. 332. Flower of the common Mallow (*Malva rotundifolia*), showing the monadelphous stamens; *in*, involucel; *ca*, calyx; *cor*, corolla; *an*, anthers; *st*, stigmas; *fil. mon*, the united filaments.

tree, growing to the height of forty feet; but its girth is entirely out of proportion to its height, some trees being thirty feet in diameter, becoming contracted towards the top. Humboldt speaks of it as the "oldest organic monument of our planet;" and Adanson, a botanical traveler, in 1794, made a calculation that one of these trees, thirty feet in diameter, must have been at least five thousand one hundred and fifty years old. The wood is soft, and the negroes cut out chambers in the trees, which they use as places of interment. It produces a large, oblong, woody, indehiscent, capsular fruit, from eight to twelve inches, or more, long, shaped like a gourd, covered with a velvety down, and containing numerous seeds, the size of large peas, imbedded in pulp, which ultimately becomes dry and of a corky nature. It forms a great part of the food of the natives. Excellent ropes are made of the bark. As an example of the slow growth of this plant, one at Kew, though more than eighty years of age, was only four and a half feet high, but with the characteristic swollen, gouty base, six to seven inches in diameter." Several ornamental plants, as Mallows (*Malva*), Rose Mallow (*Hibiscus*), Hollyhock (*Althœa*), *Callirrhoë*, etc., belong to this family.

23. **Ternstrœmiaceæ.** The **Camellia** family comprises two hundred and sixty, mostly tropical, trees and shrubs. A common representative in conservatories is *Camellia Japonica* from China and Japan. The most important member of the family is the Tea-tree (*Thea Chinensis*), cultivated by the Chinese for ages. It is an evergreen, eight to fifteen feet high, and its leaves, picked, dried, pressed, rolled, etc., constitute the tea of commerce.

24. **Caryophyllaceæ.** The **Pink** family. Mostly

herbs, with opposite, entire leaves, and swollen joints; symmetrical flowers, four or five parted, with or without petals. Species eight hundred, widely distributed. It is a family of little economic importance; it includes many of our weeds, notably the Corn-cockle (*Lychnis Githago*),

which perceptibly injures the flour when abundant in the wheat. Among the ornamental members may be mentioned the Carnations and Clove Pinks (*Dianthus*), Mullein Pink (*Lychnis*), Catchfly (*Silene*), Agrostemma (Fig. 333), etc.

25. **Violaceæ.** The Violet family comprises two hundred and forty herbs and shrubs, with a one-spurred corolla; many of them are ornamental. The Violets (genus *Viola*) includes about one-half the species of the whole family. The Sweet Violet (*V. odorata*) and Pansy (*V. tricolor*) are universally admired, and innumerable "varieties" have appeared under cultivation.

26. **Cruciferæ.** The large Mustard family numbers

Fig. 333. A cultivated Agrostemma.

about twelve hundred species, mostly herbs, with characteristic, cruciform flowers, and tetradynamous stamens (Fig. 334). *Brassica oleracea*, originally a wild European coast plant, has been cultivated for a long time, and given rise to the "varieties" called Cauliflower (Fig. 335), Kale, Brussels-sprouts, Cabbage, and Kohl-Rabi (Fig. 336). The various kinds of Turnips, Colza, and Rape have descended from *Brassica campestris* of Europe. The Radish (*Raphanus sativus*) is a native of China. The Horseradish (*Nasturtium Armoracia*) has also been long cultivated for its roots, which are used as a condiment. White Mustard (*Brassica alba*) and Black Mustard (*B. nigra*), natives of Europe, are in common use (ground seeds) as a condiment. The commonest cultivated representatives of the family are Wall-flower (*Cheiranthus*), Stock (*Matthiola*), Rocket (*Hesperis*), Candy-tuft (*Iberis*), Honesty (*Lunaria*), Sweet Alyssum, etc. Among the weeds are Shepherd's-Purse (*Capsella Bursa-pastoris*), Peppergrass (*Lepidium*), False

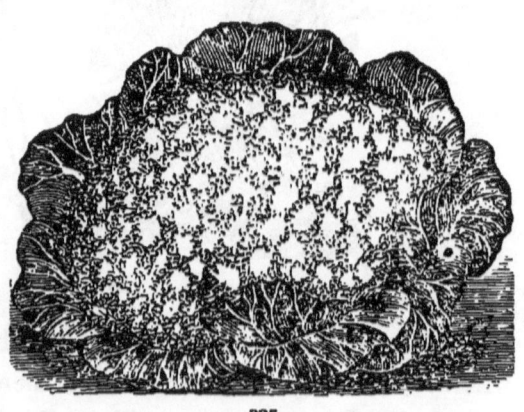

Fig. 334. Tetradynamous stamens; *a a*, long stamens; *b b*, short stamens. Fig. 335. Cauliflower. Fig. 336. Kohl-Rabi.

Flax (Camelina), etc. "The curious plant called the Rose of Jericho" (*Anastatica hierochuntica*), often sold as a curiosity, is a small annual, native of Arabia, Egypt, and Syria. The mature plant after ripening its seeds contract into a rounded mass, and is uprooted and blown about by the winds; when, however, the dry and dead plant is moistened it expands, closing again when dry. On this account it is called the Resurrection-plant.

27. **Papaveraceæ.** The Poppy family is a small group (sixty species) of herbs, and a few low shrubs, found mostly in the Temperate Zone. They have a milky juice, containing a narcotic principle, regular flowers, and indefinite stamens. The Opium Poppy (*Papaver somniferum*) is the most important representative;  it grows in the Old World, and from the green capsules the milky juice is obtained and dried. This forms the crude opium of commerce. The red juice of the Bloodroot of the United States (*Sanguinaria Canadensis*) is similar in its properties to opium. The family furnishes a few of our common ornamental plants, as the Poppies and *Argemone* of Mexico, and *Eschscholtzia* of California (Fig. 337).

28. **Sarraceniaceæ. Pitcher Plants.** This very

Fig. 337. Eschscholtzia.

small family of ten species, nine of which are indigenous in the United States, have peculiar radical leaves, which are tubular, or more or less pitcher-like in shape (Fig. 338). A common example is the Pitcher-plant (*Sarracenia purpurea*), found in peat-bogs and cranberry marshes in the Northern United States. The Pitchers or leaves are partially filled with water, in which insects often fall and from which they cannot readily, or at all, escape, because the inner wall is lined with stiff hairs, pointing downwards. After maceration this animal food is undoubtedly absorbed by the plant, and partially nourishes it.

29. **Nymphæaceæ.** The **Water-Lily** family is also small, containing thirty-five aquatic species, widely distributed. The leaves are generally peltate and floating, and the flowers solitary. The Yellow Water-Lily (*Nelumbium luteum*) and the White Water-Lilies (*Nymphæa*

odorata and *N. tuberosa*) are attractive wild species (Fig. 339), but insignificant in size as compared with the Vic-

Fig. 338. Leaf of the Pitcher-plant (*Sarracenia purpurea*). Fig. 339. The White Water Lily (*Nymphæa*).

toria Lily of the Amazon Valley (*Victoria regia*); the leaves of this plant are peltate, circular in outline, and six feet or more in diameter; the slender petioles are sometimes ten feet long; the flowers resemble those of the White Water-Lily, yet changing from pure white to a pink color when opening the second time, and measure eight to twelve inches in diameter.

30. **Anonaceæ.** The **Custard-Apple** family. Trees and shrubs, mostly tropical; calyx of three sepals; corolla of six petals in two rows; stamens many. The Custard-Apple (*Anona reticulata*), "considered by some people as one of the finest fruits in the world;" the Cherimoya (*A. Cherimolia*), Soursop (*A. squamosa*), cultivated in the West Indies and Tropical America, are the most important representatives of the group. The dry, aromatic carpels of *Xylopia aromatica* constitutes the Guinea Pepper, used as pepper. A small tree of Guiana, *Duguetia quitarensis*, furnishes the tough, elastic Lance-wood. The common Papaw of the United States (*Asimina triloba*) is a small tree, which produces an edible, though not valued, fruit.

31. **Magnoliaceæ.** The **Magnolia** family comprises seventy trees and shrubs belonging to the sub-tropical regions of Asia and America. The "pistils are many, mostly packed together, and covering the prolonged receptacle (Fig. 340), cohering with each other, and in fruit forming a sort of fleshy or dry cone." Fine ornamental, as well as timber, trees belong to the genus *Magnolia*, seven species of which grow in the Southern States. One species, the Cucumber-tree (*M. acuminata*), extends as far north as

Fig. 340. The elongated torus of the Tulip-tree flower (*Liriodendron Tulipifera*).

the great lakes; its wood is white, and prized for pump logs, wooden bowls, and a variety of other purposes. Other species of the genus, as the Umbrella-trees (*M. Umbrella, M. macrophylla*), Sweet Bay (*M. glauca*), etc., are planted for ornament wherever they can endure the winters. The Tulip-tree, or Yellow Poplar (*Liriodendron Tulipifera*), is a grand forest tree of the Eastern United States, attaining at times a height of one hundred and forty feet, and a diameter of nine feet; it furnishes a light, yellowish wood, used very extensively in cabinet-making, and a variety of other purposes. It is much prized as an ornamental tree for parks, or where sufficient space permits it to assume a beautiful and regularly conical form; the tulip-like flower, as well as the foliage, is very handsome.

32. **Ranunculaceæ.** The **Crowfoot** family. Herbs, rarely shrubs. Leaves generally alternate or radical. Sepals and petals each five; stamens many, pistils generally many, not united. Species about five hundred, many of which were formerly considered medicinal, yet but few are used to-day. Wolfsbane, called also Monkshood (*Aconitum Napellus*), of Europe furnishes the drug Aconite. The natives of India poison their arrows with a virulent poison obtained from *A. ferox*. From the Black, Fœtid, and Green Hellebores (*Helleborus niger, fœtidus,* and *viridis*) drastic and poisonous drugs are obtained. Many plants of this family are

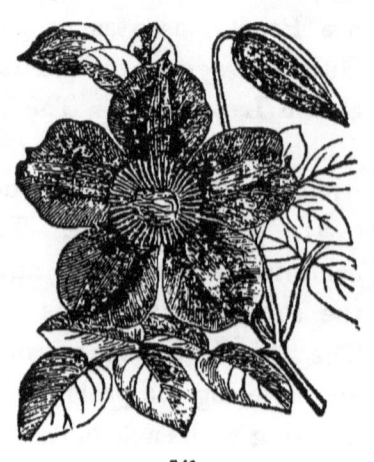

Fig. 341. *Clematis Jackmanni.*

ornamental, as species of Wind-flower (*Anemone*), Liverwort (*Hepatica*), Pheasant's-eye (*Adonis*), Columbine (*Aquilegia*), Virgin's-Bower (*Clematis*), Larkspur (*Delphinium*), Peony (*Pæonia*), Buttercup (*Ranunculus*), *Clematis* (Fig. 341), etc.

GEOGRAPHICAL DISTRIBUTION.

195. While a few species are cosmopolitan, or to be found in nearly all parts of the world, the great majority of plants are limited to areas of lesser or greater extent. This distribution of species, or, as it called, **Geogaphical Distribution**, is determined by several causes, prominent among which are Temperature, Altitude, Moisture, Soil, etc. This subject engaged the attention of Linnæus, who said: "The dynasty of the Palms reigns in the warm regions of the globe; the Tropical Zones are inhabited by whole races of trees and shrubs; a rich crown of plants surrounds the plains of Southern Europe; armies of green *Gramineæ* occupy Holland and Denmark; numerous tribes of Mosses are contained in Sweden; but the brownish-colored Algæ and the white-gray Lichens alone vegetate in cold, frozen Lapland, the most remote habitable spot of the earth; the last of the vegetables alone live on the confines of the earth."

196. That eminent scientist and traveler, Von Humboldt, characterized botanical regions as follows:

Region of	*Corresponds to*	*Contains also*
PALMS AND BANANAS	EQUATORIAL ZONE	Arborescent Grasses, Orchids, Coffee-tree, Ginger, Cinnamon, Nutmeg, Mahogany, Logwood, Ebony, Baobab, Bread-Fruit, Pine-Apple, etc.
GRAPES AND FIGS	TROPICAL ZONE	Pepper, *Convolvulaceæ*, Yam.

Region of	Corresponds to	Contains also
MYRTLES AND LAURELS	SUB-TROPICAL ZONE	Euphorbias, Cacti, Magnolias, Heaths, Zinnia, Cycas, Timber Trees, and a few Palms.
EVERGREEN TREES	WARM TEMPERATE	Fig, Orange, Pomegranate, Vine, Cistus, Smilax, etc.
DECIDUOUS TREES	COLD TEMPERATE	Oaks, Ash, Beech, Chestnut, Walnut, *Coniferæ*.
PINES	SUB-ARCTIC	*Coniferæ*, Willow, Birch, Poplar.
RHODODENDRONS	ARCTIC ZONE	Rhododendron, Azaleas, Andromeda, Pinus sylvestris, Abies excelsa, Dwarfed Willow, Alder, and Birch, many Lichens.
ALPINE PLANTS	POLAR ZONE	*Saxifraga*, Drias, Juncus. No trees, no shrubs, nor cultivable esculent plants.

197. Later study of the Floras of the different countries has resulted in the establishment of Botanical Provinces, based on the principle that each should "contain one-half the species and one-fourth the genera of some one or more natural families, and individual orders be peculiar to or reach their maximum in the region." In accordance with this, the following partial list may be indicated:

1. All the land within the Polar Circle and the two continents down to the zone of trees: Its characteristic plants are the **Saxifrages** and **Mosses**. There are also many *Gentianaceæ, Carophyllaceæ, Cyperaceæ*, and *Salicaceæ*.

2. Europe and Asia, down to the Pyrenees, Alps, Balkan, Caucasus, and Altai mountains: The **Umbelliferæ** and **Cruciferæ** characterize this province. Besides these the *Compositæ, Ranunculaceæ, Amentaceæ, Carices*, and *Fungi* are largely represented.

3. Mediterranean region: The **Labiatæ** and **Caryophyllaceæ** here abound in great numbers. Rice, Cotton, Millet, Almond, etc., are cultivated.

4. Eastern portion of North America: The characteristic plants of this province are the **Asters** and **Solidagos**. It is also remarkable for the paucity of *Umbelliferæ* and *Cruciferæ*, as compared with corresponding regions in the Eastern Hemisphere, and the absence of *Heaths*. Among the cultivated plants, Maize holds a prominent place. Some of the valuable timber trees are the Oaks, Hickories, Maples, Pines, Hemlock, Spruce, etc.

5. Western North America down to 36° North Latitude: It is characterized by the grandeur of its **Timber Trees**; as the *Sequoia* and other *Coniferæ*, among which may be mentioned *Abies balsamea, A. grandis, A. alba, A. Canadensis, A. Douglasii,* and *Pinus ponderosa, P. Lambertiana.* It has very brilliant flowers, as the *Eschscholtzia, Clarkia, Nemophila,* etc.

6. Southern region of North America: It is the region of **Magnolias**; also characterized by the paucity of *Labiatæ* and *Caryophyllaceæ*. In it are found the Tulip-tree, the Pitch Pine, Cacti, Venus's Fly-trap, *Nelumbium luteum, Tillandsia usneoides,* etc.

7. Warm temperate region of Eastern Asia (including Japan), from the thirtieth parallel northward: Its characteristic groups are the **Ternstrœmiaceæ** and **Celastraceæ**. In this province are also found the Tea-plant (*Camellia chinensis*), *Citrus, Lonicera,* and other *Caprifoliaceæ,* etc.

8. India, Ceylon, and Southeastern Asia: The **Zinziberaceæ** are characteristic plants. There are, besides, many *Leguminosæ, Cucurbitaceæ,* and *Tiliaceæ.* Other important plants are the Cinnamon, Clove, Indigo, Cotton, Pepper, Teak, Bamboo, etc.

9. Tropical Africa: The families having most repre-

sentatives are **Leguminosæ, Rubiaceæ,** and **Cyperaceæ.** The *Elæis guineënsis,* Tallow-tree, Cotton, Sugar-Cane, Ginger, Yams, Bananas, Cocoa-nuts, Papaws, Oranges, and Pine-Apples also grow in this region.

10. Central America, including Mexico and the northern part of South America: **Cacti** and **Piperaceæ** predominate. There are many Ferns and Orchids; also *Compositæ, Victoria regia,* Palms, Pine-Apple, Vanilla, Chocolate, Tobacco, Aloe, Logwood, Mahogany, *Strychnos toxicaria,* etc.

11. Basin of Amazon and Upper Parana: This is the region of **Palms** and **Melastomaceæ.** There are also Tree-Ferns, Reeds, Grasses, parasitic *Orchidaceæ, Tillandsias, Passifloras, Siphonia elastica,* and many other plants.

12. Extra-Tropical America southward: Here are found many arborescent **Compositæ;** also *Protea, Polygala, Oxalis, Aracauria,* etc., with numerous species.

13. Australia: The characteristic groups of this region are the **Eucalypti** and the **Epacridaceæ** (Ericaceæ). There are also many *Proteaceæ* and Banksias.

FOSSIL BOTANY.

198. In the strata of rocks which form the crust of the earth remains of plants, or the imprint of their leaves, stems, etc., are found. These are called **Fossil Plants.** In the uppermost layers, or those most recently formed, the plants are found to be very nearly like those now living on the earth. Often the very same species that now lives, and in other cases very nearly related species, are met with. But the further we descend, or, in other words, the older the rocks which we examine, the more unlike do the plants gradually become. When we reach the strata

or layers which were the first in order in the formation of the present crust of the earth, but few traces of plants are discernable. The interpretation of these facts is clear, when we remember that geology teaches that our earth was, at a very remote period of time, a molten mass or incandescent globe, revolving around the sun as now; in the course of time, by the gradual loss of a portion of heat, a superficial crust was formed, upon which, as soon as conditions were favorable, appeared first plants, and then animals.

199. With continued loss of heat from the earth, and other climatal changes not easily explained, the kinds of plants and animals also gradually but very slowly changed, and after a great lapse of time these were seen to be replaced by others suited to the changed environment; and such continuous modification has proceeded to this day. But the forces now operating in producing changes of the present surface of the earth were likewise acting—and, of course, with similar results—during all this immense period of time. Therefore, denudation of elevated portions of the earth's surface, and deposition of the transported material, caused a succession of layers of mud to be formed. Occasionally remains of plants and animals then living, especially the harder parts in their structure, became encased in this mud. These layers of mud afterwards became converted into rock, in the layers of which the remains of plants and animals, or their imprints (fossils), are contained, and afford to day the record—as yet but partially examined—whose reading gives the past or geological history of our earth. For convenience of study, this period of developement is divided into **Times**, called (beginning with the earliest) **Archæan** (Gr. *archein*, to

be first); **Palæozoic** (Gr. *palaios*, ancient; *zoa*, life), including the Silurian, Devonian, and Carboniferous Ages; **Mesozoic** (Gr. *mesos*, middle), including the Reptilian Age; and **Cenozoic** (Gr. *kainos*, recent), including the Mammalian Age and the Age of Man.

200. No fossil plants have as yet been found in the **Archæan** rocks, though there is reason to believe that a Flora existed at that time. There are extensive deposits of iron-ore, and the presence of organic matter is considered indispensable to the formation of Ferric Oxide and Ferrous Carbonate, which, according to Le Conte, takes place thus: The Peroxide of Iron (Ferric Oxide), which is quite generally distributed through the soil, is insoluble; but in contact with organic matter becomes deoxidized and reduced to Protoxide (Ferrous Oxide), which unites with Carbonic Dioxide (one of the products of the decomposition of organic matter), and forms Carbonate of Iron. This Ferrous Carbonate is soluble in the water which contains an excess of Carbonic Dioxide, and is, therefore, gradually washed out of the soil, and in solution appears at the surface again at springs, etc. Here the Carbonic Dioxide is replaced by Oxygen, and the iron is deposited in its original form of Ferric Oxide. Or if the iron-waters accumulate, and a deposit is made in the presence of the reducing agent (organic matter), the Ferrous Carbonate is not reoxidized, but deposited in that form. The other proof of an Archæan Flora is the occurrence of beds of Graphite, for "graphite is only the extreme term of the metamorphism of coal."

201. In the **Silurian Age** the lower forms of animals were very abundant; fully ten thousand fossil species have already been described; this is conclusive proof that plants

FOSSIL BOTANY. 237

must have existed at this time in great quantity; probably, too, in great variety. For animals depend on the vegetable kingdom for their subsistence, each animal consuming many times its own weight of vegetable food. That fossil animals are in every age found more abundantly than fossil plants is not to be taken as proof that there were fewer of the latter; it must be borne in mind that the hard parts of animals are much less destructable than any vegetable tissue, and are, therefore, oftener preserved in the fossil state. The plants which have up to the present time been found and described are a number of cellular (*marine* Algæ) and a few vascular cryptogams. Many of them were marine plants, apparently related to the genus Fucus (division *Oosporeæ*); a branching form of the Lower Silurian has received the generic name of *Buthotrephis* (Fig. 342). A representative of the division *Carposporeæ*, a plant of the genus *Corallina*, has been found in this age. In the Upper Silurian, besides many marine species, there were a number of true Land-plants, among which may be mentioned the genus *Psilophyton*, which is a representative of the Club-Mosses or Lycopods (class *Licopodiaceæ*; division *Pteridophyta*).

202. A very marked advance is exhibited in the vegetation of the **Devonian Age.** The fucoidal plants

Fig. 342. *Buthotrephis succulens* (Silurian Age).

of the Silurian continued into this age, but they were accompanied with a multitude of vascular cryptogams, and even some Phænogams (*Gymnosperms*). For the first time there was a true forest vegetation; and the great size and number of the plants thus early foreshadowed the remarkable development which took place in the next age. The groups then existing were as follows:

1. The Equisetinæ were represented by *Calamites* and *Asterophyllites* (Fig. 343). The *Calamites* had long, slender, tapering, and jointed stems, sometimes two feet in diameter, and thirty feet high. The surface was finely striated, or fluted, and at all the joints were situated whorls of scale-like or thread-like leaves. They were, except as regards size, like our living *Equiseta*, which grow generally less than three feet high and no thicker than the finger. The *Asterophyllites* were herbaceous, flexible species, with leaves arranged in whorls at the joints, as the name indicates.

2. The Ferns were represented by such genera as *Cyclopteris* and *Neuropteris*. In these the leaflets or pinnæ have no midrib.

3. The Lycopods were *Psilophyton*, already introduced in the Upper Silurian, *Lepidodendron* and *Sigillaria*. The *Lepidodendra* were gigantic plants, the surface of whose trunks and branches were regularly marked in rhomboidal patterns, or quincuncially, representing the leaf arrangement (Fig. 345); the branches were clothed with squamous,

Fig. 343. *Asterophyllites latifolia* (Devonian Age).

spinous or acicular leaves, and terminated by scale-cones, which bore spores like the Club-Mosses. The *Sigillariæ* were likewise arboreous, but their trunks exhibit longitudinal ribbing or fluting, and vertical rows of seal-like impressions representing the leaf arrangement; they were but little, if at all, branched, and clothed with numerous long, tapering leaves.

4. The Conifers were represented by the genus *Protaxites*, allied to the Yew (*Taxus*).

203. The Flora of the **Carboniferous Age**, or the vegetation of the Coal-measures, is of peculiar interest, both because of its great abundance and because of its diversity of forms. About one-fourth of all known fossil plants are from the Coal-measures. There were many marine plants, among which may be mentioned the curious Spiral-plant, or *Spirophyton*. Fungi existed at that time. But the great majority of plants may be referred to the groups Equisetinæ, Filices, Lycopodinæ, and Coniferæ.

1. **Equisetinæ.** Besides plants of the genus *Calamites*, which has already been described, there were representatives of other closely-related genera, as *Asterophyllites*, *Sphenophyllum*, etc., all of which became extinct in the last period of the Carboniferous Age.

2. The **Ferns** were abundantly represented—nearly one-half of all the plants of the Coal-measures belong to this order. Some of them had creeping stems like our common Ferns, and others were Tree-Ferns, such as are to-day found growing only in warm latitudes. A Tree-Fern of the Coal-measures, called *Megaphyton*, had its large fronds in two vertical ranks; other common genera were *Cyclopteris*, *Odontopteris* (Fig 344), *Neuropteris*, etc., whose leaflets, or pinnæ, were destitute of a midrib; *Sphenopteris*, *Hymenophyllites*, etc., whose pinnæ had a midrib discern-

240 SYSTEMATIC BOTANY.

able only towards the base, and from which the veins did not branch; *Alethopteris, Pecopteris, Asplenites,* etc., whose pinnæ presented a distinct midrib, from which the nerves branched more or less obliquely.

3. The **Lycopods** were represented by huge *Lepidodendra* (Fig. 345), and other nearly-related genera, as well as by gigantic *Sigillariæ*. The roots of these plants are often found fossil, and are distinguished by scattered, rounded depressions, or elevations. These were formerly believed to be leaf-scars on stems and branches; and the genus *Stigmaria* was formed to include them. They are yet designated by this name, but they have in many cases been found attached as roots to the *Lepidodendra* and *Sigillariæ*. Fruits also have been

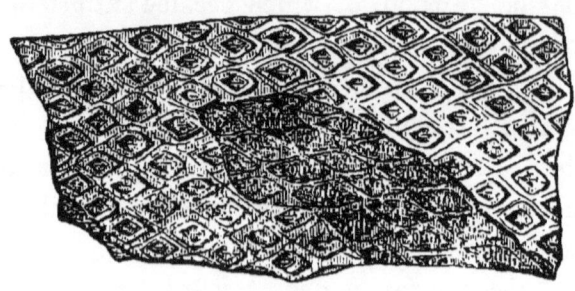

found, generally isolated, but they are believed to be the fruits of the preceding plants.

Fig. 344. *Odontopteris Wortheni* (Carboniferous Age). Fig. 345. *Lepidodendron diplotegioides* (Carboniferous Age).

4. Fossil **Conifers** are found in the form of stumps, logs, leaves, and fruits. They were very unlike the ordinary Conifers of temperate climates. They resembled more or less the tropical *Araucaria*, the broad-leaved Chinese *Salisburia* (Ginko), or the curious two-leaved African *Welwitschia*. A very interesting genus is that of *Cordaites*. It had a straight trunk, sometimes sixty to seventy feet long, and was clothed with long, strap-shaped leaves.

204. In the early part of the **Reptilian Age** (during the Triassic and Jurassic Periods) the Flora differed from the preceding age mainly in the enormous development of the Gymnosperms. These,—the *Cycads* (appearing now for the first time) and *Conifers*,—together with the *Tree-Ferns*, constituted the forest vegetation. There were also new species of Ferns and Equiseta. Diatoms and Desmids (division *Zygosporeæ*) were abundant. But it is in the latter part of this age (during the *Cretaceous Period*) that the greatest change took place. The **Angiosperms** for the first time make their appearance, and field and forest began to assume a somewhat modern aspect. Such modern genera as the Oaks, Maples, Willows, Sassafras (Fig. 346), Dog-wood, Hickory, Beech, Poplar, Liriodendron, Walnut, Sycamore, Laurel, etc., were each represented by one or more species. The families to which the Angiosperms belonged are as follows:

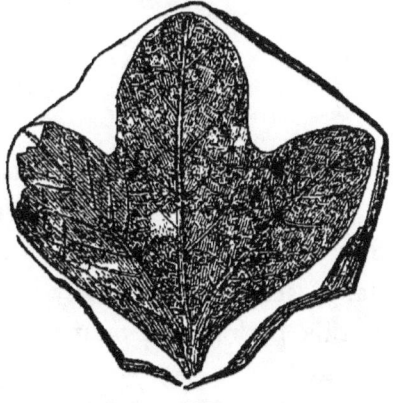

Fig. 346. *Sassafras araliopsis* (Reptilian Age).

16

1. **Monocotyledones.**—Gramineæ, Cyperaceæ, Liliaceæ, Naiadaceæ, Scitamineæ, Dioscoreaceæ, and Palmaceæ.

2. **Dicotyledones.**—Salicaceæ, Cupuliferæ, Lauraceæ, Urticaceæ, Ericaceæ, Ebenaceæ, Platanaceæ, Araliaceæ, Rosaceæ, Sapotaceæ, and Magnoliaceæ.

205. In the **Mammalian Age,** which includes the Tertiary and Quaternary Periods, the vegetation is decidedly more modern than in the preceding. In the Tertiary Period nearly all the *genera* of the Palms, Grasses, and Dicotyledones (Fig. 347) were the same as now, though most of the species are extinct. The Diatoms, too, existed in great abundance; and immense deposits, consisting wholly of their silicious shells or valves (frustules), are found in the Tertiary Period. The celebrated Bohemian deposit in Europe is fourteen feet thick, and Ehrenberg estimated that every cubic inch of the material contains forty billion shells. The Richmond deposit in Virginia is thirty feet thick, and many miles in extent. The Mosses (*Bryophyta*) and the *Protophyta* very likely existed before this time, but they have not been found in rocks lower than the Tertiary. In the Quaternary Period the plants were almost wholly identical with those now living. In this period, too, man is supposed to have appeared on the earth.

Fig. 347. *Platanus aceroides* (Manhattan Age).

206. The **Age of Man,** or the present time, exhibits a vegetation of a higher type than the preceding ages, and the species are exceedingly numerous. All countries are

not yet fully explored, and there is no means, therefore, of knowing the number of species of plants which exist. Even in countries long known new species, especially of the lower plants, are constantly being found. In 1824 the total number of species was estimated to be over seventy thousand; in 1841, over seventy-eight thousand; and in 1845, over ninety-two thousand; now the estimates are as high as one hundred and fifty thousand to two hundred thousand, or over. The affinities of the different groups—whose accuracy is at best, of course, only approximate—is shown in the following diagram (taken, by permission, from Bessey's Botany):

PART IV.

ECONOMIC BOTANY.

THE GUMS.

207. The **Gums** are usually structureless and homogeneous vegetable products, or exudations from certain trees, which arise mainly by a metamorphosis of tissue, and seldom by a chemical change of the starch contained in the cells. But few vegetable products occur so commonly as the gums. They are soluble (or soften) in water, and insoluble in alcohol. The color may be yellowish, yellow, brownish, or reddish, but seldom white or black. The powder is white. The gums are seldom pure, more or less of organic impurities always being present. They are, according to their chemical composition, carbo-hydrates, that is, they contain carbon, hydrogen, and oxygen, but no nitrogen; they are of little or no dietetic value. The important constituents are *Arabin, Cerasin,* and *Bassorin.* They are often mixed with resins, and are then resinous gums. The true gums of most importance are Gum-Arabic, Gum-Senegal and Gum-Tragacanth.

208. Gum-Arabic, called also Gum-Acacia, is obtained from several species of *Acacia,* a genus belonging to the Pulse family (*Leguminosæ*). The plants are generally small, spiny trees, or shrubs, growing in the deserts of Africa, Arabia, and other countries, sometimes forming vast forests. It was for a long time supposed that the species *A. vera* and *A. arabica* furnished nearly all the gums of commerce, but it has lately been determined that *A. verek* yields the largest quantity. That coming from Senegambia is also furnished by this species. The gums from different countries usually have different names, as Gum-Arabic, Cape Gum, Gum-Senegal, Australian Gum, etc., and differ much, too, in quality. As found in commerce, the pieces are generally roundish, with an irregular surface, which, upon fracture, is vitreous in appearance. They may be transparent or cloudy, and are often more or less colored. All the varieties, except the Cape Gum, are readily and completely soluble in both hot and cold water. The Cape Gum is not completely so. They are easily pulverized, and yield a white powder—even the impure and colored masses. The latter, therefore, are generally used for the powdered gum found in the shops. The several kinds of Gum-Acacia are heavier than water; their specific gravity varying from 1.3 to 1.6. Upon analysis they are found to contain, besides the constituents mentioned above, about twelve to seventeen per cent. of water, a small quantity of sugar, resin, and tannin. They yield about three per cent. of ash, which consists largely of calcic carbonate. Some kinds, for example, the Gum-Arabic, were used in remote antiquity. In medicine it is employed on account of its demulcent property. As a mucilage its use is very general, but the largest quantity is consumed in stiffening fabrics, and producing a glazed surface upon them. It is often added to fluids to increase their density, so that they will hold in suspension pigments, or other substances contained in them. A common example of the kind is presented in writing-ink.

209. **Feronia Gum**, or *East India Gum*, is from *Feronia elephantum*, a plant belonging to the Orange tribe

(*Aurantiæ*), in the order *Rutaceæ*. It is softer than Gum-Arabic, and entirely soluble in water. The pieces are large and glistening, and have an irregular surface. They are mostly transparent, sometimes dark and yellow, and full of minute clefts. The pieces are sometimes iridescent. It contains more than twelve per cent. of water, and five of ash. It is said to be the best gum for the preparation of water-colors. It finds the same uses as Gum-Arabic.

210. **Gum-Tragacanth** is a tasteless and odorless exudation from several shrubby plants belonging to the genus *Astragalus*, of the Pulse or Leguminous family (*Leguminosæ*). In Greece and Crete, *A. parnassi* and *A. creticus* occur; and in Asia Minor and Persia, *A. verus* prevails. The gum exudes spontaneously from the plants, and forms large, dark masses; but usually it is obtained by making incisions. When there are slits, the pieces of gum are in thin plates, striated, and more or less contorted, as is exhibited by that generally found in commerce. Or if punctures in the stem are made, the gum is in the shape of threads. It is collected in July and August. At first it is soft or half-liquid, but in three or four days it hardens. The translucent yellowish pieces are the best, the lighter pieces are more or less impregnated with air. The color varies from white to brownish-black, some species of plants yielding light, and other species dark gum. It is softer than Gum-Arabic, readily cut with a knife, and can be pulverized after drying at a temperature of 212° F. It swells up in water, but is only partially soluble. When examined under the microscope it exhibits a cellular structure, contains starch grains, etc. This would be expected from the nature of its origin, which is by the metamorphosis of the cellulose of the pith and Medullary

Rays. Its important chemical constituents are bassorin (called also tragacanthine), some arabin, cellulose, starch, water (11–17 per cent.), and mineral substances. Of the latter about one-half consists of calcic carbonate. Its uses are similar to those of Gum-Arabic. The best qualities are employed in dyeing cotton, and finishing silk and lace; the poorer sorts are used in finishing sole-leather. **Gum of Bassora**, from Bassora, near the head of the Persian Gulf, belongs to the same class of gums as tragacanth.

THE RESINS.

211. The **Resins** are the most widely occurring of all vegetable products. They are found in nearly all groups of plants, even in the mycelium of some Fungi. They occur mostly in the cortical part of plants, yet have been found in all tissue except the cambium. They are rich in carbon, contain but little oxygen, and no nitrogen. Their composition is very complex; they contain resinous acids, volatile-oil, gums, carbonaceous substances, cellulose, tannin, etc. They seem to be products of slow oxidation. As regards structure, they are mostly amorphous, though many of the turpentines contain crystals of abietinic acid. The color is usually between yellow and brown; but may be red, white or black. Some are transparent, others are opaque. They have generally a vitreous lustre, but some are lustreless. The streak they make is mostly white. Dragon's-blood and some others are exceptions. Organic inclusions are very often present. The resins either arise by a metamorphosis of tissue, etc., or are a product of secretion. They may be classified into three groups, namely: (1) Common Resins, (2) Resinous Gums, and (3) Balsams.

212. Gamboge found its way into Europe from the

East in the sixteenth century. It is obtained mainly from *Garcinia Morella*, a small tree belonging to the Gamboge family (*Guttiferæ*). It occurs in Ceylon, Siam, and Cambodia, or Cambogia (whence the name). It has opposite, entire leaves, and diœcious flowers. The yellow fruit, or drupe, an inch or two in diameter, is pulpy and edible. The resin Gamboge is obtained by making incisions into the stem, out of which it flows. It is collected in wooden vessels, as cocoa-nut-shells, bamboo-stems, etc. When fresh, it is in color a light brownish-red, and lustrous; later it becomes brown, like liver, and lustreless. After being exposed for a time it becomes coated with a green layer. The streak is citron-yellow to orange. It has no odor; and the taste, though mild at first, becomes sharp and biting. It is much heavier than water, having a specific gravity of over 1.2. Under the microscope it is found to be a homogeneous mass of gum, with granules of resin embedded in it. A greater or less quantity of impurities, as tissue, starch, etc., is present. The granules exhibit the so-called Brownian or molecular movement very beautifully. The gum in Gamboge is soluble in water, and the resin is soluble in ether and alcohol. Both of the solutions are tasteless. It is used extensively for coloring alcoholic varnishes, for making varnishes for metals, and it furnishes the yellow in water-colors. It is used also in medicine.

213. The drug **Asafœtida** is obtained from two species of plants belonging to the Parsley family (*Umbelliferæ*). One, *Scorodosma fœtidum*, growing between the Aral Sea and the Persian Gulf, attains a height of six or seven feet, and forms vast forests. It grows only in sandy soil. The other plant is *Narthex asafœtida* of Afghanistan. It is five

or six feet high, and has leaves much like the Fennel. The whole plant has the peculiarly nauseating odor of asafœtida. This substance is obtained as follows: The stem is cut off at the root, and the whitish, resinous juice exudes, and gradually hardens. This is removed, and the top of the root again cut off. After a few days, in case of *Scorodosma*, more of the resin can be removed, and the same process repeated several times with one and the same root. From the large, elevated roots of *Narthex* the resin is allowed to flow for one or two weeks into slight hollows made in the ground. At first the resinous substance is soft, but becomes hard later, and in the cold is pulverizable. In commerce it occurs in granules or in masses. The former is better, the latter containing more impurities. The odor is leek-like and nauseating; the taste bitter and persistent. Its chief constituents are gum, volatile-oil (three to five per cent.), and resin (fifty per cent). The resin contains fifteen to twenty per cent. of sulphur. In the East it is used as a condiment for flavoring sauces and food. The leaves of the plant are also eaten, and the root roasted for the same purpose. In medicine asafœtida is extensively used as an expectorant and antispasmodic or nervous stimulant.

214. The resinous gum **Galbanum**, or **Galban**, is yielded by a Persian plant called *Ferula erubescens*. It is a member of the Parsley family (*Umbelliferæ*). Galban occurs in commerce in the form of grains (tears), which are sometimes translucent or pearly white; or it may be in masses or lumps, which are brownish, yellow or sometimes greenish. It is soft, and can be kneaded in warm weather. With water it forms an emulsion, and is soluble in alcohol. The taste is bitterish, hot, and acrid. The odor, balsamic, peculiar, and disagreeable. Among its constituent substances

are about seven per cent. of volatile-oil, fifty per cent. of resin, some gum, and various impurities. Its use in medicine is as a mild counter-irritant.

215. **Gum-Ammoniacum** exudes as a milky juice from *Dorema ammoniacum*, a plant belonging, like the two preceding, to the family *Umbelliferæ*. It grows on the steppes of Asia along with the Asafœtida-plant, *Scorodosma fœtidum*. It is a fennel-like plant, with large compound leaves, and attains a height of six or seven feet. The juice exudes spontaneously (probably upon the puncture of insects). It hardens in grains or lumps. It is whitish, has a waxy lustre, and is not entirely opaque. It softens in the hands. The odor is strong and peculiar, and the taste bitter. The gum contains about seventy per cent. of resin, three or four per cent. of volatile-oil, and some gum and water. It is used in the manufacture of cement, also in medicine as a stimulant.

216. The **Turpentine** of commerce comes mainly from Europe and North America. In the former country the species *Abies excelsa*, *Ab. pectinata*, *Pinus maritima*, *P. Laricio*, *P. silvestris*, and *Larix Europœa* yield this oleoresinous substance. In North America it is obtained from the Balsam-Fir (*Abies balsamea*), White Pine (*Pinus Strobus*), Red Pine (*P. resinosa*), Loblolly or Old-field Pine (*P. Tæda*), and Broom Pine (*P. palustris*). Turpentine is found both in the cortex and in the young wood; essentially the same methods are employed in the different countries in obtaining it. With an axe, or similar instrument, wounds or cavities of considerable size are made, or holes are bored with augers, into the trunk of the tree, and in these the turpentine collects. The better kinds are thin and clear, and those of poorer quality are thick and cloudy,

on account of the water or crystals of abietinic acid contained in them. They find extensive use in the manufacture of the oil of turpentine and resin, of varnish, sealing-wax, soap, etc. The finer kinds are used in medicine. The common turpentine contains 8–33 per cent. of volatile-oil, much being lost by evaporation in collecting. The thicker it is, the more crystals of abietinic acid ; and, therefore, the less turpentine it contains. The **Venetian Turpentine**, obtained from the European Larch (*Larix Europœa*), is dark-colored, but contains no abietinic acid crystals. It has a turpentine odor, but suggestive of nutmeg and lemon. The finest of all turpentines is the **Canada Balsam**, obtained from the Balsam-Fir. It is at first colorless, but becomes yellowish with age, though remaining clear. It has a pleasant odor, and an aromatic and bitter taste. It is nearly as heavy as water, the specific gravity being a little over .99. Starch grains from the potato mounted in it are visible under the microscope, but invisible in other balsams. It is extensively used in the preparation of microscopic objects.

217. The **Common Resin**, called also *Rosin* and *Colophony*, is the mass remaining after the natural escape, or the removal by distillation, of the volatile-oil from the turpentines. It consists of resinous acids, together with a very small quantity of the oil of turpentine. Since it is soluble in alkalies it is used in the manufacture of the common kinds of soap. It is also used in the preparation of ointments and plasters, in the manufacture of varnishes, cements, etc., in sizing paper, and in lubricating machinery. Resinous wood, after yielding resin, is then often used in the manufacture of tar, illuminating gas, creosote, paraffine, and aniline. **Tar** is obtained by distillation from roots,

etc., of various Coniferous trees. It is used extensively for preserving cordage and woods from the effects of the atmosphere. From tar is produced pitch, oil of tar, creosote, etc.

218. Mecca Balsam, or *Balm of Gilead,* is obtained from a small Arabian tree called *Balsamodendron gileadense,* of the Myrrh family (*Burseraceæ*). The tree has slender branches, small bright-green leaves, and small white flowers with four petals. The fruit is an oval berry. The best quality of the balsam flows from incisions made in the twigs; but this is scarce, as only about sixty drops a day exude. The common mode of obtaining it is by boiling the twigs in water. Its taste is bitter, and the odor is that of turpentine, but suggestive of lemon and Forget-me-not. It has the consistency of pine turpentine; at first thinner, afterwards thicker. It is often of a brownish-red color, and somewhat cloudy; the best is yellowish, and has a pleasant aromatic odor. Under the microscope it is clear, and shows no solid impurities. Potato starch in it is not visible; but if olive-oil or castor-oil is added the starch grains can be seen. This, therefore, serves as a means for detecting these adulterations. It is used by the Turks in odoriferous ointments and cosmetics. It is employed in the manufacture of perfumery and in medicine. **Myrrh,** a gum-resin very similar to the last, and said to be one of the oldest medicinal articles known, is from another small tree of Arabia belonging to the same genus (*B. myrrha*). It is semi-transparent, reddish or yellowish. The taste is aromatic and bitter, the odor characteristic and pleasant. In medicine it is used as a stomachic and tonic.

219. The **Copaiba Balsam** is from *Copaifera multijuga,* a large leguminous tree (family *Leguminosæ*) of Brazil and the West Indies. A small quantity is also furnished by other species of the same genus. Deep incisions are made into the wood, out of which the balsam flows. It is said the trees are so full of it that they sometimes burst spontaneously. The balsam is of a yellow or a yellowish color. That which is thin is generally of a light-yellow, and the thicker of a golden color. In specific gravity it varies from .91 to .99. In it the starch of *Canna edulis* is invisible; that of the potato visible. It contains from thirty to eighty per cent. of volatile-oil, also amorphous resin, and crystals of a resinous (copaibic) acid. This balsam is used in making varnishes and in the manufacture of tracing-paper. It is also employed in medicine.

220. The **Elemi Resins** come from the Myrrh family (*Burseraceæ*). The largest quantity is from *Icica Icicariba* (Rio), *Icica viridiflora* (Guiana), *Amyris Plumiri* (Mexico and Yucatan), and *Bursera gummifera* (Martinique and Guadeloupe). It is not so hard as colophony, and can be kneaded with the hand. It can be cut with a knife, yet this is true of no other resin. The taste is aromatic and bitter, and the smell fennel-like. There are three kinds: (1) balsamic, which is greenish and contains but few crystals; (2) soft, which is yellowish and contains more crystals; (3) hard, which varies from yellow to white, and contains still more crystals than the last. These resins have a specific gravity of 1.02 to 1.08. Among their component elements are found both crystals and amorphous resins, and volatile-oil (3–13 per cent). They are used in the manufacture of varnish, especially that used by coach painters. In medicine their use is similar to that of turpentine.

221. A shrub or small tree, about twelve feet high and little less than a foot in diameter, growing in the Mediter-

ranean region, furnishes the resin, **Mastic**. The name of the shrub is *Pistacia lentiscus;* it belongs to the Cashew family (*Anacardiaceæ*). Nearly all the Mastic of commerce comes from the island of Chios, where a variety (*var. chia*) of the *Pistacia lentiscus* is cultivated. Sometimes the resin flows out spontaneously, and hardens in drops on the twigs. That from the twigs is better than that from the trunks; the latter are cut with a knife from the ground up as high as the branches, and the resin flows out on flat stones laid at the base of the tree. It is removed after three or four weeks, and this method of collecting it is followed about two months in a season. The amount yielded by each tree is from eight to ten pounds. The resin is a secretion, and occurs in special resin-canals in the inner cortex. Its color is yellowish or greenish, and more or less cloudy. The odor is similar to that of Galbanum; in hardness it is between Damar and Sandarac; it is heavier than water (specific gravity 1.04–1.07). Some of its important constituents are mastic acid (eighty to ninety-one per cent), mastacin, and a trace of volatile-oil. It is used in the manufacture of fine varnish.

222. **Sandarac** is from *Callitris quadrivalvis*, a small tree found in the northwest mountains of Africa. It is a member of the Pine family (*Coniferæ*). The wood is colored, hard, takes a fine polish, and is, therefore, esteemed in cabinet-work. The resin flows after incisions are made, also spontaneously from twigs and stems. It occurs in the cortex, and is probably a true secretion. The color of the Sandarac varies from a yellowish to a reddish-brown, it is harder than Mastic, and has about the same specific gravity (1.05–1.09). It has a vitreous lustre when a fresh surface is exposed. The odor is weak, aromatic, and the taste

bitter. It is complex in structure, having no less than three resinous components. It is used in varnishes to give hardness and gloss. It is also employed in medicine. From an Australian species (*C. Preissii*) a nearly related product called Pine Gum is obtained.

223. From another Coniferous tree (*Dammara orientalis*), the important resin **Damar** is obtained. The family to which this large tree belongs is the *Coniferæ*. It grows in the Moluccas, Borneo, Java, Sumatra, etc. Much of the resin exudes spontaneously. The trees are also cut low down to the ground, and the resin collects in reservoirs. In the mountainous regions of Sumatra the resin masses fall into the streams, and thus are washed down. Damar is colorless or yellow, and sometimes cloudy. The fresh surface is vitreous. It becomes sticky in the hand. It has a balsamic odor; it varies in weight, having a specific gravity from 1.04–1.12. Like the preceding, Damar is also very complex, having among its constituents several resinous bodies, a trace of gum, and a very small quantity of mineral substance. It furnishes a very clear varnish, and is often used in mounting objects for the microscope.

224. **Gum-Lac** forms a resinous crust on the twigs and branches of various trees in India. The largest amount is from *Croton laccifera*, a plant of the Spurge family (*Euphorbiaceæ*). The exudation is caused by myriads of insects (*Coccus laccæ*), allied to the cochineal insect. The females collect on the young and soft twigs and insert their long proboscis into the cortex to obtain nutriment from the plant. They then exude a resinous secretion from their entire bodies, and become enclosed in a continuous crust of resin. The twigs loose their leaves and die; in the meantime twenty or thirty larvæ develop, escape through the

back of the mother insect, and bore a hole through the resin through which to escape. If it is desired especially to obtain lac-dye (for dyeing silk and wool), the resin must be collected before the young insects hatch out, since the coloring matter is contained in the ovary of the females, and but little of it remains after the young develop. To obtain the largest amount of both dye-stuff and resin, the twigs are collected in June and November. When the resin is melted, strained through thick canvas, and spread out in thin layers, it forms shell-lac, the form most commonly found in commerce. It is tasteless, odorless, and varies in color from light to deep-brown. Its important constituents are resin, lac-dye, and waxy substances. Lac is the principal ingredient in sealing-wax, and forms the base of valuable varnishes. It is used besides in various cements, in the manufacture of felt, etc. It can be bleached, and will take delicate shades of color; dyed a golden color it is much used in the East Indies for working into personal adornments.

225. The resinous substance **Copal**, somewhat resembling Amber, comes from very many different plants. The East African Copal comes from species of *Trachilobium*, of the Pulse family (*Leguminosæ*). This is the hardest, and considered the best. It is tasteless and odorless. The surface is opaque, but within it is clear and transparent. The external crust is removed by washing, when the surface is seen to be faceted. The West African Copal is a "recent fossil," found in the sandy or clayey soil sometimes at a depth of ten feet. It is supposed to come from *Guibourtia copallifera*. The New Zealand Copal flows spontaneously from the twigs and stems of *Dammara australis* (family *Coniferæ*). It hardens quickly, is at first milky

or cloudy, and has a strong balsamic odor. That from New Caledonia is yielded by *D. ovata*. Its odor is also balsamic, its color and transparency variable. The Manila Copal flows from incisions in the trunk of *Vateria indica* (family *Dipterocarpeæ*). It hardens quickly, and has a faintly balsamic odor. The South American Copal collects in masses on the stems and roots of several plants, especially on *Hymenæa courbaril*. The surface is uneven and covered with a thick crust. The color varies from yellow to brown; it has an odor not unlike that of glue, and a bitter taste. Copal is very complex in composition. The large pieces are used in turnery. It is the most important resin for the manufacture of varnishes.

226. **Guiac,** or **Guiacum,** is yielded by *Guiacum officinale*, a tree belonging to the order *Zygophyllæ*, which is closely related to the Geranium family. The tree grows to the height of twenty or thirty feet, has very hard dark-red or blackish heart-wood, used in making ship's blocks, pulleys, etc. The resin flows spontaneously (in small grains), or after incisions are made (in large pieces). Sometimes long sticks of the wood are bored longitudinally and held over the fire, when the resin flows out and is collected in calabashes. Occasionally, but not often, it is obtained by boiling the finely-divided wood. The resin is brittle, of a brownish-black color, or greenish when long exposed. When fresh it is very lustrous. The odor is weak and peculiar, the taste pungent. It contains many resinous acids, some gum, and a small quantity of mineral substances. This resin is much used in medicine.

227. In a very limited district (Balsam Coast) of St. Salvador, *Myroxylon sonsonatense* is found, and from it is obtained the **Balsam of Peru.** This tree belongs to the

Bean family (*Leguminosæ*). When the Spaniards took possession of the island they cut down the trees to obtain the resin. Had this method not been prohibited by law, in a short time the species would have been exterminated. The mode practiced now, is as follows: At the end of the rainy season, the trees are hammered on three or four sides until the bark is loosened from the tree at those points. After a few days the bark is burned, by means of resin torches, until it is charred. It then falls off, or is removed, and the yellow, odorous, liquid resin is absorbed by pieces of cloth. When these become saturated, they are boiled in earthen vessels to obtain the resin. A tree may be thus treated two or three times in a season. By this method the black Peru Balsam is obtained. The White Balsam is said to be obtained by pressing the fruit. Balsam of Peru has a pleasant odor like that of Benzoin or Vanilla. Its taste is first mild, then sharp and biting. It is heavier than water (specific gravity 1.14–1.15). It has a variable and complex chemical composition. It finds use in the manufacture of sealing-wax, and in perfumery. It is used for flavoring lozenges and tinctures, and substituted for vanilla in the poorer kinds of chocolate.

228. A small tree of the northwestern part of South America, and belonging to the family *Leguminosæ*, namely, *Myroxylon toluiferum*, produces the **Balsam of Tolu.** Holes are bored into the trees from which the resin flows. It softens in the hand, and can be kneaded like wax. Its color is a reddish-brown; but when pulverized, pale yellow. The odor is pleasant, reminding of vanilla; it has an aromatic taste. When examined under the microscope it is found to be a homogeneous mass, with crystals of ciunamic acid embedded in it, also some remains of vegetable

tissue. The Tolu resembles the Mecca Balsam, but is more easily resinified than the latter. Among its constituents are cinnamic and benzoic acids, several resins, and a volatile-oil. Like the preceding balsam, it is also used in medicine. It is also employed in the manufacture of perfumery.

229. Liquid **Storax**, or *Liquidamber*, is obtained from *Liquidamber orientale*, a tree of Asia Minor, Cypress, etc., which belongs to the Witch-Hazel family (*Hamamelaceæ*). The tree throws off the bark in thin plates, like the Sycamore. The exposed, younger bark is removed and boiled in water. The balsam collects at the bottom of the vessel as a heavy slimy liquid, having the odor of vanilla, and a biting taste. The color becomes darker with age, becoming greenish. It is apparently homogeneous; but under the microscope can be seen a multitude of small resinous granules, remains of tissue, etc. When kept a long time, the granules disappear, and crystals of cinnamic acid are seen embedded in the otherwise homogeneous mass. The Storax in grains is obtained by the hardening of the liquid Storax. It has a brownish-black color, and a smooth lustrous surface; it becomes soft in the hands. The common Storax is a humus-like mass, with many impurities. It smells strongly of cinnamic acid. In composition it is, like many of the resins and balsams, very complex. It finds use both in perfumery and in medicine; in the latter as an expectorant.

230. A small tree, *Styrax benzoin* (family *Styracaceæ*), indigenous in India, yields the resinous gum **Benzoin**. The trees are cultivated in India, Sumatra, and other places. When they are seven years old, they yield the gum Benzoin spontaneously in small quantities, but mostly

upon incisions being made into the trunks, which are seven or eight inches in diameter. Incisions are usually made three or four times a year; after ten or twelve years the product is not so good—it is dark in color, and not very odorous. The resin occurs in the wood, in the Medullary Rays, and in the cortex. It has an aromatic, sweetish, but biting, taste. The color may be whitish, yellowish, reddish, or brownish. Several distinct resinous bodies enter into its composition. It is used in perfumery, very largely for purifying animal fat which is to receive odors of flowers, also in the manufacture of essences, pomatums, etc.

231. The resinous substance **Dragon's-blood** is produced principally by *Calamus Draco*, of the Palm family (*Palmaceæ*). It grows in India, Sumatra, the Moluccas, etc. The ripe fruits are heated over a fire, when a slimy mass exudes between the scales, which is collected in hollow canes or on Monocotyledonous leaves. In some regions that which exudes spontaneously, and is found in the shape of small grains, is collected and kneaded into balls. This is considered the best. Another mode of obtaining it is by subjecting the fruits to hot steam; sometimes the fruits are shaken in a sack, and the brittle resin is separated from the shells by a sieve, and heated in the sun or in hot steam. The best sorts of Dragon's-blood are of a deep red or blackish color; the poorer, brick-red. The streak is blood-red; it has a sweetish taste; its specific gravity is about 1.2. It is soluble in alcohol, alkalies, and acetic acid. In it are found a red resin called Dracin (ninety per cent.), benzoic acid, calcic oxalate, calcic sulphate, and cellulose. It is mostly adulterated with Damar and gum. It finds extensive use as a coloring for alcoholic varnishes, for staining marble and horn, preparing gold

lacquer, for tooth-powders and washes. In medicine it is used for its astringent property.

232. The resin called **Botany Bay Gum**, or *Grass-tree Gum*, covers the stems of several Australian species of *Xanthorrhœa*, of the Lily family (*Liliaceæ*). The red resin is from *X. australii;* it has a color very similar to that of Dragon's-blood. It is very lustrous, and the streak is orange. The yellow resin (called also Black Bay Gum) is *X. hastilis*. It is, when fresh, yellowish to brownish; when old it has a crust of a deep brown color. This gum has its origin in a metamorphosis of tissue, and is very complex in chemical composition. It is used for coloring alcoholic varnishes, and especially for varnishes for metalic objects.

THE CAOUTCHOUC GROUP.

233. In the **Caoutchouc Group** are included Caoutchouc, Gutta-Percha, and Balata Gum. These occur, in the form of granules, in the milky juice of many plants belonging to the orders *Euphorbiaceæ, Apocynaceæ, Asclepiadaceæ, Sapotaceæ, Compositæ, Lobeliaceæ,* and *Artocarpaceæ*. Some fresh juice sent in sealed vessels from South America to Faraday, and by him analyzed, showed the following composition:

Caoutchouc. . . . . 31.70 per cent.
Wax, etc. . . . . 7.13 per cent.
Gum ? (soluble in water). . . . . . . 2.90 per cent.
Soluble Albuminoids . . . . 1.90 per cent.
Water, Acetic Acid, and Salts . . . . 56.37 per cent.

1. Caoutchouc was used by the Indians of Brazil and Guiana from remote times, in the manufacture of vessels, shoes, etc. The natives of East India likewise used it, from time immemorial, for lining baskets for holding liquids, for torches, etc. Caoutchouc, from South America, was first described by La Condamine in 1751. It was employed for a long time simply to erase lead-pencil marks, a use first pointed out by Magellan. When the process of vulcanizing the Caoutchouc was invented—which consists of impregnating a small quantity of sulphur with it, which has the effect of hardening it, and extending its elasticity to wider limits of temperature—its uses were greatly multiplied, and now it is in the arts one of the most important of all vegetable products. It was, therefore, sought for in other plants than those from which it was obtained by the Indians. It is now obtained from *Siphonia braziliensis* (family *Euphorbiaceæ*), in Brazil; *Urceola elastica* (family *Apocynaceæ*), in East India; *Ficus elastica* (family *Urticaceæ*), in East India; *Vahea gummifera* (family *Apocynaceæ*), in Madagascar. A very small quantity is collected from swamps, which has spontaneously exuded and hardened. It is mostly obtained by making incisions into the trees. A horizontal incision is made, and from this upwards a vertical incision and many oblique ones are made. The juice then flows out, and is collected in earthen vessels, or wooden ones lined with clay. It is worked at once, ammonia being added to prevent its coagulation. A fire is built with the fruits of a Palm (*Atalea funifera*), and over it are held wooden paddles, or earthen forms, previously dipped in the milky juice; when the liquid is evaporated, a thin dark-colored layer of Caoutchouc is found deposited, and the process is repeated very many times till a thick coating of Caoutchouc is formed. Then the earthen form is broken, or the Caoutchouc is cut down on one side and removed from the paddle, and in this form is exported. Another method in some places is followed, which is as follows: The liquid is diluted with four times its volume of water, and stirred.

After twenty-four hours the Caoutchouc collects on the surface, alum is added, it hardens, and is finally pressed. It is said that old trees yield more than young ones, and the juice flows more in cold than in hot weather. The Caoutchouc from South America is brown or blackish; that from Madagascar, bluish or yellowish; that from India, white or yellowish; and that from China, reddish. The odor is peculiar, but not strong, and it has no taste. It cannot be cut with a knife. It has a specific gravity of .92 to .96, is a "non-conductor" of electricity, and insoluble in water; it swells up in alcohol, oil of turpentine, carbon disulphide, ether, and benzine. It is not attacked by acids at ordinary temperatures. Under the microscope it presents a homogeneous appearance, without any cavities. It is used in the manufacture of optical and surgical instruments; for buttons, combs, stoppers, tubes; for making water-proof clothing, air-pillows, etc. *Ebonite*, which contains more sulphur and is harder than ordinary Caoutchouc, is used for those instruments and other objects for which the latter would be too soft.

2. **Gutta-Percha** is not so widely distributed as Caoutchouc; it occurs in the milky juice of plants only which belong to the family *Sapotaceæ*. The largest quantity comes from *Isonandra gutta*, a tree of India and the Sandwich Islands, usually three or four feet in diameter, and sixty to eighty feet high. It has a straight trunk, numerous ascending branches, with oblong, petiolate leaves, crowded at their extremities. The flowers are small and white; the wood is soft, fibrous, and of a pale color. Gutta-Percha was known for a long time, and used by the natives for handles for knives, weapons, etc. It was introduced into Europe in 1843. The trees were felled, cut up,

and the juice collected in vessels; but a more rational method of obtaining it is followed now, namely, the same which is employed in getting Caoutchouc. From the same tree Gutta-Percha may be obtained for several years. The juice hardens to a porous, spongy mass, to which water is added, and then it is kneaded. The Gutta-Percha when pure is nearly white, or with a shade of red or yellow; when impure, it is of a reddish or dark color. It is tasteless, and has a peculiar odor when warm. It can be cut with a knife; it is not so elastic as Caoutchouc, and is a poor conductor of electricity. It is partially soluble in alcohol and ether, and completely so in warm oil of turpentine and benzine. Its best solvent is a mixture of benzine and carbon disulphide. It is not attacked by alkalies nor weak acids. When examined with the microscope it is found to be full of minute cavities. It is more complex in composition than Caoutchouc, and contains pure gutta, resins, acids, volatile-oil, casein, and coloring and mineral substances. It is used in immense quantities to cover sub-marine cables. It is also employed in the manufacture of shoe-soles, bands for machinery, tubes, vessels, water-proof cloth, for taking copies or casts of objects, etc. Like Caoutchouc, it also can be vulcanized.

3. **Balata Gum** has been used since the middle of the present century as a substitute for Caoutchouc and Gutta-Percha. It comes from Guiana, and is yielded by *Sapota Muelleri* (family *Sapotaceæ*). The milky juice of the tree has been used for a long time as food by the natives. To obtain the juice for the Balata Gum, the trees were at first felled, placed on supports, the bark cut at short distances, and the exuding juice caught in vessels placed below. A rational method is generally followed now, which is as

follows: A narrow, vertical strip of bark is removed, whereupon the juice flows out. The following year the tree is again wounded in the same manner, but at a different point. The amount of Balata yielded annually is about one pound to the tree. The juice flows mostly in the rainy season. It is collected in wooden vessels; metal vessels are not employed, for the juice becomes black when in contact with the metal. After standing a while a porous, spongy mass is formed, which is stirred and worked with wooden sticks. The color of the gum is whitish, tinged with red or brown. It is tasteless, and when warm has the odor of Gutta-Percha. It can, like the latter, be cut with a knife. As to solubility, it behaves like Gutta-Percha. It is not attacked by alkalies, and can be vulcanized. It is used for bands for machinery, soles and heels for shoes. For surgical purposes and as insulators it is said to be better than Gutta-Percha. For the latter, as well as for Caoutchouc, it can be employed in general as a substitute.

OPIUM AND CATECHU GROUP.

234. The dried, milky juice of the white Poppy (*Papaver somniferum*) constitutes the **Opium** of commerce. The plant belongs to the Poppy family (*Papaveraceæ*). It is extensively cultivated in Egypt, Asia Minor, Persia, and India. A few days after the petals fall from the flowers, the pods are sliced horizontally (so as to sever the laticiferous vessels), when the milky juice exudes, and hardens over night to a doughy mass. It is collected in masses, and rolled in leaves. It is then dried in the sun, or over the fire. It is usually adulterated with dock fruit (*Rumex*), tragacanth, or other gums. It has a deep brown

color, a peculiar stupefying odor, and a bitter, burning taste. It is heavier than water, and partially soluble in it. Under the microscope it is seen to be partially crystallized (the narcotin). In chemical composition it is very complex and variable. It usually contains from nine to twenty-four per cent. of water, and eight per cent. of ash. Of its numerous alkaloids, the most important are morphine, papaverin, and narcotin. Its use in medicine is well known. From the seeds a medicinal oil is expressed; it is yellowish to golden-yellow, and has a specific gravity of .92. It is a drying oil, and dries more readily than flaxseed-oil. The seeds contain from fifty to sixty per cent. of this oil.

235. The inspissated juice of several species of the genus *Aloe* (family *Amaryllidaceæ*), especially *A. vulgaris*, *A. socotrina*, etc., constitutes the drug **Aloes**, used in medicine and in dyeing. The plants grow in Africa, have showy, tall, flowering spikes, and thick fleshy leaves, from which, when incisions are made, the juice exudes. Sometimes the leaves are cut off and pressed, or boiled; and a third mode of obtaining the juice is to sever the leaves close to the ground, and stand them, with the cut ends downwards, in vessels, into which the juice flows. The juice is boiled down in shallow pans. The Aloes may be lustrous, of a grayish-yellow color; and when pulverized light yellow, with no crystals (*Aloe lucida*); or blackish or brown, and containing crystals (*Aloe hepatica*). The odor is peculiar, reminding of saffron; the taste is bitter and unpleasant. Aloin is the active, bitter principle.

236. From *Acacia catechu* (family *Leguminosæ*) is obtained **Catechu**, or *Cutch*, the old name for which is

Terra Japonica. The tree grows in India, Ceylon, etc., and attains at times a height of fifty or sixty feet and a diameter of over two feet, but usually it is much smaller. The resinous substance is contained in the old heart-wood, which is finely cut and boiled in kettles. The product is boiled down to a doughy mass, then rolled in Monocotyledonous leaves to harden. Catechu has a brown or blackish color, and is lustrous on the fresh surface. The odor is weak, the taste bitter and astringent. The hot water solution of Catechu is reddish-brown, not clear, and slightly acid. The important constituent is Catechin; it contains besides about fifteen per cent. of water, and two to four per cent. of ash. Catechin is a very astringent medicine, and an important black dye. It is also used in tanning poor and heavy leathers.

237. The inspissated juice of *Nauclea gambir* is the **Gambier,** also called by tanners Terra Japonica. The plant belongs to the Madder family (*Rubiaceæ*); it is a climbing shrub, with oblong or oval-lanceolate leaves, two or three inches in length. The flowers are greenish, and form axillary, globular heads. It is indigenous in India and the neighboring islands. It is also extensively cultivated, when it is pruned to a shrub six or eight feet high. When three years old, twigs and leaves are collected from it; this is continued twice a year till the plant is about thirty years old. The twigs and leaves are boiled in water in kettles five or six hours. When of the consistency of syrup, it is poured out to harden in wooden troughs or bamboo-stems. It is then cut into cakes, and dried in the sun. When fresh, Gambier is whitish, but it becomes darker in a few weeks, and finally assumes a reddish-brown color. It is lustreless, easily reduced mechanically, and has scarcely

auy odor; the taste is at first astringent, then sweetish. It is soluble in hot water. Its important constituent is Catechin. Gambier is used, like Catechu, in dyeing and tanning.

238. Another substance similar in properties and uses to Catechu and Gambier is **Gum-Kino**, which is yielded by several species of plants. That called Malabar, or Amboyna Kino, is from a leguminous tree, *Pterocarpus marsupium*. It is said to flow from incisions, and resembles red currant jelly. This is evaporated, dried in the sun a few hours, and then exported. It is lustrous, and has a blackish or reddish color. Under the microscope it is amorphous and full of clefts. It is soluble in hot water, alcohol, and caustic alkalies. The solution is ruby-red, and has an acid reaction. The Botany Bay Kino is from several Australian species of *Eucalyptus* (family *Myrtaceæ*). It is called also Blood-wood Gum, Spotted Gum, and Black-beetle Gum. It is said to occupy cavities in the trunks of the trees, and is collected by wood-splitters and sawyers. It varies in color from red to yellowish. It is odorless, has an astringent taste, and is soluble in hot water and alcohol. Bengal Bay Kino, or Red Gum, is yielded by a leguminous plant, *Butea frondosa*. It is slightly lustrous, and swells in water. In medicine it is chiefly used in the form of tinctures.

VEGETABLE FATS AND WAX.

239. From the fruits of the Palm, *Elæis guineënsis* (family *Palmaceæ*), is expressed the **Palm-oil** of commerce. The plant is found in Africa, the West Indies, and Brazil. It is generally less than twenty feet high, and crowned with pinnate leaves. It lives many years,

and produces annually bunches of thickly-clustered fruit two or three feet long. The fruits are plum-shaped, about the size of walnuts, and have a red rind. The fleshy part encloses a hard nut. The oil is contained both in the fleshy fruit-hull and in the nut. The oil is usually obtained by pressure. It is orange-yellow in color, and may be bleached by heating (oxidation). It melts at 79°–87° F. When examined under the microscope it is found to consist of a yellowish oily mass, with crystals and reddish granules. The crystals (acid) are in greater quantity when the oil is rancid. The most important constituents are palmatin, olein, and glycerin. The oil is soluble in alcohol and ether. It is very extensively used in the manufacture of candles (stearine candles) and soap, and in lubricating machinery. The natives of the countries where the oil is produced use it for food.

240. **Cocoa-nut-oil**, or *Cocoa-nut Butter*, is from the Palm, *Cocos nucifera*, which grows on all tropical coasts. The tree attains a height of fifty to one hundred feet, and has long pinnate leaves. It affords the inhabitants food, drink, and domestic utensils, and materials for building and thatching. The fruits are taken from the shell, dried in the sun, or put in hot water, and, after being reduced mechanically, the oil is extracted from them by pressure. This is white, has an unpleasant odor, and a peculiar bland taste. It melts at 64°–68° F. It contains, as shown by the microscope, needle-like crystals. It is soluble in alcohol and ether, and saponifies with alkalies. It contains cocinin, olein, and many other substances. It is employed in the manufacture of soap. In pharmacy it is used as a substitute for lard, and in medicine as a substitute for cod-liver oil.

241. The Tallow-tree, *Stillingia sebifera* (family *Euphorbiaceæ*), has black seeds as large as Hazel-nuts, which are covered with what is called **Chinese Tallow**. The tree grows to the height of twenty to forty feet, has long and flexible branches, with long petiolate leaves, resembling those of the Poplars. The monœcious flowers are in dense terminal spikes, and the fruit is a three-lobed capsule, with a seed in each cell. The seeds are collected in November and December, and reduced in stone mortars. The mass is then pressed through straw. The tallow melts at $98°-109°$ F. It has a specific gravity of $.81-.82$; its color is greenish or white, and its reaction acid. It contains palmatin, stearine, etc. It finds use in the manufacture of candles, soap, etc. It has also been employed as a substitute for linseed-oil, and for burning in lamps.

242. The Olive-tree (*Olea Europæa*), of the Olive family (*Oleaceæ*), is found wild in Western Asia. There are two forms of it: (1) *var. silvestris*, which has thorns and grows wild; and (2) *var. culta*, destitute of thorns and extensively cultivated, and has itself given rise to numerous so-called "varieties." From the latter the **Olive-oil**, or *Sweet-oil*, is obtained. The tree is an evergreen, rarely exceeding twenty feet in height. The wood is yellowish and fine-grained, and used in small cabinet-work, in inlay work and in turnery. It has lanceolate, or lance-oblong, leaves, which are pale-green above and pale beneath. The flowers are axillary, small and white, and the fruit is an oily drupe. When ripe, the Olives are dark-violet or black. If collected at this time they yield the best yellow and sweet oil used as food. The oil from unripe fruits is greenish and tart; that from over-ripe fruits is yellowish or colorless, but sour and unpleasant. To obtain the best edible oil, the ripe fruits are picked, the seeds are removed, and the flesh pressed. Usually the fruit is shaken or knocked off. More oil is obtained when the fruit is put in heaps and allowed to ferment. The oil is at first cloudy, but later it becomes clear; colorless oil is obtained by clarification with animal charcoal, or by exposing to air and light for a long time; the fruit which has remained on the tree all winter yields colorless oil. In every case, however, the oil is rancid; therefore, not edible, yet valuable for all other purposes. The oil is solid generally at $50°$ F. That obtained by cold and gentle pressing, with little palmatin and much olein, is solid at lower, and that obtained by warm and strong pressing, with much palmatin, is solid at higher, temperatures. Its specific gravity is .86–.91. Its chemical composition is complex. It is used extensively in the manufacture of soaps, and in illumination, also for lubricating machinery. Watchmakers keep the oil in stoppered bottles, in which a piece of lead is placed, upon which a viscid whitish mass collects, leaving the oil more pure for their use.

243. The Wax Palm, *Copernica cerifera*, is found in Brazil. The natives eat the bitter fruits, and from the leaves they extract a fibre for making hats, thatching, and clothing. The hard wood is used in cabinet-making. The root is diuretic, and used medicinally. The wax, called **Cerea Wax**, or **Carnauba Wax**, forms a coating on the leaves, which, under the microscope, is found to consist of prismatic and cylindrical rods perpendicular to the surface. The leaves are carefully cut from the tree and shaken to obtain the grayish-white powder, which is then melted. The raw wax is of a dirty, yellowish-green, filled with small air bubbles. It is hard, brittle, odorless, and taste-

less. The pure wax has a pale greenish color, and is hard and brittle; when melted, it is clear and slightly aromatic. It has a specific gravity of .999, and melts at 174°–206½° F. It is soluble in boiling alcohol and ether. It is used in the manufacture of candles and wax-varnishes, and is often substituted for beeswax. Another Wax Palm, *Ceroxylon andicola*, grows on the highest mountains of New Grenada. It is a tall tree, with pinnate leaves, fifteen to twenty feet long. The *Palm Wax* forms a crust on the stems, from which it is scraped after the trees are felled. Each tree yields about twenty-five pounds. Sometimes the bark is boiled to obtain the wax; it is yellowish-white, of complex composition, and melts at 161° F. It is mixed with tallow, and then used to make candles.

244. The Bayberry, *Myrica cerifera*, a shrubby plant of North America, with a grayish bark, many branches with numerous entire petiolate leaves, and flowers in aments; and other species of the same genus (family *Myricaceæ*), growing in South America and Africa, have a coating of wax, in the form of a crust or powder, on the spherical berries. This, called **Myrica,** or **Myrtle Wax,** or *Bayberry Tallow*, is obtained by boiling the fruits in water; the fruits sink, and the wax floats on the top. The wax is greenish in color—due, perhaps, to chlorophyll contained in it. It is as tenacious as, and harder than, beeswax, and can be saponified. It has the same uses as beeswax, for which it is sometimes substituted.

CAMPHOR.

245. The Camphor-tree, *Laurus camphora*, is an evergreen, much resembling the Linden-tree, and belonging to the Laurel family (family *Lauraceæ*). It is a native of

Eastern Asia, and is cultivated for ornament in warm regions. The tree bears red berries. **Camphor** is obtained in China, Japan, Formosa, etc., by putting the twigs and finely-divided wood in kettles of water and applying gentle heat. Over the kettles are placed dome-shaped covers, in which the camphor is deposited by sublimation. It is afterwards purified in glass flasks, or in cast-iron vessels; in these is put with the camphor some coal or sand or quicklime; when heat is applied, the camphor sublimes. The odor is strong and peculiar, and noxious to insects; the taste is bitter and burning. Camphor is soft and tough, difficult to pulverize, and has a specific gravity of .99. It is used in pyrotechnics and in medicine.

STARCH AND SUGAR.

246. Starch is found in great abundance, and is very widely distributed. It is in all green parts of plants, from which, though originating there exclusively, it is never obtained for commerce. The principal source is the bulb, the tuber, fruit, etc. The color of starch is generally white, but in some plants it may be red, yellow, etc. Some starches (as that of Horse-chestnut) are impregnated with tannin. The fineness of starch depends on the size of the grains. Its specific gravity is about 1.5. When fresh it contains thirty per cent. of water; and when air-dry, seven to eighteen per cent. The quantity of ash varies from .2–.6 per cent. When heated over 240° F. starch is converted into paste. Diastase (a principle developed in germination of seeds), acids, and alkalies, as well as heat of over 320° F., converts starch into dextrine and grape sugar. Its formula is $C_{12} H_{20} O_{10}$, a chemical composition the same as that of cellulose. From bulbs and tubers it is,

18

in general, obtained as follows: These are reduced between large cylinders, and the pulp is washed in sieves. The starch thus washed out is then dried in heated chambers, and finally reduced between crushers. The pulp, in which more or less starch remains, is used in feeding; or from it starch-sugar, or whisky is manufactured. Another mode is to slice the bulbs, etc., macerate in warm water, and pile in heaps, when fermentation takes place, by which, perhaps, the cell-walls are dissolved—a process chemically not well understood. The mass is then washed as above. From grains (of wheat) the starch is obtained by crushing between cylinders, after soaking the grains for ten or fifteen days, then washing in sieves. Starch so obtained is not pure white; therefore the following process is usually resorted to: Water is added to the mass reduced as above, and fermentation (first alcoholic, then butyric) takes place. The starch is then washed, and found to be pure white. Starch is used extensively as food. When green (not dry), it is used in the manufacture of dextrine and sugar; when dry, it is employed as paste for finishing cotton and linen fabrics, as a thickener of colors and mordant in dyeing, and for many other purposes.

247. The **Starch of Wheat**, *Triticum vulgare* (family *Gramineæ*), is in the endosperm of the grains. The grains are (1) large and lenticular, the layers very indistinct or invisible, the commonest size of which is .0011 inches; (2) small and many-sided, and sometimes irregular, layers not visible, with an average size of .00028 inches; and (3) compound grains, composed of two to twenty-five easily-separable partial grains. The grains are distinguishable as such with the aid of a lens. Those of wheat, rye, and barley are

STARCH AND SUGAR. 275

very much alike, but readily distinguishable after very many grains are measured. The size of each kind is as follows:

		Minimum.	Maximum.	Commonest.
WHEAT. . . .	large grains .	.00055 in.	.00154 in.	.0011 in.
	small grains .	.00008 in.	.00032 in.	.00028 in.
RYE	large grains .	.00055 in.	.00185 in.	.00142 in.
	small grains .	.00008 in.	.00035 in.	.00024 in.
BARLEY. . . .	large grains .	.00039 in.	.00126 in.	.00079 in.
	small grains .	.00004 in.	.00024 in.	.00016 in.

248. Potato Starch, from tubers of *Solanum tuberosum* (family *Solanaceæ*), is distinguishable from wheat starch by the naked eye. The grains are so large that they are recognized as such even without the aid of a lens. The paste made from it is not so stiff nor so viscid as that made from wheat starch; it has also an unpleasant smell. The grains are mostly, but not always, simple, large and oval, and the layers are very distinct (Fig. 348). The nucleus is near the narrow end; the eccentricity varies from one-fourth to one-sixth.

Fig. 348. Starch grains from the Potato.

249. Rice Starch, from *Oryza sativa* (family *Gramineæ*), often has a yellowish color, but sometimes (the finest) is dazzling white. It is often bleached with chlorine compounds. It appears to the unaided eye like wheat starch; but with the simple lens no grains are visible. The grains are (1) single, and of the same size as the partial grains; and (2) compound, which are oval and consist of 2–100 parts. Instead of a nucleus, they have a cavity, which is often more or less star-shaped. No compound grains intact are found in the rice starch of commerce. This resembles the starch of oats, but may be distinguished from it at a glance, for in the latter the compound grains are not wanting.

250. Corn Starch, from grains of Indian Corn (*Zea Mays;* family *Gramineæ*), is much like that of wheat. The paste, however, is thicker, and the starch is more readily converted into grape sugar. When used in finishing cloth, it does not give so fine a polish as the wheat starch. The grains are perceptible with a strong lens; the size varies between .00032 and .00122 inches. Some grains are simple, polyhedrical, or roundish. The compound grains are composed of two to five parts. When fresh, they exhibit a nucleus; but when dry a cavity instead. The layers are not often perceptible.

251. West India *Arrow-root*, or **Maranta Starch**, is from the white, scaly, tuberous rhizomes of species of *Maranta* (family *Scitamineæ*). They are tropical or sub-tropical plants. *M. arundinacea* is indigenous in the West Indies and South America; cultivated in the Bermudas, Guiana, Ceylon, etc. *M. indica* is indigenous in the East Indies; cultivated in the East Indies and adjacent islands. The starch has been used by the natives from time immemorial. It is obtained by washing the rhizomes and soaking the pulp in water; the starch can then be washed out. The size of the grains is variable; the largest diameter .00043–00276 inches. The shape is oval, elliptical, or irregular; the grains are both simple and compound. This furnishes a simple food for invalids.

252. The East India **Arrow-root Starch** is from two species of *Curcuma* (*C. angustifolia* and *C. leucorrhiza*), belonging to the Banana family (*Scitamineœ*). They are extensively cultivated in India for the rhizomes, from which the starch is obtained. The grains are very large, elliptical, and flat; their width is about two-thirds their length. The layers are remarkably plain.

253. *Manihot utilissima*, of the Spurge family (*Euphorbiaceœ*), a woody-stemmed plant of Tropical America, is cultivated in many tropical lands for its large, fleshy, parsnip-like roots. These are peeled, carefully washed, then ground. From this reduced mass the starch is washed out, which is sometimes called *Brazilian Arrowroot*. The dried, ground mass is **Cassava**, also highly prized as food. The starch grains are generally double, or consist of two to eight parts. **Tapioca** is made by moistening the starch, granulating it by means of sieves, and heating it on metal plates. These three forms of food are extensively used, and considered very nutritious. The root in its raw state is poisonous.

254. The Sago Palms, *Sagus Rumphii* and *S. lœvis*, grow in the East—in Siam, the Indian Archipelago, etc. They attain a height of thirty to fifty feet. There is a soft white pith which is removed after splitting the stems. This is reduced mechanically, placed in water, washed repeatedly, and strained with sieves, by which means a pure pulpy paste is obtained. It is granulated with sieves, and the grains are rounded in rotating drums. They are then heated by hot steam or otherwise, which partially converts the starch grains into paste.

255. **Sugar-Cane** (*Saccharum officinarum*) is a native of Asia, but now cultivated in all warm regions of the world. It belongs to the Grass family (*Gramineœ*), and in size and appearance is much like Indian Corn. Its height

is six to fifteen feet (with forty to sixty joints), and diameter one and a half to two inches. It was not known in North Europe till the time of the Crusades. It went to the West Indies in 1506; the juice is a watery solution of sugar (seventeen to twenty per cent.), with traces of aleurone grains, glutin-like substance, vegetable wax, etc. It is pressed from the cane, and boiled to the point of crystallization; the crystals which then form are the *brown sugar*, and the amorphous residue forms the *molasses* of commerce. The brown sugar when refined constitutes the *white sugar*, which may be in large masses, broken lumps, granulated or pulverized. A considerable quantity of sugar is now manufactured from the beet. Although the quantity of sugar produced annually amounts to billions of pounds, "yet five hundred years ago it was but little known to our European ancestors, and even a century and a half ago it was one of the luxuries."

FIBRES.

256. The various Fibres used in the manufacture of fabrics, cordage, etc., may be (1) *hairs*, as cotton, silk-cotton, vegetable silk; (2) *fibro-vascular bundles* (of Monocotyledonous plants), as New Zealand Flax, Manila Hemp, Tillandsia; and (3) *parts of fibro-vascular bundles* (of Dicotyledonous plants), as Hemp, Flax, Jute, etc. They are mostly whitish in color, but may be yellow, green or gray, snow-white or black. Some are lustrous, and others are not. They are composed almost exclusively of cellulose; sometimes they are partially lignified, and are then more brittle. The amount of ash varies from .5 to 5.5 per cent. The hairs are generally unicellular, filled with air, and covered with a more or less distinct cuticula. The fibres

consistiug of fibro-vascular bundles may be composed of bast-cells aloue, or bast-cells with parenchyma, sieve-tubes and woody ducts. These component parts are so characteristic of the plants to which they belong that by microscopic examination the source of the fibres can be determined with certainty.

257. The vegetable fibres are used in the manufacture of (1) **Cordage**, (2) **Yarns** and **Woven Tissues**, and (3) **Paper**. For cordage (ropes, cables, and strings), the fibres may be coarse, but they must be very strong, and not suffer from the alternation of heat and moisture. They must have such flexibility that they will not break when bent at a sharp angle, otherwise the rope would break at a knot when a sudden jerk or strain is applied. For cables, besides possessing the above-mentioned qualities, the fibres must readily absorb tar. Yarns are finer than ropes or strings, and their fibres should be of considerable length and fineness. They must possess the "spinning quality," or glossy surface, else they would not readily slide against each other and through the teeth or comb of the machinery, by this means their parallelism is secured preparatory to twisting; considerable tenacity is also essential. The fibres for paper should be thin and short, suitable for felting together when in a wet state. A curly disposition, so as to catch each other and become entangled, gives, tenacity to the paper; this is increased if the ends of the fibres are lacerated into numerous fibrils.

258. The most important of all fibres used in spinning is **Cotton**. It was cultivated in Egypt five hundred years before the Christian Era, but was not known to the Ancient Egyptians. It has been known in India from time immemorial. It is now cultivated in nearly all

warm regions, as far North as 40° North Latitude (in Crimea 45°), and as far South as 30° South Latitude. Cotton consists of hairs on the seeds of several species of *Gossipyum*, of the Mallow family (*Malvaceæ*). The important species cultivated are: (1) *G. herbaceum*, probably indigenous in East Asia, cultivated in Turkey, Greece, Asia Minor and India; (2) *G. arboreum*, a native of South Asia, cultivated in East India, China, Egypt, West Indies, and North America; (3) *G. hirsutum*, native of West Indies and Tropical America, and widely cultivated; (4) *G. barbadense*, indigenous to West Indies, but cultivated in all cotton-growing countries; (5) *G. religiosum*, indigenous in China, and cultivated in China, East Indies, etc. The quality of the cotton depends somewhat on the species; that from the arboreous species is better than that from the shrubby, and that from the shrubby, better than that from the herbaceous species. The climate, soil, mode of culture, etc., has also an influence on the quality of the cotton as well as the habit of the plant. *G. arboreum* lives fifteen to twenty years in its native country, and yields annually two harvests. In Malta this species begins to fruit the second year, and after two years of productivity dies. The size and length of cotton of different species is as follows:

	Commonest length of fibre.	Maximum width.	Commonest width.
G. herbaceum	.79 in.	.00047–.00087 in.	.00075 in.
G. barbadense	1.58 in.	.00075–.00110 in.	.00098 in.
G. arboreum	.98 in.	.00079–.00150 in.	.00118 in.
G. religiosum	. . . .	.00087 in.	.00130 in.

The cell at first is round, and is more or less flattened when dry, as is best shown in a transverse section (Fig. 349). The cell-wall is thicker than in most hairs, hence its strength. Cotton is readily distinguished from Flax by reference to the comparative thickness of their cell-walls, the presence of a cuticula, and by the form of the cell. When air-dry, it contains 6.6 per cent. of water; in an atmosphere saturated with moisture, it contains 20.9 per cent. of water. The ash constituents amount to 1.8 per cent. For determining the quality, the important properties are: (1) Length—long staple is one inch, middle staple and short staple, less than one inch; (2) Silkiness—which depends on the minimum development of the cuticula; (3) Fineness and softness— that from *G. barbadense* being the best; (4) Purity and homogeneity, and the color.

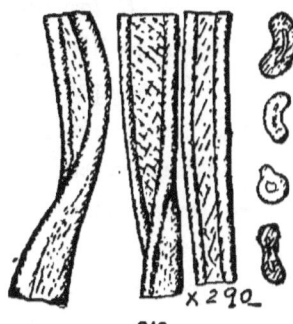

259. The **Silk-Cotton** is from the seeds of several trees (*Bombax*) belonging to the Mallow family (*Malvaceæ*). *B. hepatophyllum*, of South America and the West Indies, furnishes the largest and straightest hairs. They have a lustrous appearance like silk, but are not very strong nor durable. The silk-cotton is seldom used alone in spinning; it is, however, often mixed with cotton. It is seldom pure white; it verges into yellowish or brownish. The hairs are generally unicellular, but occasionally two-celled; the length varies from .39 to 1.18 inches. The greatest diameter is .00075–.00016; mostly .00083–.00114. The thickness of the wall is to the diameter of the cell as one to ten; cotton has relatively four times as thick a wall. The cuticle is evident under the microscope. The commonest use of silk-cotton is in stuffing cushions, etc.

Fig. 349. Cotton fibres.

260. Many other plants produce hairs which often find an economic use. The substance called **Pulu**, which is used somewhat in upholstery, consists of the long woolly hairs of several species of Fern, *Dicksonia* (family *Filices*), growing on the Sandwich Islands. On a Fern of the Azores, *Balantium calcita*, beautiful, soft, silky hairs grow, used by the natives for stuffing cushions. Several species of Asclepias (family *Asclepiadaceæ*) have long hairs on their seeds, but they have been found to be too brittle to come into extended use in spinning. The seeds of *Beaumontia grandiflora*, of the Dogbane family (*Apocynaceæ*), have lustrous, slightly yellowish, hairs, which, like the preceding, are used in upholstery, or mixed with cotton. All kinds of vegetable silk (or hairs) can be readily dyed.

261. The fibre longest used in spinning, namely, **Flax**, is the bast of *Linum usitatissimum*, a species of the Flax family (*Linaceæ*). It is a slender annual, growing from two to six feet high, and has small, alternate, lanceolate leaves, and blue flowers. It probably came originally from the Caucasus, or from Eastern Asia. It is extensively cultivated in many lands; other species are found in cultivation, but to a very limited extent. In warm regions more seeds and less fibre, and in colder regions more fibre and less seed, are produced. The Flax is harvested before the seeds are ripe, when the bast at the base of the stem begins to turn yellow; later, lignification sets in, to the detriment of the fibre. The unripe seeds may be used for oil, but not for planting. The plants are pulled out of the ground, and subjected to a process of retting, either by dew, cold or warm water, or steam, by means of which the bast is loosened from the stem, and more or less decomposed into fibres. These are 8–55 inches

in length, with equal fineness; the longer the fibre, the better. The width varies between .00177–.02440. The color is a light blonde to gray or yellowish. The best Flax is very lustrous; that which is lustreless is contaminated with cortical parenchyma. When air-dry, it contains 5.7 to 7.2 per cent. of water. The bast-cells, of which it is composed, have pointed ends and walls so thick that the cavity is almost closed; their length is 8–16 inches, their maximum width .00047–.00102, and commonest width .00059–.00067 inches. They are not bleached till after their manufacture into cloth.

262. The very important textile fibre, **Hemp**, consists of the bast of *Cannabis sativa*, a diœcious species of the Nettle family (*Urticaceæ*), growing six to twelve feet high, having large pedate leaves, with five leaflets and inconspicuous flowers. It is supposed to be a native of the warm parts of Asia, and is found in cultivation in Africa, North America, Australia, and elsewhere. It has been used in Europe several hundred years. It must be harvested for the fibre before maturity of the seed; the latter can then be used for obtaining oil. The pistillate plants when grown for the seed must be allowed to ripen. The process of retting is similar to that employed in case of Flax. The fibre of Hemp is longer and coarser than that of Flax. The color is often white, but the gray is the best. It is lustrous. The cells of the fibre are two-fifths of an inch or more in length, with mostly obtuse ends, and in transverse section are round. The cavity of the cell is about one-third its diameter; width of the latter, .00059–.00110 inches. The Hemp plant is used as an intoxicant for chewing and smoking by over three hundred million people. Its narcotic effect is due to a gum-resin existing in the leaves

and flowers; it is called "*Hasheesh.*" The seeds of Hemp contain thirty-four per cent. of oil, most of which may be extracted by pressure. It is a drying oil, greenish at first, then becoming yellow, and used in mixing paints, making soap, etc.

263. The bast-fibre of several species of *Crotalaria* (family *Leguminosæ*), especially *C. juncea*, a native plant of India and adjoining islands, is the so-called **Sunn**, or **Bombay Hemp**. It is found in cultivation in Southern Asia, Borneo, Java, etc. The plant is an annual, growing eight to twelve feet high, has silvery hairy leaves and bright yellow flowers. The fibre is removed by beating and washing, after the plants have steeped in water a few days. The fibres when air-dry contain 5.3 per cent. of water; in an atmosphere saturated with moisture they contain 10.9 per cent. of water. The color is pale, the lustre less than that of Jute. The bast-cells composing the fibre have a length of .0197–.2716 inches, and a width of .00079–.00165. The ends are very obtuse. The thickness of the wall is one-ninth to one-third the diameter of the cell. This Hemp finds a use similar to ordinary Hemp.

264. China Grass, *Bœhmeria nivea*, and *B. tenacissima*, perennial herbs, belonging to the Nettle family (*Urticaceæ*), have been cultivated in India since very early times, for their excellent fibre called **Ramie**. It cannot be readily separated from the epidermis and surrounding tissue. The bast-cells have a very large diameter. They are dirty green, whitish, yellowish, or light-brown, and are very tough and strong. Their length is very great, amounting sometimes to nine inches. The maximum diameter is .00158–.00315 inches; mostly .00197 inches. The Ramie or China Grass fibres contain when air-dry 6.5 per cent. of

water; in a saturated atmosphere, 18.2 per cent. of water. It is used for cordage; in India it is extensively employed for making fishing-nets. The finest fibre, even rivaling Flax in fineness and durability, is woven into cloth. *B. nivea* is now cultivated in the Southern States and in California.

265. One of the most important vegetable fibres, namely, **Jute**, is the bast of *Corchorus capsularis*, and other species of the Linden family (*Tiliaceæ*). It is an annual herb, growing to a height of eight to twelve feet, bearing simple jagged leaves and small yellow flowers, extensively cultivated in India, China, Egypt, Guinea, etc. For its best growth there must be a hot, moist climate, with abundant rain-fall, and a rich alluvial soil. The leaves are used in India as a pot-herb. The plant is harvested while in flower; for if allowed to stand till in fruit, the quality of the bast is not so good; as in case of Hemp, Flax, etc., so here also, the strength and flexibility decrease from the time of the appearance of the flowers till the ripening of the fruit, in consequence probably of lignification of the cells, which takes place during this time. The fibre is separated from the plants by retting (*maceration*)—bundles are thrown into water, and after a few days the bast readily separates from the stem. It is then washed and dried; this simple method suffices to obtain the Jute as clean as Hemp is made by heckling, but it is very rough and rigid; an attempt, therefore, is now being made to render it soft and flexible. "For this purpose bundles are laid upon one another, sprinkled with water and fat (commonly train-oil), and are allowed to remain, according to the warmth, twenty-two to forty-eight hours, or till the water has been sucked up and the fat has covered the surface. Prepared in this manner, the stalks are strongly squeezed between rollers and heckled in strong heckling machines, whereby the fibres, now to be wrought up like Hemp, are isolated." The fibres (consisting of many bast-cells) measure generally four to six feet, though there are many much shorter. The cells when isolated vary in length between one-fortieth and one-eighth of an inch. It is easily distinguished from Flax and Hemp by its silky lustre; it is also much more intensively colored by aniline. Fresh Jute has but little color; from whitish it varies into yellowish; exposed to the atmosphere, and especially to dampness, it becomes deeply colored, as seen in that long used for coffee-sacks, wool-sacks, etc. Fresh white Jute has been found by analysis to contain about six per cent. of water; used brown Jute contains seven or eight per cent. The ash constituents amount to about one per cent. When examined with the microscope, Jute is found to consist of bast-cells, which appear as shown in transverse section in

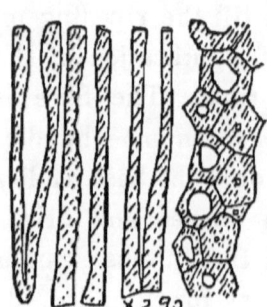

350a 350

Fig. 350. The walls vary much in thickness in adjacent cells; and, when examined in longitudinal section, it is found that each individual cell or fibre has at one place thin, and at another place thick, walls, as shown in Fig. 350a. Jute has been used since olden times, in those countries where it is indigenous, in the preparation of ropes and fabrics. Only within the last half century, however, has it come into extended use. From it is manufactured coarse cloth in great quantity, used for packing and transporting all manner of goods. Even carpets and cloth

Figs. 350, 350a. Cells of the Jute fibre in transverse (350) and in longitudinal section (350a), magnified.

of considerable fineness are now made from it. It is sometimes woven with silk.

266. A few plants yield **Bast** in wide long strips, which need no further preparation for weaving into mats or for wrapping certain wares. It is the inner bark which is the *bast*, and is called the *endophlœm*. The bast-cells may be in rows, or single in the parenchyma. They vary much as to length, strength, etc. In Europe (especially in Russia) large quantities are obtained from the Linden-tree, *Tilia parvifolia* (family *Tiliaceæ*). The tree is cut and the bark removed in May. This is thrown in water, and left for several weeks; when taken out and dried, it separates into thin layers, corresponding to the annual rings of growth. A tree of moderate size yields about ninety pounds, from which ten or twelve mats are made. The finest are made from the inner layers. The bast from *Sterculia villosa* (family *Sterculiaceæ*), a tree of India, has long been used for ropes, strings, etc. It is composed of many annual rings, or layers, like the Linden bast, but not so easily separated as that. The bast of *Holoptelea integrifolia* (family *Urticaceæ*), of the West Indies, is thicker than Linden bast, for which, however, it is often substituted. Bast is obtained for various purposes from numerous other trees in different countries.

267. From the leaves of the Flax-Lily, *Phormium tenax*, of the Lily family (*Liliaceæ*), the **New Zealand Flax** is obtained. The plant has firm leaves four to six feet long. The scape bearing the panicles of red flowers is sometimes more than ten feet high. Cook, in his first voyage around the world, gave information of this New Zealand plant. It is now cultivated in the East Indies, Australia, etc. The fibres in the leaves are numerous, amounting to about

twenty-two per cent. The crude fibre is yellowish or whitish, and has a length sometimes of over three feet. According to Labillardiere, the comparative strength of Silk, New Zealand Flax, Hemp, and Flax are represented by 100, 60, 48, and 34½. The New Zealand Flax is used extensively in making ropes, mats, etc.

268. Several species of *Aloe*, especially *A. perfoliata*, of the family *Liliaceæ*, yield the **Aloe Fibre**. This is whitish and somewhat lustrous; it is soft and flexible, has a length of eight to twenty inches, and a maximum thickness of .00295–.00413 inches. It contains when air-dry ten per cent., and when in a saturated atmosphere eighteen per cent., of water. The fibre consists simply of bast-cells having thick walls, the cavity being one-third the diameter of the cell. The cells are cylindrical and pointed. The common Aloe fibre is used in the manufacture of ropes and cables, and the finest in the manufacture of cloth (Aloe-cloth).

269. *Musa textilis* (family *Scitamineæ*) is much like the Banana-tree, fifteen to twenty feet high, with dark-green leaves. It is cultivated on the Moluccas, the Philippine Islands, etc. From it and other species of the same genus the **Manila Hemp**, called also *Siam Hemp*, *Plantain Fibre*, and *White Rope*, is obtained. The leaves contain fibres, but they are not very strong, and are not used. Those of the stem or trunk are obtained as follows: The tree when five or six inches in diameter is felled and subjected to a process of retting and then passed through iron combs. The fibres in the centre of the stem are finer than those near the periphery. The fine fibres have a length of two yards, and the coarse ones are longer; the usual thickness of the former is one-half inch; of the latter,

four-fifths of an inch. The amount of water contained, when in a dry atmosphere, is twelve per cent.; when in a saturated atmosphere, fifty per cent. The fibre consists mainly of bast-cells, whose walls are little or much thickened. It is used extensively for cordage; it is very useful for cables for ships on account of its durability in water. The old worn ropes are then used in the manufacture of paper.

270. Of all the kinds of "vegetable horse-hair," none are so valuable as the **Tillandsia Fibre**, or **Long Moss**, *Tillandsia usneoides*, a member of the Pine-Apple family (*Bromeliaceæ*). It grows in tropical and sub-tropical regions. It is an epiphyte, "very common in the low countries, from the Dismal Swamp, Virginia, to Florida and Louisiana, hanging in long, dark gray tufts and festoons from every tree." It has a three-parted green calyx and three colored petals. In elasticity, strength, durability, and appearance the Tillandsia fibre approaches true horse-hair. It consists of the decorticated stems of the plant, the epidermis being readily removed by a simple process of retting. The fibres are sometimes an inch long, and have a thickness of .004–.005 inches. The color is black or brown; when dry it contains nine per cent. of water; the amount increases to twenty per cent. in an atmosphere saturated with moisture. The ash forms over three per cent. It is used in stuffing cushions, mattresses, etc.

271. Fibres from which **Paper** is manufactured must be obtainable in immense quantities, must also be soft, fine, and readily bleached. Those most used are cotton, linen, Hemp, Jute, Straw, Wood, young Bamboo-trees, bast of Paper-Mulberry, Esparto Grass, etc. The textile fibres are not used generally until the cloth into which they

have been woven is worn out. The oldest paper made from straw is Chinese-paper, made from rice straw. Now straw of all kinds (Wheat, Rye, Barley, Oats) is used. Wood must be a white, soft, fibrous kind, as that from the Pines, Poplars, Maples, and Linden. The inner bark of the Paper-Mulberry, *Broussonetia papyrifera* (family *Urticaceæ*), a native of the islands of the Southern Ocean, is now extensively used in paper-making. The bast is separated from the tree in large, white, flexible pieces, which can be separated into long, fine fibres, from which, in Japan, paper, flexible like cloth, is made, which is used for handkerchiefs, napkins, etc. The plant is now cultivated in many countries. The Alfa, or Esparto Grass, is also much used in paper-making. There are two species, *Stipa tenacissima* and *Lygeum Spartum* (family *Gramineæ*). They grow wild on the high grounds of North Africa. The cells are remarkably firm and short, and manifest a tendency to curl. They have the merit over wood-pulp of absorbing printing ink more rapidly.

272. The **Papyrus** of the ancients was made by slicing the pith of a Sedge, *Cyperus papyrus*, or *Papyrus antiquorum* (family *Cyperaccæ*), and gluing the thin slices together under pressure. The plant grows on the marshy banks of rivers, etc., in Abyssinea, Syria, Sicily, etc. It has large rhizomes, which grow in the mud, and send up triangular stems six to ten feet high; these are an inch or more in diameter, and their "pith," or inner tissue, is snowy white, and can be cut almost as readily as elder pith. The large flower-cluster is highly prized by the natives for decoration; the pith is eaten as food. The stalks are used in the manufacture of wicker-work, boxes and baskets, and from the bark are made cordage, mats, and cloth.

THE CORTEX, OR BARK.

273. The **Cork Oak,** *Quercus Suber* (family *Cupuliferæ*), is found in the southern part of Europe and the northern part of Africa. It has oval, dentate, evergreen leaves. The thick mass of cork which it develops is removed periodically, and constitutes the cork of commerce. A corky layer, or periderm, begins to be developed when the tree is two or three years old. The first cork that is produced is very inferior, but after its removal good cork is yielded. When the tree is five years old, the first worthless layer can be removed without injury to the phellogen, or cork-producing cambium. This is done by making vertical and horizontal incisions, reaching almost to the generating layer of cells or phellogen, within; the bark is then carefully pried off. This process cannot be performed with safety during the period of rest of vegetation, nor during the active renewal of growth in the spring; it can be done, however, between May and October without in the least harming the phellogen, provided the latter is not exposed to rain. The layers become two-thirds to one inch (or more) thick, and are removed every eight or ten years. When the trees are fifteen years old, a valuable layer may be removed. Cork continues to be produced till the trees are one hundred or one hundred and fifty years old; that is best, however, which is removed from trees between fifty to one hundred years old. The cork that grows in warm regions is better than that produced in cold climates; and that from trees on the mountains is better than that from trees in swamps. It is said that the thick branches and the south side of the trunk yield better cork. When removed, the layers of cork are placed in piles and weighted with stones and allowed to dry, thus losing fifteen per cent. in weight. The outermost and innermost sides are then removed with a knife or file, and the slabs placed in boiling water five to six minutes. They are then dried, and found to have gained one-fifth in volume. In Spain the cork layers or slabs are sometimes drawn through a flaming fire, when they take on externally a blackish and internally a deep grayish-brown color. The cork slabs or plates are sometimes nearly two inches thick; they are plainly stratified, i.e., the annual rings of growth are plainly seen. The cork-cells are in section generally four-sided; their walls are very thin, and seldom lignified. The hard, brittle portion of the cork consists of sclerenchyma. Cork contains more carbon and less oxygen than cellulose; its important chemical constituent is Suberin. The various uses of cork are well known, and require no further mention.

274. Of the various **Tanning Barks** used in different countries, none compare with those from several species of Oak (*Quercus*). The most valuable species in Europe are *Q. pedunculata* and *Q. sessiliflora*. These have for centuries supplied the tanners with bark, by use of which leather of the best kind, both as to color and wear, is made. The quality of Oak bark is better when the trees grow on good clay soil; poorer, when on calcareous soil. It has been shown by analysis that Oaks of fifty years growth yield thirteen per cent., and those one hundred years old yield but eight per cent., of tannin. The inner bark of the Cork Oak (*Q. Suber*) contains much tannin, and is used in Spain for tanning. The Oran, or African Oak (*Q. coccifera*), yields fifteen per cent. of tannin, and is extensively imported for tanner's use. In Russia, one of the most

important tanning barks is furnished by Willows. In this country most of the bark used in tannery comes from White Oak (*Q. alba*), Red Oak (*Q. rubra*), Scarlet Oak (*Q. coccinea*), Black Oak (*Q. tinctoria*), Burr Oak (*Q. macrocarpa*), the Hemlock (*Abies Canadensis*), and Birch (*Betula alba*). The Oak and Hemlock barks make the leather firm and hard, and give good weight. Mimosa bark, from species of *Acacia* (family *Leguminosæ*), growing in Australia, is now extensively used in tanning. The Mangrove bark (*Rhizophora Mangle*) has been much used, but the leather obtained from it is inferior in color and quality. The Mangrove-tree grows in low places in all tropical countries. The table below gives the percentage of tannin in the barks most commonly used. It is to be remembered, however, that the absolute amount of tannin does not determine the color, solidity, pliability, and other properties constituting good leather, which are also to be considered in selecting tanning materials.

Name of Plant.	*Tannin.*
British Oak (*Quercus pedunculata*, and *Q. Robur*)	10 per cent.
Cork Oak (*Quercus Suber*)	12 per cent.
Hemlock (*Abies Canadensis*)	11 per cent.
Mangrove-tree (*Rhizophora Mangle*)	27 per cent.
Red Oak (*Quercus rubra*)	6 per cent.
White Oak (*Quercus alba*)	8 per cent.
Black or Quercitron Oak (*Q. tinctoria*)	7 per cent.
Mimosa (*Acacia dealbata*, etc.)	27 per cent.
Burr Oak (*Quercus macrocarpa*)	8 per cent.

275. The important dye, **Quercitron**, is obtained from the Black Oak, *Quercus tinctoria*, a North American tree, growing to a height of eighty to ninety feet, and attaining a diameter of four or five feet. The bark is deeply furrowed, of a deep brown or black color, and yellow within.

The leaves are six or more inches long, lobed, with the broadest end towards the apex. The acorn is seven-eighths of an inch in diameter, in a large scaly cup. The species was originally called *Quercus citrina,* and by a corruption of this the name *Quercitron* was formed, which is used to designate the yellow dye obtained from the bark. The quality of the dye is excellent, and besides can be obtained in immense quantity. For these reasons it has almost entirely superseded the *Genista, Reseda,* and other yellow dyes, formerly used very extensively in Europe. The dyeing capacity of Quercitron is said to be four times as great as that of the yellow wood (*Maclura*), and eight or ten times as great as that of *Reseda.* The outer bark of the tree is removed, the inner is then ground between millstones. The odor is weak, peculiar, but not disagreeable; the taste is bitter. The Quercitron resides mainly in the parenchymous tissue of the middle and inner bark. The important constituent is *Quercitrin,* which consists of sulphur-yellow crystals, soluble in alcohol, scarcely soluble in water, and not at all soluble in ether. The Quercitron is used both in dyeing and tanning.

276. The bark of *Cinnamomum zeylonicum,* of the Laurel family, is the **Cinnamon** of commerce. The plant is cultivated in India, Ceylon, Sunda Islands, West Indies, and South America. It is a small tree, twenty to thirty feet high, with oblong-lanceolate leaves. The trees are topped, every one or two years, like basket-willows, and thus from the main stem many shoots are produced; from these the bark is easily removed in the spring, after a rainy period, when the activity of the cells in the cambium zone is greatest. Circular incisions are made at considerable distances from each other, and connected by a longitudinal

incision. The bark is then removed by the help of the knife-blade. When partially dry, the outer bark is scraped off; the bark or bast is then whitish, but as soon as dry presents the peculiar cinnamon color. If vigorous growth takes place in November and December, the bark can be again removed, but it is inferior. The refuse parts, together with the leaves, are used in the manufacture of oil of cinnamon, of which the bark contains .5 to 1 per cent. This is used in perfumery. Cinnamon finds extensive use as a spice; in medicine it is used as an aromatic and moderate stimulant.

277. Another tree of the same genus as the last (*C. Cassia*), growing in Southern Asia and neighboring islands, yields the **Cassia bark** and **Cassia buds**. Cassia bark is thicker than, but otherwise much the same as, the cinnamon; the taste, however, is not so fine and strong. The bark of the young twigs is cut longitudinally on two sides, when the cambium is full of sap. After twenty-four hours it is removed, the outer bark at the same time spontaneously separating from it. In drying, the bark rolls up into tubes like the cinnamon. Cassia bark contains .8 to 1.5 per cent. of volatile-oil.

278. Several arboreous species of the South American genus Cinchona (of the Madder family, *Rubiaceæ*), as *C. calisaya*, *C. lutea*, *C. micrantha*, etc., furnish the **Cinchona bark** of commerce, the most important febrifuge known. It is also called **Peruvian bark**, or **Jesuits' bark**. In the mountainous regions of New Grenada, Bolivia, and Peru, the bark is collected by half-civilized Indians. They cut their way into the forests, clear the parasitic and climbing plants from the Cinchona trees, remove the bark from the trunk, then fell the tree and collect the bark

from the branches. It is then dried to prevent moulding. This irrational method of procedure must eventually end in the annihilation of the Cinchona supply. Successful attempts have, therefore, been made in the cultivation of the trees in the East Indies. If the bark is dried too much, the amount of alkaloids decreases. At first it is pale yellow, then becomes deep yellow, red, or brown. The outer part of the bark of old trees is removed as worthless; the entire bark of young trees or stems is used. The taste of Cinchona bark is intensely bitter, but the odor is weak. Among the numerous constituents are found cellulose, gum, sugar, starch, mineral constituents (mostly calcic and sodic carbonate), and many alkaloids. Of the latter, *Quinia* is the most important; it is crystallizable, slightly soluble in water, soluble in alcohol, ether, and chloroform; forms crystallizable salts, with several acids. The sulphate of Quinia, or Quinine, fine, white, silky, is the form most used in medicine. The next most important alkaloid constituent is *Cinchonia*, which is about one-half less powerful than *Quinia*. Various preparations of the bark and alkaloids are made, and used medicinally as tonics and febrifuges.

WOOD.

279. The **Wood** or lignified stems, trunks, and branches of Gymnosperms (as Pines, etc.), of some Monocotyledons (as Palms), and of Dicotyledons are used in architecture, ship-building, manufacture of vehicles, machines, implements, tools, furniture, ornaments, in the construction of bridges, fences, for fuel, etc. A great variety as regards color, strength, hardness, weight, porosity, durability, flexibility are offered by the numerous species of woody plants.

The following list contains some of our most important kinds of wood, or indigenous timber trees:

Yellow Poplar, *Liriodendron Tulipifera* (*Magnoliaceæ*).
Linden, or Basswood, *Tilia Americana* (*Tiliaceæ*).
Sugar-Maple, *Acer saccharinum* (*Sapindaceæ*).
Oregon Maple, *Acer macrophyllum* (*Sapindaceæ*).
Flowering Locust, *Robinia Pseudacacia* (*Leguminosæ*).
Kentucky Coffee-tree, *Gymnocladus Canadensis* (*Leguminosæ*).
Honey Locust, *Gleditschia triacanthos* (*Leguminosæ*).
Wild Black Cherry, *Prunus serotina* (*Rosaceæ*).
Black, or Sour Gum, *Nyssa multiflora* (*Cornaceæ*).
White Ash, *Fraxinus Americana* (*Oleaceæ*).
Red Elm, *Ulmus fulva* (*Urticaceæ*).
Mulberry, *Morus rubra* (*Urticaceæ*).
Butternut, *Juglans cinerea* (*Juglandaceæ*).
Black Walnut, *Juglans nigra* (*Juglandaceæ*).
Shell-bark Hickory, *Carya alba* (*Juglandaceæ*).
Pignut Hickory, *Carya porcina* (*Juglandaceæ*).
White Oak, *Quercus alba* (*Cupuliferæ*).
Douglas Oak, *Quercus Douglasii* (*Cupuliferæ*).
Burr Oak, *Quercus macrocarpa* (*Cupuliferæ*).
Red Oak, *Quercus rubra* (*Cupuliferæ*).
Black Oak, *Quercus tinctoria* (*Cupuliferæ*).
Chestnut, *Castanea vesca* (*Cupuliferæ*).
Beech, *Fagus ferruginea* (*Cupuliferæ*).
Iron-wood, *Ostrya Virginica* (*Cupuliferæ*).
Paper, or Canoe Birch, *Betula papyracea* (*Betulaceæ*).
Red Pine, *Pinus resinosa* (*Coniferæ*).
White Pine, *Pinus Strobus* (*Coniferæ*).
Douglas Spruce, *Abies Douglasii* (*Coniferæ*).
Red Cedar, *Juniperus Virginiana* (*Coniferæ*).

Redwood, *Sequoia sempervirens* (*Coniferæ*).

Larch, or Tamarack, *Larix Americana* (*Coniferæ*).

Cypress, *Taxodium distichum* (*Coniferæ*).

280. *Hæmatoxylon Campechianum* (family *Leguminosæ*), the pulverized wood of which constitutes **Logwood**, or **Campeachy-wood**, is a tree of Central and South America, forty to fifty feet high, with a diameter of fifteen to twenty inches, and having a rough bark. The flowers are in axillary racemes; the calyx is purplish, and the corolla yellow; the sap-wood is whitish; the heart-wood is of an intense blood-red color, and when exposed to the atmosphere becomes a deep violet or blackish. It was first brought into commerce by the Spaniards, and early found its way into England, where, in the time of Elizabeth, its use in dyeing was prohibited by a special act of Parliament. This continued in force for a hundred years, until by new processes more durable colors from it could be made. The wood is very hard and difficult to split. The annual rings are scarcely distinguishable, and the Medullary Rays are visible only with the aid of a lens. The fresh wood has a sweetish taste and a slight odor. It gives with water a colored solution. The important constituent is Hæmatoxylin. Logwood is used in dyeing, and in staining anatomical preparations for the microscope. In medicine it is a mild astringent. The wood is employed in cabinet-work.

281. A large, crooked, and knotty tree of South America, *Cæsalpina echinata* (family *Leguminosæ*), with fragrant red flowers and small leaves, furnishes the **Brazil-wood**, called also *Pernambuca-wood*. The heart-wood is of a deep red color, very hard, heavier than water, and takes a fine polish. The annual rings and ducts, but

no Medullary Rays, are visible to the naked eye. The reduced wood, shaken in cold water, gives only a trace of red substance; more is yielded on boiling. The important constituent is Brazilin, which is soluble in water and alcohol. Brazil-wood is used in dyeing red; the color is not permanent unless fixed with mordants. Red ink is prepared by boiling the wood in water and adding a little gum or alum. Paper saturated with it is used in chemical analysis as a test for sulphurous acid, by which it is bleached; also for fluorine, which turns it yellow. The wood is used in fine cabinet-work.

282. *Pterocarpus santalinus* (family *Leguminosæ*), of India, is the **Red Sandalwood**. The tree grows to a height of twenty or thirty feet, and has a heavy, close-grained wood. The heart-wood is of an intense red color; exposed to the atmosphere it becomes brownish and blackish. In a transverse section of the wood isolated ducts are visible, but no Medullary Rays can be seen ; the latter become visible in a radio-longitudinal section. The coloring matter is contained in the tissue of the Medullary Rays, ducts, and parenchyma. It is but slightly soluble in cold water. With ammonia-water, a carmine red, and with alcohol, a light yellowish-brown extract, is obtained. The important constituent is Santalin. This wood is used both for dyeing and in cabinet-work.

283. The wood of *Rhus cotinus* (family *Anacardiaceæ*) is called **Young Fustic, or Zante Fustic, or Fustet**. The plant is shrubby, or arborescent, and is found in the Mediterranean region. The heart-wood is golden-yellow, sometimes inclining to greenish. The small pith is brownish. The annual rings are evident to the naked eye, but the Medullary Rays are scarcely distinguishable without

the aid of a lens. The heart-wood has a silky lustre, is soft and light, difficult to split, and when fresh has a turpentine odor. The important constituent is Fisetin, which is nearly related to Quercitrin. Young Fustic is used in dyeing wool and leather.

284. The **Boxwood-tree**, *Buxus sempervirens*, of the Spurge family (*Euphorbiaceæ*), is an evergreen shrub, or small tree, of Southern Europe and Asia Minor. The leaves are small, oval, and opposite; the flowers are diœcious and inconspicuous. The pith, annual rings, and five Medullary Rays are visible to the naked eye. Under the microscope the rings are scarcely recognizable; on the convex or outer side of the ring is a row, one or two cells thick, whose cells are compressed radially, and whose cavities are reduced to a line. Though these cells are not visible to the naked eye, yet they have a peculiar color, which makes the annual ring distinguishable. The ducts are regularly distributed, and vary from .0008–.0016 inches in width. Each Medullary Ray is composed of one or two, seldom three, rows of cells. The wood is hard, fine, homogeneous, yellowish, and lustreless. It is very difficult to split and very durable. Its specific gravity varies from .99 to 1.02. It finds extensive use in making wood-cuts for pictures and illustrations. It is also highly prized in turnery, and in the manufacture of musical and mathematical instruments.

285. The **Mahogany**, *Swietenia Mahogani* (family *Meliaceæ*), is a large spreading tree of the West Indies and South America. It grows about fifty feet high, and has a diameter of four or five feet. The leaves are pinnate and shining; the flowers are small, greenish-yellow, in axillary panicles, which are three or four inches long; the

fruit is oval and large. The wood found its way into Europe at the end of the sixteenth century; about a hundred years later it was in use over the world generally. The wood is brown, when exposed becoming very dark. The annual rings are very indistinct. The fine Medullary Rays are visible to the naked eye. The wood is difficult to split; its specific gravity is .56–.88. It is a valuable wood for cabinet-making.

286. The **Cork-wood** of Jamaica, *Ochroma Lagopus*, belonging to the Mallow family (*Malvaceæ*), has wood so soft and elastic that it is used as a substitute for cork. The trees attain a height of forty feet, and grow along the coast on the West India Islands and Tropical America. The fresh wood is whitish, but becomes somewhat reddish-brown when exposed. The large ducts and narrow Medullary Rays are visible to the naked eye. The wood is so soft that it can readily be impressed with the finger-nail; it cuts like cork, and has a slightly silky lustre. The specific gravity is equal to that of cork.

287. Several species of *Diospyros*, of the Ebony family (*Ebenaceæ*), especially *D. Ebenum*, furnish the valuable wood called **Ebony**. The trees are large, but slow-growing; the leaves are entire, coriaceous, and dark-colored; the flowers are axillary and diœcious. The heart-wood is deep black in color, very hard, firm, and heavy (specific gravity 1.18–1.24). In transverse section the rings of annual growth are scarcely visible. Both the ducts and Medullary Rays can be seen only with the aid of a lens. The wood is used for knife-handles, piano-forte keys, fine cabinet-work, inlaying, etc.

288. The **Teak-tree** (*Tectona grandis*), belonging to the Verbena family (*Verbenaceæ*), is indigenous in India.

On account of its great value it is extensively cultivated; it is said the cultivated trees furnish better wood than those growing wild. It is a magnificent tree, with opposite, ovate or elliptical leaves six to eight inches long; they are rough on the upper surface, and are used for polishing; they also yield red dye. The trees are cultivated; when forty to sixty years old they attain a height of sixty feet and a diameter of four feet. The Teak-wood when fresh is a light brownish-red; upon exposure it becomes brown, or brownish-black. The annual rings are not clearly marked; the Medullary Rays are irregular in their course and distribution. The wood is heavy (specific gravity .9), hard, and splits with difficulty. It is said to contain much silex. It is highly prized in ship-building. "It is said to resist the attacks of *Limnoria terebrans* when exposed in sea-water." It is employed in building temples, dwellings, etc.

289. The yellow dye called **Fustic**, or *Old Fustic*, is the wood of *Maclura tinctoria*, a large tree of the West Indies, belonging to the Nettle family (*Urticaceæ*). The heart-wood is yellowish, brown, or orange-yellow. Neither the annual rings nor the Medullary Rays are plain to the naked eye. The ducts become visible when examined with a lens. The important constituents of the wood are Morin and Maclurin, both soluble in alcohol and slightly soluble in water. The dye is obtained by boiling the wood, and is used "for converting silks, woolens, and light fabrics already dyed blue to a green."

290. The curious tree called **She-Oak**, or **Iron-wood** (*Casuaria equisetifolia*), a representative of the Beef-wood family (*Casuarinaceæ*), is found on the South Sea Islands and Indian Archipelagoes. It is also cultivated in the

Tropics. It is a leafless tree, with smooth bark; the branches are cord-like, pendulous, striate, and have sheathing joints, much resembling the stems of the Scouring Rush (*Equisetum*). The flowers are inconspicuous, the staminate in spikes or catkins, and the pistillate in heads, eventually becoming a woody cone. The wood is brown in color, and has many small ducts. The Medullary Rays are not visible to the naked eye. The wood is difficult to split and cut. The bark furnishes a dye, and the ashes are used in the manufacture of soap. It is a valuable timber for ship-building. This tree and other species of the same genus are cultivated as ornamental curiosities.

ROOTS AND RHIZOMES.

291. The dye **Madder** is furnished by a small plant of the order *Rubiaceæ*, namely, *Rubia tinctoria*. Its roots are perennial; they send up annually slender-jointed, square stems, a few feet high; the leaves are whorled, and the plant resembles some species of *Galium*. The flowers are in clusters, and have a rotate yellow corolla. Madder was known to the ancient Greeks and Romans. It is now cultivated in Europe, Asia, Australia, and America. It is seldom raised from the seed, but usually from stolons; after two years the slender roots can be used. The outer cortex of the root is reddish-brown. All the membranes or cell-walls are yellow or red. The coloring matter exists dissolved in the cell-sap; and in drying, the walls become tinged. Many chemical constituents are contained in the root, among which may be mentioned Rubian, a brown, amorphous, gummy substance, soluble in water and alcohol, but insoluble in ether. After the roots are dug, they are dried, then flailed to remove the cuticle; they are then crushed and ground. Madder is used for dyeing red.

292. *Anchusa tinctoria*, of the Borrage family (*Borraginaceæ*), yields the red dye called **Alkanet**. The plant is perennial, and has pretty blue flowers. It is a native of Southern Europe, and extensively cultivated for the roots, which are yellowish within, and dark violet on the surface. The important constituent and coloring matter is Anchusin, a resinous, purple-red substance. Alkanet is much used in coloring fats, alcohol, and varnishes. An alcoholic extract is used in dyeing linen, cotton, and silk; for dyeing goods violet they must be previously prepared with alum mordants, and for coloring gray the fabrics must have been prepared with iron mordants.

293. *Curcuma longa*, a member of the Banana family (*Scitamineæ*), is a native of Southern Asia, and is cultivated in India, Ceylon, Java, the West Indies, etc. Many different varieties have arisen under cultivation, which furnish the dye **Turmeric** in varying qualities. The rhizome is tuberous, and from it arise leaves, some being roundish, others narrow. It is heavier than water, and yellow or orange in color. The taste is somewhat pungent and spicy, the odor aromatic. The coloring matter resides both in the cell-walls and also as an amorphous mass within the cells. Its most important constituent is Curcumin, in the shape of prismatic crystals; it is soluble in ether and alcohol. Turmeric (the yellow rhizome) is used in dyeing paper, wood, and leather, and in coloring varnishes. It is much used in cookery, also in medicine. Turmeric paper, or unsized paper colored with a decoction of Turmeric, is used in the chemical laboratory as a test for free alkali, which turns it brown.

294. The Ginger-plant, *Zinziber officinale* (family *Scitamineæ*), has been cultivated, from time immemorial, in

India, in which country it is probably indigenous. It has recently come into cultivation in the West Indies and other tropical lands. It is an annual plant, with stems two or three feet high and leaves two or three inches long. The flowers are yellowish, and have an aromatic odor. The rhizome, powdered or otherwise, constitutes the **Ginger** of commerce. It contains about one per cent. of volatile-oil, which is thin and reddish-yellow. The rhizome contains also starch, resin, etc. It is used in obtaining the oil, which is employed in cooking, for flavoring liquors, etc. Ginger is a mild stimulant and carminative, and has been used as a spice from early times.

295. The Sweet Flag (*Acorus Calamus*) has a fleshy aromatic rhizome called **Calamus**. The plant grows in Europe, Asia, and North America, in marshy or wet places. It has a spadix of greenish flowers; the leaves are long, radical, and sword-shape. The rhizome is collected in the fall, when it contains the largest amount of reserve material. It is then washed and dried, and used in the manufacture of oil of calamus, yielding about one per cent., which is found mainly in the cortex; or if to be employed in medicine the cortex is removed. The odor as well as taste of the rhizome is aromatic. It is used by confectioners, also in preparing aromatic vinegar and some other articles.

LEAVES.

296. The **Dyer's-weed** or **Weld**, *Reseda luteola* (family *Resedaceæ*), is an erect, herbaceous, European plant, about two feet high; the leaves are small, alternate, lanceolate, with a tooth on each side at the base; the flowers are greenish-yellow in a long spike. This plant has been

cultivated from ancient times for coloring yellow; but since the introduction of Quercitron it has not been so much used. The important constituent is Luteolin, consisting of yellow, prismatic crystals, soluble in alcohol; the solution is bitter and the reaction acid.

297. The **Tea-plant**, *Camellia chinenses* (family *Turnstrœmiaceœ*), has been cultivated for ages, and its native country is now no longer known. It is an evergreen shrub or very small tree, generally kept dwarf by pruning. The branches are very numerous, bearing elliptical or lanceolate leaves, which are two or three inches in length. The plants yield a small picking when three years old, but the maximum yield is in the eighth or tenth year. The leaves are carefully picked, heated in pans, and rubbed with the hands into the form they retain. The processes of heating, airing, pressing, rolling, and drying are continued alternately till the desired changes take place in the leaves. The rapidity of this operation and the age of the leaves when picked determines the quality of the tea; young leaves, quickly prepared, give the best green teas. Old leaves, subjected to a less rapid operation, yield the black teas. Among the many constituents found by analysis, may be mentioned carbo-hydrates, albuminoids, tannin, caffein, aromatic oil, and mineral substances. Tea (an infusion of the leaves) has been used by the Chinese as an exhilerating beverage for centuries. Recently it has found its way into nearly all countries, and is used almost universally now by rich and poor.

298. **Tobacco**, *Nicotiana Tabacum* (family *Solanaceœ*), was used by the Indians long before America was discovered by Columbus, for in old Indian mounds smoking utensils have been found. It was taken to Spain by

de Oviedo in the early part of the sixteenth century, later to France by Nicot, and to Germany by Gessler. Although sometimes prohibited by edicts, smoking soon became general all over Europe, passed into other countries, and finally found its way into Australia; and tobacco is now "used by all civilized nations of the globe." It is a native of South America, but cultivated in many countries, being easily acclimated. The plant grows from three to six feet high, and bears long, broad, soft, hairy leaves. The flowers are terminal, rose-color, and showy; the capsule is two-celled and many-seeded. The culture, soil, and climate affect the quality of the tobacco very much. The best is grown in light soils exposed to the sun, the leaves having then less mesophyll. The largest yield is obtained about 32° North Latitude; it is cultivated, however, in western North America at 40°, in Japan at 52°, and in Europe at 62° North Latitude. The plants are cut while yet green, dried, and prepared for chewing, smoking, etc. The most important alkaloid contained is *Nicotine;* it is strongly alkaline, heavier than water, and very poisonous. The ash varies from fifteen to twenty-seven per cent., and of this twenty-five to fifty per cent. is lime, seven to fifteen per cent. magnesia, three per cent. potash, etc.

299. **Peppermint,** *Mentha piperita* (family *Labiatæ*), native of Europe, cultivated in several countries, is a small square-stemmed plant, one to three feet high, with ovate-lanceolate and serrate leaves. The spikes are oblong, or cylindrical, and obtuse; the corolla is purplish. A volatile-oil exists in all parts of the plant to the amount of one per cent. That obtained from the leaves alone is finer than that obtained from the whole plant. The specific gravity is .89–.92.

FLOWERS.

300. From the petals of several species of Rose, *Rosa centifolia, R. gallica, R. damascina, R. sempervirens*, etc. (family *Rosaceæ*), **Attar of Roses** and **Rose-water**, etc., are manufactured. For this purpose roses are cultivated in great quantities in several warm countries. On one acre of ground, ten thousand rose plants may stand, and these produce annually about five thousand pounds of rose leaves (i.e. petals), and this quantity of petals yields one pound of oil or Attar of Roses. The flowers are collected before they are fully expanded. From the petals, by a simple process of distillation, *Rose-water* is obtained. The process in the manufacture of the Attar (called also Ottar and Otto) is much more complicated. It is seldom to be found pure, being mixed with oil of geranium and olive-oil. *Spirit of Roses* is obtained by distilling the petals with a small quantity of alcohol. The dried petals infused in vinegar is called *Rose of Vinegar*. By beating up the fresh flowers in boiling water, and adding an equal weight of honey, *Honey of Roses* is obtained; and *Conserve of Roses* is made by beating up the petals with sugar.

301. The **Orange-tree**, *Citrus aurantium* (family *Rutaceæ*), is cultivated both for its delicious fruit and fragrant flowers. It is an evergreen shrub or small tree, native of India; it has a greenish-brown bark, and bears oblong leaves, with winged petioles; the sepals and petals are five each, and the versatile anthers about twenty or more. The fruit is a berry, the well-known *Orange*. The flowers are solitary, or in axillary clusters, and very fragrant. From their fragrant white petals the oil of

Neroli is obtained, which is used in perfumery, and the hard close-grained wood is used for inlaying.

302. "The most beautiful, the most elegant, the most precious of all trees" is the *Caryophyllus aromaticus*, which produces the **Cloves** of commerce. It is a member of the Pink family (*Caryophyllaceæ*), and grows to the height of forty feet. The trunk is straight; the bark is smooth, and of a light-olive color; the crown of the tree forms a perfect cone. The Clove-tree is a native of the Moluccas and New Guinea, and cultivated in many tropical lands. The cloves are the unexpanded flowers, or flower-buds; these, attached to their pedicels, are collected when they contain the most and best oil, which amounts to from sixteen to twenty-five per cent. They also contain a large amount of tannin. When dry, the stems are broken off, and from them about four per cent. of oil is obtained by distillation. The oil is slightly yellowish or brownish. It is found in drops, in intercellular spaces, in all the tissues, and even in the filaments. Cloves are extensively used as a spice, and in medicine furnish a stimulant to the digestive organs. The oil is used in perfumery and in flavoring liquors.

303. Three or four species of *Lavendula* (family *Labiatæ*) are cultivated for the flowers, from which the **Oil of Lavender** is obtained. The species commonest in cultivation is *L. vera*, an evergreen shrub about two feet high; it has grayish-green, hoary leaves, which are linear and sessile. The flowers are in long spikes; the bilabiate corolla is pale violet or blue; the corolla and calyx are covered with stellate hairs, among which are shining, oily glands, to which the fragrance is due. Lavender is a native of the mountainous regions bordering on the Mediterranean; it is easily acclimated, and found in cultivation in Europe and

North America. The volatile-oil amounts to about three per cent., and is contained very largely in the glands of the calyx. About one and a half per cent. is yielded on distillation. It is of a pale yellow color and of a pleasant odor; it is soluble in alcohol. The best oil is obtained by distilling the flowers alone, without the stems. A larger amount is obtained when the flowers grow in dry, bright weather. The oil of Lavender is used in perfumery.

304. *Carthamnus tinctoria*, **Safflower**, has been cultivated from time immemorial for the flowers, which are used for dyeing. It belongs to the Composite family, found native in the East Indies, and cultivated in Persia, Egypt, East Indies, Australia, Mexico, etc. It is an annual, but becomes biennial under cultivation; many "varieties" have arisen. It grows two or three feet high, is prickly, has stiff leaves, and produces a head of red flowers. Filamentous chaff, or pales, are found among the florets. It is harvested two or three times a year by collecting the flowers, or florets, as far as possible free from the other parts. These are simply dried, or first washed and then dried, but not in the sun, for then they lose a part of the coloring matter. The important constituent is called Carthamnin (.3–.6 per cent.), a deep reddish-brown, amorphous powder, which is insoluble in water, but soluble in alcohol. Safflower is used in dyeing, especially silk; the shades of color vary between red and yellow. From the seeds an oil is obtained (eighteen per cent.), which is used in illumination and for food. It is a cathartic, and saponifiable.

305. The stigmas of *Crocus sativus*, Iris family (*Iridaceœ*), constitute the dye **Saffron**. The plant is cultivated in Europe, Africa, America, etc. It has blue or purple flowers, and linear, radical leaves. The long flower-tube is almost sessile on the bulb; the pistil is about four inches long, surmounted by three clavate-crested stigmas; in these the coloring matter resides. These stigmas are picked out of the flowers, and about twelve thousand of these are required to obtain a single ounce of Saffron. Crocin, or Safranin, is the important constituent; it is a red, amorphous substance, soluble in water and alcohol. Saffron is used as a spice, and also medicinally. It is used for coloring cheese, liquors, confectionaries, etc.

306. *Anthemis nobilis*, **Chamomile**, is a European herb, of the Composite family. It is a prostrate, woolly plant, with compound leaves, the leaflets cut into linear or subulate segments. The involucre is hemispherical; the ray flowers are numerous and white. The plant has a strong and agreeable odor, and a bitter, aromatic taste. It is cultivated for the flowers, which have tonic and anodynous qualities, and for the oil which is extracted from it.

SEEDS AND FRUITS.

307. The **Almond**, *Amygdalus communis* (family *Rosaceæ*), is a native of the Caucasus, and has been long in cultivation. It is a low, spreading tree, with lanceolate-serrate leaves. The flowers are sessile, in pairs, and precede the leaves in the spring. The seed consists of two cotyledons and a caulicle, surrounded by a hard pericarp. In the *Bitter Almonds* 1.5–3 per cent. of Amygdalin is contained, a bitter, crystallizable substance; besides this, oil (thirty-five to forty per cent), sugar, gum, albuminoids, cellulose, acetic acid, and coloring matter are contained in both *Bitter* and *Sweet Almonds*. The oil is light yellow, with a specific gravity of .92. The purer sorts of almonds are used in the manufacture of oil, which is used for flavoring

liquors, for perfumery, and in medicine. They are also used for food.

308. The **Peanut,** *Arachis hypogæa* (family *Leguminosæ*), is supposed to be a native of South America; it has been cultivated for a long time in all warm countries. It is an annual plant, with clover-like leaves, and yellowish axillary flowers on erect peduncles. After fertilization these bend downwards, and the ovary is thrust into the ground, where the pod ripens; this is an indehiscent legume, coriaceous, veiny, and tough. The seeds have an oily taste; analysis shows that they contain forty-three to fifty per cent. of fat, twenty-seven or twenty-eight per cent. of albuminoids, thirteen per cent. of starch and cellulose, and some gum and sugar. The oil when cold-pressed is colorless, of a pleasant odor and taste, and thinner than olive-oil; when warm-pressed it is yellowish, and has an unpleasant odor and taste. The plant is cultivated for the fruit, which is consumed in large quantities as food. The oil which is manufactured from the seeds is used for food, also for illumination, and in the manufacture of soap.

309. The **Coffee-plant,** *Coffea Arabica* (family *Rubiaceæ*), is indigenous to Abyssinia, where it is called Coffa, and within a few hundred years has come into cultivation in many other countries. It is an evergreen tree, eighteen to twenty feet high; it has white, papery bark, and slender, horizontal branches. The leaves are oblong-ovate, acuminate, smooth and shining, six inches long, and nearly one-half as wide. The evanescent flowers are in axillary clusters; they are pure white, and have a rich, fragrant odor. The fruit is a cherry-like berry, becoming of a dark-red color as it ripens; the pulp within is yellow, and encloses two plano-convex seeds, the *Coffee* of commerce. The constituents of coffee are as follows: Caffein, eight per cent.; fat, ten to thirteen per cent.; cellulose, thirty-four per cent.; water, twelve per cent.; trace of oil and ash, 6.7 per cent. The use of coffee was prohibited by the Koran, it being regarded as an intoxicant. Coffee-houses were opened in Constantinople in the sixteenth century, and were met with violent hostility on the part of ecclesiastics. The first coffee-shop was opened in London in 1652; the use of coffee met with opposition here also. At about the same time cocoa and tea were introduced. Coffee is now used in immense quantities. Statistics show that the approximate amount used annually per inhabitant in France is 2.73 pounds; in Belgium, 13-48 pounds; in Holland, 21 pounds; in Italy, 1 pound; in Denmark, 13.89 pounds; in Russia, .19 pounds; in Switzerland, 7.03 pounds, and in the United States, 7.61 pounds.

310. The **Castor-oil Plant** (Fig. 351), *Ricinus communis* (family *Euphorbiaceæ*), supposed to be a native of India, is now cultivated in the East Indies, Africa, North America, and some other countries. Many "varieties" have arisen under cultivation. In cold countries it is an annual; in warm countries it becomes perennial, woody, and arborescent. The stem is glaucous, bearing very large leaves, with serrated lobes; the flowers are apetalous and monœcious in terminal

Fig. 351. The Castor-oil Plant (*Ricinus communis*).

panicles; the stigmas are feathery and the capsules are prickly. The seeds are the size of a small bean, with a shell sprinkled brown and gray. They contain in the endosperm a large quantity of albuminoids. The oil in the seeds, for which the plant is cultivated, amounts to forty or forty-five per cent.; it is a thick fluid, of pale color, slightly nauseating odor, and oily taste. It is used for illumination, especially in the East; it is employed in the manufacture of soap, and used in medicine as a mild cathartic.

311. The **Flax-plant**, *Linum usitatissimum* (described in paragraph 261), is cultivated mainly for the fibre, but the seed is also an important product, because of the oil which is expressed from it. Each capsule has ten small brown seeds, which are flattened, smooth, shining, and oblong. These are found by analysis to contain eight per cent. of water, thirty-three per cent. of oil (twenty-seven per cent. being usually expressed), twenty-five per cent. of albuminoids, a trace of tannin, and four or five per cent. of ash. The *Flaxseed-oil* is a drying oil, used in the manufacture of printer's ink, varnishes, soap, and for food.

312. For a long time the seeds of cotton, *Gossypium herbaceum*, etc. (see paragraph 258), were regarded as useless refuse, but from them lately an *Oil* has been expressed. The seeds, after the removal of the coating of hairs (cotton), are seen to be oval, their cotyledons much folded, and contain forty-five per cent. of oil, and grains of aleurone. The oil has a specific gravity of .93; it contains palmatin and oleic acid; unrefined it is brownish; refined it is yellowish or whitish. It is used as a machine oil, for illumination, and in the manufacture of soap, etc.

313. The **Chocolate-tree**, of Tropical America, *Theobroma cacao* (family *Sterculiaceæ*), is a small tree sixteen

to twenty feet high, having large oblong leaves, thin and papery. The small flowers are followed by the elongated, ribbed fruits, each containing fifty or more oily seeds, arranged in five vertical rows. The tree blooms almost constantly; the fruits are collected twice a year. The almost colorless seeds when dried become reddish-brown; they are elliptical, slightly flattened, and exalbuminous; the cotyledons are of a deep brownish or violet color, filled with drops of oil and grains of aleurone. The constituents of the seeds are cocoa-butter, thirty-four to fifty-six per cent.; the alkaloid Theobromine, which imparts the bitter taste; sugar, cellulose, starch, and albuminoids. The seeds are used in the manufacture of *Butter of Cocoa* (used in perfumery) and of *Chocolate* and *Cocoa*. The seeds are roasted, then ground into a paste; to this are added vanilla, sugar, etc., forming chocolate, or without these various ingredients it is cocoa.

314. The **Mustard-plants**, *Sinapis nigra* and *S. alba* (family *Cruciferæ*), native annuals of Europe, have stems three to six feet high, with lyrate, pinnate, or dentate, petioled leaves. The flowers are yellow, the fruit is a silique, smooth, and with a four-sided beak, in case of *S. nigra*; hispid, and with an ensiform beak, in case of *S. alba*; the seeds of the former are roundish, or elliptical, and deep brown; of the latter, large and yellow. Their taste is at first oily, then burning; the taste of the black seed being the stronger. They contain three per cent. of fixed oil, which is odorless and tasteless. The oil is expressed from the seeds. *Mustard-seed* has been used in medicine very many years, being mentioned by Theophrastus and by Galen. It is used externally as a cataplasm, and internally as a diuretic and irritant. The pulverized seeds are also used as a condiment.

315. The **Nutmeg-tree**, *Myristica moschata* (family *Myristicaceæ*), is a native of the Indian Archipelago, now cultivated in many tropical lands. The tree is twenty to thirty feet high, and has the aspect of a Pear-tree. The bark is smooth and gray, and within has a yellowish juice. The slightly aromatic leaves are alternate and petiolate, oblong, with an acute apex, entire, dark-green, and somewhat shining. The staminate flowers are very fragrant, in clusters of three to five, much like those of the Lily of the Valley, and have about eleven stamens; the pistillate flowers are much like the others, but usually solitary, and have a single pistil, with a two-lobed stigma. The seed has a hard, dark-brown shell, about a line in thickness, enclosing the kernel, which is the *Nutmeg* of commerce. Surrounding the seed is a lacerate, red aril, which forms the spice *Mace*. The kernel, or endosperm, is furrowed, and into these depressions the delicate inner testa sinks, giving in section a marbled appearance. The endosperm is very hard, heavier than water, and consists of parenchymous cells, filled with fat, starch, and aleurone grains. It contains myristica-butter, and six per cent. of volatile-oil. The aril is dried after being removed from the seed, and the red color is exchanged for a dull orange-yellow; it becomes horn-like, and contains four to nine per cent. of oil. The plants, if raised from seed, bear when eight years old, and continue to bear until seventy or eighty years old. The fruit is collected (1) in March, or early in April, when both the nuts and mace are in greatest perfection; (2) in July and August, when the fruit is most abundant; (3) and collected again in November, when the fruit is smaller, but the mace is thicker. The nuts are dried over the fire till the seeds rattle in the shell; the brittle shells are then

broken with a hammer. The average annual product of a tree is five pounds of nutmegs, and one and a half pounds of mace.

316. Caraway, *Carum carui,* of the Umbel or Parsley family (*Umbelliferæ*), is cultivated for its aromatic fruit or mericarps. The cultivated plant has larger and more odorous fruit than the wild; it is biennial, has a stem two to four feet high, smooth, striate, and bears dissected leaves and white flowers in umbels. The wild plant contains three to five per cent., and the cultivated plant nine per cent., of volatile-oil. The oil is pale yellow, thin, has a bitter taste and strong odor; it is used in flavoring liquors and articles of food, also in perfuming soap. Caraway is used as a spice, and in medicine as a stimulant to the digestive organs.

317. Anise, *Pimpinella anisum* (family *Umbelliferæ*), a perennial herb of Asia and Africa, cultivated in Europe, etc., has pinnately-parted leaves and large umbels of white flowers. The mericarps are used in confectionery and in the manufacture of *Oil of Anise,* which is obtained both by distillation and by pressure. The oil is colorless when fresh, and yellow when old; its specific gravity varies from .98 to 1.07; it consists mainly of *Anethol.* It is used in medicine, being aromatic and carminative.

318. Coriander, *Coriandrum sativum* (family *Umbelliferæ*), is an annual plant, both indigenous and cultivated in the Mediterranean region. It is two or three feet high, has bipinnate leaves, and white flowers in umbels. The fruit is globular or roundish, the two mericarps do not separate. When fresh the odor is very strong and unpleasant; dried, it is pleasant, spicy, and aromatic. The volatile-oil contained (which is obtained by distillation) is less than one per cent. in amount, and has a pleasant odor. Coriander is used in confectionery, for liquors, and medicinally.

319. **Fennel**, *Fœniculum vulgare* (family *Umbelliferæ*), is a European plant, cultivated for the pleasant aromatic quality of its leaves, which are used in flavoring sauce. It grows from three to six feet high, has a round stem much branched and glaucous, biternate leaves finely dissected, yellow flowers, and turgid, ovate, oblong fruit, which is warmly aromatic. All parts of the plant are impregnated with oil to the amount of three per cent.; but it is extracted from the fruit only. The *Fennel-oil* is yellowish in color, has a pleasant odor, and a sweetish taste; its specific gravity is .9 to 1.0. The principal constituent of the oil is Anethol. It is used medicinally.

320. The **Hop-plant**, *Humulus Lupulus* (family *Urticaceæ*), grows wild in Europe, Asia, and North America, and is also extensively cultivated. It is an annual twining plant with a rough stem; the leaves are long-petiolate, three-lobed, and very rough on the surface. The staminate flowers have five sepals, five stamens, dehiscent by a pore; the flowers are numerous, greenish and panicled; the pistillate flowers have one sepal and two styles, are small and inconspicuous, but they are subtended by large, entire, concave and imbricated bracts, which form a cone, or cone-like ament. The fruit-clusters are the *Hops;* they have on the upper side of the scales or bracts golden-yellow glands, which are many-celled, oval or roundish, and contain a volatile-oil. The wild Hops are larger than the cultivated ones, but have scarcely any glands. A bitter principle called Lupulin (or Humulin) is contained in the glands; the latter are sometimes isolated by shaking

in a sack and carefully sifting; one ounce of glands may be obtained from one pound of Hops. Hops are found by analysis to contain volatile-oil (two per cent.), resin, gum, malic acid, tannin, etc. The ash amounts to 8.5 per cent. By distillation with water the Hops yield nine per cent. of oil. Hops are used in large quantities in brewing beer and in medicine. The plant was introduced into the United States about two hundred and sixty years ago, but extensively cultivated only within the last seventy-five years. In Sweden, a fibre is obtained by boiling the Hop-plant in alkaline-water for a few hours, then in acetic acid; from it is manufactured a strong, white and durable cloth.

321. The **Vanilla-plant**, *Vanilla planifolia*, is a member of the Orchid family (*Orchidaceæ*). It is an epiphyte, growing on trees in Tropical America, now cultivated in India, East Indies, and elsewhere. It has thick, laurel-like leaves and inconspicuous flowers. The fruit is a fleshy capsule five or ten inches long; it is gathered before maturity, wrapped in wool, and heated, then exposed; this process is often repeated till the fruit is dry, and the odor and brown color in the meantime becoming fully developed. Upon analysis the following constituents have been found: tannic acid, resin, fat, wax, gum, sugar, and an aromatic substance, namely, Vanillin. The flowers of the Vanilla-plant when cultivated out of its native country must be artificially fertilized. It is propagated by attaching scions to trees, which produce fruit after three years, and continue to bear thirty to forty years. Its culture is carried on in connection with the culture of the Chocolate-tree, on which the Vanilla-plant grows.

322. **Vegetable Ivory** is the endosperm of *Phytelephas*

macrocarpa (family *Phytelephasieæ*, nearly related to *Palmaceæ*), a plant found in the tropical region of America. The tree has a stem six or eight inches in diameter, and pinnate leaves eighteen to twenty feet long. The diœcious flowers are enclosed in a spathe; the cluster of fruit is globular, six or eight inches in diameter, and contains about forty nuts, each nut as large as a walnut, ovate, slightly flattened, and contains within the brittle shell the endosperm, which is nearly as hard as ivory; it is composed of parenchyma, whose cells have very thick walls. This, called Vegetable Ivory, can be readily turned and colored, and is used extensively in the manufacture of toys, buttons, handles, door-knobs, and other small objects for which ivory is used.

GALLS AND CRYPTOGAMS.

323. Galls are pathological, often more or less globular, outgrowths on the stems, twigs, or leaves of many plants, caused by the punctures or stings of insects. The best Galls of commerce are collected from an Oak of the Levant, *Quercus infectoria* (*Cupuliferæ*). A species of *Cynips*, an insect belonging to the suborder *Hymenoptera*, inserts its ovipositor in the leaves and twigs and deposits its eggs. An unnatural multiplication of parenchymous tissue takes place, forming the excrescence or Gall with the eggs, now hatched into larva, within. A large amount of tannin is contained in the tissue, and the Galls are, therefore, used in tanning, dyeing, making ink, etc. In Europe a large quantity of Galls is obtained from *Quercus pedunculata* and *Q. sessiliflora*. The Chinese Galls come from a species of Sumac (*Rhus*). Curious red-horned Galls, used for tanning morocco leather, are obtained from the Chio Turpentine-tree (*Pistacia Terebinthus*). Galls called "Padwus" are produced in India on a species of Tamarisk (*Tamarix Furas*). Under the name of *Valonia*, the acorn-cups of *Quercus Ægilops*, of the Mediterranean region, are found in commerce, also used in tanning.

324. Carrageen, or **Irish Moss,** is the Sea-weed or Alga *Chondrus crispus* (division *Carposporeæ*). It grows on the rocky North American and European Atlantic coast. It is greenish-yellow to dark purple in color, and soft and gelatinous in texture. It is washed and dried, when it becomes horn-like, yellow, and translucent. It contains thirty-three per cent. of mucilaginous substance, ten per cent. of albuminoids, and fifteen per cent. of mineral constituents, in which is a large amount of iodine. It forms a jelly in twenty to thirty times its weight of boiling water. Carrageen is used occasionally as an article of food (*blanc mange*), and to thicken colors for printing calico. In those regions where it grows, it is often employed as cattle food. The Dulse, *Rhodymenia palmata* (division *Carposporeæ*), growing in places similar to the last, is also used as human food, and as a remedy in scrofulous complaints.

325. *Roccella tinctoria* is a foliaceous Lichen (division *Carposporeæ*), which grows in tufts in rocks. It is found all over the world, often growing on high perpendicular cliffs, from which it is collected by men lowered with ropes. From this and other species of Lichens, **Orchil** and **Litmus** are obtained. The former was at one time very much used in dyeing, but has recently been largely replaced by dyes of the coal-tar products. Litmus is used as a chemical test for acids and alkalies.

326. Iceland Moss, *Cetraria islandica,* like the preceding, is a foliaceous Lichen, three or four inches high, with branches channeled or rolled into a tube. It grows in the mountains of the North, and is characteristic of the lava slopes of Iceland. It contains seventy per cent. of Lichenin, or Lichen-starch, a substance isomeric with starch, but destitute of structure. It also contains cetraric acid, which gives a bitter taste. It forms a nutritious and easily-digested food, and is a mild tonic. In Iceland it is used, however, as food only in times of scarcity.

APPENDIX.

327. For the study of ORGANOGRAPHY no extensive outfit is required. It is desirable to collect an illustrative specimen of each and every thing mentioned in the text, both as an aid to a clear understanding of the object in question and as a means of impressing and fixing it in mind. To do this a digging instrument, as a trowel, or a very large knife, is needed to obtain roots for examination, and a strong knife is also necessary to get woody specimens, flowers, fruits, etc. For carrying these a covered box of strong pasteboard, or other material, will be necessary; or what is, of course, in every respect more advantageous, a *Botanical Collecting-box* (such as shown in Fig. 352). This is made of tin, about eighteen inches long and four to six inches in diameter, being elliptical in transverse section. The lid is nearly as large as the side of the box, and close-fitting so as to prevent escape of moisture,  thereby preserving specimens fresh for a long time. The box is generally carried by a strap thrown across the shoulder, and fastened to the ends of the box. For making sections of stems and other parts, as buds, ovaries, etc., for examination, a very sharp knife (or a razor) is needed. A pocket lens should be carried invariably; it is almost indispensable in the examination of minute flowers,

Fig. 352. The Vasculum, or Collecting-box.

324 APPENDIX.

sections of anthers, ovaries, seeds, etc. The lens shown in Fig. 353 is very convenient; the lens can be slipped off the rod B. and carried in the pocket. As represented in the figure it can be used as a "dissecting" microscope, the specimens being placed on the base below the glasses and the latter slipped up or down till it is in focus, or can be plainly seen; with mounted needles, or similar instruments in the hands, a small object or delicate specimen

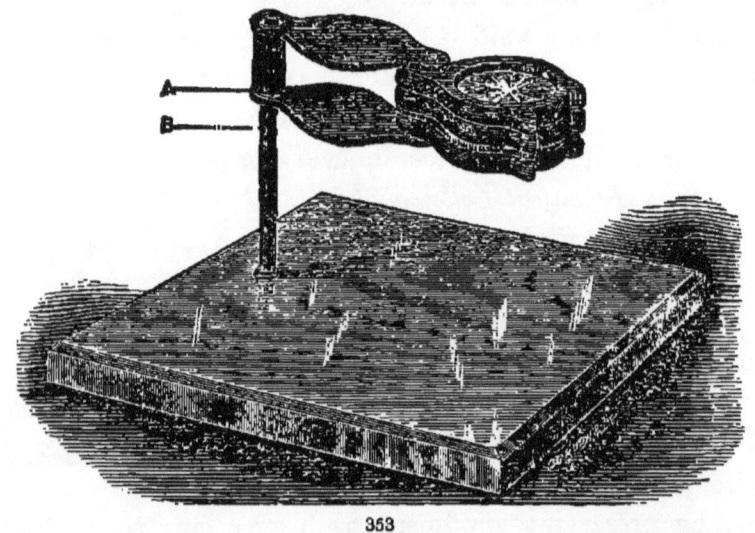

can be turned and examined at will. When parts are too delicate to be held between the fingers in making sections, they can be clamped between two pieces of elder pith; or, better, slit a short piece of the pith nearly its whole length and insert the piece to be cut, pressing the pith between the thumb and fingers as before when cutting.

328. In order to watch the process of germination and follow the development of the organs, seeds may be planted in the soil out of doors if the study is carried on during

Fig. 353. A Pocket Lens, mounted as a dissecting microscope.

the growing season. In cold weather seeds may be sprouted and plants grown in a box of moist soil kept in a warm room. If the germination only is to be observed, the seeds may be placed on anything which is kept moist, as a layer of cotton on water in a small vessel; in an unglazed earthen dish, as a saucer of a flower-pot placed on a plate or in a shallow dish containing water, etc. In such case the plantlets will grow only as long as there is nourishment in the seed to draw from. It is desirable to preserve specimens for later study or reference. As a general thing, they need simply be dried, in which case they retain, more or less, their natural appearance. Delicate parts, as leaves, flowers, etc., must be dried between papers under pressure, otherwise they become distorted and unsightly. Collections of twigs, showing various kinds of buds, their variation in shape, size, etc., and specimens of leaves and flowers after being dried, can be fastened on stiff paper for preservation and further use. The specimens may be sewed on the paper, or fastened by using narrow strips of gummed paper, placing a sufficient number across the specimen to hold it in place; another common mode of mounting (as this is called) is to glue the specimen to the paper, using common white glue, or a mucilage of gum-arabic. Specimens should invariably be accompanied by illustrations made from fresh specimens, which may be mere outline figures, such as every pupil with a little practice can readily draw. The drawing of figures of specimens daily studied, on the black board as well as on paper, should be constantly practiced.

329. The study of HISTOLOGY, or minute anatomy, can be made much more profitable by the aid of the microscope. This instrument, for studying the most of the cells, tissues, etc., mentioned in the text-book, numerous as they

are, need not be an expensive one. Formerly microscopes of any value cost at least fifty or sixty dollars; now very satisfactory ones may be had for half that money. It is not the high magnifying power that should determine the choice of microscopes or lenses, but mainly their penetrating and defining power, the flatness of the field, etc. The system of combination of lenses at the lower end of the tube is called the *objective*. Objectives are generally named or designated by their focal distance: thus, two inch, one inch, one-half inch, one-quarter inch, one-eighth inch, etc. The first being of very low magnifying power, the next higher, the third still higher, and so on. The combination of lenses and the frame which holds them at the upper end of the tube of the microscope is called the *eye-piece*. The instrument without eye-pieces and objectives is called the *stand*. The plate below the objective, on which the object to be examined is placed, is called the *stage*. In the middle of it is an aperture, a short distance below which is placed a small, round *mirror*, generally reversible, the one side having a plane and the other side a concave reflecting surface. It is movable, and is to be so adjusted that it will reflect the light up through the object which is placed on the stage to be examined. The tube holding the eye-piece and objective is movable either by smoothly sliding through a supporting tube or by means of a rack-and-pinion. This is called the *coarse adjustment*, and by it the objective is brought to a certain point near the object, at which the latter can be most clearly seen; or, as it is said, brought into focus. With only very low-powered objectives, however, can this point be readily attained without a *fine adjustment*. This is secured by means of a fine screw, or otherwise. The object when in exact focus is seen within a circular space, called *the field of view.*

330. Many objects, as pollen grains, spores, hairs, etc., require no special manipulation preparatory to their examination. They need simply to be placed on a narrow slip of glass, which should be perfectly clear, called a *slide.* The commonest size of glass-slides is one by three inches. A preferable form is that now coming into extended use; it has a size of twenty-five by forty-five millimetres. Over the object must invariably be placed a very thin piece of glass, called the *cover-glass.* As a rule, objects must be placed or mounted (as it is called) in water, alcohol, glycerine, or balsam. Other reagents, as all these substances are called, are often needed, as potash, acetic and other acids, iodine, hæmatoxylin, and other staining reagents. The use of alcohol in preparing objects for examination is important, as will early be learned by experience. It is invaluable for driving out bubbles of air that are entangled in the tissues or other objects to be examined. These air bubbles are the great pest of the microscopist, and even alcohol will not always expel them entirely. They appear as round, transparent bodies, bordered by a dark line, and will doubtless be seen, even if not recognized, in the first specimen mounted by the amateur. The potash solution tends to clear specimens that are dark, and is indispensable when judiciously used. Iodine has many uses, and should be invariably at hand. Glycerine is one of the most convenient and valuable of the mounting fluids. All these and other reagents are supplied in small bottles by those who deal in microscopes and microscopists' supplies.

331. The cutting or making thin sections of tissues

for examination with high powers is difficult, but with some practice it can usually be well done. For this purpose a razor is used. The object or specimen to be cut is held between the thumb and fingers of the left hand; if it is delicate or thin, as a fragment of leaf or piece of wood, etc., it can be clamped in a slit piece of elder pith, or of cork. The section must be made exactly at right angles to the longitudinal axis of the stem, leaf, etc., and the knife or razor must be drawn with the right hand steadily (better rather quickly) and obliquely to the blade towards the person. A drop of water or alcohol should be placed on the blade before cutting, in which the sections can at once float; if they become dry, they are worthless. After making very many sections, three or four of the best ones can be carefully lifted with the point of a scalpel, mounted needle, or otherwise, and transferred from the razor to the glass slide, previously cleaned and wiped with care, and on which a drop of the mounting fluid has been placed. Over these place a clean cover-glass, and remove any superfluous fluid which may be at the edge of the cover-glass with a piece of bibulous paper. Then the object is ready for examination; place it on the middle of the stage and move the tube of the microscope down till the objective is supposed to be at about the proper point for clear vision. Then look through the eye-piece, and at the same time move the mirror until it is so adjusted as to reflect the proper amount of light up through the specimen. Now with the fine adjustment focus accurately and examine the object *ad libitum*. Sketch what is seen, which will be both a test as to correct observation and a means of better fixing the image in mind.

332. Mounting specimens for preservation and subse-

quent use is still more difficult, yet with a little patient practice every person can do it satisfactorily. More care should be exercised to secure good specimens, and every air bubble must be expelled. The mounting medium should be, as a rule, glycerine, yet for some objects Canada balsam is better. Other media are used, but the beginner need not now encumber himself with them. Proceed as directed above, but more care must be exercised in putting on the cover-glass, so as not to entrap any air bubbles. The superfluous fluid must also be more carefully removed, and the slide wiped till thoroughly dry; then with a small camel's hair brush, dipped in asphalt or other cement manufactured for this purpose, run a line along the edge of the cover-glass, cementing it to the slide; set it aside, protected from dust, for a day or two, or till dry, and run another line of cement over the first, and perhaps ultimately a third one to thoroughly secure it. Square cover-glasses will be found to be much more convenient than round ones. The mounted slides must be kept free from dust, for they are difficult to clean. It should be remembered that if strong alkalies or acids have been used in the preparation of specimens, they must be thoroughly washed to remove every trace of the reagent, otherwise the specimen will be worthless. Neutralize acids with weak ammonia, and alkalies with acetic acid. Dry mounts are such as are made without the use of any mounting medium. Pollen grains, spores, and a few other objects may be so prepared. For detailed directions for manipulating the microscope, preparing and mounting objects, one must have recourse to the various works on such subjects, and for material of all kinds apply to manufactures and dealers of such wares. It is quite desirable to have small forceps, such as represented in Fig. 354, mounted needles, small scalpels, etc. These, and accessories to the microscope, are described in catalogues of microscopes.

333. Material for examination is so extensively abundant that it remains necessary to mention but a few objects most likely to be overlooked. Many isolated cells exhibit a variety of form as well as of sculpture or markings. Pollen grains of various plants and spores of different Cryptogams should be examined. Thin longitudinal sections of various stems should also be made; for stellate cells make sections of Rush (*Juncus*) stems. The cells from the Dahlia root from hard nuts, knots in pears, etc., in section, exhibit stratification; a rather high power must be used in their examination. The rotation of the protoplasm within the cell can be seen in leaves of *Vallisneria*, and a few other water plants mounted in water; the circulation of the protoplasm in the stamen-hairs of the Spiderwort (*Tradescantia*), in the stinging hairs of Nettle, etc., but with difficulty. The grains of chlorophyll will be easily seen in green tissue, but for beautiful spiral bands, rings and stars, one must examine our numerous fresh-water Algæ, or the "green slime" in streams, ponds, etc. For examination of starch grains thin sections of tissue can be made, or the cut surface scraped; the mass should be mounted in water; upon the addition of iodine the grains become blue. The stratification is very evident in potato

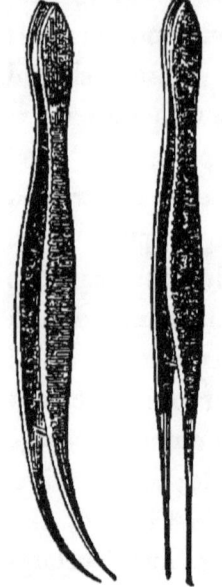

Fig. 354. Figures of Forceps.

starch. Raphides are abundant in the garden Rhubarb, Evening Primrose, Balsam, etc. Other forms of crystals will often be met with, especially in *Begonia* leaves, scales of Onion bulb, etc.

334. For examples of cell-rows the Algæ above spoken of must be resorted to. Cell surfaces or single layers of cells are illustrated in the leaves of the Mosses. For *collenchyma* make sections of Potato stems, Dock, Cucumber, etc. In the rhizome of a Fern, the Common Brake, (*Pteris aquilina*) will be found if thin longitudinal sections are made, examples of *sclerenchyma*, as well as of other tissue. It is also illustrated in stony nuts, shells, etc. For primary *meristem*, longitudinal sections through buds or the growing-point must be made, which consumes much time before success can be expected. Very often the epidermis can be pealed off, and when spread out and looked at will exhibit the *stomates*. It is also necessary to make thin sections in order to understand both the epidermis and the stomates. No difficulty will be met with in obtaining different specimens with the *fibro-vascular bundles*, but scarcely so much can be said as to making sections of them so as to exhibit all the points of structure mentioned in the text. Common cork stoppers can be examined, also the bark of many plants, as Birch, etc., for cork-cells; in the latter case the walls are thicker. Very small *intercellular spaces* will be seen, if thin sections of leaves, pith of Indian Corn, etc., be examined with a high power. Large canals are seen often with the naked eye in stems and petioles of many water plants. Resin canals may be looked for in Pine leaves, orange and lemon rind, many of the Labiatæ, etc.

335. When a leafy stem is cut off it wilts unless put in

water; to see that liquids actually pass up into the stem to supply the loss by evaporation, place the stem in a colored solution, as the juice of Poke-berries. Grow plants in the dark, change them from light to darkness, and vice versa, to verify statements in the text. Grow some plants by "water-culture" as follows:

Take of Potassic phosphate . . . . 12 milligrams.
" Sodic phosphate. . . . . 12 milligrams.
" Calcic chloride . .   . . 27 milligrams.
" Potassic chloride . . . . 40 milligrams.
" Magnesic chloride. . . . . 20 milligrams.
" Ammonia nitrate . . . . 10 milligrams.
" Ferrous chloride . . . . a few drops.

Dissolve the above in nearly a quart (one litre) of water. Sprout the seeds and support them in the wide-mouthed bottle containing the solution, so that the roots only will dip in the solution; provide a fresh solution every week or two, and thus grow the plant to maturity. Vary the experiment by omitting one or more of the elements of food or substances in the above list, and note the result.

336. While pursuing the SYSTEMATIC BOTANY, it is desirable as far as possible to collect representatives of the several groups from the native flora. Specimens should not only be collected but preserved for subsequent use and reference (directions for collecting, pressing, poisoning, and mounting specimens of "flowering plants" will be found in a companion volume to this book). The same remark may apply to some extent in reference to the study of ECONOMIC BOTANY. The objects and specimens when studied in the text should, by all means, be at hand for actual examination. A small sample of nearly all that is not native or produced at home can be obtained at the shops at a trifling cost.

GLOSSARY.

A (as a prefix): without or destitute of; as Apetalous, without petals.
Aberrant: departing or wandering from the type or usual form.
Abnormal: of unusual or unnatural form or structure.
Abortion: non-development.
Abortive: not developing; or if so, but slightly.
Abruptly pinnate: having a pair of terminal leaflets.
Acaulescent: without an evident stem.
Accessory: added to; as Accessory buds.
Acerose: needle-like.
Achenium: a dry, indehiscent, one-seeded, seed-like fruit.
Achlamydeous: without any perianth.
Acicular: finely needle-shaped.
Acotyledonous: destitute of cotyledons.
Acrocarpous Mosses: those bearing the fruit at the apex of the stem.
Acrogen: top-grower; as Ferns, Mosses, etc.
Acrogenous: growing at the top.
Acropetal: towards, or approaching the top.
Aculeate: having prickles.
Acuminate: with a sharp, drawn-out point.
Acute: sharp-pointed.
Adelphous: united; as filaments of stamens.
Adherent: growing together of different parts; as calyx and ovary.
Adnate: growing fast to a different organ or part.
Adnate anther: attached by its whole length to the apex of the filament.
Adnation: the growing fast, or together, of different parts or organs.
Adventitious: appearing at an unusual place.
Adventive: accidentally introduced, but hardly naturalized.
Æcidiospore: a spore of the Æcidium. Æcidial stage of certain Fungi.
Æcidium: the first stage (formerly considered a genus) in the development of the Cluster-cup Fungi (Uredineæ).
Aerial: not growing on or in the soil; deriving nourishment from the air.
Aërophytes: aerial plants; epiphytes.
Æstivation, or *Præfloration:* arrangement of the parts in a flower-bud.
Affinity: close and natural relationship.
Aggregate: collected together.
Air plants: those deriving nourishment wholly from the air.
Akene: achenium.

Ala: wing or side petal of a Papilionaceous corolla.
Alate: winged.
Albumen: endosperm or reserve material stored in the seed.
Albuminous: having an endosperm or reserve material stored in the seed outside of the embryo.
Alburnum: sap-wood.
Aleurone: albuminous granular bodies in seeds, having the same reaction as protoplasm.
Alliaceous: like the Onion (Allium).
Alpine: growing on mountains.
Alternate: one above, or between, the other.
Alveolate: with pits like honey-comb.
Ament, or *Catkin:* a scaly spike of flowers.
Amentaceous: having aments or catkins.
Amorphous: without definite form; not crystalline.
Amphicarpous: having fruit of two kinds.
Amphigastria: the small leaves or scales on the underside of Liverworts.
Amphitropous ovule: inverted, with a short raphe, and the hilum near the middle of one side.
Amplexicaul: clasping the stem.
Amylaceous: starchy.
Analogy: resemblance as to function.
Anastomosing: uniting end to end, and forming a net-work, as veins.
Anatropous ovule: inverted, so the hilum is close to the orifice and the chalaza at the top.
Andrœcium: the stamens taken collectively.
Anemophilous flowers: those whose fertilization (or pollination) is effected by the agency of the wind.
Angiocarpous: with the hymenium (or spore-bearing layer) immersed in a cavity (perithecium).
Angiosperm: an angiospermous plant, or one with an ovary.
Angiospermous: with seeds in ovaries.
Angular divergence: the angle formed by vertical planes passing through the leaves and the centre of the stem.
Annual: yearly; living but one year; fruiting and dying the first year.
Annular: ringed; having rings; ring-shaped.
Annulus: the thickened ring in sporangia of many Ferns, and at the mouth of the spore-cases of Mosses.
Anther: the part of the stamen which contains the pollen.
Antheridium: the male reproductive organ in Cryptogams, whose function corresponds to that of stamens in Phænogams.
Antheriferous: bearing anthers.
Anthesis: flowering; the time or act of flowering.
Antispasmodic: that which prevents spasms or convulsions.
Apetalous: without petals.
Apex: the top; the point of the leaf opposite the petiole.
Aphyllous: destitute of leaves.
Apical: pertaining to the apex.

Apocarpous: when carpels of a gynæcium are separate, as in Ranunculus.
Apothecium: the reproductive part or sporocarp of a Lichen.
Appendage, or *Appendix:* a part which is added; a projection.
Appendiculate: having an appendage.
Appressed: close pressed; as leaves, etc., to the stem.
Apterous: destitute of wings.
Aquatic: growing in water.
Arachnoid: like a spider's web; clothed with soft fibres.
Arbor: tree
Arboreous: like a tree; dendritic.
Arborescent: almost a tree; growing into a tree.
Arboretum: a place in which a collection of trees is cultivated.
Archegonium: the flask-shaped reproductive organ of Mosses, Ferns, etc., corresponding in function to a pistil.
Arcuate: curved like a bow.
Areolate: having small spaces, or areolæ marked out.
Areolation: small spaces bounded by veins of leaves, or cell-walls, etc.
Argentate: resembling silver.
Arillate: having an aril.
Aril: a fleshy growth (like a third integument) more or less covering the seed.
Arista: awn; beard of Wheat, Barley, etc.
Aristate: having an awn or long bristle.
Articulated: jointed; having joints or articulations.
Artificial classification: that which is based on one or a few characters regardless of affinity.
Ascus: the cell or sac in which the spores arise in some Fungi (Ascomycetes).
Assimilation: conversion of inorganic into organic matter.
Assurgent: ascending or rising obliquely.
Astichous: not in rows.
Atropous: orthotropous; not bent.
Attenuate: long drawn out.
Auricle: an appendage, or expansion somewhat ear-shaped.
Auriculate: having ear-like appendages.
Autogamy: close-fertilization, or the fertilization of the ovules by the pollen of the same flower.
Auxospore: the spore resulting from copulation in Desmids, and by which the individual is increased in size.
Awn: beard of Wheat, Barley, Grasses, etc. (Arista.)
Axil: the angle formed by the leaf and stem.
Axillary: in the axil; belonging to the axil.
Axis: the root and stem; a central organ to which others are attached; central line.

Baccate: like a berry; pulpy like a berry.
Banner: the upper petal of a Papilionaceous corolla (vexillum).
Barbed: having a barb or double hook; with projecting hooks or prickles.

Barbellate: having short, stiff hairs, as the pappus of some Compositæ.
Bark: that part of the stem or trunk external to the wood.
Basal: attached or belonging to the base.
Base: that part of an organ by which it is attached.
Busidiospore: a spore, as in the Mushrooms, which is supported by a little pedicel of the basidium.
Basidium: the enlarged terminal portion of the hymenial hyphæ, bearing spores on sterigmata.
Basipetal: towards or approaching the base.
Bast, or *Bass:* the inner fibrous bark.
Bast-cells: the long-pointed thick-walled cells of bast.
Beaked: terminating by a long narrow tip or beak.
Berry: a pulpy or juicy fruit.
Bi, or *Bis* (as a prefix): two; as bilobed (two-lobed), bifid (two-cleft).
Biennial: lasting two years; fruiting and dying the second year.
Bifid: two-cleft to near the middle.
Bifoliate: with two leaflets.
Bifurcate: forked into two branches; twice forked.
Bilabiate: two-lipped (labiate).
Bilocular: two-celled, or having two cavities.
Binary: composed of two elements; in two's.
Binomial nomenclature: naming by two (the generic and specific) names.
Biology: the science which treats of plants and animals.
Bipartite: two-parted.
Bipinnate: twice pinnate.
Bipinnatifid: twice pinnatifid.
Bisected: cut in two; divided in two parts.
Biseptate: having two partitions.
Bisexual: having both stamens and pistils (hermaphrodite).
Bisulcate: two-grooved; having two furrows.
Blade: the thin expanded portion of a leaf (lamina).
Bloom: the fine white powder (of wax) on some leaves.
Botanical Province: a geographical region having characteristic groups of plants.
Botany: the science which treats of plants.
Botryose: of the racemose type.
Bract: small leaf or scale from whose axil a flower or pedicel proceeds; the reduced leaves in a flower-cluster, etc.
Bracteate: having bracts.
Bracteolate: having bractlets.
Bractlet: the bract or scale situated on the pedicel.
Branches: the divisions of a stem or trunk; limbs.
Branchlets: very small branches; divisions of a branch.
Breathing pores: stomates.
Bristle: stiff, sharp hair.
Bristly: having bristles.
Bryology: that division of botany which treats of Mosses.

Bryophyta: the division including the Mosses and Liverworts.
Bud: the undeveloped branch; the "growing point" with its covering of scales.
Budding: producing an outgrowth by some Cryptogamous plants, which separates and grows into a form like the parent.
Bud-scales: the scales or modified leaves of a bud.
Bulb: a shortened axis or bud with fleshy scales.
Bulbiferous: bearing bulbs.
Bulblet: small bulbs above ground; as in axils of Lily.
Bulbous: bulb-like.
Bullate: blistery or bladdery.

Caducous: falling off very early.
Callose: hardened; having callosities.
Calycine: belonging to the calyx.
Calyculate: having an additional outer calyx, or calyx-like bracts.
Calyptra: the hood or covering over the operculum of Moss capsules.
Calyx: the outer whorl of the floral envelopes; the sepals taken collectively.
Cambium: the generating tissue between the wood (Xylem), and bark or bast (Phloëm).
Cambium zone: the continuous layer of cambium surrounding the wood in Exogens.
Campanulate: bell-shaped.
Campylotropous ovule: curved upon itself so that the micropyle is brought towards the funiculus.
Canaliculate: channeled or with a long groove.
Cancellate: like lattice-work.
Canescent: grayish-white.
Capitate: with a globular apex; forming a head.
Capsule: a pod; any seed or spore vessel.
Carina: keel; the two lower (anterior) petals of a Papilionaceous flower, joined so as to be keel or prow-like.
Carinate: keeled.
Carminative: remedy for colic, or expelling wind from the body.
Carpel: a simple pistil, or one of the parts or leaves of which a compound pistil is composed.
Carpellary: pertaining to a carpel, or part or leaf of which a compound pistil is composed.
Carposporeæ: a division of the vegetable kingdom characterized by the formation of a sporocarp.
Caryophyllaceous: pink-like.
Caryopsis: the grain or one-seeded fruit of Grasses.
Cataclasm: poultice.
Catkin: a scaly spike of flowers (ament).
Caudate: tailed; pointed like a tail.
Caudex: a trunk like that of Palms; an upright root-stock.
Caudicle: the little stem or pedicel of pollinia (pollen masses).
Caulescent: having an evident stem.
Caulicle: the rudimentary axis of the embryo.

Cauline: pertaining or belonging to the stem.
Cauline bundles: those fibro-vascular bundles in the stem which have no connection with those in the leaf.
Caulome: that which answers in general to a stem.
Cell: the minute body consisting of a wall or membrane enclosing protoplasm, etc., which is the proximate constituent element of vegetable tissue; a vessel or cavity, as anther-cell.
Cellular: consisting of cells.
Cellulose: the substance of the cell-wall or cell-membrane.
Centrifugal: from the centre outwards.
Centripetal: towards the centre.
Cereal: pertaining to the grains; as Wheat, Rye, etc.
Cernuous: nodding.
Chaff: the bristles or scales on the receptacle of Compositæ; the glumes of Grasses.
Chalaza: the point of the ovule where the integuments and nucleus unite.
Channeled: hollowed out like a gutter; furrowed.
Character: any distinguishing point or property.
Chlorophyll: the green coloring substance in plant-cells.
Choripetalous: with petals not united with each other.
Chorisepalous: with sepals not united with each other.
Cicatrix: a scar left by the fall of a leaf or other organ.
Cilia: long hairs like eye-lashes; hair-like prolongations of protoplasm.
Ciliate: fringed with cilia, hairs, or bristles.
Cinereous: ash-gray.
Circinate (or *Circinnate*): rolled inwards from the top.
Circulation of protoplasm: a streaming or current movement in the protoplasm in cells.
Circumscissile: divided by a circular line around the sides.
Cirrhiferous: bearing tendrils.
Cirrhose: bearing tendrils.
Clavate: club-shaped; thickened above.
Class: a group; one of the groups which form a division; as class Gymnosperms, of division Phænogams.
Classification: grouping, or putting in groups or classes.
Claw: the narrowed base or stem-like part of some petals.
Cleistogamy: close-fertilization in unopened flowers.
Cleistogamous: characterized by cleistogamy.
Cleistogamic: pertaining to cleistogamy; exhibiting cleistogamy.
Cleft: divided almost to the middle.
Closed-bundles: fibro-vascular bundles destitute of cambium.
Close-fertilization: fertilization of the ovules by pollen of the same flower.
Club-shaped: clavate; thickened above.
Clypeate: shaped like a buckler.
Coalescent: growing together.
Cœnobium: a cell colony; cells loosely united into a family.
Coherent: connate; growing together of like parts.

Cohesion: union of like parts or organs; as petals with each other.
Cohort: a division of a sub-class; as Cohort Glumales (Grasses and Sedges of sub-class Monocotyledons).
Coleorhiza: the root-cap.
Collar, Collum: the point of junction of stem and root.
Collenchyma: tissue whose cells are thickened at the corners and situated under the epidermis.
Colored: not green.
Columella: the slender, elongated torus, as in Geranium; the central column of a sporangium or capsule.
Column: the tube of monadelphous stamens; the body formed by the union of stamens and pistil, as in Orchids.
Coma: a tuft; a tuft of hairs.
Commissure: the face by which two carpels cohere; as in Umbelliferæ.
Common bundles: those fibro-vascular bundles which pass below into the stem, and above into the leaf.
Complanate: flattened.
Complete flower: one having the four parts—calyx, corolla, stamens, and pistil.
Complicate: folded upon itself.
Composite flower: one which consists of a head of florets, as in Compositæ.
Compound: not single; composed of several parts.
Compressed: flattened lengthwise, or on two opposite sides.
Conceptacle: cavities in the tissue in which the reproductive organs are contained; as in the Florideæ.
Confluent: blending together.
Conidia: non-sexual spores; often borne on aerial branches or hyphæ.
Coniferous: bearing cones.
Conjugation: fusion of the contents of two cells to form a new cell or spore, as in some Algæ; union of two cells equal in size and appearance.
Connate: united, or grown together from the first.
Connate-perfoliate leaves: opposite, with bases grown together through which the stem passes.
Connective: the part of the filament between the two anthers.
Connivent: coming in contact or converging.
Contorted: twisted, same as convolute.
Contracted: narrowed or shortened.
Convolute: (in vernation) rolled up from one edge; (in æstivation) twisted, or with one edge of each petal overlapping that of the next.
Copulation: union of swarm spores, etc.; fusion of two masses of protoplasm.
Cordate: heart-shaped.
Coriaceous: leathery.
Cork: a kind of tissue with firm, dry cell-walls, destitute of cell-contents and impermeable to liquids and gases.

Cork cambium: phellogen, or meristematic cells which produce cork-cells.
Corky: like cork; having cork.
Corm: a solid bulb.
Cormophyte: plants with stem, root, foliage, etc.
Corolla: the inner set or whorl of the floral envelopes; the petals taken collectively.
Corona: a crown; the appendage at the top of the claw of some petals.
Coronate: having a corona or crown.
Corpuscula: the elongated bodies in ovules of the Gymnosperms in which the germ-cells originate.
Corrugate: wrinkled.
Cortex: the rind; the part of the stem external to the wood or fibro-vascular bundles.
Cortical: pertaining to the cortex, or rind.
Corymb: a level-topped flower-cluster with centripetal inflorescence.
Corymbose: in corymbs, or like corymbs.
Costa: a rib.
Costate: ribbed; with ridges.
Cotyledons: the seed-leaves, or first leaves of the embryo.
Crateriform: goblet-shaped.
Crenate: scalloped, or having rounded teeth.
Crenulate: similar to crenate, but finer.
Crested: with a crest-like appendage.
Cribriform, or *Cribrose:* sieve-like.
Cross-fertilization: the fertilization of the ovules with pollen from a different flower.
Crown, Corona: the appendage at the top of the claw of some petals.
Cruciferous, Cruciform, or *Cruciate:* having the form of a cross.
Crustaceous: crust-like; hard and brittle.
Cryptogam: a plant destitute of flowers and producing spores instead of seeds.
Cryptogamous: destitute of flowers and producing spores instead of seeds.
Crystalloids: crystal-like albuminous bodies in aleurone grains.
Cucullate: hooded, or hood-shaped.
Culm: the stem of Grasses and Sedges.
Cuneate, or *Cuneiform:* wedge-shaped.
Cupule: the cup of the acorn; a little cup.
Cupuliferous: having a cupule.
Cuspidate: having a sharp, stiff point.
Cut: incised or cleft.
Cuticle: same as cuticula.
Cuticula: the thin continuous external layer of the epidermis-cells.
Cutting: a severed portion of a plant used for bud-propagation.
Cycle: circle; one turn of a helix or spire.
Cyme: a flower-cluster with centrifugal inflorescence.
Cymose: having cymes, or like a cyme.

Cystolith: a projection of cellulose into the cell-cavity which is impregnated with calcic carbonate.
Cytoblast: a name formerly used for the nucleus of the cell.

Daughter-cells: the new or young cells arising from existing cells.
Deca (as a prefix): ten; as decandrous, with ten stamens.
Decandrous: having ten stamens.
Deciduous: falling off early, as deciduous petals; falling off at the end of the season, as deciduous leaves.
Decompound: several times compounded.
Decumbent: lying on the ground, but the summit tending to rise.
Decurrent: prolonged downwards on the stem.
Decussate: in pairs which cross each other, or placed at right angles.
Definite: of a fixed number, (in inflorescence) same as centrifugal.
Dehiscence: opening; mode of opening, as of anthers, etc.
Dehiscent: opening regularly.
Deliquescent: repeated branching till the trunk disappears in branches.
Deltoid: triangular.
Demulcent: a bland mucilaginous substance which protects the tissue from irritation.
Dentate: toothed; with teeth pointing outwards.
Denticulate: with small teeth.
Depressed: as if flattened from above.
Dermatogen: the epidermis of the growing point.
Determinate: fixed; definite.
Di, or *Dis* (in Greek compounds): two or double.
Diadelphous: filaments united into two sets.
Dialypetalous: same as choripetalous or polypetalous.
Diandrous: having two stamens.
Dichasium: a two-parted or two-rayed cyme.
Dichlamydeous: having a calyx and corolla.
Dichotomous: divided into two forks.
Dichogamous, Dichogamy: maturity in a perfect flower of either the stamens or the pistils in advance of the other.
Diclinous: when flowers are of separate sexes.
Dicotyledon: an exogenous plant, or one whose embryo has two cotyledons.
Dicotyledonous: having two cotyledons.
Didynamous: having two pairs of stamens, with one pair shorter.
Diffuse: much and irregularly spreading.
Digitate leaf: one with the leaflets attached at a common point or end of the petiole.
Dimorphism, Dimorphous: having two forms, as two sets of flowers, one with long stamens and short pistil, and the other with short stamens and long pistil.
Diœcious: with staminate and pistillate flowers on different plants.
Dipterous: winged.
Disciform: depressed and circular, like a disk or quoit.
Discoid, or *Discoidal:* without rays.

Disc, or *Disk*: an elevated rim of the torus.
Disc-flowers: the florets of a Composite flower, which are on the receptacle and have no rays.
Dissected: finely divided or cut.
Dissepiment: partition of an ovary or fruit.
Distichous: two-ranked; in two rows.
Distinct: not cohering; not united with each other.
Divaricate: extremely divergent.
Divided leaf: one with the blade divided to the midrib.
Dodecandrous: with twelve stamens.
Dorsal suture: the outer suture, or that corresponding to the midrib.
Double flower: one with the petals multiplied.
Downy: having short and soft hairs.
Drupe: a stone fruit.
Duct: fused cells which form a continuous vessel or tube.
Duramen: the heart-wood.
Dwarf: diminutive.

E, or *Ex* (as a prefix): destitute of.
Eared: having ear-like appendages.
Ebracteate: destitute of bracts.
Ebracteolate: without bractlets.
Echinate: with prickles.
Echinulate: with small prickles.
Ectoplasm: the hyaline layer surrounding the naked protoplasm.
Edentate: toothless; not toothed.
Efflorescence: anthesis; flowering.
Elaters: the threads interspersed with spores of Liverworts, etc.
Eleutheropetalous: petals free or distinct; polypetalous or choripetalous.
Elliptical: oblong with regularly rounded ends.
Emarginate: with a notch at the summit.
Embryo: the rudimentary plantlet in the seed.
Embryo-sac: the enlarged cell of the ovule in which the embryo arises.
Emersed: raised above water.
Endocarp: the inner layer of a fruit.
Endochrome: coloring matter in cells, especially that in Algæ.
Endogen: a plant with woody fibres (or bundles) and pith commingled; a Dicotyledonous plant.
Endogenous: arising or growing within; like an endogen.
Endosperm: the albumen, or part of the seed which develops within the embryo-sac.
Endospore: the inner wall of a spore.
Ensiform: shaped like a sword.
Entire: even; not notched nor toothed.
Entomophilous flowers: those whose fertilization (pollination) is effected by insects.
Ephemeral: lasting but a day.
Epi (as a prefix): upon.

Epicarp: the outer layer of a fruit.
Epidermis: the outer layer of cells.
Epigynous: situated upon the pistil or ovary.
Epipetalous: upon the petals.
Epiphyte: a plant growing on another, but not receiving its nourishment from it.
Episepalous: upon the sepals.
Equitant: astride.
Erose: gnawed.
Ergot: a horn-like sclerotium of the hyphæ of the fungus *Claviceps purpurea*.
Estivation: same as æstivation.
Etiolated: blanched.
Evergreen: not deciduous; remaining green all winter.
Ex (as a prefix): destitute of.
Exalbuminous: with no endosperm or albumen external to the cotyledons.
Excurrent: running out to the very top or beyond the apex; as the trunk of a tree, the midrib of a leaf, etc.
Exhalation: transpiration or evaporation through the stomates.
Exo (as a prefix): outwards.
Exocarp: the outer layer of the pericarp.
Exogen: a plant with pith, surrounded by a ring of wood or fibro-vascular bundles, and this by a bark or cortex; a Dicotyledonous plant.
Exogenous: with the structure of an endogen; outside growing.
Exospore: the outer wall of a spore.
Expectorant: that which promotes discharges from the throat and lungs.
Exserted: protruding.
Exstipulate: destitute of stipules.
Extine: the outer layer of a pollen grain.
Extrorse: directed or turned outwards.
Eye: the bud on a tuber.

Falcate: shaped like a scythe.
Family: a group of allied genera.
Farina: starch.
Farinaceous: like, or containing starch.
Farinose: covered with a meal-like powder.
Fasciate: banded; abnormally flattened stems.
Fasciation: a monstrosity in which the stem broadens and flattens.
Fascicled: in a bundle.
Faveolate: same as alveolate; like a honey-comb.
Feather-veined: pinnately veined; veins branching from a midrib.
Feathery: plumose; beset with hairs along the sides.
Ferruginous: like iron-rust in color.
Fertile: pistillate; producing.
Fertilization: the process which results in the formation of the embryo.

Fibre: an elongated cell, or fine filament.
Fibril, Fibrilla: a very small fibre or thread.
Fibrous: containing, or like fibres.
Fibro-vascular bundles: woody threads or bundles composed of fibrous, vascular, and parenchymous elements.
Filament: the thread-like portion of the stamen which supports the anther.
Filamentous: thread-like, or bearing slender threads.
Filiform: thread-form.
Fimbriate: fringed.
Fission: division of any body into two parts by gradual constriction.
Flabellate, Flabelliform: fan-shaped.
Flagellum: a long whip-like filament or cilium.
Fleshy: succulent, composed of pulp or flesh.
Floating: swimming on the surface.
Floccose: with tufts of woolly or long soft hairs,
Flocculent: diminutive of floccose.
Funiculus: the stem or stalk which supports the ovule in the ovary.
Fuscous: grayish-brown.
Fusiform: spindle-formed.

Galeate: helmet-shaped.
Gamo (as a prefix): united.
Gamopetalous: petals united.
Gamosepalous: with sepals united.
Gemmæ: a mass of cells forming a body similar in function to a bud.
Gemmation: budding.
Genera: plural of genus.
Generic: relating or pertaining to genus.
Genetic: by inheritance; genealogical.
Genus: a group of allied species.
Geotropism: turning towards the earth.
Germ: a young bud; point of growth; that from which anything originates.
Germination: sprouting; sending out a filament; the development of the plantlet at the expense of the nourishment contained in the seed.
Gibbous: swollen at one point.
Glabrous: smooth; not hairy.
Gland: a cell, or mass of cells which secretes something.
Globoids: round bodies similar in occurrence and behavior to the crystalloids.
Globular: spherical, or nearly so.
Globule: the male organ or antheridium of the Characeæ.
Glossology: explanations of technical terms.
Glumes: the husks or bracts which are inserted at the base of a spikelet.
Glutinous: viscid; sticky.
Gonidia: the green bodies in the thallus of the Lichens.
Grain: a caryopsis; the fruit of the Gramineæ.

Gramineous: pertaining to grain or the Gramineæ.
Granulose: the most readily soluble constituent of a starch grain.
Guard-cells: the two cells surrounding a stomate.
Gymnos (as a prefix): naked.
Gymnocarpous: with a disc-like, exposed hymenium, as in some Lichens, etc.
Gomnosperm: a plant with naked seeds (not enclosed in an ovary).
Gymnospermous: having naked seeds.
Gynandrous: the stamens united with the pistil.
Gynœcium: the pistil or pistils of a flower taken collectively.

Habit: the general appearance of the plant.
Habitat: the place where a plant grows.
Hackle: same as heckle.
Hairs: outgrowths from cells; hair-like appendages.
Hairy: having hairs.
Hastate: with a spreading lobe on each side at the base.
Haustoria: outgrowths from hyphæ, which penetrate the cells for the purpose of obtaining nourishment.
Heart-shaped: ovate with a sinus at base; cordate.
Heart-wood: the mature wood of exogenous trees, generally more or less colored and destitute of sap.
Heckle: to draw through teeth or a comb in order to separate the fibre.
Heliotropism: turning towards the sun or light.
Hepta (as a prefix): seven.
Herb: a plant in which no woody tissue develops.
Herbaceous: like an herb; of the texture of an herb.
Herbarium, Herbal: a collection of dried plants.
Hermaphrodite: having both stamens and pistils in the same flower.
Heteros (as a prefix): diverse or various.
Hex (as a prefix): six.
Hilum: the scar of the seed, or point of its attachment in the ovary.
Hirsute: having stiffish or beard-like hairs.
Hispid: having stiff hairs; bristly.
Histology: that department of botany which treats of minute anatomy or of tissues.
Hoary: grayish-white.
Homologue: that which corresponds in structure.
Homologous: of similar or corresponding structure.
Hybrid: a cross-breed between two species.
Hymenial layer: the spore-bearing layer of hyphæ in Fungi.
Hymenium: same as hymenial layer.
Hyphæ: the vegetative threads or filaments of Fungi.
Hypo (as a prefix): under; beneath; lower.
Hypoderm: thick-walled or otherwise peculiar cells immediately below the epidermis.
Hypogynous: inserted under the pistil.
Hypocotyledonary: under or below the cotyledons in the embryo, as hypocotyledonary stem.

Imbricate: overlapping, like shingles or tile on a roof.
Immersed: under water.
Imperfect flower: one which is destitute of either stamens or pistils.
Incised: cut; jagged; cut irregularly.
Included: not protruding; enclosed.
Incomplete flower: with one or more of the four parts wanting.
Indefinite: of no fixed number; (in inflorescence) centripetal or in the direction of the apex or top.
Indehiscent: not opening of itself.
Indeterminate: not definite, (in inflorescence) same as indefinite.
Indigenous: native; not introduced.
Induplicate: with edges folded in, or turned inwards.
Indusium: the thin membrane sometimes covering the sori.
Inferior: below; attached below.
Inflated: swollen or bladdery.
Inflexed: turned inwards.
Inflorescence: arrangement of flowers on the stem; flowering.
Innate anther: one attached by its base to the apex of the filament.
Inserted: attached.
Insertion: mode or place of attachment.
Inspissated: thickened by evaporation.
Intercalary growth: that which takes place at an intermediate point and not at the apex.
Intercellular spaces: spaces arising between cells.
Internode: the portion of the stem between the nodes or joints.
Intine: the inner coat or membrane of the pollen grain.
Introrse: turned inwards or towards the axis.
Intussusception: interstitial reception of particles.
Involucel: a small or partial involucre.
Involucrate: having an involucre.
Involucre: a whorl of bracts or leaves below a flower or other part.
Involute: rolled inwards.
Irregular flower: one in which some of the members or any one or more sets of organs are unlike the others in shape or size.

Keel: a projecting ridge; the two anterior petals of a Papilionaceous flower.
Key-fruit: samara, as the fruit of the Maple.
Kingdom: the most comprehensive group in nature, as Vegetable Kingdom.

Labellum: the odd (more or less modified) petal of an Orchid flower.
Labiate: lip-shaped; bilabiate.
Lamella: a flat plate or thin layer; blade.
Lamina: blade; a plate.
Lanate (Lanose): woolly, or with soft entangled hairs.
Lanceolate: shaped like a lance.
Latent: not developed; dormant; concealed.
Latex: the juice (usually milky or colored) in vessels of plants.
Laticiferous: having latex.

Leaf-blade (*Lamina*): the thin expanded portion of a leaf.
Leaflet: one of the divisions or parts of a compound leaf.
Leaf-scar: the scar on the stem after the leaf has fallen.
Leaf-stalk (*Petiole*): stem of the leaf.
Legume: a simple ovary or pod which at maturity splits along both ventral and dorsal sutures.
Leguminous: having legumes; like a legume.
Lenticel: an elevated portion or spot on Elder and other stems, consisting of a corky mass, which replaces the stomate.
Liber: the inner or fibrous bark of exogenous plants.
Ligneous, or *Lignose*: woody.
Ligule: the ray or strap-shaped corolla of some flowers of Compositæ; the appendage at the summit of the leaf-sheath in Grasses.
Ligulate: strap or tongue-shaped.
Liliaceous: like a Lily.
Limb: the blade of a petal, border of a corolla, etc.
Linear: narrow and flat.
Lip: the principal division, or lobe of a labiate corolla and calyx; the labellum.
Lobate: having lobes.
Lobulate: diminutive of lobate.
Loculicidal: splitting down the middle of the back of each cell or cavity.
Loment: a pod which separates transversely into joints or parts.
Lomentaceous: like a loment.
Lunate: crescent-shaped.
Lyrate: lyre-shaped.
Lyrate leaf: a leaf with the terminal lobe large and roundish, and the lower lobes small.

μ (Greek m): in measurement one thousandth of a millimetre.
Macro (as a prefix): large.
Macrospore: the larger of two kinds of spores, as in some Lycopods.
Maculate: spotted.
Medullary: relating to the pith.
Medullary Rays: the lines or portions of parenchymous tissue regularly interspersed in the wood, and radiating from the pith.
Membranaceous, or *Membranous*: like a membrane; thin, and more or less translucent.
Mericarp: one of the closed half-fruits of the Umbelliferæ.
Meristem: generating tissue, or tissue capable of growth by cell-division.
Meristematic: having or like meristem.
Meros (in compound words): parted.
Mesocarp: the middle one of three layers of the pericarp.
Mesophyll: the parenchymous tissue forming the interior of the leaf-blade.
Mesophlœm: the middle bark.

Metamorphosis: change ; a gradual change into something else.
Metastasis: all the chemical changes after assimilation.
Micropyle: the opening in the ovule by which the pollen-tube enters.
Microspore: the smaller of two kinds of spores; as in some Lycopods.
Midrib: the large vein or rib in the middle of the leaf.
Monadelphous stamens: those united by their filaments into one set.
Moniliform: necklace-shaped ; contracted at intervals.
Mono (as a prefix): one or (sometimes) united ; as monopetalous.
Monoclinous: hermaphrodite.
Monocotyledon: a plant having seed with but one cotyledon
Monocotyledonous: having but one cotyledon.
Monolocular: one-celled ; having one cavity.
Monœcious: having staminate and pistillate flowers on the same plant.
Monopodial branching: the new branches are lateral, the original growing point of the stem not dividing, as in dichotomous branching.
Monstrosity: a form which deviates greatly and abnormally from the usual.
Mordant: a substance which unites firmly both with fabrics or organic fibres and with dyes, thus fixing the latter.
Morphology: that which treats of forms especially in a comparative sense; sometimes used in place of metamorphosis.
Mother-cell: that cell which gives rise directly to new cells.
Mucronate: with an abrupt sharp point.
Multi (as a prefix): many.
Muscology: the department of botany which treats of Mosses.
Mycelium: the vegetative threads or filaments of Fungi.
Mycology: that part of botany which treats of Fungi.

Naked: wanting some usual covering.
Napiform: shape of a turnip.
Narcotic: (in small doses) relieving pain and causing sleep; (in large doses) producing stupor.
Natural classification: that according to affinity, or that which is based on all the characters.
Nectar: the honey or sweetish substance secreted by nectaries.
Nectary: the tissue or organ usually in connection with the flower, which secretes a sweetish substance called nectar.
Nectariferous: bearing nectar.
Nerve: veins of leaves especially when parallel.
Netted-veined: the veins anastomosing so as to form a net-work.
Node, Joint: the place on a stem from which a leaf or pair of leaves springs.
Nodose: knotty.
Nomenclature: see *binomial nomenclature.*
Normal: usual ; according to rule; typical.
Nucleolus: the body within the nucleus of a cell.
Nucleus: the body of the ovule ; the small denser body in the protoplasm of a cell.

Nucule: the female organ of Characeæ.
Numerous: indefinite.
Nut: a hard indehiscent, mostly one-seeded fruit.

Ob (as a prefix): reversely.
Obcompressed: flattened opposite to laterally.
Obcordate: broadly notched at the apex.
Oblanceolate: lance-shaped, but tapering downwards.
Oblong: much longer than broad, the two ends rounded.
Obovate: ovate, with the broad end upwards.
Obtuse: blunt.
Ochrea: the sheathing stipule as in Polygonum.
Ochreate: with ochreæ or sheath-like stipules.
Ochroleucous: yellowish-white.
Octo (as a prefix): eight.
Officinal: having an approved use in medicine.
Offset: branches at the ground which take root.
Oligos (as a prefix): few; as oligandrous, few stamens.
Oögonium: a large cell which is the female reproductive organ in the Oösporeæ.
Oösphere: a rounded mass of protoplasm within the oögonium.
Oöspore: the fertilized and ripened oösphere, having a cell-wall.
Oösporeæ: the division of plants which are characterized by the production of an oögonium.
Open bundles: those fibro-vascular bundles which contain cambium.
Operculum: the lid of the capsule or theca of Mosses.
Opposite: on opposite sides of the stem, (of stamens) in front of petals, etc.
Orbiculate, or *Orbicular:* in outline round, or nearly so.
Orchidaceous: like an Orchid.
Order: a group of allied genera.
Organ: any part that has a special function to perform.
Orthos (as a prefix): straight.
Orthotropous ovule: erect; with the micropyle at the apex or opposite the chalaza.
Oval: broadly elliptical.
Ovary: the lower part of the pistil which contains the ovules.
Ovate: egg-shape, with the broad end downwards; as ovate leaf.
Ovule: the body in the ovary which develops into the seed.

Palet (Pale): a chaff or chaff-like bract, as in Composite flowers; that which corresponds to a sepal in the grass-flowers.
Palmate leaf: with the leaflets attached at the top of the petiole and spreading like the out-stretched fingers of the hands.
Panicle: an open cluster or compound raceme.
Papilionaceous: more or less butterfly-shaped; the upper petal is called the Banner or Vexillum, the two side petals Alæ, and the two anterior ones the Keel.
Papilla: a minute elevation.

Pappus: the bristles, scales, teeth, or chaff crowning the achenium of many Compositæ.
Parasite: a plant situated on another from which it draws its nourishment.
Parasitic: drawing nourishment from another plant.
Parenchyma: the soft tissue in the leaf; tissue whose cells are roundish, or if elongated not having pointed ends.
Parenchymous: having or like parenchyma.
Parietal: attached to or belonging to the wall.
Parted: divided almost to the base or midrib, etc.
Parthenogenesis: production of seed without the intervention of pollen.
Pauci (as a prefix): few.
Pectinate: finely divided, like the teeth of a comb.
Pedate: like a bird's foot.
Pedicel: the branch of the peduncle which supports the flower.
Pedicellate (or *Pedicelled*): having a pedicel.
Peduncle: the flower-stem or stalk supporting one or many flowers.
Peltate: shield-shaped.
Penta (as a prefix): five; as pentamerous, five-parted, etc.
Pepo: the Gourd fruit, or fruit like the Melon or Cucumber.
Perennial: persisting from year to year.
Perfect flower: one with both stamens and pistils.
Perfoliate leaf: with the base extending around the stem so that the latter appears to pass through the leaf.
Peri (as a prefix): around.
Perianth: the floral envelope, especially when the distinction between the calyx and corolla is not evident, as in Lilies.
Periblem: the portion immediately under the dermatogen and which becomes the cortex.
Pericarp: the wall of the ovary or fruit.
Periderm: a continuous corky layer surrounding the stem.
Peridium: an investing cellular layer or wall, as in case of the fruit of some Fungi, as Puff-balls, Cluster-cups, etc.
Perigynous: situated on the calyx.
Perisperm: the portion of reserve material of the seed which, in a few cases, is stored up outside of the embryo-sac.
Peristome: the circle of teeth around the orifice of the capsule or theca of Mosses.
Persistent: remaining longer than the usual time.
Perithecium: the wall of the fruit or sporocarp of some ascomycetous Fungi.
Petal: one of the parts or leaves of the corolla.
Petiolate: having a petiole.
Petiole: the stem or stalk of a leaf.
Phænogam: a plant which produces flowers and seeds.
Phænogamous: having flowers and producing seeds.
Phellogen: cork-cambium; meristem which produces cork-cells.
Phenogam: same as phænogam.
Phloëm: the bast portion of a fibro-vascular bundle.

Phycoerythrine: the red pigment in some Algæ (*Florideæ*).
Phycology: that department of botany which treats of Algæ.
Phycoxanthine: the brownish or yellowish coloring matter in Diatoms.
Phyllotaxy: leaf arrangement.
Phyllome: that which in general answers to a leaf.
Pileate: having a pileus or cap.
Pileus: the cap or sporocarp of Toad-stools (*Agaricus*).
Pileorhiza: the root-cap.
Pilose: having soft slender hairs.
Pinna: a primary division of a pinnate, bipinnate leaf, etc.
Pinnate-leaf: having the leaflets on two sides of a common petiole.
Pinnatifid: pinnately-cleft.
Pinnule: a division of a pinna.
Pistil: the central organ of the flower in which (ovary) the seeds are produced.
Pistillate: having pistils, but no stamens.
Pith: the parenchymous tissue in the centre of an exogenous stem.
Pitted: having pits, or depressions.
Placenta: the line or part of the ovary to which the seeds are attached.
Plasmodium: the naked protoplasm of the Slime Moulds (*Myxomycetes*).
Plerome: the central cylindrical mass directly behind the growing point and enclosed by the periblem.
Pleurocarpous Moss: one whose fruit is borne laterally and not from the apex of the stem.
Plicate (Plaited): like the plaits of a fan.
Plumose: feathery.
Plumule: the bud terminating the caulicle in the embryo.
Pod: a legume, or any kind of a capsule.
Pollen: pollen-grains; the powdery fertilizing grains of the anther.
Pollen-tube: the tube emitted by the pollen grain which grows down through the stigma and style.
Pollination: the conveyance of the pollen from the anther to the stigma.
Pollinia: agglutinated pollen masses.
Poly (as a prefix): many (or separate, as in polypetalous).
Polygamous: some of the flowers perfect and some imperfect.
Polypetalous: of separate (distinct) petals; petals not united.
Polysepalous: of separate (not united) sepals.
Pome: a fleshy fruit; like the apple, pear, etc.
Posterior: behind; (in axillary flowers) next to the axis of inflorescence.
Præfloration: æstivation.
Præfoliation: vernation.
Primine: the first or inner integument of the ovule.
Primordial: first.
Primordial cell: a naked or membraneless cell.
Primordial epidermis: the first formed epidermis over the growing point.

Primordial leaves are those of the plumule.
Primordial utricle: the thin protoplasmic sac lining the walls of cells which have very much cell-sap.
Process: a projection.
Pro-embryo: the filamentous or cellular mass which sometimes grows directly from the spore, and from which a plant directly or indirectly springs.
Promycelium: a filamentous growth from some spores which bears sporidia.
Prosenchyma: tissue with long and pointed cells.
Prosenchymous: like or having prosenchyma.
Protandrous: same as proterandrous.
Proterandrous: said of flowers whose stamens precede the pistil in maturing.
Proterandry: stamens maturing before the pistil.
Proterogynous: having flowers whose pistils precede the stamens in maturity.
Proterogyny: ripening of the pistils before the stamens.
Prothallium: the growth from the Fern-spore, and on which the organs of reproduction develop.
Protista: those low organisms not clearly referable either to the group of animals or plants.
Protogynous: same as proterogynous.
Protonema: the filamentous growth from the Moss-spore from the buds of which the Moss-plants develop.
Protophyta: the lowest division of plants.
Protoplasm: the nitrogenous semi-fluid mass in cells.
Protos (as a prefix): first; one; lowest.
Pseudo (as a prefix): false; spurious.
Pseudopodia: protrusions or branches from naked protoplasm.
Pteridophyta: the division which includes the Ferns and their allies.
Pteris: wing.
Pubescent: hairy; especially having soft hairs.
Punctate: having dots or apparent holes.
Punctum vegetationis: the covered growing point of stem or root.
Pungent: terminating in a rigid sharp point.
Putamen: the shell of a nut; the endocarp of a stone fruit.
Pyriform: pear-shaped.

Quadra (as a prefix): four.
Quaternary: consisting of four elements.
Quinque (as a prefix): five; as quinquefoliate, five-leaved.

Race: a marked "variety" or "form" perpetuated by seed.
Raceme: a flower-cluster with an elongated axis bearing pedicelled flowers, centripetal in development.
Racemose: like a raceme, or in racemes.
Rachis: the axis of a spike, of a compound leaf, and the like.
Radiate: having rays.
Radical: to or from the root, or from a root-like (subterranean) stem; pertaining to the root.

Radicle: the lower part of the caulicle in the embryo which develops into the root.
Radix: root.
Ramose: branching.
Raphe: the seed-stalk or funiculus when applied (adhering) to the ovule, as in an anatropous ovule.
Raphides: needle-shaped crystals in the cells.
Ray: a marginal flower, especially if ligulate.
Receptacle: the enlarged end of an axis or peduncle which supports a head of flowers.
Reflexed: bent backwards.
Regular flower: the members in each whorl alike in shape and size.
Rejuvenescence: one process of cell-formation, as by all of the protoplasm in a cell contracting and itself becoming a new cell.
Reniform: kidney-shaped.
Repand: with a wavy margin.
Repent: creeping.
Resting spore: a zygospore.
Reticulate: netted; as reticulate veins.
Retrorse: directed downwards or backwards.
Retting: the process of preparing Flax, etc., by maceration or otherwise in order to effect a separation of the fibre from the stem.
Retuse: with a shallow or obscure notch in a rounded apex.
Reversion: petals changing back to sepals, stamens to petals, etc.
Revolute: rolled backwards.
Rhachis: the axis of a compound leaf, flower-cluster, etc.
Rhaphe: the funiculus or seed-stalk when confluent with the side of an anatropous ovule; raphe.
Rhizoids: hairs which, as in Mosses, etc., perform the function of roots.
Rhizome: root-stock; subterranean stem.
Rib: a prominent vein in a leaf; a ridge
Ribbed: having ribs.
Ringent: gaping.
Root: the descending axis of a plant, tipped with a root-cap, destitute of leaves, etc.
Root-cap: the mass of cells at the tip of the root covering its growing point.
Root-hairs: the minute hairs or outgrowths from surface cells of the root.
Rootlet: a little root, or branchlet of a root.
Rootstock: rhizome; root-like stem or trunk on or under ground.
Rosaceous: like a rose.
Rostellate: with a small beak.
Rostellum: a beak; the protuberance in Orchid-flowers in which the lower ends of the caudicles of the pollinia are enclosed.
Rostrate: beaked.
Rotate: wheel-shaped.
Rotation of protoplasm: mass movement of protoplasm in cells.
Rugose: wrinkled.

Runcinate: with coarse teeth pointing backwards.
Runner: a slender, prostrate rooting branch.

Saccate: having a sac or purse-shaped cavity.
Sagittate: shaped like an arrow-head.
Salver-form: with a border spreading at right angles to the tube.
Samara: a wing fruit; as in Maple.
Saprophyte: a plant feeding on decaying organic matter.
Sap-wood: the younger wood, still containing sap.
Sarcocarp: the soft or fleshy part of a stone fruit.
Scabrous: rough or harsh.
Scalariform: like the rounds of a ladder.
Scale: a very much reduced and more or less rigid or membraneous leaf.
Scandent: climbing.
Scape: a peduncle coming from the ground; as in acaulescent plants.
Scarious: thin, dry, and membranous.
Scion: a twig used for grafting.
Sclerenchyma: tissue in which the cells have thickened and indurated walls.
Sclerotium: a compacted and hardened mass of hyphæ.
Scurf: minute scales.
Scurfy, or *Scurvy:* having scurf.
Secundine: the second or inner coat of the ovule.
Seed: the fully developed ovule containing the embryo.
Seed-leaves: cotyledons; the leaf or leaves of the embryo.
Segment: a division or lobe.
Semi (as a prefix): half.
Sepal: one of the leaves or parts of a calyx.
Sepaloid: like a sepal in texture, etc.
Separated flowers: those having only stamens or only pistils.
Septate: divided by partitions or septa.
Septicidal: where the dehiscence is through the partitions or dissepiments.
Septifragal: where the walls of the ovary or valves break away from the partitions.
Septum: partition.
Sericeous: silky.
Serrate: with teeth pointing forwards or towards the apex.
Sessile: attached directly to the stem or stalk; without a foot-stalk.
Seta: a slender bristle-like body; the supporting filament of the Moss-capsule, etc.
Setaceous: like a seta; bristle-like.
Setiform: in the form of a bristle or seta.
Sheath: the base of leaves, etc., which invests the stem.
Shrub: a small woody plant; smaller than a tree.
Shrubby: woody; like a shrub.
Sieve-cells, or *Sieve-tubes:* those having holes or sieve-like openings in their partitions.
Silicle: the short pod or pouch of the Cress family (Cruciferæ).

Silique: like a silicle, but much longer.
Silver-grain: the glittering plates (Medullary Rays) in exogenous wood.
Simple: not compound; of one piece or part.
Sinuate: with deep waves.
Sinus: a recess or space between two lobes or projections.
Smooth: not hairy nor hispid.
Sori: plural of sorus.
Sorus: the fruit-dot or mass of sporangia in Ferns.
Spadiceous: having a spadix.
Spadix: a fleshy spike.
Spathe: a large bract which envelops a flower-cluster.
Spatulate: widened at the top like a spatula.
Species: all the individuals of one kind, descended as such from common parents.
Spermogonium: cavity which contains the filaments that bear the spermatia.
Spermatia: the spore-like bodies produced in the spermogonia.
Spermatozoids: the protoplasmic bodies or cells developed within the antheridia.
Spicate: like a spike.
Spike: a flower-cluster similar to the raceme, but with sessile flowers.
Spikelet: a secondary spike; the cluster of flowers in Grasses surrounded by glumes.
Spine: thorn; an indurated leaf or branch.
Spinose: having spines.
Sporangium: the organ in which spores develop.
Spore: the body resulting from fructification in the flowerless or Cryptogamous plants; destitute of an embryo, but having a function similar to that of the seed.
Spore-case: sporangium; capsule containing the spores.
Sporidia: secondary spores, or those produced on the pro-embryo, or what develops directly from the spore.
Sporiferous: bearing spores.
Sporocarp: the reproductive as opposed to the vegetative part in Cryptogams.
Sport: an individual deviating much from the type, but whose characters are not transmitted.
Spur: a projecting, more or less horn-like, appendage.
Spurred: like or having spurs.
Squamate, Squamose: having or like scales.
Stamen: the floral organ which produces (in the anther) the pollen.
Staminate: having stamens.
Staminodium: a sterile or abortive stamen.
Stellate: star-shaped.
Stem: the ascending axis of the plant.
Stemless: acaulescent; having no apparent stem.
Sterigma: the slender stalk or support of the spores in some Fungi.
Sterile: unfruitful.
Sterile flower: one with stamens but no pistils.

Stigma: the upper end of the pistil which receives the pollen.
Stipe: stem of a Mushroom, etc.
Stipel: a stipule of a leaflet.
Stipulate: having stipules.
Stipules: appendages on either side at the base of some petioles.
Stolon: a trailing, rooting shoot.
Stoloniferous: bearing stolons.
Stoma (pl. *Stomata*), or *Stomate:* the orifice or breathing-pore in the epidermis of leaves, etc.
Stone-fruit: a fleshy fruit with a hard or stony endocarp.
Stratification: alternate denser and less dense layers in a thickened cell-wall.
Streak: appearance of a mineral when scratched; the line made by marking with a mineral.
Striate: having longitudinal grooves or furrows.
Striation: layers at right angles to those of stratification.
Strobile: a cone-like multiple fruit; as of the Hop and Pine.
Style: the part of the pistil between the ovary and stigma.
Stylospore: stalked, and apparently non-sexual, reproductive bodies or spores, as in some Fungi.
Sub (as a prefix): nearly or under.
Suberose: like cork.
Submersed: growing under water.
Subulate: awl-shaped; broad at the base and pointed at the apex.
Sucker: a shoot of subterranean origin.
Suffrutescent: slightly shrubby.
Suffruticose: low and shrubby at base.
Sulcate: having deep longitudinal furrows.
Superior: above.
Suspensor: the elongated growth in the embryo-sac on the lower end of which the embryo is formed.
Suture: the line of junction of two parts or two edges.
Swarmspore: a motile, naked spore.
Symmetrical flower: one in which the members of the different whorls are the same in number.
Syncarp, Syncarpine: a multiple fruit.
Syncarpous: composed of two or more united carpels.
Syngenesious: stamens with anthers united into a tube.

Tap-root: the primary root with a stout body.
Taxology, Taxonomy: that which relates to classification and its rules.
Tegmen: inner coat of a seed.
Teleutospore: a thick-walled winter spore of some Fungi (Uredineæ).
Tendril: a filiform coiling body for assistance in climbing.
Teratology: that which relates to unnatural forms or monstrosities.
Terete: round.
Terminal: at or belonging to the end or apex.
Terminology: glossology; technical nomenclature.
Ternary: in threes; having three elements.
Testa: the outer, more or less firm, seed-coat.

Tetra (as a prefix): four.
Tetradynamous: having six stamens, two of which are shorter than the others.
Tetraspores: non-sexual spores; as of the Florideæ; mostly in fours.
Thalamus: the receptacle of a flower.
Thallophyte: a Cryptogamous plant which has no differentiation of stem and leaves.
Thallus: a cellular expansion without differentiation into caulome and phyllome.
Theca: the sporangium or spore-case; as in Mosses.
Throat: the opening in a Gamopetalous corolla.
Tissue: any union of cells.
Tomentose: with woolly hairs.
Torus: the upper end of the peduncle which supports the floral organs.
Tracheary tissue: ducts or vessels with thickened and variously perforated walls.
Tracheïdes: cells with markings similar to the ducts.
Transpiration: same as exhalation or evaporation.
Tri (as a prefix): three or thrice.
Triadelphous: the stamens united by their filaments into three sets.
Tribe: a group under an order or family.
Trichogyne: the filamentous prolongation of the carpogonium in some Cryptogams.
Trichome: a hair.
Trifoliate: a compound leaf with three leaflets.
Triple-veined: with a large vein on each side of and approximately parallel with the midrib.
Trisulcate: three-grooved.
Truncate: as if cut square off.
Tuber: an enlarged portion of a subterranean stem.
Tunicate: coated.

Umbel: a flower-cluster in which the pedicels have a common point of insertion.
Umbellate: in or like umbels.
Umbelliferous: bearing umbels.
Undulate: wavy.
Under-shrub: a very low shrub.
Unguiculate: having a claw.
Uni (as a prefix): one.
Unsymmetrical flower: one in which the number of parts in each set is dissimilar.
Uredospore: a thin-walled "summer" spore of the Uredo stage, formerly considered as a distinct genus; as in the Uredineæ.
Utricle: a seed like an achenium, but with a loose or inflated pericarp.

Vacuole: the cavity in the protoplasm of the cell filled with a watery fluid.
Valvate: having valves; (in æctivation) edges meeting without overlapping.

Valve: a lid; one of the pieces into which a pod, etc., splits.
Variety: a group of individuals having some character in which they differ from the typical form of the species.
Vascular: having or like vessels or ducts.
Vasculum: the botanist's collecting-box.
Vegetative cone: same as growing point.   *Punctum vegetationis.*
Vegetative point: same as growing point.
Vein: a branch of the skeleton or frame-work of a leaf.
Veinlet: a small vein.
Venation: the veining or pattern of veining in a leaf.
Ventral: on the side next the axis or centre; opposite of dorsal.
Vernation: the arrangement of leaves in the bud.
Versatile: attached at a point so as to allow swinging to and fro.
Verticillate: whorled; in whorls.
Vesicle: a little sac or bladder.
Vesicular: bladdery.
Vessel: duct.
Vexillum: the upper petal or "banner" of a Papilionaceous corolla.
Villose: having long soft hairs.
Viscid: sticky; adhesive.
Vitreous: glassy.
Vittæ: oil-tubes in the fruit of the Umbelliferæ.
Viviparous: germinating or sprouting from seed or bud while yet on the parent plant.
Voluble: twining.
Volva: an external covering or veil; as in many Fungi.

Water-pore: an orifice similar to a stomate, but with immovable guard-cells, filled with water.
Whorled: verticillate; in whorls.
Wing: a thin expansion.
Winged: with a wing or thin expansion.
Woolly: with long entangled hairs.

Xanthos (in compounds): yellow.
Xylem: the woody portion in the fibro-vascular bundle.

Zone of life: the cambium in exogenous stems.
Zoöspore: naked motile cells (spores) in some Cryptogams.
Zygospore: sexual spores with thick walls; as in the Conjugatæ, etc.
Zygosporeæ: the division whose representatives produce "resting" spores or zygospores.

"THE BEST TEXT-BOOK ON ENGLISH LITERATURE."

ENGLISH LITERATURE

AND

LITERARY CRITICISM.

A Practical Guide to Systematic Literary Study.

With Typical Selections, Illustrative Criticisms, and Exhaustive Analyses of the Best and most Notable Works in the English Language. Showing What to Study, How to Study, and How Best to Apply the Knowledge Acquired Thereby.

By JAMES BALDWIN, A.M.,

Superintendent of Public Schools, Huntington, Indiana.

English Prose.........................(580 Pages).......................$2.00.
English Poetry........................(608 Pages).......................2.00.

The citations from authors are made with taste and judgment; the critical and explanatory remarks are sound, without being wearisome; and the quotations from the best critics and essayists are stimulating and suggestive. I shall take pleasure in commending it to students and others.—MELVILLE B. ANDERSON, Professor of English Literature, Knox College, Galesburg, Ill.

I think there are many points in which Baldwin's English Literature is to be commended above any other work of like kind that I have examined. Its arrangement is unique and sensible. The list of books and studies suggested to the student at the close of each chapter is most excellent. The selections from the works considered are well made, and calculated to awaken in the student a desire to read the whole. The work is a valuable addition to our list of school books.—MATILDA C. BARNS, Vice-Principal, and Teacher of Literature, Girls' Normal School, Philadelphia, Pa.

This is the best text-book on poetry for general use, as well as for students, that we have ever read, for many reasons, which will be apparent to every one upon examination, and we hope that it will be generally introduced. The volume treating of prose, perhaps, better makes its commendable features apparent. Its arrangement is excellent. This work is one of the best to meet popular needs, as it adopts several good ways of securing interest, and really gives an excellent general survey, which leaves the beginner firmly grounded, and develops accurate literary taste.—*The Globe*, Boston, Mass.

The system adopted by the author of this work has two features which distinguish it from other books on the subject, giving it a peculiar and genuine interest of its own. The first is its arrangement. The other is the free use of quotations from the best critics. Still another noticeable feature is that the illustrative selections are never trite. In short, Prof. Baldwin's book has been put together with admirable skill and judgment, is free from dullness, and an excellent work.—*Good Literature*, N. Y.

JOHN E. POTTER & CO.,

PUBLISHERS,   **PHILADELPHIA.**

FRENCH SYNTAX.

A CRITICAL STUDY OF THE FRENCH LANGUAGE.

By JAMES A. HARRISON,
Professor of Modern Languages in Washington and Lee University. Author of a History of Spain, Greek Vignettes, etc.

New Edition,
WITH PRACTICAL EXERCISES PREPARED BY
M. W. EASTON,
Professor of Comparative Philology in the University of Pennsylvania.

12mo, Cloth. 677 Pages. Price $2.00.

This is the most important book for a thorough Study of French which has yet been published in the English lauguage. It is the work of an experienced teacher, whose scholarship and literary skill are of the highest order, done for the benefit of students and other teachers. In it every doubtful point which can arise in the study of the French language is considered and every difficulty is solved. The basis of the book is Edouard Mätzner's celebrated Französische Grammatik, supplemented by Dr. Carl Ploetz's Syntax und Formenlehre der Neufranzösischen Sprache. To this a syllabus of Working Forms and an ample Historical Section have been added, and also a sketch of French Prosody and twelve appendices, which will be found of the greatest service.

For the new edition, Prof. M. W. Easton of the University of Pennsylvania, has prepared a series of seventy-five Practical Exercises, together with French-English and English-French Vocabularies—the object of which is to provide suitable material for the practice of translating into French.

"It seems to be beautifully done."
>> PROF. F. BÔCHER, of Harvard.

"So far as I am aware there has been nothing hitherto in English that filled anything like the same place. It should be in the hands of all teachers, and introduced into those classes to whose scale of study it is adapted."
>> PROF. WILLIAM D. WHITNEY, of Yale.

"I shall expect to derive great help from Prof. Harrison's Syntax, and shall recommend it to my classes."
>> PROF. ALONZO WILLIAMS, of Brown.

"I shall require the University booksellers to have the book on hand in numbers, and I shall strongly recommend all French students to get the book and study it carefully."
>> PROF. SCHÈLE DE VERE, University of Virginia.]

From *The Dial*, Chicago.

"Attention has already been called in these columns to Professor Harrison's admirable *"French Syntax"* (John E. Potter & Co.). A new edition now comes to us, adapted to the use even of beginners by the addition of a series of "Practical Exercises" from the competent hands of Prof. M. W. Easton, of the University of Pennsylvania. The essential rules and directions are printed with the exercises, to which full vocabularies are appended. After the exercises for beginners, a number of well-annotated and varied anecdotes, etc., for translation into French, provide for the needs of the more advanced student. No one should be misled by the too modest title to suppose this work to be merely an exhaustive syntax: the addition of full chapters upon phonology, etymology, historical grammar, and prosody, together with a great number of convenient tables and lists of various kinds, make the book a cyclopedia of exact information concerning the French language. All students will appreciate the advantage of having between the covers of one book answers to all the questions that it can ever occur to the most curious to ask. Teachers should be thankful that they can at last put into the hands of beginners the best French grammar in the world, and proud that they owe this privilege to an American scholar."

JOHN E. POTTER & CO.,

PUBLISHERS,   **PHILADELPHIA.**

CHOICE TEXT-BOOKS.

THE SCIENCE AND ART OF ELOCUTION;
OR,
HOW TO READ AND SPEAK.

A Series of Exercises for Gesture, Calisthenics, and the Cultivation of the Voice; and a Collection of nearly One Hundred and Fifty Literary Gems for Reading and Speaking. NEW AND ENLARGED EDITION. BY FRANK H. FENNO, of the National School of Oratory. 12mo, Cloth, Extra. Price $1.25.

This work is designed to furnish both a theoretical and practical knowledge of elocution and oratory. The principles of good reading and speaking have been carefully and minutely investigated by the author, and are presented in a simple and concise form, within the comprehension of the ordinary student, so that, with proper study and diligent practice, the art of good reading and good speaking may be thoroughly acquired. For convenience of study, the work has been divided into four parts: THEORETICAL, VOCAL CULTURE, HELPS TO THE STUDY, and READINGS and RECITALS.

I do not hesitate to give my unrestricted commendation of "Fenno's Science and Art of Elocution." I consider it the best work of the kind published—well adapted to the common school, academy, and college, and this I say after a thorough test of its merits in our classes.—PROF. J. W. RUST, President of Bethel Female College, Hopkinsville, Ky.

It seems to me a very valuable book both for students and for teachers of advanced Elocution.—ELLEN BISHOP, Teacher of Elocution, Normal School, Albany, N. Y.

THE ARTIST AND HIS MISSION.

A Study in Æsthetics. Designed for the use of Schools and Colleges. By REV. WILLIAM M. REILY, PH.D., Professor of Ancient Languages, Palatinate College. 12mo, Cloth, Extra. Price, $1.50.

A thoughtful contribution to the literature of æsthetics is "The Artist and his Mission," by Professor William M. Reily, of Palatinate College. It is written with the utmost modesty, and makes no pretence to original investigation; but it represents, in point of fact, no small amount of reading and reflection. The author's views on the true object and purpose of art are clear and true, and are faithful to the conception of duty. Moral beauty as well as physical is recognized in this treatise, which is creditable both to the learning and the spirit of its author. —*Good Literature.*

EASY LESSONS IN GERMAN.

A Manual of the Language, especially adapted for Beginners. By AUGUSTIN KNOFLACH, Teacher of Languages. 12mo, Cloth, Extra. Price, $1.00.

The order of arrangement is logical, and agrees with that followed by English grammars. The book carefully gives only those rules and classifications that are of practical value, and calculated to aid the student in the early portion of his German course.

JOHN E. POTTER & CO.,
PUBLISHERS,   PHILADELPHIA.

3065. *[One-third actual size.]*

THE ABOVE CUT REPRESENTS

THE AMATEUR MICROSCOPE.

SOLD BY

JAMES W. QUEEN & CO.,

924 CHESTNUT STREET. **PHILADELPHIA.**

Price with one (No. 2) eye-piece, and one one-half inch objective (this is divisible, giving powers of 50 and 110 diameters), in walnut case with handle and lock, $23.00.

The same as above, with the addition of a one-sixth objective, giving a range of powers up to 360 diameters, $28.00.

☞ List of our ten catalogues will be sent by mail upon application.

(365)

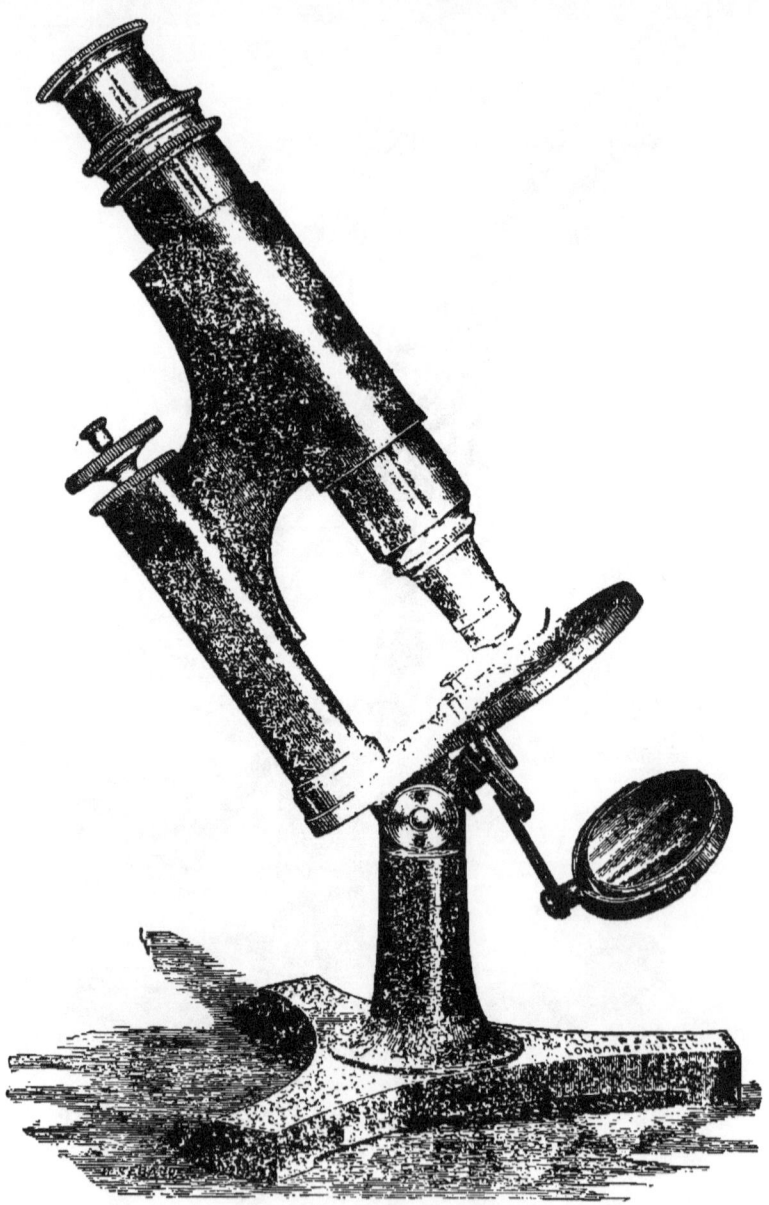

No. 342.   *One-half actual size*

THE SCHOLARS' MICROSCOPE.

MADE BY

R. & J. BECK,

1016 CHESTNUT STREET.   PHILADELPHIA.

Price with one (No. 2) Eye-piece, and dividing Objective of one inch and one-quarter inch, giving powers from 40 to 285 diameters, in handsome Mahogany case, $25.00. This instrument has Draw-tube, extending to ten inches; coarse and fine adjustments of focus, and Diaphragm. The Mirror swings above the stage for the illumination of opaque objects. Illustrated Price Lists mailed *free* to any address.

www.ingramcontent.com/pod-product-compliance
Lightning Source LLC
Chambersburg PA
CBHW020228240426
43672CB00006B/458